2004
T3-BXA-887
University of St. Francis Library
3 0301 00214723 5

Women in Western Intellectual Culture

Women in Western Intellectual Culture, 600–1500

Patricia Ranft

LIBRARY
UNIVERSITY OF ST. FRANCIS
JOLIET, ILLINOIS

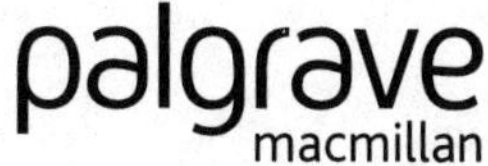

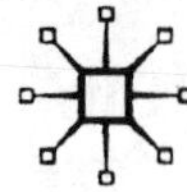

WOMEN IN WESTERN INTELLECTUAL CULTURE, 600–1500

© Patricia Ranft, 2002

All rights reserved. No part of this book may be used or reproduced in any manner whatsoever without written permission except in the case of brief quotations embodied in critical articles or reviews.

First published 2002 by
PALGRAVE MACMILLAN™
175 Fifth Avenue, New York, N.Y. 10010 and
Houndmills, Basingstoke, Hampshire, England RG21 6XS
Companies and representatives throughout the world

PALGRAVE MACMILLAN is the global academic imprint of the Palgrave Macmillan division of St. Martin's Press, LLC and of Palgrave Macmillan Ltd. Macmillan® is a registered trademark in the United States, United Kingdom and other countries. Palgrave is a registered trademark in the European Union and other countries.

ISBN 1–40396–139–5 hardback

Library of Congress Cataloging-in-Publication Data
Ranft, Patricia.
Women in Western intellectual culture, 600–1500/Patricia Ranft.
p. cm.
Includes bibliographical references and index.
ISBN 1–40396–139–5
1. Women—Intellectual life. 2. Intellectual life—History. 3. Women intellectuals—History—To 1500. I. Title.
HQ1143.R35 2002
305.4—dc21 2002025827

A catalogue record for this book is available from the British Library.

Design by Newgen Imaging Systems (P) Ltd., Chennai, India.

First edition: December, 2002
10 9 8 7 6 5 4 3 2 1

Printed in the United States of America.

305.4
R195

To my sisters
Marion, Joanne, Terry and Peggy
for all they taught me

And to my brothers
Raymond, Donald, Robert and Richard
who learned early in life how intelligent women are

"Knowledge is not given as a gift but by study."
—Laura Cereta, Letter to Bibolo

Contents

Introduction

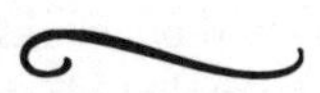

In an excellent study of medieval English women writers, literary historian Laurie A. Finke concludes that the evidence she examined proves once and for all that "women were not silent in the Middle Ages" and that the women she studied "deserve to be included in any account of the English language, English history or English literature, alongside of the men who are usually credited with the development of English culture."[1] When women's history started in earnest in the 1970s the reverse was almost automatically assumed. It was supposed, first, that women were indeed very silent; second, that women did not contribute to or participate in intellectual history; and, third, that the few women writers we knew about were rare and exceptional in ability. Many also assumed that while women might earn a place within a women's history they did not deserve one in a general account. Even when groups of women scholars were found researchers often held on tight to one or all of these assumptions. In the 1980s, for example, Margaret L. King and Albert Rabil undertook a study of women humanists in Quattrocento Italy. They admitted that these women were not silent and that they did participate in the intellectual developments of their day, but then King and Rabil concluded that the women were rare and exceptional. Thus, they argued that these women's historical heritage lay in this exceptionality and in their introducing a new notion into Western society, "that women could participate creatively as intellectuals in the shaping of culture."[2] What more recent studies have proved, however, is that women humanists could not have introduced this new notion, because it was not new. Women had been participating creatively in the intellectual community throughout the entire Middle Ages.

The difference largely responsible for the disparity between the conclusions of earlier historians and more recent ones does not lie in ideology as much as it lies in the actual texts. Early historians did not have available to them the numerous texts penned by women and often did not have knowledge of the many ways in which women participated in intellectual activities. The sheer number of critical editions and translations of women's writings published since the 1980s is extraordinary and is one of the chief accomplishments of the late twentieth-century academic community. Just as no one expected to find such a wealth of treasures when scholars first began exploring the medieval era at the turn of the last century, so too are we all elated at the amount of source material only a few decades of research has yielded. Prior to the outstanding work of modern editors and translators, an intellectual history of women would barely have been possible and then only after literally a lifetime of ferreting out long-forgotten manuscripts in obscure places. Now the once forgotten works of women intellectuals are readily accessible to us all. Certainly the debt I owe those hundreds of editors and translators of women's works is apparent on every page of this study. New critical editions continue to be published at an impressive rate even as I write, and, given that reality, the reader should realize how swiftly this work may be outdated. So be it.

With the influx of such an imposing number of women's texts into the academic world it is not surprising that a debate soon began over the authorship of those texts. Were women the true authors of those works, or were they merely instruments through which the voice of patriarchy spoke? Many argue that even in the texts undeniably written by women we are not hearing women speak. Rather, we are hearing "a vague echo of more theoretically powerful works by orthodox males or a species of 'false consciousness' that reflects merely patriarchal repression."[3] While the basic point is well taken, that the true voice of a written work must be determined at the outset of any critical analysis of a text, in the case of women's history this a priori assumption has had an unfortunate result. It has contributed to the modern silencing of past women's voices. By positing a priori that all texts emitting from a patriarchal society contain de facto patriarchal voices and only patriarchal voices, many twentieth-century scholars have (unintentionally?) muffled the utterances of historical women. Similarly, universal statements such as Andrea Dworkin's provocative stance that all men are agents and all women are victims,[4] have disturbingly helped keep women outside mainstream intellectual history. In its place we are often offered histories of gendered relationships in which women are passive recipients on the historical stage. While such an approach has inherent value in the history of gender, if we allow it to deny the presence and the contributions of women in all intellectual matters, it then becomes oppressive; it oppresses women's true history, negating even the possibility of women's participation in intellectual history.

There are many adherents to this approach to women's studies, and I certainly risk alienating potential readers of this book by stating forthrightly in the Introduction that I see more disadvantages than advantages in such an approach. I am not alone in this belief, though, for increasingly scholars are recognizing, first, that such an approach renders women more impotent and insignificant in history than they in fact were, and, second, that the vast majority of women's texts do actually contain women's voices.[5] One would be hard-pressed today to find a scholar of Hildegard of Bingen, Margery Kempe, or Catherine of Siena, for example, who would argue that these women did not possess an articulate, independent voice of their own, despite the fact that they did not personally write the works attributed to them but dictated them to male scribes. Even in instances where confessor-spiritual directors instructed women to write, it is clear that many women's voices still emerge clear and untainted;[6] Teresa of Avila is a prime example here. Surely there is room for both approaches, just as there is room for gender studies and women's history. They are not mutually exclusive, but, to the contrary, need each other. Carolyn Walker Bynum's research offers us an example of such mutual benefits. While pondering the role gender plays in late medieval texts she concludes that "a careful and comparative reading of texts by male and female authors from the twelfth to the fifteenth century thus suggests that it is men who develop conceptions of gender, whereas women develop conceptions of humanity."[7] This is a conclusion of immense significance in gender history, yes, but also in Western intellectual history, because it demonstrates women's proclivity to abstract thought.

What is needed at this early stage of women's intellectual history is, in fact, rather elementary. First, the general public must be made aware of the quality and quantity of women's participation in intellectual matters throughout the course of Western history. Before we can determine if it is a woman's authentic voice in a particular text, we must identify the text. The identification and organization of all appropriate texts and authors is a necessary first step. Second, in light of this quality and quantity we must cease approaching individual woman's contributions as if they were exceptional or rare. I long ago lost count of how many scholars of women's history introduce their subject with a remark about how exceptional that subject's intellectual achievements were. The most efficient way to prove that each woman's achievement is not a rarity but part of a long tradition coterminous with Western intellectual history is to document that tradition in one place for all to see and contemplate. The overwhelming amount of evidence will easily convince even the skeptic. Third, we must examine each woman's work for its distinctive contribution. This will provide a base for future historians to use in their determination of the proper position of that contribution in Western intellectual history.[8]

There is a danger in a work such as this for the reader to conclude that I am over-emphasizing the importance of these women. I in no way mean to imply that every act of participation is equal. It is not, and I certainly do not mean to imply that every woman's contribution is equal to every man's, any more than it is correct to maintain every man's contribution is equal to every woman's. Both conclusions would border on the absurd. In any intellectual history there will always be some ideas and contributions that are more important or influential than others. So too is this true for women's ideas and contributions within Western intellectual history. My purpose here is simple to gather in one place the many ways women did participate in the intellectual community. Once it is gathered, then we can begin debate about what is historically significant, what is not, and what is the relationship of these women's works to the whole of Western intellectual tradition.

1

The Early Renaissance

In the magisterial work, *Thought and Letters in Western Europe A.D. 500 to 900,* historian M. L. W. Laistner reviews the intellectual contributions made during that period according to the following categories: classical grammatica, history and biography, hagiography, geography, dogmatic theology, scriptural exegesis, pastoral theology, political ideas, philosophy, Latin and vernacular poetry, and prose.[1] Laistner's topics are indeed comprehensive, but the contemporary student picking up the book for the first time would immediately be struck by an absence that previous generations ignored: There are no women in the narrative. Besides one fleeting reference in the epilogue to Hrotsvitha of Gandersheim's dramas, women are absent from the history. Three generations of scholars considered this silence warranted, but, thanks to recent advances in medieval studies, the current generation now knows the silence is undeserved. Almost every category that Laistner examines contains at least one important work by a woman. Hrotsvitha of Gandersheim wrote two historical epics of political import, *The Deeds of Otto* and *The Founding of Gandersheim Monastery;* she was a prolific hagiographer with eight *vitae* to her credit, and she was, of course, an accomplished poet and dramatist. The renowned Queen Radegund wrote an autobiographical poem, *The Thuringian War,* in an era singularly void of autobiographies, while the little known Baudonivia, a nun in Radegund's monastery, wrote a *vita* of the queen that surely rivals the more famous Venantius Fortunatus. Hugeberc, an eighth-century abbess, created a new approach to geographical writing, the travelogue, while Dhuoda, a ninth-century Carolingian lay woman, wrote a sophisticated educational manual for her son which includes lessons in scriptural exegesis, pastoral theology, political ideas, grammar, and numerology. Women were not as absent from the field of early medieval intellectual endeavor as Laistner led us to believe.

Perhaps the larger problem facing the early medieval intellectual historian is not whether to mention women's accomplishments, but rather how to situate their works in the context of a period which historians have often called intellectually sterile.[2] The recent examination and analysis of women's thought and literature has not led us to any radical revision of the period's intellectual productivity. It has, however, revealed benefits to be gained by approaching the topic less restrictively. Patrons, collaborators, oral informants, correspondents, transmitters of learning, spiritual directors, and translators, in addition to the traditionally recognized intellectuals, are now readily acknowledged to be part of intellectual history. The result is a broader understanding of how the intellectual foundation of the West was laid which in turn enables us to better evaluate the contributions of women to that foundation. We begin our exploration of the early medieval period by looking at those moments in early medieval Western history which past historians have labeled renaissances[3]—the Anglo-Saxon renaissance, the Carolingian renaisssance, and the Ottonian renaissance—for women's involvement in and contribution to them.

The Anglo-Saxon Renaissance

The Anglo-Saxon renaissance is generally understood to be rooted in a Celtic renaissance of sorts. Marcia Colish calls the early medieval Irish people the earliest emissaries of classical traditions, a surprising fact given the lack of Roman imprint in Ireland.[4] The Celtic Church, specifically the monasteries, gave refuge to Latin intellectual culture, although why and how is still unclear. During the sixth century male monasteries such as those at Clonard, Bangor, Derry, and Iona became "study centers,"[5] as did such female monasteries at Kildare, Sliab Cuilinn, and Cluain-Credhuil. Cluain-Credhuil had a school for boys that educated so many future ecclesiastical leaders that the monastery's founder Ita is known as the foster mother of Irish saints.[6] We know only the barest skeleton of what was taught at these schools. There is evidence that the study of rhetoric, grammar, computus, and some secular Latin authors was undertaken in both male and female monasteries,[7] and that men did not have any qualms about asking women for instruction.[8] The literary output of the Irish monks was not particularly original, but the works that have survived preserve evidence of the transmission of past scholarship. The anonymous treatise *Concerning the twelve abuses of the age* (ca. 630–650) reveals familiarity with Isidore of Seville, the *Vulgate,* the Benedictine Rule, Gregory the Great's *Pastoral Rule,* homilies by Caesarius of Arles, and some biblical commentaries of Jerome. On the other hand, Adamnan, abbot of Iona (670–704) wrote *Concerning holy places* and what is considered to be one of the best *vitae* in medieval hagiography, *Life of Columba.* Laistner judges these works to be undeniable proof of the excellence of the Irish monastic educational system.[9]

Bede tells us that Irish literary culture found its way to northern England in 635 when King Oswald sent a request to the Irish elders with whom he had lived "while in exile, asking them to send him a bishop whose teaching and ministry" might benefit the English people.[10] They send Aidan, and Oswald then "appointed the island of Lindisfarne to be his see." Oswald continued to welcome Irish missionaries after Aidan came, and soon there were numerous endowed monasteries populating the countryside of Northumbria where "the English, both noble and simple, were instructed by their Scots teachers."[11] At the same time the pilgrim Fursey, "of noble Irish blood and even more noble in mind" came among the East Angles and "built himself a monastery in which he might devote himself more freely to sacred studies."[12] Sometime around 650 a nun in the Frankish monastery of Chelles named Hilda "was recalled home by Bishop Aidan and was granted one hide of land" to establish a monastic community. "After this, Hilda was made abbess of the monastery of Heruteu [Hartlepool]," and almost immediately after was "appointed to rule" another monastery in Calaria. There she "quickly set herself to establish a regular observance following the instructions of learned men." Her most important monastic foundation was the next one, the monastery at Whitby (she founded one more house at Hackness right before her death in 680). Bede tells us that here "she established the same regular life as in her former monastery," which meant that "those under her direction were required to make a thorough study of the Scriptures." Five of Hilda's students later became bishops, all of which Bede implies were quite well educated. He offers as an example one bishop, Oftfor, who "devoted himself to reading and applying the Scripture in both Hilda's monasteries" and then continued his studies under Archbishop Theodore of Canterbury. Hilda's reputation as a learned, wise leader was so great "that not only ordinary folk but kings and princes used to come and ask her advice."[13] Caedamon, one of only two English poets known by name and who could quickly turn any passage of Scripture "into delightful and moving poetry in his own English tongue,"[14] was taken under the wing of Hilda once she discovered his talent. She "advised him to abandon secular life" and "admitted him into the Community as a brother." Her patronage did not stop there; "she ordered him to be instructed in the events of sacred history," which he "stored up in his memory" and "turned it into such melodious verse that his delightful renderings turned his instructors into auditors."[15] We see here that Hilda's monastery had numerous teachers ready to instruct the uneducated. There is evidence in an anonymous *vita* of Gregory the Great written at Whitby ca. 704 (and the first book to be written by an Englishman) that Hilda had assembled a respectable library at the monastery.[16] Even after she was struck down with her final illness in 680 "she never ceased to give thanks to her maker or to instruct the flock committed to her."[17]

The Celtic renaissance also left an imprint in Wessex where education flourished in double monasteries, such as Barking and Wimbourne,[18] and in the male monasteries of Malmesbury and Glastonbury. The work of Aldheim (639–709), the first English writer, reveals a close relationship among the educated in these male and female monasteries. A student first of the Irish scholar Marldruib and then of the African Hadrian, Aldheim was a product of both Celtic and Roman intellectual traditions. Hadrian and the Greek Theodore of Tarsus had established a renowned center of learning at Canterbury in 671, while three years later the famed monasteries of Jarrow and Wearmouth were founded. Benedict Biscop combined his Roman training with the Celtic intellectual legacy predominant in the area[19] to produce two monasteries that were "the heirs of Vivarium."[20] This was the home of Bede, a figure unequalled in the Anglo-Saxon renaissance. It is because of his inclusion of women's activities in his *A History of the English Church and People* that we know so much about women's intellectual contributions of the day. While he obviously appreciated women's role, neither Bede nor his school at Jarrow had any known interaction with women scholars. On the other hand Bede's contemporary Aldheim did. Aldheim's chief work, *In praise of virginity,* was addressed to the women at Barking monastery. That in itself is significant, but the content of the work also reveals much about the involvement of the Barking women in intellectual pursuits. First of all, given the level of discourse and subject matter of *In praise of virginity,* it is evident that Aldheim was writing to a well-educated audience. He mentions ten women by name, so we know that he was sure of at least this minimum number among his readers: "Hildilid and likewise Justina, Cuthberga, and Osburga, who contributes much to me through close friendship, Aldgida and Scholastica, Hidburga and Burngida, Eulalia and Tecla, renowned for much holiness like an ornament of the Church." His salutation continues praising the women's "erudition in the sacred sciences, scholars as wise as ancient philosophers."[21] This is an appraisal to be reckoned with, for Aldheim was, according to Colish, "probably the best-read person in Europe in his day after Isidore of Seville."[22]

Aldheim's praise arises from Barking monastery's extensive intellectual activity. He makes it clear that the women corresponded with him and that their letters included discussion of intellectual pursuits: "Just as I was getting ready to go with my fellow brethren to an episcopal council, I received your kind letter with pleasure, filled with good news of heavenly rewards and in a style not only worthy of a monastic community filled with faith, but one where they clearly still engage in the sweet study of Holy Scripture."[23] Aldheim then describes in detail some of that scholarship, how the women engaged in the full course of studies in "theological commentaries by the catholic Fathers, the innermost nuclear spiritual core of the evangelists, using traditional fourfold approach to biblical study held by the Church—historical, allegorical, tropological, and anagogical—now carefully searching the pages of historical narratives and chronological studies, that have recorded the changes of the past and are revered in memory; now studying the rules grammarians and orthographers, the tone and time of accentuation, fixed in poetic feet by colons and commas, that is, in pentameter verse and heptameter verse."[24] The women's curriculum was indeed extensive, as extensive as any found in contemporary male monasteries.[25] After a long scholarly discussion on the main topic of virginity, Aldheim ends his treatise apologizing for "the faults of this letter" and adding a final tribute to the women: "And so farewell, flowers of the Church, sisters of the convent, disciples of learning" ["*alumniae scholasticae*"].[26] The letter was so well received that Aldheim was encouraged to send the women another copy of the treatise, this time in verse.

Aldheim also had close ties with the women at Wimbourne,[27] a monastery which had numerous interactions with the intellectuals of the day. Founded ca. 705 Wimbourne Abbey in Wessex was first ruled by Abbess Cuthburga, sister of Wessex king Ine and the former wife of King Alcfrith, whom Bede tells us was instructed by Wilfrid, "a very learned man."[28] Since Cuthburga began her monastic life at Barking in all likelihood she is the same Cuthburga that Aldheim addressed in his treatise's salutation. From its foundation, therefore, we can surmise that intellectual activities were encouraged. Within one generation its reputation as a place of learning was established. Thanks to Rudolf of Fulda's *vita* of Leoba, missionary partner of Boniface, we have a detailed description of life at Wimbourne under the reign of Tetta, another sister of King Ine.[29] It was under Tetta that Leoba was trained after receiving preliminary schooling under Abbess Eadburg at Minster-in-Thanet.[30] Between Rudolf's *vita* and the extant correspondence of fourteen women to English missionaries in Germany, particularly the letters from Wimbourne and Thanet, we possess a rather detailed picture of the intellectual activities of eighth-century Anglo-Saxon nuns. Boniface, appointed by Pope Gregory II in 719 "to preach to those people who are still bound by the shackles of paganism" and to "instil into their minds the teaching of the Old and New Testaments ... with arguments suited to their understanding,"[31] was especially dependent on the Anglo-Saxon women for their intellectual support and eventually their service. As early as 720 Boniface was asking one of the women[32] to send him books, a practice he continued for years. "And know also that I have been unable to obtain a copy of your beloved *The Passions of the Martyrs* which you asked me to send you, and provided that I stay healthy, I shall send it." She continues: "And you, my most beloved, guide my thoughts with a small consolatory treatise, like you promised in your delightful letter, that is, choose something appropriate from Holy Scripture," thus indicating that a good part of their relationship involved intellectual give-and-take.[33] He later replies in kind: "But about writing down my thoughts, as you asked, you must indulge my sins, for because of pressing work and continual journeys I have not been able to write as you asked; but I will complete it presently and send it to you."[34] Boniface tells Abbess Eadburga that "often your kindness lifts one up out of sadness, whether you help me with comforting books or with vestments. And so I pray that you fertilize what you began to grow, by copying in gold the Epistle of my lord St. Peter the Apostle, so that Holy Scripture will be held in honor and reverence before pagan eyes."[35] Another time he thanks her for "sending presents of spiritual books."[36] Another letter to Boniface contains evidence of a certain degree of familiarity with ancient sources; its author, a woman of unknown origin called Eangyth, makes references to Virgil's *Aeneid* four times, to Jerome twice, and to contemporary Aldheim of Malmesbury twice.[37] The more famous of these letters, though, is from Leoba, his distant relative. After calling upon their kinship ties and asking if she can "regard you as my brother," Leoba asks for his prayers and then adds:

> Would you also, if you please, correct the homely style of this my letter and send me as a model a few words of your own, for I deeply long to hear them. The little verses written below have been composed according to the rules of prosody. I made them, not because I imagine myself to have great ability, but because I wish to exercise my budding talents. I hope you will help me with them. I learned how to do it from my mistress Eadburga, who continues with increasing perseverance in her study of the Scripture.[38]

She concluded her letter with four hexameters, modeled on the poetry of Aldheim.

The relationship grew during the ensuing years, and when Boniface realized he needed women as well as men to complete his missionary goals, he wrote Abbess Tetta of Wimbourne "asking her to send Leoba to accompany him on this journey and to take part in this embassy; for Leoba's reputation for learning and holiness had spread far and wide."[39] It is clear from Leoba's *vita* that Rudolf, its author, firmly believed it was Leoba's intellectual acumen that Boniface was counting on, and it is equally clear from Boniface's correspondence and his many requests for books that he considered the conversion process to include a strong intellectual component.[40] Boniface "received her with the deepest reverence," not because "she was related to him" but because of "her holiness and wisdom."[41] Leoba was made abbess over the monastery at Tauberbischofsheim, where she educated a large community, both spiritually and intellectually. In Rudolf's description of her rule we have the quintessential portrait of an eighth-century educated woman.

> So great was her zeal for reading that she discontinued it only for prayers or for the refreshment of her body with food or sleep: the Scriptures were never out of her hands. For, since she had been trained from infancy in the rudiments of grammar and the study of the other liberal arts, she tried by constant reflection to attain a perfect knowledge of divine things so that through the combination of her reading with her quick intelligence, by natural gifts and hard work, she became extremely learned. She read with attention all the books of the Old and New Testaments and learned by heart all the commandments of God. To these she added by way of completion the writings of the church Fathers, its decrees of the councils and the whole of ecclesiastical law. She was deeply aware of the necessity for concentration of mind in prayer and study, and for this reason took care not to go to excess either in watching or in other spiritual exercises. Throughout the summer both she and all the sisters under her rule went to rest after the midday meal, and she would never give permission to any of them to stay up late, for she said that lack of sleep dulled the mind, especially for study.[42]

One of the most remarkable works we have from this period was a product of the same type kind of intellectual environment that Rudolf describes here. Walburga (710–779) was born into a royal and holy family in Wessex. Her father, mother and two older brothers, Wynnibald and Willibald, are revered as saints. When her father and brothers decided to make a pilgrimage to the Holy Land in 720 she entered the same esteemed monastery as Leoba, Wimbourne, and was thoroughly educated according to the standards of the day under Abbess Tetta. There she remained, a reputation for learning growing around her, until in 750 Boniface requested Tetta to send Leoba and other women to establish monasteries and schools in Germany, because he knew that by their "holiness and wisdom [they] would confer many benefits by [their] word and example." Walburga was among those who "were trained according to [Leoba's] principles in the discipline of monastic life and made such progress in her teaching that many of them afterwards became superiors of others."[43] Walburga became abbess of a double monastery founded by her brother Wynnibald, that of Heidensheim. The hagiographic *Miracles of St. Waldburga* by Wolfhardi Haserensis hints at the extent Walburga's wisdom was appreciated in the area, particularly her medical knowledge.[44] No works of hers are known to have survived, but her place in intellectual history was assured when she commissioned one of her nuns to write the lives of her two brothers. The identity of the woman was unknown until historian Bernhard Bischoff discovered it hidden within the text in a cryptogram: The author was Hugeberc (ca. 740–ca.790).[45] That Walburga chose one of the women educated in her own monastery for what she obviously considered to be a momentous task is testimony to the scholarly standards she held her monastery to, especially when numerous literate males in Boniface's entourage would have been willing and able to write the *vita*. In fact, in her preface to Willibald's *vita* Hugeberc humbly confesses that even she knows that: "I know that it may seem very bold on my part to write this book when there are so many holy priests capable of doing better." Moreover, she tells us that the facts upon which the *vita* is based were repeated to her in the presence of two deacons who were presumably capable of writing the *vita* themselves.[46]

Walburga's choice was excellent, for Hugeberc produced a work truly worthy of Walburga's trust. Besides the value it has as hagiography, it is also significant for its contribution to pilgrimage literature. Hugeberc seems personally dedicated to the task of preserving Willibald's description of "the scenes where the marvels of the Incarnate Word were enacted," for "it did not seem right to allow these things to pass into oblivion, nor to be silent about the things God has shown to His servant." Recognizing the value of Willibald's experience Hugeberc proclaimed that "I would like to record something of their deeds and travels for future ages."[47] Elizabeth Alvilda Petroff claims that in so doing Hugeberc was thus "inventing a new genre, a new literary form, the first travel book written by an Anglo-Saxon;"[48] C. H. Talbot says it is the only extant travelogue to the Holy Land from the eighth century and fills in a wide gap between the pilgrimage narrative of Arculfus in 670 and that of Bernard the Monk in 865.[49] Since scholars have long lamented the scarcity of geographical works written during the seventh and eighth centuries,[50] Hugeberc's contribution is all the more significant.[51] While Hugeberc's work is not without its grammatical and stylistic problems, other geographical writings of the period pale in comparison to Hugeberc's vivid and interesting narrative.[52]

Hugeberc is very conscious that her role is that of author, not simply that of scribe. She sees one of her primary tasks to be that of organizer. She must take Willibald's "faithful description" of his travels as told to her and the two deacons "on the twentieth of June, the day before the summer solstice" and combine it with "a brief account of [his] early life."[53] She tells us she will accomplish this by "combining and putting into order the few facts that there are and weaving them into a continuous narrative." When she sees herself straying from this order she is quick to act. When narrating events surrounding his birth she gets distracted momentarily with speculations about his destiny and then recalls herself thus: "But let us return to the early infancy of the blessed man."[54] She is not content merely organizing Willibald's description into a coherent story, though, for she always is interested in motivation. Here she is most helpful. She places Willibald's initial interest in travel in his desire to live the monastic life. After entering the monastery at Waldheim "night and day he pondered anxiously on the means of monastic perfection and the importance of community life." How he got from a desire for monastic perfection to traveling for ten years in Rome and the Holy Land is explained thus: "Next he began to inquire how he could put these ideas into effect so that he could despise and renounce the fleeting pleasures of this world and forsake not merely the temporal riches of his earthly inheritance but also his country, parents and relatives. He began also to devise means of setting out on pilgrimage and travelling to foreign countries that were unknown to him." In the end he did not abandon his family, but instead "asked his father to go with him," as well as his brother Wynnibald. In Willibald's mind, travel was a form of asceticism, fit only for the "servant of Christ" willing "to brave the perils of the pathless sea" to experience "this hazardous enterprise and to undertake this difficult mode of life."[55] In this he was correct, for extensive travel during the eighth century entailed much suffering. In numerous places "they grew so weak through lack of food that they feared their last day had come."[56]

It was not only an ascetic impulse, however, that drove Willibald to plan his journey. It was also curiosity. In this we are most fortunate, since Willibald's curiosity and Hugeberc's recognition of its importance result in vivid descriptions of things rarely or never recorded elsewhere. Hugeberc's vignette of the pilgrims' visit to Jerusalem is an example:

> Then they came to Jerusalem, to the very spot where the holy cross of our Lord was found. On the site of the place called Calvary now stands a church. Formerly this was outside Jerusalem, but when Helena discovered the cross she placed the spot within the walls of Jerusalem. There now stand three crosses outside the church near the wall of the eastern end, as a memorial to the cross of our Lord and those who were crucified with Him. At present they are not inside the Church, but outside beneath a pent roof. Nearby is the garden in which the tomb of our Saviour was placed. This tomb was cut from the rock and the rock stands above ground: it is squared at the bottom and tapers towards a point at the top. On the highest point of it stands a cross, and a wonderful house has been constructed over it. At the eastern end a door has been cut in the rock of the sepulchre, through which people can enter the tomb to pray. Inside there is a slab on which the body of our Lord lay, and on this slab fifteen lamps of gold burn day and night; it is situated on the north side of the interior of the tomb and lies at one's right hand as one enters the tomb to pray. In front of the door of the sepulchre lies a great square stone, a replica of that first stone which the angel rolled away from the mouth of the sepulchre.[57]

The strength of this curiosity as a motivating factor is apparent in Hugeberc's account of the pilgrims' visit to a volcano called the Hell of Theodoric. There "Willibald, who was inquisitive and eager to see without delay what this Hell was like inside, wanted to climb to the top." The ashes on the edge of the crater prevented him from doing so, but "all the same, he saw the black and terrible and fearful flame belching forth from the crater." Only "after they had satisfied their curiosity" thus, did "they weighed anchor and sailed."[58] In another graphic sketch of a night spend in the open, we see the full powers of Hugeberc's literary talent in retelling Willibald's tale. "After praying there [at Corazain], they departed and came to the spot where two fountains, Jor and Dan, spring from the earth and then pour down the mountainside to form the river Jordan. There, between the two fountains, they passed the night and the shepherds gave us sour milk to drink. At this spot there are wonderful herds of cattle, long in the back and short in the leg, bearing enormous horns; they are all of one colour, dark red. Deep marshes lie there, and in the summer-time, when the great heat of the sun scorches the earth, the herds betake themselves to the marshes and, plunging themselves up to their necks in the water, leave only their heads showing."[59]

Hugeberc emphasizes that curiosity about the unknown world and its people ran both ways in the eighth century. While the pilgrims were traveling in Saracen territory, they were arrested "because they were strangers" and the native population "knew not to which nation they belonged." A merchant found out about their detention and tried to have them released. When he failed he tried to make their life easier by feeding them, sending his son every Wednesday and Saturday to take them to bathe, and taking them every Sunday to church. While on these trips they went through the market places and "the citizens of the town, who are inquisitive people, used to come regularly to look at them, because they were young and handsome and clothed in beautiful garments."[60] Finally, a Spaniard with "a brother at the king's court" became curious about the prisoners "and made careful inquiries about their nationality and homeland." He interceded for them "and they were let off scot-free."[61]

Along with curiosity, however, came the xenophobia which Hugeberc is equally quick to point out. We just noted that the Saracens imprisoned the group only because they were strangers. At the summit of Libanus the pilgrims discovered it "guarded and closed; and if anyone comes with a pass the citizens arrest him immediately and send him back to Tyre." In Tyre "the citizens arrested them, put them in chains and examined all their baggage to find out if they had hidden any contraband."[62] In Salamias and Emesa they needed letters of safe conduct to travel about.[63] Monasteries, however, were always hospitable to them. Willibald and Tidbercht, a friend "who travelled everywhere with him," visited Monte Cassino where they were welcomed by the community and stayed for ten years.[64]

Hugeberc concludes her work by noting a special concern of hers. She wants posterity to judge her work to be historically accurate and so reiterates the source for the narrative and its verification. "We have tried to set down and make known all the facts which have been ascertained and thoroughly investigated," Hugeberc insists. "These facts were not learned from anyone else but heard from Willibald himself; and having received them from his own lips, we have taken down and written them in the Monastery of Heidenheim, as his deacons and other subordinates can testify." Then Hugeberc makes a statement in which we can see how earnestly she wanted her work to be judged scholarly: "I say this so that no one may afterwards say that it was an idle tale."[65]

Talbot told us a half-century ago that when assessing the Anglo-Saxon renaissance of the seventh and eighth centuries there was no reason why women should not share center stage.[66] One must remember that the intellectual activity of Anglo-Saxon men as well as women was limited and rarely speculative or original.[67] Within those limits the women's contributions are significant. We have met women letter writers and creative authors. We know that women's monasteries copied books and educated their own members to the highest standards of the day. With the exception of Jarrow and Wearmouth the monastic schools of women were on par with those of men. This is not a new conclusion, but one that Talbot penned in 1954:

> The prominent part played by women in this intellectual renaissance is remarkable .... Their literary attainments were considerable, comparing favourably with those of the men, if we except Bede and others of the same rank; and the biography of Leoba tells us that she was so deeply versed in the Scriptures, the writings of the Fathers and canon law that she was consulted by abbots, bishops and kings. It is no coincidence that of all the companions who surrounded Willibald in his bishopric in Eichstatt it was a nun who undertook the task of

> recording for posterity the description of his journeys and the founding of his diocese. The degree of freedom and independence which these nuns enjoyed, the influence they were able to exert and the confidence they inspired in such men as Boniface, Lull and Willibald, is no small tribute to the strength of the monastic traditions in which they were trained.[68]

The only thing current research has done is to reinforce this basic appraisal. Talbot adds the evidence that given the information in letters among Leoba and Boniface's circle and the manuscripts themselves with women's names written in some flyleaves and margins, "we must conclude that the production of books . . . was their particular province."[69] Bischoff has proved the presence of a female scriptorium on the continent in Chelles,[70] while Rosamund McKitterick has argued extensively and persuasively in a study of eighth-century English scriptoria that "the production of books, therefore, could readily become an essential part of the monastic and devotional life and there seems little doubt that both kinds of religious community, male and female, took advantage of it."[71] Hugeberc's sole authorship and collaboration with Willibald is undeniable, as is Walburga's patronage in the production of the *Hodoeporicon of St. Willibald.* Evidence that women were teachers of both women and men is abundant; it was so common that one woman, Abbess Eangtha, complained to Boniface that "ministering to so many minds . . . of either sex and every age" was at times overwhelming.[72] The equal relationship that the studious Boniface had with Leoba is but one example of a man and a woman sharing intellectual pursuits. That none of this resulted in a woman producing a speculative masterpiece or literary classic should not be surprising, for in general early medieval societies were rather sterile in abstract thought. Their rational powers were by force of circumstance focused on concrete realities, and an outstanding job they did with this more crucial task. Borrowing, adopting, adapting, selecting, and demolishing, they slowly but carefully merged the best of antiquity, Christianity, and Germanic culture into a new civilization.[73] Furthermore, very few men produced speculative or literary masterpieces either. Intellectuals of the seventh and eighth centuries were engaged in a more significant task, that of building a foundation upon which all future generation would depend. They were sowing the seed of a strong, distinctive, intellectual culture, one dependent yet independent of their Greco-Roman predecessors. In Pierre Riché's words, they were organizing "a new kind of Christian studies and offered their contemporaries and successors a formula that would contribute to the building of medieval culture."[74] Given the durability and long-lasting influence of that intellectual culture it is not too bold to assert that the contributions of Anglo-Saxon renaissance women and men together comprised genius. It was an elusive genius, sometimes nigh invisible and most often sparsely documented, but genius nevertheless. On these small beginnings of intellectual life in the West the seeds of the future were planted.

The Carolingian Renaissance

Just as the roots of the Anglo-Saxon renaissance are easily discernible, so too are the roots of Carolingian intellectual activity. The Carolingians, like the Anglo-Saxons, benefited from the Irish, but they also benefited from the fruits of the Anglo-Saxons who preceded them. As Riché says, "the honor for having first successfully applied the principles of Christian culture belongs to the Barbarian Celts and Anglo-Saxons" through whom "the West rethought its culture."[75] The Carolingians' job was to expand on that success. This they did. Intellectual activity increased in quantity and quality under the Carolingians. Still, their accomplishments were limited. The concrete world demanded and got more of their attention than the abstract world.

The reputation of Celtic and Anglo-Saxon scholars was well known on the continent in large part because of the missionaries who established monasteries there. Columban and twelve Celtic monks had arrived in Burgundy ca. 590 and founded monasteries at Annegray, Luxeuil, and Fontaines. This began a tradition of learning and education which left a permanent imprint on Frankish intellectual life.[76] Likewise, Boniface, Leoba, and their circle of educated missionaries, "among them readers, writers and learned men trained in the other arts,"[77] left a lasting impression in the northern territory of the German people. German monasteries quickly became centers of study on par with those in England. Leoba's monastery at Tauberbischofsheim, Chunihilt and Berthgyth's in Thuringia, Walburga's at Heidenheim, and Tecla's at Kitzingen were noted centers for women in Germany, while the Frankish communities of Chelles, Brie, and Andalys actually predated much Anglo-Saxon intellectual activity. Many of the women in these Frankish monasteries were the educators of women who later participated in the Anglo-Saxon renaissance when they returned home.[78] The key to maintaining such centers was, as it is today, libraries, and abbots and abbesses were always shopping for books. We have quoted Boniface's request for books from Anglo-Saxon nuns[79]; he also requested books from two of the most famous libraries of the time, those at Jarrow and York. Benedict Biscop, founder of Jarrow, had collected books for his monastic library at every opportunity and knew well that "the fine and extensive library of books which he had brought back from Rome and which were so necessary for improving the standard of education in this Church should be carefully preserved."[80] His six trips to Gaul and Rome in search of books resulted in the transmission of ancient texts to people, especially monks, north of the Mediterranean who had previously been eclipsed by intellectual activity. Ancient works were not the only type of literature that eighth-century intellectuals were interested in; Boniface asked Abbot Cuthbert at Jarrow and Abbot Egbert at York to send him Bede's work.[81] From a Laon manuscript we gain insight into the kinds of books found in Frankish monasteries of the time: Scripture, missals, commentaries, saints' lives, religious poetry, sermons, patristic writings, penitentials, and medical writings.[82] According to Bischoff, some of these manuscripts may have been copied in house, although much work needs to be done before we know the full extent of women's contributions as scribes.[83] McKitterick argues from somewhat ambiguous evidence that Chelles, which Bischoff conclusively proved did operate a scriptorium "was not wholly exceptional," and that because production of books was so compatible with monastic life "there seems little doubt that both kinds of religious community, male and female, took advantage of it."[84] The ninth-century biographer of two eighth-century women, Herlindis and Reglindis, paints a picture of rather accomplished women. They studied "divine doctrine, human arts, religious studies, and sacred letters," read books and memorized lectures, had "extensive knowledge" of chant and ecclesiastical ceremonies, "and, what is more admirable in our day, of even copying and illuminating." This is in addition to the more domestic skills of spinning, weaving, designing, and embroidering.[85]

One of the few new aspects born in this intellectual milieu was in hagiography. During the seventh century Frankish women authors altered hagiography when they augmented the traditional model of female sanctity manifested by the virtues of humility, chastity, and asceticism with the gendered roles of mother, wife, and daughter. A comparison of Baudonivia's *vita* of Radegund with Venantius Fortunatus' *vita* of Radegund reveals how significant this change is. Venantius Fortunatus' saint is not an ideal wife but "more Christ's partner than her husband's companion."[86] Baudonivia's Radegund is a saint mainly because she transferred her true love of family and husband to the community.[87]

Aside from such small, qualified advances such as this example, the continent was ripe for an intellectual revitalization. It came in the form of a legislated revival of education during the reign of Charlemagne. The political needs of Charlemagne were such that he believed his survival as a ruler hinged on whether he could forge unity among all the diverse peoples under his control. He also possessed a seemingly sincere desire to improve the intellectual life of his people; one of the more active scriptoria of the period was at his sister Gisela's monastery at Chelles.[88] The establishment of ecclesiastical schools could address both problems. Romanization of all liturgy and ritual in a uniform manner could foster unity among peoples whose only common denominator was Christianity. This, in turn, could be accomplished by educating scholars capable of achieving this goal. To this end Charlemagne invited numerous foreign scholars to his court. Peter of Pisa, Paulinus of Aquileia, Paul the Deacon, Theodulfus of Spain, and Alcuin of York responded to his call. It was Alcuin whom Charlemagne asked to head his Palace school, and it was a wise choice. Soon the school was fulfilling every one of Charlemagne's goals. Alcuin remained head of the school from 782 to 796, and during his tenure he spearheaded the effort to revise the *Vulgate* and eliminate disparities between different translations. He also carried on extensive correspondence with the educated women of his day. Gisela, Charlemagne's sister, Rotrud and Bertha, Charlemagne's daughters, and Liutgard, his fourth wife, as well as numerous abbesses and nuns from the continent and from England, all engaged in correspondence with Alcuin.[89] Other educational centers raised their intellectual standards at the same time. Legislation that mandated that catechumens be instructed was not a mandate for universal education, but it raised people's consciousness enough for several bishops and councils to strongly recommend schooling for all children.[90] It certainly contributed to a growing awareness among the people that the intellectual level of society should be raised. A decree issued by a Roman synod in 826 was but an echo of those ordinances issued by Charlemagne and his successors:[91]

> From certain places it has been brought to our notice that there is an absence of teachers and of interest in the study of letters. Consequently, in all bishoprics and the parishes subordinated to them, and elsewhere that it may be necessary,

> careful and diligent measure shall be taken to appoint teachers and learned persons who, being conversant with letters, the liberal arts, and sacred theology, are regularly to teach these subjects, because in them above all the divine ordinances are made clear and manifest.[92]

It is within this environment that a lay woman produced one of the major surprises of the era, the *Liber manualis* of Dhuoda. While the work reveals much about Dhuoda's inner self little is known about the externals of her life other than that she was married to Bernard of Septimania on June 29, 824 and was the mother of two sons, William and Bernard. We do not know where or how much she was educated, only that she was well educated, for she wrote her manual "according to the Hebrew speech and to Greek letters and to the Latin language."[93] Examination of the text shows she had a thorough knowledge of scripture, particularly the Psalter,[94] and knew Ovid,[95] Prudence,[96] Augustine, Gregory the Great,[97] Donatus,[98] Alcuin, Ambrosius Autpertus, Jonas of Orléans, Paulinus of Aquileia, Rabanus Maurus, Lupus of Ferrìeres, Isidore of Seville, Venantius Fortunatus, Gregory of Tours, the Rule of St. Benedict, and many lives of the saints.[99] She was so well read that her reliance on these works is often hard to discern, because she internalized them so thoroughly that their phrasings became part of her speech patterns. Scholars in the past have assumed that Dhuoda's educational level was exceptional, but recent historians have permanently put that claim to rest. Whereas historian Suzanne Wemple argues that the Carolingian renaissance bypassed women, and JoAnn McNamara claims that it was even a regression,[100] the leaps and bounds made by scholars in researching early medieval literacy, scriptoria, and manuscript identification have shown us how unexceptional Dhuoda was.[101] Riché has even established that Dhuoda's intellectual background was representative of Carolingian lay education and typical of her peers.[102] As historian M. A. Claussen says, her only uniqueness in this area lay in the fact that her "book has managed to survive."[103] That Dhuoda is representative of her class socially and educationally is one of the reasons why her *Liber manualis* is so crucial to our understanding of the period, for it gives us a view of the intellectual life outside the clerical, professional scholar circle of monastery and cathedral.[104] The genre she chose to write in is not unique either, but has a long history distinguished by such works as Augustine's *Enchiridion on Faith, Hope, and Love.*[105] Even her clever use of the acrostic in the incipit, "Dhuoda dilecto filio Wilhelmo salutem: Lege," has a long and revered history.[106] Unfortunately, her grammar is also representative of the times, and its limitations have contributed to past scholars dismissing her value outright.[107] If one accepts that limitation in her education, however, and is able to look beyond the limits of presentation to the manual's intellectual strengths, then Dhuoda's niche in intellectual history is evident.

Inclusion of works within an intellectual history, after all, can be based on many different criteria. Explanation of phenomena, solution of problems, invention of technology, and determination of cause and effect all involve rational thought and are customarily included in intellectual history. Rational activity, however, does not have to be new or even original to merit inclusion. It can also deserve inclusion if it is representative of its age, class, gender, or society, if it changes society, if it is influential, if it provokes action or changes behavior, if it provides insight into change, if it demonstrates processes difficult to discern, or if it offers a definitive expression of commonly held beliefs. Sometimes a work is entitled to inclusion simply because it bears witness to a great intellect otherwise limited by the restrictions of its age. When we examine *Liber manualis* we find that it deserves inclusion chiefly for one reason. Like the work of John Scotus Erigena, Dhuoda's manual exercised little influence that we know of, it did not change society, nor did it provoke action, but, also like John Scotus, Dhuoda demands the attention of the intellectual historian. The works they both produced give testimony to the creative minds of their authors and provide us with an opportunity to see what such minds could produce even in a limited intellectual environment.

We will start by examining Dhuoda's political thought, a somewhat neglected aspect of the manual. By "political thought" I mean those ideas that pertain to the organization, duties, obligations, or actions of individuals who seek to control the actions of other individuals or communities.[108] The situation that gave rise to her writing was deeply political. Dhuoda is "far away from you, my son William,"[109] because her husband Bernard "has given you as a hostage to the lord king Charles." While "in the midst of the many struggles and disruptions of the kingdom" Bernard also "constrains me to remain in this city" of Uzes.[110] One of the lasting lessons this tumultuous time taught her was that "in this world we speak as though everything is under our own power, but this is not so." She has seen too many relatives fall from power, too many "who had the appearance of power in the secular world, but are not powerful now."[111] Worldly power is not rooted in sanctity, but "in the physical world, in their action here." Holiness will make them "mighty before God" but not necessarily before society.[112] Moreover, worldly power comes with a high price and is not dependable. Personally she went "greatly into debt" trying "to defend the interests of my lord and master Bernard,"[113] while she warned William that his father might decide not to "command that you be enriched" by his kin's inheritance "because of his many pressing obligations."[114] Dhuoda was thus well aware that humans "struggle here to render faithful service both to your several earthly lords and to that singular Lord,"[115] but her knowledge of the political conflict of interest did not result in contempt for the world. Rather, she manifests a healthy reverence for all that is secular throughout the manual. In strong contrast to the *contemptus mundi* tradition that flourished both before and after her,[116] Dhuoda embraces the world, specifically the political world, as indispensable to salvation. This is clear throughout the manual. We see this theology forming her statement of purpose in the prologue as she explains "what is essential" to William: "that you show yourself to be such a man on both levels that you are both effective in this world and pleasing to God in every way."[117]

Dhuoda's embrace of the world is based on her understanding of creation and the Incarnation, two doctrines intimately intertwined. The Incarnation flows directly from creation: "God is the maker of all good things in heaven and earth, but he deigned to show his presence even here below for the sake of the least of his creatures. For as the learned say, even though he is the Most High and the creator of all things, he deigned to take on the form of a servant… in order then to raise them up to a higher state." Through the Incarnation all of creation becomes good as "every higher creature with the faculty of reason" should acknowledge; creation is the means through which God "who loves the human race [*ipse humani generis amitor*] ... does not fail to enrich."[118] God embraces the world to give humans the complete happiness of God, just as humans must embrace the world to enjoy the complete happiness of God: "The Lord is here and everywhere."[119] She explains her deeply held belief in one of her most powerful passages:

> Believe that he is above, below, within, and without; for he is higher, deeper, inside, and outside. He is above in that he oversees and rules us. He is "high," and as the Psalmist says, *his glory is above the heavens.* He is below, for he supports us all: *in him we live, and move, and are,* and we exist in him always. He is within, for he fills and satisfies us with his good things, as is written: *the earth shall be filled with the fruit of thy works; and thou fillest with blessing every living creature.* He is outside, for he surrounds us with an impregnable wall, fortifies us, protects and defends us, as is written: he girds us with a wall and puts on his crown like a shield. I, your mother, although I may be worthless in the smallness and the shallowness of my understanding—I believe that he who is God is such.[120]

With such an understanding of the creator's presence and action in the world, it is not surprising to see Dhuoda espouse the value of the secular world for "earthly things teach what heavenly ones are."[121] Salvation can be attained only in and through this world. All of Dhuoda's advice and instruction to William is guided by this optimistic philosophy. One does not run away from the world and its politics but uses it, for in it is the key to happiness. "Seek out, hold close, and observe faithfully the examples of great men in the past, present, and future" if salvation is desired, but not just the example of the holy recluse. Seek instead those "who are known to be pleasing in their faith to both God and this world." The twelve patriarchs enjoy eternal happiness because "they undertook and accomplished worthy ends through thought and deed" in this world.[122] Dhuoda devotes the greater part of her manual instructing William how to live in this world, because that is the only way to gain ultimate happiness.

While Dhuoda believes in the efficacy of grace and discusses it at length in Book Four, she also believes that "among the human race [*in specie humanitatis*] to attain perfection requires the application of great and constant effort."[123] This means that because William's role is to "fight in this secular world among all the earth's confusion"[124] under Charles the Bald "who God and your father, Bernard, have chosen for you to serve,"[125] he must exert tremendous effort to serve well. "Serve him not only so that you please him in obvious ways, but also as one clearheaded in matters of both body and soul," Dhuoda advises. "Be steadfastly and completely loyal to him in all things." William must learn that loyalty is an indispensable commodity in the political world of his day. If he keeps "this loyalty as long as you live, in your body and in your mind" then "the advancement that it brings you will be of great value both to you and to those who in turn serve you." He must avoid "the madness of treachery" at all costs and instead spend his time trying to "discover how you may serve your lord" and "devote yourself to the faithful execution of your lord's commands. Look around as well and observe those who fight for him loyally and constantly. Learn from them how you may serve him."[126] A good soldier, though, does more than remain loyal to one lord. His duties extend to "the great and famous relatives and associates of your royal lord—those who are descended from his illustrious father's side as well as those related to him by marriage."[127] Such loyalty is essential for the preservation of society. Faithfulness must be complete and unquestioned, "for God chose them and established them in royal power." A soldier's duty is to his lord "whatever sort of lord he may be—and to his worthy relations of both sexes and to all those of royal origins." William must learn to "serve them to good ends."[128]

Dhuoda also offers William specific suggestions on how he can become useful in the political world of the court. Authority is always essential for the preservation of society. Although Dhuoda does not analyze the power exercised by secular lords, she does discuss the ways in which ecclesiastical leaders must exercise power in this world:

> Bishops, after the model of the true and sublime Lord, are the bearers of authority above, below, within, and outside. They have authority above for the reason that they give protection by looking out afar, as they take up a point of observation at a distance. For through their learning and by the example of their chastisement, the Lord gathers us together from far-off lands. And bishops have authority below because they are the feet that bring peace, announce good tidings, preach salvation, and speak to Sion. They have authority within because we are imbued with the example of their worth and wisdom; we are made learned and satisfied by them. And they have authority outside because through their constant prayer, staying as they do close to God, we are found worthy to be surrounded, fortified, protected, and kept safe, so that evil spirits do not seize us.[129]

The authority of the priest is similarly broad and extends over the whole person: body and mind in addition to soul. "I urge you to entrust your mind and body to the hands of priests," Dhuoda proclaims.[130] In the face of authority of any kind, ecclesiastical or secular, everyone must show respect: "As for the magnates and their counselors—and all those like them who serve faithfully—show them your love, affection, and service often. Do so to them together and individually, to whomever is important at court." Thus we find Dhuoda encouraging William to participate in the politics of the court. He should "learn from those elders" how to respond to and gain power, so that "you may be pleasing to God before all else and then be useful to man."[131]

What we are examining here is one of the earliest formulations of the chivalric code, certainly the earliest by a lay woman. Throughout the manual Dhuoda advises William on how to combine the needs of body and soul to become a moral Christian soldier. In fact, the Incarnation serves as Dhuoda's model for the Christian soldier. Christ took on the form of a servant "and if he who is so great acts thus even toward the least of men, what should we who are ourselves of small importance do for those who are even lesser? Those who can give aid should do so," even soldiers like William who "may be the least in stature among those who fight."[132] The good soldier, in short, imitates Christ. "I wish that as you grow patiently in worthy virtues among those who fight alongside you, you may always be slow to speak, and slow to anger," Dhuoda writes. "Therefore I direct you that, with gentleness, justice, and holiness, you perform your worthy service to him . . . . If you encounter a poor man, offer him as much help as you can, not only in words but also in deeds. I direct you likewise to offer generous hospitality to pilgrims, widows and orphans, children and indigents and to be quick to lift your hand to help those who you see are in need."[133] These acts of charity are not independent of the soldier's life but are an essential part of it, because the secular duties are an essential part of spiritual duties. Dhuoda is very insistent throughout the manual that William realize that he must fulfill the obligations of the secular world to meet the obligations of the spiritual world. William must try "to improve your own self," not solely in spiritual terms but "both in public and in your own mind."[134] Dhuoda emphasizes that each person has two births, "one of the flesh, the other of the spirit" and that "among the human race one cannot exist without the other." Hence Dhuoda's goal is "to set in order your earthly experience, so that you may act calmly and confidently, without dishonor, while you serve as a warrior or embrace the contemplative life."[135] This is Dhuoda's goal, because she believes success and right behavior in the secular world are necessary for happiness in the spiritual world. As Dhuoda summarizes, "And if your loyalty toward your father and your earthly lord leads you to respect and love them as well as the magnates and all your peers, old and young alike, and if you do not participate in insults to them or shameful contention against them, the spirit of the fear of God will certainly rest upon you."[136] The Christian soldier obeys the mandates of the spiritual world because it will make him a better soldier, and he fulfills the obligations of the secular world because it will bring him salvation: "I wish that you may act as you serve on earth among your fellow soldiers so that in the end you may be found worthy to be included as a free soul among the free, with the servants and soldiers of Christ who serve together and not alone, in that kingdom without end."[137]

In the political world of Dhuoda and William no figure loomed larger that the father, and no group was more important than family. Dhuoda provides us with entry into these two constructs, but as we shall see, she also adds a variation of her own to the traditional structures. First of all, as Claussen points out, Dhuoda's use of the words "pater" and "patres" is deliberately ambiguous, and can refer to Bernard as William's biological father, other fathers, God, or the patriarchs.[138] Dhuoda starts Book Three with a command that William "in every matter be obedient to your father's interest and heed his judgment."[139] While she does tell William to "love, fear, and cherish your father," she follows that mandate immediately with the reason why he must: "Keep in mind that your worldly estate proceeds from his." Moreover, "it is a fixed and unchangeable truth that no one, unless his rank comes to him from his father, can have access to another person at the height of power."[140] Dhuoda reminds William that "many others who have been obedient to God and mindful of the commands of a devoted father have been honored and respected in the secular world."[141] When she contemplates the source of power she situates it firmly within patriarchal structure: "Consider, my son, how strong those are in the secular world who are worthy of God's blessing because of their parents' merits and because of their own filial obedience."[142] But Dhuoda also talks at length about communities where fellowship rather than dominance prevails. In exegeting Psalm 41, "As the hart panteth," she uses Acts 4:32, 34 to explain:

> The point is not obscure to the learned, for everything is immediately clear in their sight. In the harts' mutual support—in their changing places in line—they

> show that human beings [*in generi humano*] too must have the brotherly fellowship of love for greater and lesser men alike, in all ways and in all circumstances. We read this was fulfilled in the past by many men [*per omnia*], especially among the holy apostles and those like them. It is written, "For neither was there any one needy among them, but all things were common unto them." They had "one heart and one soul" in God, always feeling brotherly compassion for each other in Jesus Christ.[143]

Even in society like the Carolingian that supported a class system, a community like the first Christians was possible. "What more could I or might I say to you," Dhuoda asks, "by way of example of those who are of differing status—subjects or equals or even those of low estate—but joined together by love?"[144] Acts 4:32–35 became the center of the *vita apostolica* movement of the eleventh- and twelfth-century monastic renewal,[145] but such a call for the *vita communis,* no less for the *vita apostolica,* was unusual in the ninth century, to say the least.[146] Even Dhuoda's call for corporeal works of mercy is done out of awareness of community "lest you forget fraternal compassion for those who are beneath you."[147] We see Dhuoda's concept of community placing all people on a level field when she discusses justice: "Each inquity or injustice returns to him who committed it. It is so among kings and dukes, and so also among bishops and other prelates who live badly or vainly and who not only perish for their own injustices but also cause others to fall headlong by allowing them their wrongdoings." Thus it is the duty of all "who share the same faults" to "correct each other."[148] Thus throughout the manual Dhuoda, without attacking the patriarchal structure directly, is offering William a substitute model, "one informed by ideals of mutual charity, cooperation, self-sacrifice."[149]

This stance is consistent with Dhuoda's understanding of marriage and motherhood. She chooses to quote a poet's reflections on marriage to support her own views of it: "The two will be one flesh, commanding all that is subject to them, raising their estate by the use of reason."[150] She also writes that "the word 'flesh' signifies the state of brotherhood in which all of us take our origin."[151] Marriage raises rather than diminishes both man and woman. In this she is consistent with other Carolingian theologians who stressed the equality of people in marriage.[152] Thus when she talks about William's future decision about whether to "keep your body in virginity" or "in the chastity of the union of marriage," she advises him to remember that "learned authors do not refuse sacred marriage to the union of the flesh" nor do Hebrew patriarchs "and all the others who struggled to keep their hearts pure in Christ in the union of marriage."[153] That Dhuoda argues for the good of marriage frequently in the text might surprise us, because she also gives frequent testimony to the trials endured in her own marriage.[154] Dhuoda is, however, quite capable of distinguishing the particular from the universal, as well as of separating emotional reactions from intellectual judgments. This is most clear in Dhuoda's treatment of parenthood. She judges William's biological father an unworthy parent and makes this clear to William when she compares Bernard to the biblical patriarchs.[155] She also lets us know that her personal history does not interfere with her intellectual ability to recognize the inherent worth of the role. We see this reverence for parenthood in her discussion of Theoderic, William's godfather,[156] and in her use of the model in her presentation of spiritual direction. In a book devoted to "instructing you how to direct your soul's service to perfection," she tells William that every person has two births, physical and spiritual. Obviously only women can give physical birth (she urges William to consult the Greeks if he needs the facts of life explained further[157]) but both parents can give spiritual birth. "One man may be the father of many others in this second birth," just as there are many "mothers to their children in both the first birth and the second birth in Christ." Here we see another instance of an equality that extends into both worlds, secular and spiritual, as Dhuoda tells us how parents can give spiritual birth to their children "in their teaching of the Church holy doctrines and the example of their conversion to good works."[158]

The distinction Dhuoda is making here helps us understand her own self-perception. First and foremost Dhuoda sees herself primarily as a human being. In Book One she feels obligated to justify her teaching to her audience. What is most significant in this passage is that she thinks she needs to justify her work not as a woman but as a frail human [*humanae fragilitatis meae*], composed of dust and ashes, a condition common to all humanity. She talks about the "happiness of the human condition" [*felicitas humanae conditionis*] and about the need "among the human race to live both a fleshly and a spiritual life" [*in genere consistere humano*].[159] Her frailty, her happiness, and her needs are common to all humanity, not just women or lay people.[160] Yet, the family of humanity is composed of individuals, and Dhuoda always perceives herself to be very much an individual. In this matter we are very indebted to Dhuoda, for she reveals her individuality in ways we do not see again for many generations. As Peter Dronke concludes, "none of the major Carolingians, in my view, can match Dhuoda in showing us a mind and presence of such sensitive individuality." Dronke goes on to argue that many of the limitations intellectual historians accuse her of are deficiencies of her critics who fail to realize that she is simply communicating much that was beyond the ken of her contemporaries.[161]

Secondly, she sees herself as both a biological parent and a spiritual parent. Biological parents are limited by the restrictions of the secular world, whereas spiritual parents are not. Spiritual parenthood is indeed superior to the biological, because its goals are. They have such strong obligations and responsibilities to their children that the restrictions of the secular world do not apply to them as they go about their tasks. Thus Dhuoda has no hesitation in claiming a magisterial authority over William that far exceeded the norms of a biological mother in a patriarchal society. She was justified because, she declares, "I will act as your mother in spirit as well as in body."[162] This is not merely a clever way of circumventing societal limitations placed on women but is a strongly held belief, one that leads her to advocate repeatedly throughout the manual that William must assume the same position of spiritual parent in relation to his brother:[163] "Read the words I address to you, understand them and fulfill them in action. And when your little brother, whose name I still do not know, has received the grace of baptism in Christ, do not hesitate to teach him, to educate him, to love him, and to call him to progress from good to better."[164] These are the tasks of a spiritual parent, ones that Dhuoda fulfills for William, and, therefore, her appropriation of the role of writer, teacher, and counselor are entirely within her rights. Her claims for these rights are sometimes couched in the topos of humility,[165] but she also sincerely believes that she has the right to these roles: "You and I must seek God out, my son; we take our existence from his approval, we live, and move, and are. Even I; unworthy and frail as a shadow, seek him as best I can and unceasingly call upon his aid as best I know and understand it. It is absolutely necessary for me to do so in all things."[166] This unworthy and frail woman then continues her self-justification by exegeting the story of the Syro-Phoenician woman and her child (Mt 14:21–28 and Mk 7:24–30) in a very personal way.[167] As "it often happens that an insistent little bitch, scrambling under the master's table with the male puppies, is able to snatch up and eat such crumbs as fall," so too Dhuoda places herself among the educated clergy "under his table—that is, within his holy church" to "gather words for both you and me, my son William—clear, worthy, beautiful words from among their intellectual and spiritual crumbs." It is God who "opens my understanding, giving me insight."[168]

Such is Dhuoda's justification of her participation in the intellectual life and the education system. She certainly has no concerns that she is transgressing any ecclesiastical or Pauline prohibition of women theologians. In her opening remarks in Book One she "humbly suggest[s]" that no one "condemn me or hold it against me that I am so rash as to take upon myself so lofty and perilous a task as to speak to you about God," and then proceeds to theologize throughout the manual never once worrying that her theology will be challenged.[169] She even exegetes Heb 5:12 ("For though by this time you ought to be teachers, you have need again for someone to teach you the elementary principles of the oracles of God, and you have come to need milk and not solid food") to show further support of her theological lesson on the beatitudes and gifts of the Holy Spirit. It is almost as if Dhuoda is endowing herself with an authority higher than sacerdotal, a quasi-scriptural authority.[170] It is in this vein that Dhuoda compares herself to Moses. After she rhetorically asks why she should be able to comprehend the mysteries of life when so many others have failed, she answers for us. As Moses at the burning bush could not see the face of God, so too Dhuoda's "desire is burning" because she too is unable to see God completely.[171] This similarity between herself and Moses is reinforced by her repeated use of such imagery. When she says that her "burning, watchful heart" desires to help William with "helpful words,"[172] she is implying that like Moses who was chosen to lead his people Dhuoda was chosen to lead William. If this scriptural authority is not enough, then Dhuoda offers the combined authority of Moses, biological motherhood, and spiritual parenthood to convince the doubter: "My son, my firstborn son—you will have other teachers to present you with works of fuller and richer usefulness, but not anyone like me, your mother, whose heart burns on your behalf."[173]

It is interesting to note that although Dhuoda repeatedly insists that "from the beginning of this book to the end, both in form and in content, in the matter and rhythm of the poetry as well as the prose passages here—know that everything, through it all, is intended entirely for you, for the health of your soul and body,"[174] this does not preclude her from intending her work to have a larger audience. She wants William to show this handbook to his little brother "when the time has come that he has learned to speak and to read."[175] In Book One she addresses her opening remarks "to those to whom you may offer this little book for perusal."[176] That she intended her manual to instruct people other than her son does indicate that she believed her authority to teach rested on more than or even primarily on motherhood. Interspersed throughout the manual is a theme that demonstrates yet another source of her teaching authority: her ability to think, read, and learn. If she was forced today to identify her most important qualification to teach, I believe she would chose her intellectual abilities, particularly her ability to "seek by thinking;"[177] she firmly believes that "if you live by thinking well and speaking well and acting well"[178] a person reaches perfection. And if we were to ask her what the most important qualification was for a student she would undoubtedly answer reading. Reading shapes thought and thoughts shape behavior in this world, and behavior in the secular world determines life in the spiritual world. That is why Dhuoda instructs William to "read and reread this volume from time to time."[179] Time and again she repeats this lesson: "Read the words I address you, understand them and fulfill them in action."[180] It is not just her writings that she promotes but reading in general. If her exposé of the Trinity is not intellectually satisfying, then "read the volumes of the orthodox saints" for thus not only will William be intellectually satisfied but he will start "flying away with laughter."[181] One must "read and consider," "read and pray often," read "with appropriate concentration," and then "read, ponder, contemplate, study and understand" some more.[182] Even at William's young age ("only four times four years' growth"[183]) Dhuoda urges that he "not be distracted by the mundane cares of this earthly world from acquiring many volumes. In these books you should seek out and learn" about even more things than Dhuoda includes in her manual.[184]

What we have in Dhuoda's emphasis on reading is a rare peek at a society in the process of becoming literate. The process in the West is complex, with many steps forwards and backwards before Western society becomes predominantly literate many centuries later, but we certainly gain a better understanding of how literacy enters into a lay culture after studying Dhuoda's work. I know of no other work that affords us this opportunity, hence once again underlying the importance of Dhuoda's inclusion in intellectual history. She assumes "an unlettered man wish[es] to become learned."[185] She tells William of the power of reading, where "you will learn how you must pray" and "everything will be clear to you there."[186] She writes that if he wants "to overcome [his] faults with ease" he should "read the eight beatitudes aloud and then keep them always in your heart."[187] If William will read and study then "your mind will be filled with great joy throughout all time,"[188] and he will "be truly rich."[189] He must let "the words of the saints shape his thought."[190] Her "great concern" is "to offer you helpful words."[191] In her exegesis of the Syro-Phoencian woman we saw her argue that at the lord's table (a clear reference to the Eucharist) she "can gather words for both you and me."[192] Indeed, reading "the words of the holy gospels and the writings of the other Fathers" will lead to knowledge of "the virtues, the elements, and the senses of the body."[193]

Because Dhuoda's main desire is to educate her sons and possibly some of their peers in body and soul she has some rather definite ideas about the type of pedagogy necessary to the task. Educational pedagogy must be based on tradition yet be flexible. And it must address the specific needs of the intended audience. "The knowledge of this little book is partly derived from several other books, but my loving intent here has been to refashion their content in a manner appropriate to your age."[194] That her teaching method is age-appropriate is a major concern of hers, and she explains this again in her introductory remarks of Book Six. "My intent here is to set forth and explain in turn those eight beatitudes linked, respectively, to the seven graces of the Holy Spirit," she begins. "In doing so, I have seen fit to address myself to you, who are only a boy, in the childish terms appropriate to my own understanding. I have done so as if you were unable to eat solid food but could take in something only like milk. Climbing little by little, as if on a stairway, you may then progress easily from lesser to greater things."[195] If William were older, then her teaching method would be different: "And if in twice as many years and half again I were to see your image, I would write to you of more difficult things, and in more words."[196] The student might respond differently too. "Study carefully the volumes of his scriptures," Dhuoda instructs, "with appropriate concentration."[197] The two best methods of teaching are by word and by example. In nearly every book Dhuoda cajoles William to "seek out, hold close, and observe faithfully the examples of great men in the past, present and future,"[198] and, of course, avoid "the example of evil men."[199]

Dhuoda also acknowledges the need to challenge the mind to higher levels in her discussion of numerology: "What the differences are among these various calculations, my son, is too long to explain step by step, but I will set it forth for you briefly so that you are at least familiar with this sort of reasoning."[200] Her extensive exegesis of the psalms should also be placed within her pedagogy. If, as religious historian E. Ann Matter contents, exegesis was "the major intellectual activity of Carolingian culture" and "was shaped by the educational needs of each generation,"[201] then Dhuoda is a near-perfect example of an exegete using biblical interpretation to further the education of her students. She constantly employs the language, images, and symbols of the bible to teach William things such as social responsibility, a sense of community, worldly obligations, and love of family.[202] Sometimes she uses a scriptural passage as the basis of her lesson which she then restates. For example, she writes, "My son, if you love justice and do not allow evil men to do evil deeds, you will be able to say confidently with the Psalmist, 'I have hated the unjust, and have loved thy law.' "[203] At other times she uses scripture to prove her lesson valid: "It profits a man nothing, if he gains the world and loses himself, for 'the world passeth away, and the concupiscence thereof.' "[204] Dhuoda at times incorporates scriptural language into her lessons so thoroughly that it is often difficult to separate her voice from that of the bible, as, for instance, in her lesson on anger: "I wish that, as you grow patiently in worthy virtues among those who fight alongside you, you may always be *slow to speak and slow to anger*."[205] She sometimes inverts a scriptural image to make a point, as in her use of the pregnancy and nursing imagery in Mt 24:19, or uses the symbols of scripture, such as the Lord's table in the Syro-Phoenican parable, to evoke a whole theological tradition.[206] What is common to all her exegesis is its use in Dhuoda's pedagogy.

Even after this lengthy discussion of Dhuoda's manual much still remains that deserves the attention of intellectual historians. There is a highly developed soteriology, in part original, in part derived from Irenaeus' works.[207] I have mentioned Dhuoda's status as a theologian and as a lay person; she articulates a rather sophisticated lay theology which seeks salvation in and through the secular world. She has a great respect for history and the models it gives us; she finds virtue and reward in the secularism of court life; and she encourages stewardship, community, and the rights of the individual. She defines authority and political power quite differently than do monastic or clerical circles and places the parenthood of mother and father center stage. Furthermore, Dhuoda is most persistent in her demand that the body, mind, and soul are equally essential to human perfectibility. Dhuoda's God is the god of the Incarnation who fully embraces the whole of creation. The god who dominates the pages of her manual is not transcendent but immanent. A corollary of Dhuoda's concern with lay theology is her moral or "practical" theology;[208] the whole of Book Four is devoted to the construction of practical theology. Her sacramental theology is likewise well developed, particularly baptism, marriage, the Eucharist, and penance. While speculative thought is not Dhuoda's forte, she is more than capable of engaging in it. In a very lengthy discussion on the term "*quasi*" ("as though") in Book Five, for example, Dhuoda attempts to reconcile the temporal order with the eternal. It is a discussion historians of philosophy should note, because at minimum it reveals a level of interaction between the intellectual elite and the educated laity. Finally, Dhuoda's anthropology contradicts many of the stereotypes we have of early medieval society's social beliefs, as in all the above-mentioned topics. Future scholars must take Dhuoda's manual into account and adjust their generalizations accordingly.

The Ottonian Renaissance

Dhuoda completed her manual on February 2, 843,[209] the same year that the division of the Carolingian Empire into three kingdoms was formalized in the Treaty of Verdun. The treaty did little to bolster the political stability of the area, and it did not provide a structure strong enough to withstand the onslaught of destructive incursions by Magyars, Muslims, and Scandinavians into the area. In 895 the Magyars were in Hungary, and during the next half-century they continued to plunder Bavaria, Saxony, the Danube, Alsace and Rhine regions, and even Reims, until they were defeated at the battle of Lechfeld in 955 by Otto I of Germany. The bulk of the Scandinavian invasions were felt in the British Isles where raiders had struck as early as 787. Within seven years the great educational center and library of Jarrow had been plundered and razed. During the course of the ninth century the Scandinavians spread their terror throughout western Europe and settled permanently in England. Alfred the Great (871–899) of Wessex eventually organized Anglo-Saxon resistance enough to check Scandinavian dominance somewhat, and when he insisted peace was contingent on their conversion to Christianity he paved the way for Scandinavian assimilation into Anglo-Saxon culture. The year 843 also saw Muslim forces threaten but not conquer Rome; they had previously conquered Sicily, Corsica, Sardinia, and parts of the Rhône River delta region. Muslims occupied bases on the Italian peninsular until the Byzantine army expelled them in 915.

Since the Middle Ages themselves scholars have debated about the effect these events had on the intellectual life of the tenth century. That libraries, schools, monasteries, and cathedrals were destroyed is certain, but it is also certain that many new schools were built to offset the losses.[210] In England few if any women's monasteries survived the invasions, but when Alfred restored order to Anglo-Saxon society he and his wife Elswitha busied themselves with the building of monastic houses, among them the women's monasteries at Shaftesbury and Nunnaminster.[211] Monasticism and hence education was injected with new life with the establishment of Cluny by Count William (interestingly, the grandson of Dhuoda[212]). The greatest concentration of women's monasteries during the ninth and tenth centuries, however, was in Germany. Wemple tells us that men and women nobility preferred to establish women's houses rather than men's; in the diocese of Halberstadt six male monasteries were founded in the tenth century, while twelve female houses were.[213] In northwestern Germany the great houses of Gandersheim, Essen, Quedlinburg, and Nordhausen thrived and encouraged intellectual activity, especially under abbesses Richburga of Nordhausen, Hathumod and Gerberga II of Gandersheim, Matilda of Quedlinburg, and Matilda of Essen. Recent scholarship has argued that all four abbesses inspired or commissioned major historical works that were produced by women: *The Foundation of the Gandersheim Community, Deeds of Otto, Annales of Quedlinburg, Life of Queen Matilda Antiquor, Life of Queen Matilda Posterior,* and a Latin translation of the *Anglo-Saxon Chronicle.*[214] Historian Elizabeth van Houts goes further and argues that women's contributions to historiography extended beyond these works into what she calls "commemorative activity." Tenth-century Ottonian women commissioned chronicles, read them, orally transmitted information for them, collaborated with writers, and served as memory banks in the service of dynastic interests.[215] Most abbesses of the great Ottonian monasteries conscientiously kept records of their ancestors and considered it their duty to keep the memory of the past alive.[216] This is not an activity traditionally included in intellectual histories but one that should be, for without their contributions the chief historical works of this period would not have been written. Some abbesses, such as Hathumod of Gandersheim, were revered in *vitae* that spoke of their intellectual gifts. "No one could show greater quickness of perception," Agius wrote, "or a stronger power of understanding in listening to or in expounding the scriptures,"[217] thus indicating the women engaged in exegesis at a time when, according to historian Beryl Smalley, "bible study represented the highest branch of learning."[218] This is not meant to imply that women studied only scripture. We know from the writings of Hrotsvitha that her education included the study of Jerome, Prudentius, Venantius Fortunatus, Sulpicius Severus, Bede, Notker, Ekkehard, Virgil, Lucan, Statius, Terence, Boethius, Isidore of Seville, *vitae,* the *Vulgate,* liturgical texts, Greek apocryphal gospels and acts, probably Ovid, and possibly Donatus.[219] As historian John Newell says, Hrotsvitha's training in this classical works "seems fairly representative of well-educated writers of the tenth century."[220]

The literary evidence extant at Essen allows us an opportunity to judge the level of intellectual activity that these women engaged in on the eve of the Ottonian renaissance. Whether or not there was a scriptorium there has not been definitely settled, but there is much evidence to claim there was.[221] Marginalia leaves us no doubt that the women could write, that they were well educated and comprehended much, and that they were literate in both Latin and their vernacular. In two very thorough studies of one of Essen's most famous codex, *Sammelhandschrift,* historians Steven Stofferahn and Bernhard Bischoff both claim that much can be gleaned from the manuscript. Its unique contents consist of works from Augustine, Claudius of Turin, Alcuin, Ambrose, Old and New Testament, Bede, Gregory I, anonymous commentaries and sermons, lives of Euphrosynae and Marina, a hymnary, Book of Songs, Ephraem, and Pseudo-Ambrose.[222] Bischoff argues that the unique musical notation script in the manuscript points to the existence of an independent intellectual tradition flourishing at Essen in the late ninth century;[223] Stofferahn argues that curious notes on a flyleaf support the thesis that women's intellectual activity was not exceptional but mainstream.[224] The flyleaf contains this petition written by a schoolgirl to her teacher: "Mistress ["*domina magistra*"] Felhin, give me leave to keep vigil this night with mistress Adalu, and I affirm and swear to you with both hands that I shall not cease either reading or singing on behalf of our Lord the whole night through. Farewell, and do as I ask."[225] The presence of the message in the manuscript, first of all, tells us that girls were being educated. Second, it tells us that schoolgirls were reading the manuscript and that they read and wrote fluently. Third, the passage evokes "images of actively and intellectually engaging women" whose education was thorough enough for them to utilize it in the course of everyday life. Finally, the girl's education was so extensive that it "gave her the power to add her own unwitting testimonial to this manuscript's extraordinary ability to communicate the effectiveness and creativity of Carolingian women's education to students and teachers a millennium away."[226]

There is testimony in other manuscripts that confirms that girls were regularly educated in the major women's monasteries of the late ninth and tenth centuries. The *vita* of Liutberga relates how the saint instructed girls in an extern school of some type, because after their education the girls returned to their homes.[227] In Queen Matilda's *vita* the author informs us that Matilda entered the monastery of Herford to study, not to become a nun, hence no dispensation was needed when she left to marry Henry I.[228] Hrotsvitha tells us of her monastic teachers and a bit of the methods women used in their teaching. Her comments also let us see how monasteries gave women the freedom to pursue intellectual goals:

> Unknown to others and secretly, so to speak, I worked alone. Sometimes I composed with great effort, again I destroyed what I had poorly written; and thus I strove according to my [*sic*] ability, scarcely adequate though it was, nonetheless, to complete a composition from the thoughts in the writing with which I had become acquainted within the confines of our monastery of Gandersheim: first through the instructive guidance of our learned and kindly teacher Rikkardis, and of others who taught in her stead; and then through the gracious considerations of the royal Gerberga, under whose rule as abbess I am living at present. Though she is younger in years than I am, yet, as befits a niece of the emperor, she is farther advanced in learning, and she it was who right kindly instructed me in those various authors whom she herself studied under the guidance of learned teachers.[229]

LIBRARY
UNIVERSITY OF ST. FRANCIS
JOLIET, ILLINOIS

Hrotsvitha also mentions "the loving care of my teachers ["*magistrorum*"]," which Dronke insists in its context is testimony to Hrotsvitha having male teachers as well as female.[230] Further evidence of widespread education of Carolingian and Ottonian women is found in records of book ownership and borrowing,[231] an addition to the numerous extant private charters that give witness to women's literacy.[232] McKitterick argues for the possibility of another contribution to intellectual activity on the part of German nuns: "In Niedermünster, Meschede, Kitzingen, Gandersheim, Freckenhorst, Herford, Quedlinburg, or any of the other leading houses of religious women in the Ottonian Empire, there is no reason to suppose that the women were not capable of producing their own books."[233] McKitterick offers evidence of another nature, iconography, for her thesis. In a study comparing Carolingian illustrations of women to Ottonian, she shows that a striking feature in Ottonian manuscripts is the increased representation of women, particularly representations which portray women in favorable intellectual light.[234]

It is important to acknowledge all these activities, for together they combine to produce the intellectual atmosphere in which the Ottonian renaissance arose. Henry I (919–936) established the Saxon dynasty as rulers of Germany, and under his son Otto I (936–973), called the Great, Germany experienced relative prosperity, at least enough to support increased intellectual activity. Such activity received encouragement from another direction, too, first from that of Otto I's wife Adelheid of Burgundy and then from the wife of their son Otto II, Theophano. Adelheid was well educated and during her stay in Italy prior to the marriage she had been exposed to Byzantine intellectual culture. Theophano was also well educated, the granddaughter of Constantine VII, Byzantine emperor and author of *The Book of Ceremonies*.[235] The Byzantine connection resulted in numerous scholarly activities. The writing of Liutprand of Cremona is one example, and his *Embassy to Constantinople* is a worthy product of any age. Grammarian Stephen of Pavia, theologian Rather of Verona, poet Leo of Vercelli, translator Notker of St. Gall, and the educator Notker of Liège all flourished during this period, producing works of varying degrees of merit.[236]

In 1888 William Hudson summarized his contemporaries' view of the tenth century thus: "It is a generally expressed opinion that it was during this period that the intellectual darkness of the Middle Ages reached its deepest."[237] After a century of research in areas like those just discussed, we now know that intellectual activity was not completely stilled. There was an Ottonian renaissance. Yet, Hudson's statement is comparative, and thus the thrust of the opinion remains valid. In comparison with past and future periods, even in comparison with the immediately preceding Carolingian renaissance and the immediately succeeding twelfth-century renaissance, the Ottonian renaissance was more limited. It was not, however, sterile, and, therefore, it is erroneous to view Hrotsvitha, the century's brightest light, as exceptional. The genius that she displayed in her work was unique, as is all genius by definition, but the work she engaged in was not per se unique or exceptional.

While many judgments have been offered concerning the work of Hrotsvitha I believe the true significance of her work as it bears on intellectual history is in its originality. We know that Hrotsvitha borrowed, imitated, and copied much from the literary canons of the past, so I am obviously not suggesting that Hrotsvitha was writing on a *tabula rasa*. Her originality, rather, rests on the type of originality that her age was in dire need of. A major lesson from the failed Carolingian Empire was that the new peoples of the West could not simply recreate the West of the past. The solutions of antiquity were answers to problems peculiar to antiquity. Tenth-century society had different problems that needed different solutions. Only if and when they realized this would they survive as a cultured society. This did not necessitate the complete abandonment of all that was ancient, but it did demand that tenth-century people chose only those elements of the past that could contribute to the structure of a new culture and reject those elements which did not directly help. New vehicles of thought, new modes of communication, new sets of relationships, and new definitions of self had to be created if the new West was to survive its birth. In Hrotsvitha's writings we see this type of originality. She combined the best of the old with the best of the new in such an original, creative manner that it became part of the foundation of Western literature. Sometimes she accomplished this in the most simple way.[238] For centuries the legends of the early martyrs had circulated in the West, yet it took until the tenth century for anyone to realize the dramatic value of these narratives. Hrotsvitha recognized how effective they would be in dialogue and set about doing just that, creating the first Christian dramas as a result.[239] Moreover, she appears conscious of the nature of her talent and of her potential contribution to society.

Hrotsvitha addresses both the issue of originality and the nature of her contribution in the prefaces she wrote for her works.[240] She is aware that she is sailing in uncharted waters yet proceeds full speed ahead. "At present I am defenceless at every point, because I am not supported by any authority," she acknowledges. That, however, is the price one pays when something new is pursued. Creating something new but imperfect is certainly a lesser fault than not creating at all. "Why should I fear the judgment of others" for any mistakes she might make in her ventures, Hrotsvitha asks in the preface to her epics, when, in reality "I should deserve blame if I sought to withhold my work."[241] She realizes that humility and courage are needed for creativity, and she surely demonstrated courage when she decided to baptize pagan literature as she simultaneously embraced it. Her dramas, the first ones written since antiquity, merge elements of classical and patristic literature with themes and presuppositions of her Christian world to produce a distinctly different type of literature, peculiar to the need of her time and destined to become the seed which blossoms into medieval morality plays.[242] She accomplishes this by accepting the best of the old and turning it into something new. She explains how and why she did this in reference to Terence.[243] Many of her contemporaries enjoyed reading Terence, because of "the sweetness of his style and diction," but, unfortunately, his subject matter leaves them stained by learning of wicked things in his depiction. "Therefore, I, the strong voice of Gandersheim, have not refused to imitate him in writing" but not in subject. She simply changed Terence's "shameless acts of lascivious women" into Christianity's "laudable chastity of sacred virgins." It was not an easy task, one that demanded skill and imagination, "but had I omitted this out of modesty I would not have fulfilled my intent"—the creation of the first Christian dramas. "Doubtlessly, some will berate the worthlessness of this composition as much inferior, much humbler, on a much smaller scale, and not even comparable to the language of him whom I set forth to imitate,"[244] but so what? Hrotsvitha concludes that what is gained by the creation of a new genre is more important that what is lost in literary style and skill. She is well aware that she is not as linguistically skilled as Terence. That realization does not discourage her, for she believes the old forms of antiquity are not adequate to the needs of her day. Another example of this is found in her *Gesta Ottonis,* where she relates the story of Queen Adelheid's escape for Italy before her marriage to Otto I. Edward Zeydel argues that this narration provides us with insight as to how Hrotsvitha used earlier sources to construct her own unique literary works; she is not a "slavish imitator" of others but borrows carefully, always retaining "her integrity as an independent literary artist."[245]

Hrotsvitha knows that there is a thin line between over-confidence and lack of courage and the dilemma is often painful for her: "I am torn between two contradictory emotions: joy and fear; I rejoice with all my heart that God, by whose grace alone I am what I am, is praised in my art; but I also fear to appear to be more than what I am. I am convinced both would be wrong: to deny God's gracious gift to one; and to pretend to have received a gift when one has received none. I do not deny that by the gift of the Creator's grace I am able to grasp certain concepts concerning the arts because I am a creature capable of learning."[246] Once she realized her potential she felt obligated to actualize her talents in meaningful ways. "I was eager that the talent given me by Heaven should not grow rusty from neglect, and remain silent in my heart from apathy,"[247] Hrotsvitha confides, so she challenged herself to master as much subject matter as she could. She even challenged herself to learn new forms of communication: "Although prosody may seem a hard and difficult art for a woman to master, I without any assistance but that given by the merciful grace of Heaven (in which I have trusted, rather than in my own strength) have attempted in this book to sing in dactyls."[248] Sometimes she appears overwhelmed by the obstacles each new task imposed. In her preface to *Gesta Ottonis* Hrotsvitha describes the frustration she experienced as she pushed the Christian epic into new areas of expression and historical narration:[249] "I was like a person in a strange land wandering without a guide through a forest where the path is concealed by dense snow. In vain he tries to follow the directions of those who have shown the way." Still, she trod onwards despite the fact that "there were things of which I could not find any written record, nor could I elicit information by word of mouth which seemed sufficiently reliable."[250] The overall impression one gets from the preface is that Hrotsvitha had, in Dronke's words, "a positive sense of doing something wholly new."[251] This is particularly evident in her history of Gandersheim in which she portrays herself as "the new vision of sparkling light" announcing the history of her monastery.[252] Even self-deprecating remarks are either deliberate over-statements for effect or "have a twinkle about them"; all such remarks are made in a context of self-confidence in herself as "the strong voice of Gandersheim."[253]

How Hrotsvitha achieves originality can be seen when her plays are compared to her sources, the passions of saints. She changes the mood of the sources from passive to active by using dialogue. This invites the audience to participate.[254] She gives central characters minor roles, and minor character move center stage. Strong, controlling males are replaced with weak buffoons, and weak, meek, feeble female victims are replaced with dominating, intelligent female heroes. For example, the drama *The Passions of the Holy Virgins Agapes, Chionia, and Hirena,* commonly known as

Dulcitius, is based on the ancient passion of St. Anastasia. Dulcitius is the chief male protagonist in the passion and is portrayed as a bright, powerful ruler intent upon bending the will of three sisters toward evil. In Hrotsvitha's hand Anastasia disappears completely. By juxtaposing Dulcitius' opening remarks that the sisters are angry with his reason for declaring them mad, their Christianity, Hrotsvitha immediately elevates the women to superior intelligence over the men in the drama. The sisters are further elevated in stature when Hrotsvitha describes them as so "firm in faith"[255] that they "will never give in to evil persuasion."[256] Dulcitius, on the other hand, is continually reduced in stature, first, when he cannot torture the strong women into submission, second, when he mistakes pots and pans for the women while trying to seduce them, and, last, when even his wife joins the women in mocking him. The women succeeded in making "a laughingstock" out of Dulcitius,[257] while he has succeeded in nothing. Hrotsvitha's role reversal is not accomplished solely by words; the actions of her characters make the role reversal visible and concrete. Hrotsvitha's audience hears 'that noise outside the door." They "look through the crack" to see him think that "he is enjoying our embrace." They see him "appear in sight" as he "embraces the pots and the pans, giving them tender kisses."[258] Their heroic struggle as good women fighting victoriously against bad men is at the center of the plot, and they achieve their victory not by turning into males but by remaining true to their female roles as sisters. Unlike the passive women in Terence's plays, Hrotsvitha's women create and control the dramatic action throughout the entire drama.[259]

These same features are found in all her other dramas. Weak women are not immortalized by Hrotsvitha, only independent women with a strong resemblance to the woman we meet in the prefaces, Hrotsvitha herself.[260] Hrotsvitha uses her play *Sapientia* as a vehicle to showcase intelligent women. Sapientia, the mother, and Fides, Spes, and Karitas, the daughters, are all depicted as possessing superior intelligence to the men, even to the emperor Hadrian. When Hadrian asks Fides who she is mocking with her expression she answers bluntly, "It's your foolishness I deride, and I mock your stupidity."[261] Sapientia gives Hadrian a long, complex lesson in numerology in reply to his simple question, "How old are they?" Her first complicated reply leaves Hadrian "totally ignorant as to the answer to my question,"[262] while her much longer but as complicated second reply leaves Hadrian exclaiming in frustration, "What a thorough, perplexing lecture has arisen from my question concerning the children's ages!" This provides Hrotsvitha with an opportunity to summarize her attitude toward secular knowledge in reply: "Praise be thereof to the supreme wisdom of the Creator and to the marvelous science of this world's Maker, who not only created the world in the beginning out of nothing and ordered everything according to number, measure and weight, but also in the seasons and in the ages of men gave us the ability to grasp the wonderous science of the arts."[263]

Hrotsvitha does not sacrifice the women's feminine identity in order to emphasize their intellectual abilities, as was done in many of the passions. Hrotsvitha's women are women. They fully embrace their feminine roles as mothers, daughters, and sisters. When the women are placed in prison for "three days to reconsider" their refusal to worship Diana, it is their roles as women which bolster them and gives them courage. "We will never forget what we learned in our cradle sucking at your breast," Karitas promises. "It was for this that I nursed you with my milk flowing free; it was for this that I carefully reared you three," Sapientia replies, that she "may thus deserve to be called the mother-in-law of the Eternal King."[264] Spes explicitly rejects Hadrian's offer to protect her within his patriarchal clan: "I don't want you for my father; I have no desire for your favors."[265] Fides' final good-bye to Sapientia is a restatement of their most basic identity: "O venerable mother, say your last farewell to your child; give a kiss to your firstborn."[266]

So far this discussion might lead one to believe that Hrotsvitha maintains that intelligence and gender are intertwined and that she is arguing that the intellectual status of men and women should be the reverse of what classical and patristic writers maintained.[267] Actually, she is arguing something else. She is proposing that intelligence is not determined by gender. Just as we saw Dhuoda, a woman of unexceptional education or upbringing, emphasize her humanity as her chief identity, so too we see Hrotsvitha, likewise "very much a child of her century,"[268] emphasize her humanity. Hrotsvitha's main interest is in the promotion of knowledge. To that end she constructs her plays. The extensive lessons found in *Sapientia* and *Pafnutius*[269] are not distractions weakening the play's structure, but are central to her drama. Pursuit of knowledge is a very Christian thing to do. It is not whether men or women are more intelligent but that Christianity is superior to paganism, specifically because it embraces the pursuit of knowledge. This is indeed a crucial message in tenth-century Europe. Such educational lessons were rarely if ever included in hagiographic literature,[270] and certainly Hrotsvitha's sources do not include them. This is another example of Hrotsvitha's originality. Hrotsvitha's explanation in *Pafnutius* of "the dialectic method of argument" and her long discussion of music theory and its mathematical basis are done because, as she has Pafnutius say, "I was eager to share with you the tiny drops of knowledge which I drank from the overflowing cup of philosophers." Pafnutius also propounds two principles Hrotsvitha maintains must guide society. He tells his audience, first, that "there was no harm in your efforts to learn more because now you know some things of which you were ignorant before," and, second, that "it is not the knowledge of knowable things which offends God, but the wrongdoing of the knower."[271] Hrotsvitha lived by these principles.

Her desire to create, nonetheless, did not lead her to attempt tasks beyond her potential. She knew her limits. After completing the *Gesta* she tells us that "now, worn out by the journey, I am holding my peace and resting in a suitable place. I do not propose to go further without better guidance."[272] She possessed "little genius" [*talentum ingenioli*], not "genius" [*ingenium*].[273] That talent, however, allowed her to make yet another creative contribution to Western intellectual life; all these self-reflective remarks and disclosures of motives, intentions, and gifts are autobiographical in nature, and, thus, Hrotsvitha's work must be included in any history of the development of that genre.

Besides knowing her own creative limitations, she also knew the value of what she was producing and was extremely confident in its worth. We see this confidence in her defense of some questionable sources used in her legends:

> To the objection that may be raised that I have borrowed parts of this work from authorities which some condemn as apocryphal, I would answer that I have erred

> through ignorance, not through presumption. When I started, timidly enough, on the work of composition I did not know that the authenticity of my material had been questioned. On discovering this to be the case I decided not to discard it, because it often happens that what is reputed false turns out to be true. In these circumstances I shall need as much assistance in defending this little work as in improving it.[274]

In her letter to learned patrons we see how conscious Hrotsvitha was of the nature of her task: She was to weave part of the past into something new. Borrowing imagery from Boethius to demonstrate how rooted she was in tradition even while pursuing new avenues of discourse,[275] Hrotsvitha writes: "Therefore, in order to prevent God's gift in me to die by my neglect, I have tried whenever I could probe, to rip small patches from philosophy's robe and weave them into this little work of mine."[276] Only in this way would society benefit. Taken in its entirety classical literature was too filled with "the uselessness of pagan guile"[277] to serve a Christian society, but if select parts of ancient thought could be used and adapted to tenth-century Germanic thought, then the end product would be elevated, or, as Hrotsvitha says in the rhetoric of the day,[278] "the worthlessness of my own ignorance may be ennobled by the interweaving of this noble material's shine."[279] Editing pagan works is not an easy task. It takes skill to do it correctly, and Hrotsvitha openly claims that she can and will perform the necessary job. In the preface to the dramas Hrotsvitha begins by noting that Terence's fiction contains much that is good ("the sweetness of his style") and much that is bad ("wicked things in his depiction"). She then pledges to edit Terence's work accordingly so that the bad is eliminated, the good is retained and thus produces a literature that pleases. Twice she tells us her object is "to imitate him in writing, whom others laud in reading, so that in the selfsame form of composition in which the shameless acts of lascivious women were phrased the laudable chastity of sacred virgins may be praised."[280]

Her goal, in other words, was to transform classical literature into medieval literature. To a large extend she succeeded. No one before Hrotsvitha ever attempted to reinvent classical literature. Hers was a singular vision. That her literary skills were not equal to the masters of antiquity is beside the point. Hrotsvitha recognized the value of classical intellectual life. She realized that selective editing would transform them into a form more beneficial to contemporary needs, and she did it. The value of her work in the intellectual development of the West is not in the sophisticated style in which she expressed her ideas but in the idea itself. The fact that there are "those who are by far my betters in learning" does not intimidate her, nor does she hesitate to proceed with the task in order "to avoid censure." If, because "of my inelegant style," society does not get satisfaction from her work, "it was still worth the effort to me." She was content, because she knew that "even if aptitude is lacking on my part"[281] to produce a distinctly tenth-century drama by merging the classical past with Christianity, it is not only a valid desire but is the foundation for all future medieval dramas.[282] E. Blastfield and Mary Butler claim even more. They argue that Hrotsvitha's male characters are "the forerunners of the lovers, villains, and traitors of the Elizabethan drama," the likes of which are unknown in the ancient world. Furthermore, "because of their modern blend of feminine dignity and dauntless spirit, the women characters are far removed from the soft, sweet pagan heroines." Hrotsvitha's women are no longer chained to tradition but have "gone far beyond to the freedom in inquiry. Hrotsvitha's characters, as it were, stood upon the crest of the millennium."[283]

There is another area in which Hrotsvitha communicates awareness of the significance of her work, the area of history. When Abbess Gerberga commissioned Hrotsvitha to write an epic about Otto I,[284] Hrotsvitha apparently hesitated, and with good reason. For her dramas she tells us she had Terence as a model, but for a panegyric on Otto she was "without a model." Hrotsvitha means more than just that there was no existing epic on Otto for her to imitate. In fact, she admits that there may be some sources on Otto: "Many, perchance, have written and many hereafter will produce masterful memorials of your achievements."[285] She means, instead, that there were no epics she could use as models that presented the protagonist as both heroic according to classical standards and virtuous according to Christian standards. In short, she knew she was creating a new genre, the Christian epic. She wants to replace the classical heroic epic with a Christianized one. Hrotsvitha's Otto does not follow the example of Aeneas, as classical epics commonly did.[286] Rather, Hrotsvitha molds Otto into "the celebrated King David" and his son Otto II into "our Solomon," both Old Testament kings who ruled "wisely establishing the decrees of sacred laws and penetrating with profound mind into the secrets of nature."[287] When Otto learns of the deaths of his enemies his reaction is not classical but biblical. Like David, Otto laments the loss as David grieved at the death of Saul.[288] The highest praise she bestows on Otto is when she claims he was such a good ruler that "you would think that King David was ruling."[289] Gone are any descriptions of Otto as warrior-hero and present are the images of Otto as the epitome of Christian heroism. When Hrotsvitha does mention Roman imperial values it is within a Christian context. Thus, Otto is "mighty sovereign of the empire of the Caesars," but only because of "the indulgent kindliness of the eternal King."[290]

Kratz argues that Hrotsvitha also departs from the traditional Latin historical epic by "an avoidance of the language and trappings of classicizing epic, and an implied criticism of the older heroic model." We see an example of this in Hrotsvitha's refusal to describe battle scenes, which Kratz calls "the most striking departure from the epic tradition."[291] Hrotsvitha's stated reason for her declination is that she is but a "frail woman living in quiet, secluded community" who could not write about Otto's military deeds as well as the men whom she was sure would also write panegyrics about Otto.[292] Given her portrait of Otto, though, one has more than enough grounds to question whether this was her only reason. She does not deny the military responsibilities of a ruler, but she does imply by her refusal to adhere to the classical form that includes military exploits and by her projection of David as Otto's model that there is a difference between imperial rulers and Christian kings. Hrotsvitha's kings exemplify the virtues of justice, mercy, piety, and fortitude as Christianity understands them, not as pagan culture does.[293] Hrotsvitha's Christian king does battle with human nature, not just with humans. The ultimate victory is to triumph on the battlefield of temptation.

Hrotsvitha also displays an historian's keen sense of duty toward the facts of history. Long ago scholars noted how after centuries of neglect new life was breathed into historiography by medieval monks[294]; the work of Hrotsvitha necessitates a modification of that assessment to include canonesses. A prerequisite for the new secular history advanced during the high Middle Ages was a reverence for historical truth as verifiable fact. That, in turn, meant careful scrutiny of sources for accuracy. We find all these attitudes present in Hrotsvitha's works and explicitly stated in her prefaces. She writes to Abbess Gerberga that they both "know that it was impossible to collect together [Otto's achievements] from hearsay." Hearsay was not acceptable for history, even an historical epic. By way of complaining about the obstacles placed in her way as she wrote *Gesta,* she lets us see what she considered to be the two best sources for history: "There were things of which I could not find any written record, nor could I elicit information by word of mouth which seemed sufficiently reliable."[295] In a note placed before her preface to the dramas, she gives, as an example of how she considered these types of sources:

> I found all the material I have used in this book in various ancient works by authors of reputation, with the exception of the story of the martyrdom of St. Pelagius, which has been told her in verse. The details of this were supplied to me by an inhabitant of the town where the Saint was put to death. This truthful stranger assured me that he had not only seen Pelagius, whom he described as the most beautiful of men, face to face, but had been a witness to his end. If anything has crept into my other compositions, the accuracy of which can be challenged, it is not my fault, unless it be a fault to have reproduced the statements of unreliable authorities.[296]

Without authoritative sources Hrotsvitha's work was vulnerable to criticism. Hrotsvitha thus proceeded to use other methods to access authoritative truth. She persevered and, like the heroic figure wandering lost in a forest, Hrotsvitha "in like manner, bidden to undertake a complete chronicle of illustrious achievements I [have] gone on my way stumbling and hesitating, so great was the difficulty of finding a path in the forest of these royal deeds." She turned to "the eloquent treatises of the learned" for guidance.[297] She examined her own motives in writing: "No baneful presumption of mind has urged me in this matter, nor have I voluntarily played falsely by a disdain of the truth as a whole." Her chief desire was to produce an account that "is true."[298] She is also careful to assert her role in discerning proper sources, in selecting the rhetoric best suited to tell the tale, and in interpreting the past to fit the needs of the present.[299] Ultimately, though, Hrotsvitha claims the validity of her works, be they legend, drama, or epic, rests on her ultimate source, God. In *The Founding of Gandersheim Community* she does this through projecting herself into the story as the reality behind the symbolic "sparkling light" in the heavens which tells of the coming of the monastery. Hrotsvitha's task is to "set in harmonious order" those events that led to the foundation of Gandersheim "in the service of him who had filled it with such light."[300] In her prefaces she is not circumvent. She states directly that she was "without any assistance but that given by the merciful grace of Heaven in which I have trusted, rather than in my own strength." She knows that because her talent is "talent given me by Heaven" then she and everyone else must "give the credit to God" for what it creates.[301] Her insistence that her talent originates in God is not a way of belittling her role in the creative process. To the contrary, it is Hrotsvitha's way of making it nigh impossible for critics to belittle her role. How can they criticize what Hrotsvitha produces if she is merely an instrument through which God works? "Relying only on the aid of heavenly grace and not on my own powers," she explains, "my gift of ability" is "transformed into an instrument" and used to "render some little chord of Divine praise."[302] Thus she can warn men in the legend of *Basilius,* "and let him not scorn the frail sex of the women of no importance who played these melodies on a frail reed pipe, but rather let him praise Christ's heavenly mercy."[303] Her insistence that God works through her should also be seen in conjunction with her protestations of feminine weakness (all of which contain, in Dronke's works "an element of deliberate over-acting"[304]). She is playing on the biblical strength-in-weakness theme.[305] Both she and her women heroes must be understood in this context, "for the more glorious the victories of triumphant innocence are shown to be, especially when female weakness triumphs in conclusion and male strength succumbs in confusions."[306] All limitations of humanity and restrictions of society are simply and completely overcome when God's work is done.

A review of current literature on Hrotsvitha will clearly indicate how extensive her contributions are. Critics may continue to debate Hrotsvitha's literary merit, but I do not think anyone today would try to deny Hrotsvitha her rightful position in intellectual history, particularly as a pioneer. As is appropriate in a survey we have but touched the surface of her intellectual contributions. We can best end our discussion of Hrotsvitha with her own words: "I am what I am, ... the strong voice of Gandersheim."[307]

2

The Creation of a Literate Society

Slowly but surely the images of the medieval period as dark and infertile are fading from historical generalizations. Thanks to the scholarly work pursued for nearly a half century now, we know that the eleventh century was beginning an upward spiral that would ultimately lead to the modern era. Invasions ceased. Travel, commerce, and communication became easier as the second millennium proceeded. New technology affected the daily lives of people by making possible agrarian surplus, something rare in the West during the ninth and tenth centuries. The new political ties that were established during and after the Carolingian period were improved and extended, making possible the rise of small units of political stability. With their new-found prosperity and stability Western people began to expand beyond their borders, renewing contact with old neighbors such as the Byzantines or establishing new contact with new people such as the Muslims. The West was exposed to new cultures, new societies, and new customs. The relative prosperity, peace, and technological advances that the Western people experienced allowed them to establish urban centers, and urban centers provided necessary nourishment for the nascent Western culture barely kept alive during the early Middle Ages. It was within this setting that intellectual activity among Western peoples developed its distinctive medieval garb.[1]

Key to all these developments was Christianity and the monastery. It is still difficult for many secular readers of history to comprehend the role religion played in medieval society. Too often critics dismiss the contributions medieval religious made to the intellectual development of the West, because they are articulated in a religious language that seems impenetrable to modern secular minds. To some, scholasticism will always be merely theology. Such critics fail to realize how easy it is to translate the theological trappings of medieval intellectual discussions into the vernacular of today. Medieval intellectuals talk of original sin, the communion of saints, heaven, the exegesis of texts, and the like. Modern intellectuals speak of the same things but with different words: the human condition, the world community, fulfillment of one's potential, linguistic and textual analysis. In addition to using a different vocabulary most medieval intellectuals also employed different thought processes than modern intellectuals and built on different presuppositions. The dialectic, logic, mystery, progress, tradition, and personal experience are areas[2] where these differences are pronounced, and yet few intellectuals (particularly historians of philosophy) take the time to study the role of religion in medieval society before they pass judgment on its intellectual contributions.[3] The result is that highly significant contributions to the intellectual history of the West are often overlooked. This issue is especially pertinent in women's intellectual history, because women were even more restricted than men to the use of religious language. Most often (but with many important exceptions) medieval women's intellectual contributions are couched within a religious culture that needs patience, determination, and open-mindedness to breach. It is essential that this principle is remembered throughout our presentation of medieval women's thought. Women's writings on mysticism, spiritual direction, piety, morality, and doctrine are obviously religious writings, but that should not preclude us from analyzing them for their intellectual properties. It is commonplace in today's world to examine fictional works for intellectual elements. It should become as commonplace to examine religious writings in the medieval period similarly, and I will do so here. First, however, we will begin our history of the high Middle Ages with an examination of literacy and what women can tell us about that process and their role in it.

Most scholars today agree that when "written monuments exercise a jealous tyranny"[4] in intellectual history the result is a less than comprehensive history. This tyranny of the text has helped justify the near exclusion of women from intellectual history, for few of their texts have survived. Yet, we know from the handful of women's manuscripts that are extant and from innumerable references in men's manuscripts that women did contribute in very tangible ways to many areas essential to the growth of Western intellectual tradition. They created intellectual environments in their monasteries, they disseminated ideas among themselves and among the surrounding communities, and they participated in rational activities such as education and reading on a significant scale. To document these contributions, we will follow the lead of scholars who have constructed a history of literacy, because they address these issues directly. True, we have no single work that describes or records how literacy became widespread during the Middle Ages, nor does any medieval author explain explicitly how society built a community bound together by texts.[5] We know all this occurred, though, and thanks to recent research, we are beginning to understand how. Our challenge here is to extend this pioneering history of literacy into women's history and identify the specific ways in which women participated in the creation of a literate society.

Brian Stock has led the way in literacy history, and his conclusions will be our starting point.[6] Stock believes that the Middle Ages, particularly the ninth through the beginning of the thirteenth centuries, are crucial in the history of rationality. Fellow historian B. B. Price argues that during the medieval period "almost all areas of life found intellectual expression,"[7] and Stock tells us how this was accomplished. It was through the "carrier" of rationality: literacy.[8] By the eleventh century it was still common for many to be illiterate, but it was "less and less likely that they would remain out of touch with the social forces that the written word increasingly embodied."[9] This is an important distinction. Whereas classical Athens and imperial Rome had a literate class, the masses remained overwhelmingly illiterate and untouched by text. The same is not true for the medieval West. Here "the activities and practices in all areas of human endeavor took on ... an intellectual quality in their description and pursuits"[10] that touched all classes, the formally educated literate class and the uneducated illiterate masses. It was during this time that "the relationship between *ratio* and *scriptum* first became a liberating instrument,"[11] and along with the ability to read and write texts came the need to interpret them. To meet this need the West developed a new hermeneutics, one based on both oral and written traditions. Stock reminds us that the etymology of Latin *textus* is from *texo,* to weave, to plait (interestingly, Hrotsvitha used this imagery when she talked about writing her book[12]) and that medieval society perceived texts as "the material replica of a woven literary composition."[13] Oral tradition, long a domain in which the masses were familiar, comfortable, and even contributed to, entered into written tradition. Once this happened it was possible for the masses and the learned elite to build a community (Stock's "textual community"[14]) united around the common themes expressed in the text. This catapulted the West into a new phase in the history of rationality. It is interesting to note that Stock also believes that "the changes in attitude, perceptions, and thinking that literacy brought about are best observed in religion, the dimension of culture most accessible to the majority of people."[15] This conclusion supports the contention throughout this study that religious texts are of prime importance in intellectual history.

Stock also tells us the prerequisites for the creation of a literate society were set in late antiquity and the early Middle Ages with the invention of new cursive writing, book production, and the birth of linguistic communities.[16] Here research for women's role in these developments has already begun. The issue of women's role in the development of new script is largely unexplored, but we do know that the female scribes we can identify are skilled, competent, and well educated. There is no apparent reason to believe that women did not actively participate in those processes which resulted in more manageable cursive writing.[17] From almost the very beginning of women's monasticism women were involved in book production; in fact, the first monastic scriptorium we know of was in Paula and Eustochium's monastery.[18] We know that women's scriptoria existed throughout the Middle Ages, although research is incomplete and we have yet to determine the precise locations and number.[19] We have long known that women commissioned works in the vernacular[20] and that women's monastic communities formed around a common language and common texts, the same as in men's communities. In the areas of script development, book production, and linguistic communities research must continue to expand our knowledge of women's participation in these processes. While we are awaiting results, however, we can push forward in another direction, asking whether women's participation in the creation of a literate society included other areas of activity.

Did women, for instance, contribute to the merger of oral tradition to written tradition? Did they take an active part in the process that changed the West into a literate society? To find the answers to these questions we will turn to women who are usually ignored in intellectual history.[21] The first of these women is Queen Matilda of England. Matilda (1080–1118) was born of Malcolm III, king of Scotland, and Margaret, a saintly and educated woman whose biographer Turgot tells us that "doctors went from her much wiser men than when they came."[22] Margaret's intellectual life also had a profound effect on Matilda's father Malcolm. Turgot claims that whatever Margaret loved, Malcolm loved: "Hence it was that, although he could not read, he would turn over and examine books which she used either for her devotions or her study; and whenever he heard her express especial liking for a particular book, he also would look at it with special interest, kissing it, and often taking it into his hands." Books were also vehicles for the demonstration of love and power. "As a loving proof of his devotion" to Margaret, Malcolm "sent for a worker in precious metals, whom he commanded to ornament that volume with gold and gems, and when the work was finished, the king himself used to carry the book to the queen."[23] As proof of Margaret's power, Turgot narrates "one incident" above all else, the salvage of her favorite book after it was accidentally dropped in the river. "Who would fancy that the book could afterwards be of any value? Who would believe that even a single letter would have been visible?" her incredulous biographer asks. "Whatever others may think, I for my part believe that this wonder was worked by our Lord out of his love for the venerable queen."[24] Books, then, were held in very high esteem in the household where Matilda spent her early years.

Around the age of thirteen Matilda was sent to Wilton monastery for her education, the same monastery where the poet Muriel (her works have been lost) and Eve, the woman to whom Goscelin addressed his *Book of Consolation* in 1080,[25] were members. Wilton's abbess Buhtgyva also commissioned Goscelin to write the life of Matilda's great-grand-aunt, Edith. Prior to her marriage, then, Matilda lived with strong, well-educated, literate women. Once married, she continued and expanded that tradition with vigor. She was a renowned patron of literature who commissioned writings in Latin and in the vernacular during her reign as queen. She commissioned William of Malmesbury to write the *Chronicle of the Kings of England,* where he tells us how Matilda's reputation for encouraging intellectual life at court spread far and wide: "crowds of scholars, equally famed for verse and for singing, came over" from the continent.[26] In the prologue Turgot provides us with quite a detailed summation of Matilda's attitude toward oral and written traditions. He begins the *vita* by addressing Matilda's reason for commissioning the written work. "You have, by the request you made, commanded me (since a request of yours is to me a command) that I should narrate for you the particulars of the life of your mother, whose memory is held in veneration. How acceptable that life was to God you have often heard by the concordat praise of many," Turgot states. An oral tradition that contained the life story of Margaret thus existed prior to Turgot's writing. Matilda was well aware of it, but it was not enough for her. "You desire not only to hear about the life of your mother," Turgot explains, "but further: to have it continually before your eyes in writing." Here, just as Stock theorized, is a description of how and why a medieval woman slowly but surely helped an illiterate society become a literate society. Matilda commissioned Turgot to capture the oral history of her mother in written form. He was not asked to start afresh, but to use the oral tradition available to him which, Matilda tells Turgot "is especially trustworthy." Still, Turgot is aware that Matilda's task is not simple but that it demands skill to turn oral tradition into written text. He fears that "the materials, in truth, for this undertaking are more than my writing or my words can avail to set forth."[27] Yet Matilda persists in her commission regardless of the challenge. "So I am to two minds, and drawn two ways at once," Turgot confesses. "On the one hand, the greatness of the subject makes me shrink from obeying; on the other, I dare not refuse because of the authority of you who command me." He agrees finally to write it because of his love for her mother, but, more to the point, because of "the obedience which is due from me to you."[28]

A letter that Matilda wrote to her dear friend and noted philosopher, Anselm of Bec, allows us to see first-hand Matilda's attitudes toward oral and written traditions. The purpose of the letter is to persuade Anselm to take better care of his health, which Anselm is apparently not doing. "I have learned this from the frequent reports of many reliable witnesses," begins Matilda. Her concern throughout focuses on her major fear, that his fasting will inhibit his ability to speak. She fears "that his spiritually edifying voice will grow hoarse, and that this voice—which formerly used to impart with quiet and gentle discourse those things of song and speech that are sweet to God—may grow much quieter from now on. Then those persons who are at the time farther away from you may be deprived of hearing that voice and may be bereft of its benefit." For this reason alone Anselm should stop sapping his strength with inadvisable fasting "for fear that you may cease to be an orator."[29] Matilda supports her claim by citing the words of antiquity's greatest orator, demonstrating in her example how powerfully persuasive the oral and the written traditions can be when they are merged. She makes sure Anselm knows the statement comes from a text by citing the source, a practice done infrequently in medieval writing:[30] "For as Cicero says in the book he has written *On Old Age:* 'The orator's gift is not only talent, but also lung power.' " Then Matilda makes an extraordinary claim that reveals the high degree of reverence medieval people reserved for the oral tradition: "Once this is gone, your great spiritual renown would quickly be lost, and so would your great memory of the past and your ability to foresee the future. So much art, so much learning, so much invention, so much understanding of human affairs, along with the clear wisdom of the divine, would swiftly be lost."[31] Anselm's participation in the oral tradition, according to Matilda, is the source of all his wisdom. Without it, all intellectual activities will suffer. What is also most interesting here is that Matilda ties spiritual perfection to intellectual activity; if Anselm allows his intellectual life to be diminished, his spiritual life will likewise be diminished. This is indeed a passage worthy of much analysis. In two sentences Matilda—in a written form, we must remember—presents a concise argument for the inclusion of the oral tradition in the intellectual life and for the inclusion of the intellectual activities in the spiritual life.

After stating her case for the importance of the oral tradition so forcefully, Matilda addresses the need for the written tradition in the remainder of the letter. She tells Anselm that she knows how much knowledge he has received from books, that "diligent reading has often shown you" the way to truth. She includes a telling example for the life of Moses to bolster her argument. Fasting is not bad in and of itself. To the contrary it was done by great men in Scripture, including Moses, whose example Matilda is sure Anselm is following. Moses had to fast before he "merited to read the tablets written by the finger of God."[32] Since Matilda had already established that fasting weakens one's ability to share fully in the oral tradition, this passage implies that Matilda is aware that the oral tradition must be somewhat weakened before the written tradition can flourish. Only after he was weakened by fasting and, therefore, inhibited from full participation in the oral tradition did Moses "merit" participation in the written tradition. The continual creation of the written tradition came with a price, a compromised oral tradition. It is not, however, rendered impotent; the oral tradition is rather assimilated by the written tradition. Matilda ends her letter with a mandate to Anselm: "Deign to receive, read, heed, and obey this letter."[33] The strength of the written tradition was such that the price was worth paying. In another letter to Anselm Matilda lets us see that this strength came precisely because it combined various avenues of knowledge into one material representation. All the senses were involved, not merely the eyes. The written text evoked a vivid, sensual experience for the reader. "For even when you are absent, there is a certain revisiting with you, as it were, the repeated touching of your bits of writing, and the thoroughly joyful and frequent rereading of your letters, which have been committed to memory."[34] These physical letters are better than mere oratory, because they are accessible to more senses.

In evaluating the impact of Matilda in the history of literacy and rationality, we should remember who Anselm was. He is one of the stellar intellectuals of the era, possessor of one of the most original minds in the high Middle Ages. It is to such an intellectual that Matilda engages in discourse. We must also remember Matilda's political position. She was the wife of Henry I (1100–1135), and it was during the reign of her husband, the Lion of Justice, that England began its journey toward the codification of common law, a process in which the oral tradition is entered into the written tradition. The chief instrument of power that Henry I used during his reign was the royal writ, an instrument invented by Henry's Anglo-Saxon predecessors but one that Henry employed in new and extensive ways. Matilda was involved in this evolution, for numerous charters at Exeter, Canterbury, Norwich, Aylesbury, Rockingham, Cannock, Cirencester, Windsor, and Westminister all bear her signature as witness,[35] as do the royal writs she issued throughout her reign.[36] She frequently acted as regent during Henry's travels and was alone responsible for the administration of her own household and holdings.[37] Royal administration also embraced the written tradition, particularly the exchequer.[38] We know that Matilda's mother Margaret engendered a great respect for literacy within her illiterate husband Malcolm. We do not have an equivalent testimony to Matilda's influence on Henry on matters concerning the written tradition, but we do have Matilda's own statement concerning her ability to influence Henry in another matter. She believed it was quite significant. When Anselm and Henry were drawn into a quarrel, Matilda had the utmost faith that, with her urgings, Henry would relent: "With my favorable influence and my prompting him insofar as I can, he will grow more accommodating and more friendly toward you."[39] We have no reason to believe Matilda's influence in other matters, such as the championing of the written tradition, did not, like her mother before her, influence her husband. At minimum it was a positive presence in the court for the advocacy of literacy. As patron of literature and as commissioner of written works, Matilda earns a place in intellectual history. Our greater debt to her, though, is for her arguments in defense of the written tradition, both because of the influence her words had within her society and because they help clarify for us the process by which an illiterate society became increasingly literate.

To a lesser degree Bertha allows us to view the coming literacy from another perspective. Bertha (b. ca. 1020) was a canoness from the monastery at Vilich near

Cologne. The biographer of her brother Wolfhelm tells us that she possessed "the most outstanding knowledge of letters."[40] Around 1057 Bertha composed a *vita* of one of her monastery's beloved abbesses, Adelheid. It is a short work written in rhymed prose of high quality.[41] Bertha begins her *vita* by addressing the prologue to Archbishop Anno in terms that imply her equality with Abraham. "Encouraged by the example of the Patriarch Abraham who several times dared to approach God as a friend, so will I turn to address you,"[42] she writes. While Bertha does refer to "my humble work," it is evident from her introductory remarks that she believes it is of some worth. Again, she infers her equality with biblical figures, this time with the apostles. "Did not the good Teacher," she queries, defend his disciples "before those who criticized them, drew the splinters from their own eyes and other similar things with the unconquerable might of his Spirit? Thus inspired, I bring your Highness my humble work as an offering."[43] After thus establishing her work's inherent worth, she quickly adds that Anno "should corrections and improvements be necessary, edit with good counsel." She believes corrections may be in order because of the form in which she presents her history, not because of the history itself. She even goes so far as to tell Anno how to reply to any potential critics of her *vita:* "But if it is said that a work in need of correction is no offering for so venerable a lord, then we will respond thus: 'We decry the poor rustic style, yet the work is valuable; the form may be despised, yet it is acceptable because of the merit of its contents.'" Knowing how some in eleventh-century society might find it difficult to accept the vehicle she chose for the *vita* she assures the readers that "I wrote of every deed with sober words and to the best of my ability: I wrote the life of the holy Mother Adelheid."[44] She wrote the life in order to preserve the oral tradition which was in danger of dying upon the death of Adelheid's contemporaries; her chief source was the elderly "Engilrada, who, as we know well, has outstripped you all in age and thus could remember more of the story and better than any of you."[45] Bertha could have chosen to assure Engilrada's story became part of oral tradition, but she did not. She chose instead to enter Engilrada's narrative into written tradition. Hence she requests that Anno "decree that, recorded here by my pen or by some one else's, the memory of the subject discussed here will never pale and that all may hear the news of those unforgettable deeds performed with God's grace."[46] Bertha believes that she is qualified to enter the oral tradition of Adelheid's life into written tradition, because she has "reached the present strength of my mind and age" necessary to complete the task. When she summaries her reason for writing the *vita,* we also see her hint at what the future holds, the diminishment or even loss of the oral tradition, unless it is absorbed into the written tradition. "Thus I have written the life and virtue of the venerable virgin Saint Adelheid, because I deemed it an injustice that these should be covered with silence and thus fall into oblivion."[47] Bertha adds this further bit of evidence to support her contention: "After my humble pen had recorded all of this faithfully, this trustworthy witness [Engilrada] ended the journey of her life. Herein one should recognise that the unfathomable depth of divine reason had allowed her to live such a long time so that through her presence such great virtue could be made known to all the world with clarity." In other words, "divine reason" allowed Engilrada to live long enough for society to absorb her oral narrative into written tradition. If oral tradition alone was sufficient then the length of Engilrada's *vita* was inconsequential, for her narrative entered into oral tradition the first time she recounted it to anyone. But, it was not sufficient. Written tradition was needed. The future of Adelheid's memory lay within a literate society and thus needed a written form. Bertha even acknowledges that, while her fundamental thesis that society's future lies in literacy, she, being at the beginning of that tradition, might not produce a superior text. To this end Bertha sent her *vita* to her brother Wolfhelm for corrections, "so that, if later a devoted admirer should bring this life into the light with an elegant style, he would find a truthful record already written." She ends her argument with the same reminder as Matilda that reading was a multi-sensual experience. She admits her *vita* "does not glitter with artful poetry," but "credible men who are sufficiently knowledgeable in the liberal arts" have approved the book "after repeated reading and have declared it worthy to be seen by the public."[48]

There is another interesting text pertinent to our search for the history of women's participation in the creation of a literate society, an anonymous poem, *Laudis honor*. Only once is the female gender of the twelfth-century author articulated, *grata* in the penultimate line,[49] but even if the author was not a woman, the poem offers a rare view of how medieval people thought about women's engagement in intellectual activity. The poem is a particularly biting satire on the new intellectual milieu of the day, and it complains bitterly about those who would exclude women from participating in that environment. The author, speaking in a woman's voice, claims the exclusion is based on male fear of sharing the power of literacy:

> We are expelled from the new world because our concern is writing.
> Though new reading [once] pleased our leaders
> Under new leaders a new law rules.
> Formerly fierce hearts used to be softened by poetry,
> But now weak hearts are enraged by our poems.
> The poems of the poet [Ovid] earned a milder exile
> And Ceasar's anger toward poetry was less.
> Our writing provides a source of rage to ours,
> No poems now please our leaders.
> I am indicted, but in fact for what foregoing misdeed?
> If you want to know: art is my crime, and genius.
> My lofty writing gave birth to my great crime.[50]

Constant Mews argues that the one woman poet who we know experienced such censorship at this time and in the area was Heloise and that she is the author of *Laudis honor*. It is not necessary for our purposes here to determine the authorship, though, because whoever it was, she or he provides us with yet another glimpse of the difficult journey medieval society undertook in the name of literacy. The author also lets us see how well she understood the connection between literacy and rationality:

> If God is grasped by sense and grasped by reason,
> That person will grasp more in whom there is already more reason.
> Much writing will not stop me from being good,

Writing allows me, not forbids me to know God.
We believe and know rationally that God exists
And also that what we do God does not forbid.

The author champions throughout the poem the pursuit of knowledge with such intensity that centuries later we can still be affected by the earnestness of her desire for the intellectual life and her frustration with those who do not agree. Her verse touches upon the essence of the twelfth-century debate about the role of rationality in religion:

Oh new religion, holy withdrawal from life,
Now if only I knew what wickedness our writing might be.
She or he is good whose face always looks to the ground,
Who, knowing nothing, thinks that she or he is good.
Yet is that existence holy to which meditating about nothing
Or knowing nothing has brought nothing to be?[51]

Not only does the author believe firmly in the obligation humanity has to utilize the intellectual potential it was created with, but she specifically believes that this obligation is common to all humanity, women and men. Men who argue otherwise are motivated falsely: "O what new cunning—but known to us: Envy/seeks its place under the guise of correctness." For those men who claim that "it is not for holy women to compose verses/Nor for us to ask who Aristotle might be," she issues a challenge to her critics:

Compose verses, you slanderer of verse, so that I may think
That you of course can create but do not want to.
I would be acceptable to you if my writing were acceptable:
Equal genius usually reconciles two peoples![52]

While our anonymous poet permits us to see how volatile an issue literacy and the pursuit of knowledge was during the intellectual renaissance of the high Middle Ages, her statement also makes us question how deeply women were involved in that awakening. She is infuriated that "our writing provides a source of rage," revealing that she (obviously) and other women do in fact write. She bewails the fact that some do not want women studying Aristotle, again implying that women do. For too long scholars have accepted without qualification the corollary that since women were excluded from the universities, they, therefore, did not participate in or contribute to the twelfth-century intellectual renaissance. Hopefully, historians will continue to engage in research that will eventually allow us to nullify such a conclusion. It is extremely doubtful whether future research will yield evidence that women matriculated in universities, but degrees were issued on competence, not on accumulated credits and thus women could theoretically have received degrees. Marcia Colish cites the example of two women faculty members at the university in Bologna as proof of this possibility; they were "home schooled" by their law professor fathers, took their qualifying exams, defended their theses, and were granted doctorates.[53] Then there is the possibility that Trotula, an eleventh-century woman from Salerno, wrote a medical treatise for women.[54] The historical information we have about Heloise is more than enough to remind us that formal enrollment in a university was not the only way to receive an education comparable to that offered at a university. Monastic and cathedral schools co-existed with budding universities for quite a few generations before they were definitely surpassed and eventually replaced for the education of men; it was many centuries before universities played an equivalent role in the education of women. Meanwhile, the monastery and home tutoring remained the chief vehicles for women's education.

Heloise

Heloise is a product of both. The foundation of her knowledge was laid early, for both Abelard and Peter the Venerable refer to having heard of "her renown throughout the realm"[55] long before they met her. During her youth she resided for a time at the Benedictine monastery of St. Marie of Argenteuil, and we can assume much of her basic education was given there. However, Heloise also had unique training. Abelard and a contemporary chronicler, William Godel, tell us that Heloise "was exceedingly erudite in both Hebrew and Greek letters," at a time when few people in the West knew Greek, even less Hebrew.[56] We do not know how Heloise learned these languages, but Abelard tells us that her mother's uncle, Canon Fulbert, "had done everything in his power to advance her education in letters" and that he was "always ambitious to further his niece's education in letters." Around the age of sixteen Heloise left the monastic school and went to live with Fulbert in Paris. Perhaps Fulbert had her tutored in the languages upon arrival. However she learned them, her reputation as a scholar became known to Abelard. That the leading teacher of the day should tell us that "in the extent of her learning she stood supreme" must not be dismissed lightly.[57] We already appreciate the brilliance of Abelard's contributions. We must now begin to appreciate that person whom M. T. Clanchy claims was the only contemporary whom Abelard considered to be his equal or superior.[58] Heloise's writings reveal a thorough education in the trivium. Her education in grammar manifests itself in the wide range of classical authors she cited or imitated,[59] her mastery of rhetoric is judged to be superior to Abelard,[60] and she parries with the chief logician of the day on level ground.[61] She is also well educated in Scripture, patristics, and theology. The degree of learning that Heloise was able to achieve prior to the age of the university mandate her inclusion in intellectual history on that ground alone. There is, however, sturdier ground upon which she stands. Heloise is an independent thinker who has much to say about humanism, and she is an example *par excellence* of the charismatic personalities who shaped the twelfth century as it transformed itself into a literate society. As we shall see, these two aspects of Heloise are intertwined.

What seems amazing in retrospect is that study of Heloise as an independent thinker began in earnest only in the last quarter of the twentieth century. Her corpus consists of three letters to Abelard and the *Problemata* series of forty-two questions that Heloise submitted to Abelard for response. I will not consider the poem *Laudis honor* or the *Letters of Two Lovers* here as part of Heloise's corpus, even though persuasive arguments have been made in defense of her authorship[62]; the jury is still out. Heloise's contemporaries—Peter the Venerable, Hugo Mettelus, William Godel, Hugh Matel—spoke of her in light of her learning, as did Jean de Meun a century later in his controversial *The Romance of the Rose:* "She was a wise, well-educated maid. Not only had she read and studied books, but learnt of woman's nature in herself."[63] Yet already by the fourteenth century Heloise was losing her true identity to romanticism. Sometime between 1337 and 1343 Petrarch obtained a copy of Abelard and Heloise's letters, and his writing on the flyleaf of his manuscript reveal how little he considered Heloise's intellectual stature and how fixated he was on her as an idealized lover.[64] By the following century and thereafter this was Heloise's dominant image.

The inability (or refusal) to see Heloise as an independent thinker is in many ways linked to the controversies that have raged since the nineteenth century over the letters' authenticity. The first systematic attack on Heloise's authorship by an historian came in 1913 with the work of Bernhard Schmeidler. This was answered in kind by Etienne Gilson in 1938.[65] During the 1970s and 1980s the controversy stirred again, first when John Benton argued that neither Abelard nor Heloise wrote the letters, then when Benton rebutted his own hypothesis,[66] and, finally, when Hubert Silvestre claimed that Jean de Meun forged the letters.[67] Of late scholars' opinions have reverted back to the fourteenth-century assessment, that the letters are authentic.[68] It is the thesis accepted here. The authenticity of the *Problemata* has never been questioned.

Part of the reason why scholars have spent so much energy over the centuries delving into the question of Heloise's authorship, probably more than that spent on any other source, stems from a lack of knowledge of the tradition of women writers within which Heloise composed. That a woman wrote so extraordinary a source seemed in the eyes of many critics too isolated a phenomenon to be true. Once properly placed within an intellectual history of women Heloise's contributions appear less extraordinary and more credible. Heloise constructed an ethics grounded in experience, but so had Dhuoda before her. Heloise's natural genius "surpassed all women in carrying out your purpose, and have gone further than almost every man," as Peter the Venerable said;[69] so did Hrotsvitha's. Heloise displayed a deep respect for knowledge and an awareness of the power of the written word, but her contemporary Queen Matilda did also. Heloise was a very bright light in the intellectual world, but far from the only one or even the brightest. Still, she accomplished something that few writers are able to do; she wrote a timeless text that transcends its historical context. Her ability to describe the essence of selfless love has few equals in Western literature and enters into each new age as if written contemporaneously.[70] With utter simplicity and directness she expresses the essence of her love thus: "I wanted simply you, nothing of yours. I looked for no marriage bond, no marriage portion, and it was not my own pleasures and wishes I sought to gratify, as you well know, but yours." When Heloise proclaims the depth of her love we willingly believe her, so earnest are her words: "God is my witness that if Augustus, Emperor of the whole world, thought fit to honour me with marriage and conferred all the earth on me to possess for ever, it would be dearer and more honourable to me to be called not his Empress but your whore."[71] With Heloise we reach a new level of self-awareness and self-expression, but, most of all, we achieve intimate access to a personality, in degrees that only Augustine before her was able to provide.[72]

It is in this area where Heloise makes a most striking contribution to medieval intellectual history. She provides us insight into what historian C. Stephen Jaeger calls the charismatic culture of the high Middle Ages and its leaders. We have quoted Jaeger's opinion above concerning the tyranny of texts within intellectual and cultural history. He focuses on the late tenth and eleventh centuries to support this thesis and concludes that, despite the lack of intellectual textual masterpieces, "the apparent poverty of the age is misleading. The vitality and continuity in secular learning in the period 950–1100 are not found in texts and artifacts but in personalities and in the cultivation of personal qualities."[73] Once historians realize this then the achievements of this earlier pre-university period can be seen in their true light. In a charismatic culture, Jaeger continues, education is dispensed through the personality of the teacher, and the chief goal of the teacher is to instill attitudes that civilize and thus alter the behavior of the student. The teacher's most effective tool is the moral force of example. In reality Jaeger is simply identifying here a theme within the intellectual world which scholars have long recognized flourished during the same period in the religious world. During the pre-university period the church was revitalized from within by an apostolic movement, *docere verbo et exemplo*.[74] Groups of hermits in the beginning of the eleventh century began a movement which eventually resulted in significant changes in ecclesiastical and secular culture.[75] This was accomplished by charismatic leaders on the fringes of society in places "rugged, cold, sterile, isolated, inaccessible, frequented more by wild beasts than by humans."[76] Their example inspired many to imitation, and soon "there were solitaries living all over in various abodes."[77] This initial phase of the eremetic movement was short-lived, and only a few groups survived the first generation. Those that did remain became institutionalized by the second generation. The charismatic leadership of the likes of Bruno of Cologne, Norbert of Xanten, Stephen of Thiers, Robert of Molesme, and Romuald gave birth to the communities such as the Carthusians, Premonstratensians, Grandmontensians, Cistercians, and Camaldolians.[78] Little documentation exists concerning the numerous charismatic leaders' lives, and even fewer texts are known to be authored by these hermits who populated the West "like a second Egypt."[79] With the second generation we have full documentation and institutionalization. Rules, customaries, and liturgical practices were written down only after the original charismatic period ended. Without these first leaders, however, there would be no written texts, for the written texts attempted to capture the spirit of the original movement; they are not part of that first movement. There were leaders, though, in all these groups who bridged the two stages of development, and the documentation of these transitional leaders helps us learn about both.[80]

With Heloise we have a transitional leader who bridges the charismatic and institutionalization phases of the two chief movements of the high Middle Ages, the monastic renewal and the intellectual renewal. We are concerned here, of course, with the latter, but we should note Heloise's pivotal position in monastic history before moving on. The Order of the Paraclete was founded jointly by Abelard and Heloise in 1129 when she and her community were evicted from Argenteuil, the monastery where she had resided since the scandal. Abelard offered them his old oratory, the Paraclete, and there Heloise set up her community under the Benedictine Rule. She was dissatisfied with the situation, and so when Abelard reentered her life via correspondence twelve years later she and he together constructed a monastic rule more suitable for women than the male oriented Rule of St. Benedict that the community had been following.[81] Even here her objection to the Rule is partly intellectual. She argues that, because it is illogical for someone to prefer "the works of the Law" to "the freedom of the Gospel," the Rule that the community followed in the past should be modified "so that we can be free to devote ourselves to the offices of praising God."[82] It is also interesting to observe that, whereas Abelard was a dismal failure in monastic life, Heloise was a resounding success. By the time of her death in 1163/64 she had established six daughter houses, and the Order continued in existence until the Reign of Terror in 1793 closed its last house.[83]

As a transitional charismatic intellectual Heloise serves us well. Her magisterial authority rests primarily in the power of personality. It is the witness of her life that is commanding, and only secondarily the testimony of her writings insofar as they accurately reflect her life. Her cultivation of critical thinking, her demand for total surrender to love, her perception of relationships, her personal morality, her unquenchable thirst for knowledge, her need to explore psychological motives—all these qualities are, fortunately, found in between the lines of her writing. This gives us a rare opportunity to examine a figure who straddles the line separating the stages of medieval intellectual development. It was her life (and those like her) and not her writings in themselves that prodded the next few generations to institutionalize these phenomena. By the early twelfth century charismatic qualities such as those of Heloise began a process of transformation by which they were gradually "displaced at the schools and replaced by definitions and systematising, frameworks of argumentation and harmonizing of inconsistencies."[84] Bonaventure needed the spirituality of Francis of Assisi to precede and inspire him; the scholastics of the thirteenth century needed the humanism of charismatic figures of the twelfth century to precede and inspire them. Heloise was such a person.

What exactly was Heloise's understanding of humanism? Her principles are easier to discern than one might imagine. Indeed, they are so visible that again one wonders why they have been ignored for so long. Her first two letters to Abelard contain poignant revelations of her philosophy of love, and this in turn forms the basis of her humanism. She begins with her belief that love must under all circumstances be disinterested, Ciceronian love. According to Cicero, true love finds ultimate fulfillment in the giving not receiving of love.[85] Hence, Heloise declares that she has "denied myself every pleasure in obedience to your will, kept nothing for myself except to prove that now, even more, I am yours."[86] It is a love so selfless that their scandal "robbed me of my very self in robbing me of you."[87] Significantly, her love has none of the dualistic overtones that Abelard's had. Heloise sees no dichotomy in love. She loves with her body, her mind, and her soul. Abelard, on the other hand, talks of his love for Heloise solely in terms of passion. Their love affair began "all in fire with desire"[88] when passion triumphed over reason. Abelard recalls "obscene pleasures" and "the depths of shame to which my unbridled lust had consigned our bodies,"[89] while Heloise reminiscences that "the pleasure of lovers which we shared have been too sweet—they can never displease me, and can scarcely be banished from my thoughts."[90] Abelard believes that "it was wholly just and merciful, although by means of the supreme treachery of your uncle, for me to be reduced in that part of my body which was the seat of lust and sole reason for those desires,"[91] while Heloise holds God "whom I always accuse of the greatest cruelty in regard to this outrage" responsible for Abelard's physical loss. She still persists in her love for Abelard, because love is not limited to the body. Thus, it is her mind (*mens*) that is still "on fire with its old desires."[92] Heloise cannot conceive of a love that begins and ends with the body. Love for Heloise encompasses the whole person, and thus she has great difficulty accepting Abelard's position that their love ended with his castration. Her first letter is written to address this issue. She still demands that Abelard love her mind and soul even if he cannot love her body. "While I am denied your presence, give me at least through your words—of which you have enough and to spare—some sweet semblance of yourself," she reasons.[93] In fact, Abelard must devote more loving attention to her "now when I no longer have in you an outlet for my incontinence."[94]

Abelard has great difficulty understanding this type of love, because it is rooted in a concept of humanity that he does not share. Abelard sees a divide between body and mind, between passion and reason. In Abelard's scheme, evil is overcome by an act of the will. Heloise disagrees. To her, a person is a composite being, and evil is overcome by a change of heart. Loving Abelard changed Heloise's life, because the experience of love transforms and enlightens. It follows logically then that human experience is a source of knowledge. The power of reason is not denied in Heloise's epistomology, but it does have to share the stage with experience. The way in which she combines the two can be seen in her ethics. While many scholars assume Heloise merely adopted Abelard's ethics, the facts are that Abelard's *Ethics* was written years after Heloise's letters and that Heloise's ethics differ somewhat from Abelard's.[95] "It is not the deed but the intention of the doer which makes the crime, and justice should weigh not what was done but the spirit in which it is done,"[96] writes Heloise in her first letter, but then adds in her second letter that "even if my conscience is clear through innocence, and no consent of mine makes me guilty of this crime, too many earlier sins were committed to allow me to be wholly free from guilt."[97] In Heloise's ethics one's whole life and all actions must be considered as well as intention.[98]

While it is understandable why past scholars who viewed Heloise only in relation to Abelard ignored her *Problemata,* it is disappointing to see this oversight continue.[99] The format is a series of forty-two questions that Heloise asks Abelard on behalf of herself and her community, along with his replies. The bulk of the work comprises Abelard's answers, but Heloise's contributions are not negligible. First, *Problemata* exposes the collaborative nature of Abelard and Heloise's intellectual relationship. In his final years Abelard wrote many of his major works explicitly for or at the request of Heloise,[100] but the *Problemata* is the only work where Heloise's collaborative contributions are documented.

Second, Heloise openly makes the case for her status as collaborator in the introductory letter by citing precedent. "Saint Jerome greatly commended and vehemently approved of Saint Marcella's course of study," Heloise begins. Marcella did not passively receive Jerome's instruction. She initiated it and controlled the format and results. Heloise quotes the following passage from Jerome's commentary on Galatians: "Certainly, as soon as I got to Rome, no sooner did she see me, that she might interrogate me somewhat concerning the Scripture. Nor indeed, in the pythagorean manner, did she consider whatever I might respond as correct, nor did prejudged authority without reason hold any weigh for her, but she questioned everything, and with a sagacious mind considered widely, so that I felt myself to have not a disciple but rather a judge." Then Heloise wields this precedent to assure Abelard's cooperation in the undertaking: "What purpose do these things serve," Heloise asks, "but admonitions, so that because of these things you may remember what you should do, and not be sluggish in resolving your debt." Abelard's cooperation was deemed essential because of his role as co-founder of the Paraclete community and as long-time teacher of the women. Heloise is quick to add, however, a forceful reminder that in intellectual matters Marcella certainly "knew how to make progress, so that she came to distinguish herself as a teacher for others interested in learning in the same field of study," implying, obviously, that Heloise is Marcella's successor.

Heloise is also the Paraclete community's teacher, and she was good at it. Heloise concludes the letter by summarizing the community's reasons for desiring further education, thereby giving us a profile of the type of minds which fueled the medieval renaissance: "We are disturbed by many questions, we become sluggish in our reading, and are led to love less what we are most ignorant of in the sacred word, until we feel unfruitful the labor in which we are engaged." First, the women experience frustration at their lack of knowledge, and then they realize their comprehension of the written text is being limited by this gap. This situation leads to further frustration as their desire for knowledge slackens and their efforts at education become unproductive. Reading, the chief tool available for the community's internal education program, is stymied. At this point Heloise realized that a different approach is needed to break the cycle. She must enter into a dialogue with an authority. Evoking patristic imagery, Heloise specifically requests a dialogue, not a lecture. Heloise, not Abelard, will control the dialogue itself as well, by deciding the subject matter. She will "send certain small questions" not in the normal order that arise within Scripture, "but as they daily occurred" in the community. In her final words of the introductory letter she emphasizes and retains her control: "We set them down and direct that they be solved."[101] In the *Problemata* perhaps even more than in the Letters, Dronke's judgment rings true: "At all events, I think we should envisage between Abelard and Heloise literary and intellectual partnership that was not wholly one-sided."[102]

The substance of Heloise's questions reinforces this analysis. Her guiding principle here is, again, the humanism of the late eleventh- and early twelfth-century schools, a humanism grounded in classical, scriptural, and patristic training that stressed the connection between life and learning. Yet, as a transitional intellectual Heloise also points the way to the future by including both concerns. In the *Problemata* her rational concerns are easily identified. The driving force behind her questions is Heloise's near obsessions with truth. Her insistence on truth led her to reveal to all "the hypocrite I am."[103] It was her need for complete and total truth that makes her reveal her arguments against marriage, reasons that Abelard omitted in his recitation,[104] and it was her desire for truthfulness that motivated her to tell the world of her sexual frustrations and interior struggles. Her desire for a new monastic rule for her community is rooted in her need to be true to the nature of women. The *Problemata* is but a continuation, in Dronke's words, of "Heloise's passion for lucid truth."[105] In the *Problemata* she applies her reasoning powers to the inconsistencies of scripture, but what is most interesting when we read her questions is that they center on humanistic concerns. Some of her queries are elementary to daily life. She wants to know what 1 Sam 18–19 means, with its reference to a mother's garment for her boy.[106] She wonders whether "any human being [can wield] the rod of punishment, since no one is clear of sin, not even an infant";[107] whether humans will still envy "in our future life"[108] whether it is right for humans to worry about "providing for the future";[109] and whether it is proper for people to "show amazement when they see something unexpected happening."[110] She is concerned about the fairness of human justice when she asks whether "if we make an unjust judgment, we will receive an unjust one in return?"[111] Similarly, since the gospels tell us to do unto others what you would wish them to do unto you, does that mean that "if anyone should wish another to consent to him in wrongdoing," that person in return would "have to give consent to the other in a similar matter?"[112] Frustrated, she ruminates, "Against whom has an offense been committed when it can hardly be forgiven to anyone?"[113] She wonders how one is to reconcile the letter of the law and its spirit, and she seems genuinely confused when she asks, "How can anything be lacking to the Law for the perfection of its commandments, when two precepts of love of God and neighbor would seem entirely to suffice, not to lack any perfection?"[114] She seems quite preoccupied with the question of human nature and priorities, so she makes the "request that they be distinguished from each other, by which means it may become better apparent whether each will individually suffice, if they do not happen to occur in the same person simultaneously."[115] She insists that the number of children one has is quite significant in life, so she wants to know "how can it say about [Hannah's] children, that they were very many, and about the children of her friend Phenenna that they were only many [1 Sam 2:5], as if she had more children than she?"[116] In fact, the most recurring theme in the *Problemata* is maternity. *Problemata* 31–35 focus on Heloise's conception of motherhood, the joys of pregnancy, and the significance of maternal love,[117] using Hannah as her focus. One of her longest questions focuses on the role women played in the Resurrection apparitions and, by implication, women's role in salvation history. "The evangelists have left us a great deal of doubt concerning the apparitions which the Risen Lord made to women," and Heloise wants the confusion resolved.[118] True to her humanistic curiosity she also asks, "Why it is that only the beasts and the birds are recalled as having been led to Adam in Paradise, to see what he would call them, and not also the reptiles of the land, such as serpents, and the reptiles of the water, such as the fish?"[119]

On the other hand, she demands that no aspect of life contradicts logic. Her demand for logic is clearly stated in many problems. Regarding Mt 8:2 (the cure of the leper), she ponders "by what logic the Lord seems in this case to contradict the Law and at the same time to comply with it."[120] She wants apparent human dilemmas to be resolved logically: "The Lord says: 'It is not what enters the mouth that defiles a person, but what comes out of it' (Mt 15:11). Can it be then that one incurs no stain of sin from consuming stolen goods?"[121] She wants to know "by what mystery or for what reason did the Lord seek fruit on the fig tree and not find it."[122] When she perceives a contradiction in Scripture her frustration almost renders her indignant. After citing Mt 6:34 ("do not worry about tomorrow") she impatiently asks, "Could this be the same Lord who uses as an example the man who wanted to build a town and to consider his outlay?"[123] Even in the matter of salvation, the most crucial issue of all, Heloise is wary of contradiction and so succinctly asks, in regards to marriage "whether anyone can sin in doing what the Lord has permitted or even commanded."[124]

Some of Heloise's questions reflect her contemporaries' preoccupation with language, an interest born of the increased literacy of medieval society.[125] "We also ask how the Evangelists could have written so differently," she wonders, and "what did the Lord want with all His diversity of expression?"[126] In other words, Heloise wants to know whether the words themselves are real, if they signify, or if they name real things. If words are real in themselves, then diversity in expression should not be tolerated. What is the relationship of one particular stipulation to the whole law, she asks in another problem.[127] Repeatedly, she wants the words of Scripture clarified, so the precise meaning is visible: "Why is it that the Lord ... did not say of the Body, 'This is my Body of the New Covenant' (Mt 26:26), when he would say of the Blood, 'This is my Blood of the New Covenant' (Mt 26:28), as if he were recommending the Blood more than the Body?"[128] She continues this line of inquiry in her next question: "Also, what does it mean when we read in Luke of the Lord giving two cups to his disciples, or the same one twice? For it seems to be written that way."[129] That she is aware of the philosophical implications of linguistic analysis is evident in her question concerning the nature of personhood: "Why does [1 Thes 5:23: '... may you entirely, spirit, soul, and body ...'] mention spirit and soul, as if the soul were not spirit, or as if there were two spirits in a single person?"[130] Before we dismiss these ruminations too lightly, we should recall Stock's comment: "There is growing recognition that certain developments in medieval thought—not only the interpretative positions but also the theories of language on which they were based—anticipated contemporary interest in semiotics, structuralism, and hermeneutics."[131] Heloise did indeed anticipate those developments.

Jutta and Hildegard

Further proof of women's participation in the charismatic stage of the twelfth-century intellectual renewal can be gleaned in the lives of Jutta of Sponheim (1092–1136) and Hildegard of Bingen (1098–1179). Little attention is paid to Jutta, thanks to overwhelming stature of her pupil Hildegard, but if Jaeger's thesis is true, we should correct this injustice. Jutta's presence and influence in Germany is well documented. The contemporary Guibert of Gembloux's "Letter to Bovo," Theodoric of Echternach's *vita* of Hildegard, liturgical readings for the projected feast day for Hildegard, proceedings of the canonization inquiry into Hildegard, the Chronicles of Disibodenberg, and the later Chronicles of Sponheim each mention Jutta and describe her role as a charismatic intellectual, as does her own *vita, The Life of Lady Jutta the Anchoress.*[132] It is admitted right at the beginning of the text, written ca. 1146–1147 by a monk of Disibodenberg, that Jutta's *vita* is being written in order to capture in a permanent but radically different form the personal, dynamic qualities of a woman no longer active or present. "Just as when the sun declines to its setting the warmth of its rays cools down," the author begins, "the faithful, whoever they are, ought to collect examples of holy deeds as though they were collecting sticks of firewood, with which to daily enkindle in themselves inducements to the virtues." Accordingly, to preserve Jutta's charismatic presence Abbot Cuno of Disibod "considered that it was his responsibility to feed the fire on the altar of the Lord. Therefore he decided that for the coming generation a record should be made of the life of the lady Jutta, a nun and the first anchoress of modern times in this place."[133] In addition to the abbot Hildegard, Jutta's disciple "who undertook the direction of her school after her death" also requested "that a narrative of the way of life of this beloved lady be published to the praise of Christ, the edification of the generations to come, and as a memorial of her" so that "the structure of her work might not fall to ruin."[134] In this activity we see her disciples try to preserve Jutta's charismatic presence by transforming it into textual representation. Hildegard needed no *vita* while Jutta was alive, only after she was deprived of Jutta's real presence and performance. Guibert emphasizes the power of Jutta's physical presence in his "Letter to Bovo": "By the diffusion of the perfume of her sweetness, that is to say of her name, she not only fired many young women to the love and awe of God, as we mentioned before, but also attracted some of them to her presence in person. For indeed noble men and women began to flock to her, offering their daughters to her that they might take up the habit of holy religion."[135] As Jaeger claims happened repeatedly throughout society, Jutta's biographer also emphasizes how essential performance was at this stage of intellectual culture;[136] Jutta's life was nourished by the performance of others, and her stature in society grew as the significance of her own performance was recognized. "After looking around various monasteries, it was the site of the monastery of Mount Saint Disibod" where she decided to have an anchorhold built, in part because there "she had free access by day and by night to the offices of the monks at their psalmody nearby." Knowing how powerful and, therefore, potentially distracting the personal presence of an anchorite could be, she also chose this spot because she could have the anchorhold built in such a manner as to "not hinder the monks either by her own presence or by any of the visitors who approached her."[137] As Jutta was readying herself for her entombment "the holy virgin's enterprise became widely known," and Hildegard's parents approached Jutta "to take to herself their daughter whom they had set apart for holy celibacy and divine service, so that she might stay with her always." When Jutta made her decision to accept Hildegard, it was because of her personal, not because of spiritual, needs, "for it seemed she embraced the companionship of the girl as a consolation sent her from heaven."[138]

Spiritual activities permeate the life of an anchorite and are its distinguishing characteristics, yet Jutta's hagiographer repeatedly emphasizes that intellectual activity also defined Jutta's life. Her childhood, described in a short passage, dwells on the spiritual and the intellectual and on the effect of the latter on the former: "Once she had passed the tender years of her infancy, her mother handed her over to be instructed in the learning of the sacred scriptures. In these she made good progress; whatever her capacious intelligence could absorb from them she committed to her retentive memory, and thereafter strove to implement with good deeds." Even though "she was the delight of everyone," and a "young woman of comely appearance"[139] highly sought after in marriage, Jutta "resisted them all vigorously." Instead of marriage she "submitted herself as a disciple for three years to the lady Uda, a widow of Göllheim, who was living in the habit of holy religion. Instructed by her teaching, she advanced day by day."[140] After this training Jutta, age twenty, had herself and two other women enclosed at Disibodenberg. There "she taught ungrudgingly whomever she could, all that she herself had learnt from the inspiration of the Holy Spirit, the tradition of the elders and the report of the faithful."[141] Apparently it was from Jutta that Hildegard got her early training in music, because during this time Jutta was "instructing her in the songs of David, showed her how to play on the ten-stringed psaltery."[142]

Jutta continued her own education and "applied herself to reading with her mouth silent"[143] and "like the mighty heroine Judith, to whom she harks back by her very name, with the *sword of the word of God* she cut off the head of the intellectual Holofernes."[144] Soon "all those from round about of whatever rank, nobles or common people, rich or poor, pilgrims or tenants, were asking only after the anchoress, the lady Jutta; they waited on her alone as on a heavenly oracle. She was a cause of admiration and esteem to everyone for the wisdom divinely bestowed on her."[145] The number of her disciples grew to such an extent that on her deathbed, some twenty-four years after her enclosure, "she comforted her disciples, ten of them in number, with her soothing counsels."[146] During the course of her leadership "what was formerly a sepulchre [had] became a kind of monastery."[147] The transition to traditional Benedictine monastic life was completed under Hildegard who, after Jutta's death "was soon engaged in a quest for more spacious quarters to which they might transfer."[148] This follows the pattern of so many other religious groups. A charismatic individual with a desire to live an intense life in body, mind, and spirit inspires others to imitate her example. At the death of the founder the group institutionalizes the life established by that founder both in physical and literary form. In Jutta's case her own desire for an intense life experience led within one generation to the establishment of a thriving Benedictine monastery first at Disibodenberg and then at Rupertsberg. It is interesting to note what aspect of Jutta's life Guibert emphasizes in his concluding remarks about her life, and what Guibert tells us was the group's most important consideration in choosing Jutta's successor: "Now that their *magistra* had been taken from their midst and received into peace, and since no one in her school was found more outstanding in merit and holiness than Hildegard, so no one was judged more worthy to succeed her in the honour of teaching."[149] Teach them she did, as well as "giving the counsels required of her, solving the most difficult questions put to her, writing books, instructing her sisters."[150] The result was a monastery where women "apply themselves in well-fitted workshops to the writing of books, the weaving of robes or other manual crafts."[151]

With Hildegard the transition from the charismatic to the institutional stage is seen in its completed form. Five years after assuming leadership of the women Hildegard received her call to write. "O frail human, ashes of ashes, and filth of filth! Say and write what you see and hear," a heavenly voice said to her. "Explain these things in such a way that the hearer, receiving the words of [his] instructor, may expound them, in those words, according to that will, vision and instruction."[152] She hesitated and "refused to write for a long time through doubt and bad opinion and the diversity of human words" until she was "compelled at last by many illnesses" and by the encouragement of Richardis of Stade, a close friend in the community, and her second *magister* Volmar, to write *Scivias* (*Know the Ways of the Lord*).[153] Hildegard begins her writing[154] by describing in detail the source of her knowledge:

> It happened that, in the eleven hundred and forty-first year of the Incarnation of the Son of God, Jesus Christ, when I was forty-two years and seven months old, Heaven was opened and a fiery light of exceeding brilliance came and permeated my whole brain, and inflamed my whole heart and my whole breast, not like a burning but like a warming flame, as the sun warms anything its rays touch. And immediately I knew the meaning of the exposition of the Scriptures, namely the Psalter, the Gospel and the other catholic volumes of both the Old and New Testaments, though I did not have the interpretation of the words of their texts or the division of the syllables or the knowledge of cases or tenses.... But the visions I saw I did not perceive in dreams, or sleep, or delirium, or by the eyes of the body, or by the ears of the outer self, or in hidden places; but I received them while awake and seeing with a pure mind and the eyes and ears of the inner self, in open places, as God willed it. How this might be is hard for mortal flesh to understand.[155]

It is perhaps because of Hildegard's insistence on visions as the source of her knowledge that generations upon generations have excluded her from intellectual history. Even Colish refuses to consider Hildegard within the intellectual renaissance of the twelfth century and instead makes only passing reference to her in a section on mysticism and devotion. Yet, as Hildegard stresses, she is not simply a mystic nor is she only concerned with mystical union or prayer. In content *Scivias* has more in common with contemporary summas of doctrine than with any mystical writings. Hildegardian scholar Barbara Newman even claims that "if Hildegard had been a male theologian, her *Scivias* would undoubtedly have been considered one of the most important early medieval summas."[156] Perhaps that was true in medieval times, but today the visionary nature of *Scivias* keeps many scholars from reclassifying it as an intellectual work. Hildegard's constant reminder that visions, not schooling, are the source of her wisdom makes it difficult to posit otherwise. "In the purity of simplicity, write, therefore, the things you see and hear," a voice from Heaven told her, and so "I spoke and wrote these things not by the invention of my heart or that of any other person, but as by the secret mysteries of God I heard and received them in heavenly places."[157] Even the book's title had its origin in a vision: "In a vision I also saw that my first book of visions was to be called *Scivias,* for it was brought forth by way of the Living Light and not through any human instruction."[158] Yet, in the autobiographical sections of her *vita*,[159] she explains the process this way: "In this vision I understood without any human instruction the writings of the prophets of the Gospels, and of other saints and of certain philosophers, and I expounded a number of their texts, although I had scarcely any knowledge of literature since the woman who taught me was not a scholar," she wrote. "I also composed and sang chant with melody, to the praise of God and his saints, without being taught by anyone, since I had never studied neumes or any chant at all."[160] Hildegard's explanation here is remarkably reminiscent of Augustine's explanation of how he "manages to read [Aristotle's *Ten Categories*] and understand it without help,"[161] so much so that Dronke believes that Hildegard's passage may be based on Augustine's.[162] Dronke also notes that Hildegard admits here that she was quite familiar with many philosophical works and that she is denying any divine inspiration behind her writing. Dronke concludes thus: "If we make allowance for a certain element of modesty-topos, 'ad maiorem dei gloriam,' we can interpret her as saying that, because of a divinely granted intuitive gift, she could master learned texts without difficulty, notwithstanding her fairly rudimentary schooling."[163] When seen in this light, therefore, the visionary source for Hildegard's writings should not lead us to dismiss them as devotional matter, or inhibit us from evaluating their true intellectual tenor. Moreover, a good portion of Hildegard's writings is concerned with medicine and science, for which Hildegard claims no visionary basics.

Yet, there is another dimension that should be considered when trying to assess the nature of Hildegard's visionary works. We must stop and contemplate how medieval people considered visions. Because their understanding of vision was quite radically different from ours, their opinions of religious visions was consequently different. In the medieval period prior to the coming of Aristotelian translations, the dominant theory of vision was that of extromission. Platonic in origin, the theory posited that the eye emitted visual rays that lit up an object when the eye was focused on it and thus made the object visible. During the late thirteenth century another theory gained acceptance, that of intromission. Here the object emitted the rays which were directed back to the eye. In both theories vision was perceived in active terms and not in the passive terms we do today. The theory of intromission was developed further once scholars came into contact with Avicenna, for he posited that after the rays were sent back to the eye, they were sent to the brain where common sense, imagination, judgment, knowledge, and memory assessed the vision.[164] This addition increased active human participation in vision. The concept of vision in the high Middle Ages was in fact a much more dynamic concept than it is today. It actively involved the recipient of the vision, and it directly led to knowledge. Our present-day usage of the English term "I see" to mean "I understand" is rooted more in the medieval theories of vision than in modern optics. When Hildegard describes the nature of reflective knowledge, she uses sight metaphors to do so: "Knowledge shines as brightly as daylight," and "like a mirror; for as a person sees his face in a mirror and discerns beauty or blemishes," so one can look at knowledge and discern truth.[165] The senses, after all, "protect a person from harmful things and lay bare the soul's interior."[166] Two contemporaries of Hildegard from the School of St. Victor, Richard (d. 1173) and Hugh (1096–1141) developed elaborate schemas delineating the different types of eyes and kinds of vision which bring one knowledge. Hugh sometimes writes of two types of eyes, but most often he refers to three: eye of flesh, eye of reason, and eye of contemplation.[167] Richard varies Hugh's schema slightly, telling us various types of vision exist, "of which two are internal, two are external. Two are corporeal, two are spiritual."[168] The eye of the flesh views the corporeal world, the eye of reason sees all else except God. For this one needs the eyes of the mind and of faith.[169] In all but the final stage of knowledge human participation was essential to "seeing" knowledge. It is within this context of medieval understanding of optics that Hildegard's visions must be evaluated. Hildegard herself admits confusion as to the actual physical mechanics of her visions. She insists it is not mystical vision seen through the eye of faith, "for my outward eyes remain open, and I do not undergo the unconsciousness of ecstasy." She also insists that "I do not see these things with my outward eyes."[170] By denying her visions were seen by the eye of faith Hildegard is de facto arguing that she actively participated in her accession of knowledge through her eye of reason. When Hildegard talks about the senses, it is with reverence for their power and role in the spiritual life. "It is the senses on which the interior powers of the soul depend"; they "lay bare the soul's interior" and as such "the senses are to a person as precious stones and as a rich treasure sealed in a vase."[171] Of all the senses, vision is the most noble, for it teaches one "how to properly use the things of nature" and thus gain wisdom. Hildegard was, therefore, well aware of the role vision played in the attainment of knowledge; I posit that she believed her intellect played a role in the reception of vision and in understanding the vision.[172] It is the contribution that her rational powers made that must be identified and included in any assessment of medieval intellectual history.

The range of Hildegard's subjects is impressive, even in an age of summas. Dronke claims that Hildegard's uniqueness rests in the vastness of her range, noting that only Avicenna is in any way comparable.[173] Indeed, Hildegard and Avicenna's similarity is more than superficial. Both shared a materialistic and deterministic view of the physical world in tension with the transcending spiritual world.[174] Both constructed two cosmic models for comprehending these two realities, incompatible models which Hildegard only begins to resolve in a lengthy letter on music written in the last months of her life.[175] In addition to range and approach, they also share many Platonic principles, although Avicenna also adopted Aristotelian premises at times.[176] Hildegard was probably never exposed to Aristotle,[177] and shows no evidence of having been influenced by Aristotelianism. She was, in Newman's assessment, "a Platonist not only by virtue of this or that opinion, but in her most fundamental habits of thought and perception."[178] Even her musicology is Platonic.[179] Music is but a manifestation of the Divine "and so the words symbolize the body and the jubilant music indicates the spirit; and the celestial harmony shows the Divinity, and the words the Humanity of the Son of God."[180] Certainly, her constant use of images of light flow from her Platonic outlook. In her first vision while still a child God identifies himself in Platonic terminology: "I am the Living Light, Who illuminates the darkness."[181] Light imagery is employed in almost all her works. "And by the splendor that I am, the living light of the blessed angels glows, for, as a ray of light flashes from its source, so this splendor shines in the blessed angels" is the way angels are described, while prophets "foreshadowed" God. Hildegard is "a shadow of strength and health" and "all creatures shone resplendent in me, Love, and my splendor made their features visible."[182] Reflective knowledge is also perceived as a participation in light: "And the knowledge shines as brightly as daylight, because through it people know and judge their actions, and the human mind that is carefully considering itself is radiant."[183]

All this may account for some of her neglect in the centuries immediately following her death. By the end of the thirteenth century Aristotelian philosophy dominated the intellectual scene in the West, and many Platonic thinkers, or "pre-scholastics," of the twelfth century were left without immediate influence over the next generations. Hugh of St. Victor, Rupert of Deutz, and Honorius of Regensburg were as overlooked as Hildegard by the Aristotelian scholastics of the new universities. Even in certain aspects of theology Hildegard was left behind without immediate influence over the next generations, for she belonged to a sapiential Platonic tradition of divine, eternal ideas, ideal forms, microcosm and macrocosm. The next generation of theologians concerned itself with Aristotelian logic, systematic organization, and Greco-Arabic thought.

Hildegard was an influential participant in another aspect of the intellectual life of the day, though, one that radically changed the way Western people looked at the world. During the early Middle Ages resurrectional theology dominated. It had a transcendent God way up in the heavens and a devil down below in hell. Humans were but passive observers of the cosmic struggle between God and the devil for the souls of humans. Only by outwitting the devil by becoming man Himself and by triumphing over death in the Resurrection was God able to reign victorious.[184] This was reflected in art. Christ Triumphant was the artistic representation that dominated Western art during the early Middle Ages; even the crucifix corpuses were clothed in royal garments.[185] During the eleventh century we find the transcendent, resurrectional god being replaced with an immanent, incarnational god. We can trace these developments in the work of Anselm. In *Cur Deus Homo?* Anselm dismisses the god of cosmic struggle, simple because "I do not see the force of that argument, which we are wont to make use of, that God, in order to save men, was bound, as it were, to try a contest with the devil in justice."[186] Instead, we should contemplate the Incarnation and "carefully consider how fitly in this way human redemption is secured." To those who object that "we do injustice and dishonor to God when we affirm that he descended into the womb of a virgin, that he was born of woman, that he grew on the nourishment of milk and the food of men; and, passing over many other things which seem incompatible with Deity, that he endured fatigue, hunger, thirst, stripes and crucifixion among thieves," Anselm answers, no, "we do no injustice or dishonor to God." To the contrary, the Incarnation should be a source of astonishment to us, for it is "so great and unmerited." The Incarnation is the ultimate act of a loving, immanent god and as such gives "a certain indescribable beauty to our redemption as thus procured."[187]

A half-century after Anselm penned these thoughts, Hildegard echoed them.[188] She tells us what the serpent in the Garden of Eden "was saying within himself: 'I was thrown out of Heaven when I tried to fight with my angels against the army of the

Most High; I could not resist Him, and He conquered me. But now I have found Man on earth, and I will avenge myself mightily by working my wrath on him.' " Humans succumbed to the devil's art and "worshipped him instead of God." God saw the predicament of humanity and responded out of love, not out of the demands of justice. "As a person who has a beautiful jewel in a box puts it in a metal setting to show it to people, so I, Who had My Son in My Heart, willed him to be incarnate of the Virgin to save the lives of those who believe."[189] Like Anselm, Hildegard emphasizes the beauty inherent in the way redemption was procured. She asks God's help in telling "how You willed Your Son to become incarnate and become a human being within Time; which You willed before all creation in Your rectitude and the fire of the Dove, the Holy Spirit, so that Your Son might rise from a Virgin in the splendid beauty of the sun and be clothed with true humanity, a man's form assumed for Man's sake."[190]

In a society where the Incarnation dominates theology and theology dominates thought, there is a characteristic attitude towards creation that differs from one found in societies nourished by resurrectional theology. In both creation is embraced, but because resurrectional theology envisions a distant, more remote god, god's presence in creation is not as emphasized as with an indwelling, immanent god of incarnational theology. Because of the Incarnation creation is transformed. In Hildegard's words, "And, assuming humanity, He did not forsake Deity; but, being one and true God with the Father and the Holy Spirit, he sweetened the world with His sweetness and illumined it with the brilliance of His glory."[191] Such a stance has long reaching implications. It breeds new attitudes towards the world and, more importantly, towards change in the world. Christianity embraced, nay, encouraged change because the Incarnation changed everything: "There, if any man is in Christ, he is a new creature; the old things passed away; behold, new things have come" (2 Cor 5:17). Again, these changes can be easily traced in the art that emerged after this change in theological perspective. Besides the depictions of the crucified Jesus, those of Virgin and Child became less remote and regal, and more emotional. Illuminated manuscripts begin to display tenderness and maternal affection, playful innocence of children, and inherent human dignity of adults.[192] Some of the most extraordinary examples of this change in art are found in the earliest extant manuscript of Hildegard's *Scivias*. Thirty-five illuminations which almost draw the reader into Hildegard's visionary world of the text are among the most distinct, original illuminations of the medieval period. The artistic adherence to the text and its ability to clarify the author's intent has led most scholars to assume that if not painted by Hildegard, they were completed under her direction. Their style is unmistakably unique, full of original and striking energy, just as Hildegard's text is. The text of *Scivias* overflows with an appreciation and acceptance of all things created and of the interrelationships between the macrocosm and microcosm. The illuminations of *Scivias* allow readers to grasp Hildegard's interpretation—that is, her vision—of reality with their senses in addition to their intellects. Gone is the august grandeur of an awe-inspiring, impersonal god of the Carolingian and Ottonian illuminations, replaced by a new, more approachable, familiar portrait of a personal god. For example, Hildegard's eighth vision in Book Three concerns the pillar of Jesus' humanity, and in this pillar was "an ascent like a ladder from bottom to top, on which I saw all the virtues of God descending and ascending."[193] In the text she explained the vision thus: "This is to say that in the incarnate Son of God all the virtues work fully, and that He left in Himself the way of salvation; so that faithful people both small and great can find in Him the right step on which to place their foot in order to ascend to virtue."[194] The illumination accompanying the text includes a variety of familiar human figures, a suffering crucified corpus, two Mother and Child figures, and the Shining One, all warmly and unsophisticatedly drawn in such a manner as to convey a sense of immediacy. In each of the illuminations for the visions of soul and body, the soul and her tabernacle, the synagogue, the mother church, and church as the net of Christ, the Incarnation is recalled by the figure of a woman giving birth.

It is in her so-called minor works on music, medical and scientific writings, and her letters that we see the extent of Hildegard's embrace of incarnational theology and the effect such a theology has on one's view of creation. Even the imaginary language she constructed is intimately bound to her incarnational theology. Scholar Jeffrey Schnapp goes so far as to argue that incarnational theology was responsible for bringing the Middle Ages into a "golden age of neologism and verbal invention,"[195] for it gave medieval society permission of sorts to name or rename creation, because it was reborn under the New Law. Hildegard's invention of terms for things created in the Garden of Eden, such as penis, vulva, sweat, and feces, suggests that because of the Incarnation Hildegard wanted to start over anew and eliminate the residue of the Fall, including the language of the Old Law.[196] The result, Hildegard's imaginary language, *Lingua ignota,* "is the only systematically constructed imaginary language that has come down to us from the Middle Ages."[197] It is not simply in its conception that it is incarnational but in its structure also. Hildegard invents some 1010 terms which she divides into categories. All of the terms are for physical things created, and the vast majority of them have to do with the human and natural world. According to Schnapp's analysis, 25.74 percent (261 terms) name the elements in the natural world, 26.53 percent (269 terms) refer to things present in the lives of humans, and 16.96 percent (172 terms) name body parts and conditions and kin.[198]

A preoccupation with creation and the embrace of it in Hildegard's imaginary language is likewise evident in her other works. "God cannot be perceived directly," Hildegard reasons, but thanks to the Incarnation "he is known through creation, through humankind alone which is a mirror of all God's wonders."[199] The desire to know God thus becomes the desire to know creation. Even in an era of summas and authors with encyclopedic ambitions the breadth and depth of Hildegard's writings on the natural world is unusual. Sometime between 1150 and 1160 she wrote *Subtleties of the Diverse Natures of Creatures,* although the work is better known by the common name of its two parts, *Physica* (*Natural Things*) and *Causae et curae* (*Causes and cures*). The former describes the beneficial and detrimental effects of herbs, plants, animals, elements, rocks and metals, and the latter is a medical compendium within cosmic scale; both embrace the goodness of the world in order to better understand it. Between 1163 and 1173 she composed what some consider her most impressive achievement, *The Book of Divine Works;* here she developed a history of humanity in relationship to cosmos, a cosmos in which divine immanence is a major theme.[200]

The implications of her incarnational approach toward the world are explicit here. Hildegard's universe is a changing, dynamic world in nature, culture, and history. As early as the first book in *Scivias* Hildegard established that creation "had been created for the service of humanity."[201] By the time she wrote *Physica* she had added an essential corollary: "The elements willingly served humanity because they sensed that people were endowed with life, just as people worked with them."[202] Work is what makes the world tolerable for humans, and, as such, it is mandated. As she wrote the *Book of the Rewards of Life,* her philosophy of work had matured. "God created all things and made all living creatures,"[203] Hildegard begins, and "when God created man, he told him to work with the other creatures. Just as man will not end unless he is changed into ashes and as he will rise again, as also his works will be seen, the good, of course, for glory."[204]

This responsibility to work is "part of his divine plan,"[205] but in Hildegard's thought work is not punitive. It is creative. Work is the means by which humans participate in creation and share in God's power. "Let the faithful man seize a plow with oxen so that he may, nevertheless, look at God who gives greenness and fruit to the earth"—greenness (*viriditas*) connotes the creative principle of life for Hildegard—"and let him walk according to the commands of his master so that, cultivating earthly things, he does not desert heavenly things." Work is rewarding and satisfying, and it makes earthly life more pleasant. "If we do not have care of earthly things, the earth will sprout thorns and thorny plants. We would then be sinning since the earth is supposed to feed all the animals but could not do so if we did not care for it," Hildegard argues. "A faithful person pays attention to these things and remembers them well."[206] Work creates conditions conducive to happiness. For instance, "justice comes about through the good works of people at which time it enters God's deepest knowledge where it is spread out among wondrous things, because God knows about the works of the holy and does not forget them."[207] Work is also a means by which creatures see the Creator. If humans work as they should, "when they sow their seeds in the earth and those seeds are bathed with the dew and the rain so that they grow," they will "have seen him in the light of good knowledge and in the light of the temporal sun."[208] Moreover, work creates permanent change, "but just as the work of God, which is man, will endure and not be ended, so also the work of man will not vanish because the work of man, which reaches to God, will shine in heavenly things." Humans must be discerning in their work though, for work which does not produce good, work "which reaches to the devil, will remain in punishments."[209] As such, humans must remember that they "are more changeable in their actions than any other type of creature,"[210] and thus must perform only work that changes them for the better. It is not only easy for humans to discern proper works but if they do not choose wisely, if they refuse to work, then creation will become hostile. "The elements bring their complaints to their Creator with great crying aloud," Hildegard maintains, for they "are not strong enough by themselves to travel the ways and to fulfill the duties given them by God since they can be overturned by the injustices of other men."[211] When Adam and Eve fell in the Garden "primordial sin rashly and deceitfully choked off human work."[212] In a reversal of the traditional, Hildegard here regards work as a reward for a virtuous life, not a punishment for sin.

As beneficial as work is, humans must not "put all their effort and care into their present life while they are alive" and put no "effort into their future life,"[213] because the purpose of work is, among other things, to enter into the life of the Creator. Out of love of humanity "God gave man the ability to work," and as a result "man should look forward to what is useful."[214] Work has the power to alter creation and, therefore, work engenders in people a reverence for creation. Work is a most powerful tool. "I could destroy all things I did not make or create or give knowledge to," Hildegard admits, but reverence for creation forbids it. "All the things God created please me. I do not hurt anything," nor will Hildegard tolerate anyone who does.[215] Hildegard thus displays a sensitivity towards the dignity of work, the role work plays in maintaining the ecological balance, and the fundamental creative nature of work which is indeed advanced for the era. Work is one of the greatest gifts of God to humanity and a key to its happiness: "So you have the knowledge of good and evil, and the ability to work. And so you cannot plead as an excuse that you lack any good thing that would inspire you to love God in truth and justice. You have the power to master yourself."[216]

Hildegard communicates these principles in another manner in *Causae et curae* when she discusses creation. Throughout the discussion she employs working metaphors, particularly the metaphor of cooking. Not only is the work she chooses for her metaphors mundane work with little inherent glamor, but it is also work done either by men and women or predominately by women. Hildegard uses the reality of personal experience to reinforce the validity of her thesis concerning the dignity of work. At creation "Adam was made out of the earth, called forth by fire, filled with air, and water poured over him, and he was stirred. Then God put him to sleep, and cooked [*coctus est*] him into a man."[217] Adam was created with a soul, which in turn possesses a will. This will is most powerful, "for the will is like a fire, baking each deed as if in a furnace. Bread is baked so that people may be nourished by it and be able to live. So too the will is the strength of the whole work, for it starts by kneading it and when it is firm adds the yeast and pounds it severely; and, thus preparing the work in contemplation as if it were bread, it bakes it in perfection by the full action of its ardor, and so makes a greater food for humans in the work they do than in the bread they eat."[218] Once Adam is finished cooking and woman is also created, "God gave to man the power of creating, that through his love—which is woman—he might procreate children." When procreating the woman experiences "a sense of heat in the [woman's] brain, which brings with it sensual delight, communicates the taste of that delight." The love of man differs somewhat from the love of woman, and Hildegard explains the difference by using cooking imagery: "The man's love, compared with the woman's, is a heat of ardour like a fire on blazing mountains, which can hardly be put out, whilst hers is a wood-fire that is easily quenched; but the woman's love, compared with the man's, is like a sweet warmth proceeding from the sun, which brings forth fruit."[219] The man's semen is "only a poisonous foam until the fire, that is the warmth, warms it." This happens "through the warmth of the mother" whose oven-like womb "holds the flesh [of the unborn child] together with a bloody slime and a constant moisture just as food is cooked in a pot by the fire."[220] By thus mixing the acts of creation and procreation with the acts of cooking Hildegard elevates the work of the cook to new heights. She even continues the metaphor by describing the work of the Holy Spirit as the work of a cook: "Just as ordinary dishes are changed into better-tasting dishes by the addition of seasonings and peppers . . . so is the ordinary nature of a person transformed through the fire of the Holy Spirit into a better sort."[221]

Hildegard's work metaphors are plentiful throughout all her works, because she realizes the potential of work. In a letter to Abbot Adalard she writes of the Living Light telling her, "you are like the potter who molds many vessels but who fails to fire them properly. Learn from this analogy that your works should not fail to possess the sheen of love." Then she switches to the kitchen again. She should "follow the example of the saints" who "gave food to men which they could swallow with joy. For if they were given thorns instead of bread, they cannot eat them." Every religious superior, therefore, "must sift the words of his teaching with maternal sweetness so that his subordinates will gladly open their mouths and swallow them." Immediately following, she employs the imagery of farm work: "The millstone grinds grain and brings forth various kinds of meal. In the same way, the planters of the Church took legal precepts from the Old and the New Law. . . . The millstone is the Old Law, which brought forth every grain of truth in Christ, and the pure wheat, sifted clean of all contamination, is virginity."[222] In another letter to an abbess Hildegard uses a parable to present other aspects of her philosophy of work:

> Listen now to a wise man's parable: A certain man wanted to dig a cave, but while he was working with wood and iron, fire burst forth from a rock he had dug into. And the result was that this place could in no way be penetrated. Nevertheless, he took note of the location of the place, and with great exertion he dug other tunnels into it. And then the man said in his heart: "I have toiled strenuously, but he who comes after me will have easier labor, because he will find everything already prepared for him." Surely, this man will be praised by his lord, because in length and breadth his work is much more useful than work done in arable land that is turned by the plow. And so his master will consider him a mighty knight competent to be in charge of his army, and so he puts him in charge of the other farmers who present him fruit in their due season. For whoever has labored first is preeminent over the one who succeeds him. Indeed, the Maker of the world undertook creation first, and thus set the example for His servants to labor after His fashion.[223]

After reading this and grasping the mentality behind it, it is easier to understand the dynamic nature of twelfth-century Western society. Hildegard sees the power of work and, most importantly, the power of pioneering work in new fields. How and why the West set about creating its medieval culture is somewhat easier to grasp in light of Hildegard's writings. She embraced the world, she embraced work in the world, and she embraced the change work in the world brings about. Given the extensive network of contacts that she developed during her life, it is no wonder that her contemporaries recognized her wisdom and were influenced by her.[224]

The dignity Hildegard bestowed on work flowed over to the worker. In Hildegard's scheme humans, even after the Fall, enjoy great dignity. She holds that men and women, not just men, are made in the image of God.[225] "The human form is to be seen in the inmost nature of the Deity, where neither angels nor any other creatures appear,"[226] and these humans "are widely divergent in bodily form."[227] Large or small, martyr or sinner, "humanity is powerful in soul. Humanity's head is turned upward and its feet to the solid ground, and it can place into motion both the higher and the lower things."[228] The dignity of the relationship between man and woman is forcefully emphasized in Hildegard's anthropology: "Male and female were joined together, therefore, in such a way that each one works through the other. The male would not be called 'male' without the female, or the female named 'female' without the male. For woman is man's work, and man is the solace of woman's eyes, and neither of them could exist without the other."[229] What she describes is a relationship of mutual dependency: "Woman was created for the sake of man, and man for the sake of woman. And she is from the man, the man is also from her, lest they dissent from each other in the unity of making their children; for they should work as one in one work, as the air and the wind intermingle in their labor."[230] Humanity possesses gifts not given to the rest of creation, because man alone was created "to worship God with all his strength and all his might and with all the devotion of his intelligent reason."[231] Humanity, for example, was imbued with "five senses for the sake of the work of God."[232] With special treatment, however, comes special conditions. Thus, humans only are tested by God to see if they are worthy of their unique gifts. "Hence, O foolish humans, how can that which was made in the image and likeness of God exist without testing? For Man must be examined more than any other creature, and therefore he must be tested through every other creature." The tests are hard and thorough but necessary if humanity is to retain its dignity and attain eternal happiness. "Spirit is to be tested by spirit, flesh by flesh, earth by water, fire by cold, fight by resistance, good by evil, beauty by deformity, poverty by riches, sweetness by bitterness, health by sickness," and so on; "Hence, Man is tested by every creature in Paradise, on earth and in Hell, and then he is placed in Heaven."[233]

Creatures, too, have a dignity in God's universe, as do the elements. Specifically "created for the service of humanity" in the primordial Garden, after the Fall creation "now opposed" humanity.[234] Humanity needs creation, though, because the physical world "contains the seeds for everything that germinates and sends forth flowers of green strength" and "produces and nourishes man" as well as "sustains and supports all the things that man uses." In these statements Hildegard is articulating the ancient Judeo-Christian belief encapsulated in Genesis' account of creation in which "God created man in His own image, in the image of God he created him, male and female He created them" and then gave them the command to "fill the earth, and subdue it; and rule over the fish of the sea and over the birds of the sky, and over every living thing that moves on the earth" (Gen 1:27–28). Hildegard does not stop here, though. She argues that because humanity "has the power of reason and the spirit of intelligence," humans must support "the development of these things" of the earth.[235] Acceptance of the status quo is not enough; humans must overlook the development of creation with their intellect. Here, once again, Hildegard gives us insight into the motivations and intentions behind the medieval intellectual expansion.

How it stimulated Hildegard intellectually can be seen in her writings on natural science. Research into this area of Hildegardian studies lags behind most other aspects of her corpus, but the little that has been done places Hildegard squarely in the same class as better-known medieval scientific pioneers such as Albertus Magnus. Historian Laurence Moulinier even claims that Hildegard's presentation of the animal world in *Physica* makes that book perhaps the most original and important zoological study in the entire Middle Ages.[236] Other scholars are not quite as efflorescent but still insist that Hildegard is a key pioneer in the development of a modern scientific approach in zoology. As historians Kenneth Kitchell and Irven Resnick say, Hildegard "passed beyond the randomness of the *Physiologus* and bestiary tradition and has imposed further order on the Hexaemeron tradition in an early attempt to see the world in a structured fashion;" as such, she "serves as a significant and individualistic bridge between the older learning and that which was to come."[237] To prove their thesis they compared Hildegard's chapter on fish to Albertus Magnus' discussion of fish in his *De animalibus* and concluded that Hildegard's earlier work "is clearly part of the same process that led to later, more precise 'science' " in the work of Albertus Magnus.[238] The content of *Physica* indicates in itself Hildegard's encyclopedic approach. There are nine chapters of varying length in *Physica,* each on a distinct species or element. Her presentation of plants is the longest in the book, and her interest throughout focuses on their medicinal properties. She treats trees in another long book, again focusing on their medicinal aspects. Fish, birds (which include flying insects), mammals and reptiles each have their own chapter, most of them short; Hildegard completes her discussion of creation with chapters on the elements, stones, gems, and metals.[239] The details of her discussions indicate that Hildegard had a special interest in nature, particularly in plants. How much of Hildegard's work was based on personal experience and how much was taken from ancient or local sources is hard to determine until more critical research on the text is done, but its worth no matter how it was compiled is undeniable. Hildegard records for posterity descriptions of species now unknown and perhaps extinct, of spawning practices in Hildegard's region and of uses humans made of nature. Hildegard's taxonomy is somewhat weak, based in part on the six days of creation and on observation. The fact that she places them in a scheme at all makes her work significant, though, for it distinguishes her work from the bestiary tradition of her immediate precedessors and contemporaries and points us towards the natural philosophy that gained prominence in the thirteenth century. [240]

The overall picture of nature that Hildegard presents in her medical and scientific works is one of harmony. The natural world is in harmony with itself and with humanity. This harmony is reinforced by Hildegard's theory of microcosm and macrocosm that permeates all her works. In *Scivias,* her first work, Book One presents creation and the Fall, the universe, soul and body, the synagogue, and angels through the imagery of macrocosm and microcosm. Everything in the macrocosm is created for and understood by the microcosm. For example, "at certain times the report of the Creator's miracles comes to all of God's creation, so that miracle is piled on miracle in a great thunder of words; and then Man, struck by the greatness of these miracles, feels the impact on his mind and body, and in these wondrous deeds considers with astonishment his own weakness and frailty."[241] In *Causae et curae* she explains it thus: "O man, look to man. For man has the heavens and earth and other created things within him. He is one, and all things are hidden within him."[242] In one of her antiphons she expresses this relationship between humans and creation poetically and musically:

> O how wonderful is the prescience of the divine heart,
> who foreknew every creature.
> For when God looked on the face of man,
> whom He had made,
> all his works
> He saw completed in his form.
> O how wonderful is the breath
> which brought man to life.[243]

In *On Divine Works* Hildegard offers yet another view of the macrocosm/microcosm relationship between humanity and the world: "For man is the work of God perfected, because God is known through him, and since God created all creatures for him, and allowed him in the embrace of true love to preach and praise him through the quality of his mind. But man needed a helper in his likeness. So God gave him a helper which was his mirror image, woman, in whom the whole human race lay hidden." Hildegard thus argues, "therefore, as said above, such is the form of man, body and soul, the work of God brought together with all creation."[244] All human qualities find their equivalent in the macrocosm. Humans love in the microcosm; in the macrocosm Love is described thus: "I am the fiery life of the essence of God; I flame above the beauty of the fields; I shine in the waters; I burn in the sun, the moon, and the stars. And, with the airy wind, I quicken all things vitally by an unseen, all-sustaining life."[245] Humans possess reason; reason also exists at the cosmic level, as Reason itself explains: "Mine is the blast of the resounding Word through which all creation came to be, and I quickened all things with my breath so that not one of them is mortal in its kind; I am life. Indeed I am Life, whole and undivided—not hewn from any stone, or bundled from branches, or rooted in virile strength; but all that lives has its roots in me."[246]

In probably her most famous letter, written only months before her death to the prelates of Mainz, Hildegard articulates her cosmic views of harmony in reference to music. During a conflict over the burial of a certain nobleman, the ecclesiastical rulers of Mainz placed Hildegard's monastery under interdict, which included a ban on music. Because Hildegard adheres to a Platonic, Augustinian worldview which sees music as the microcosm echo of eternal harmony,[247] the forfeiture of music made her "greatly distressed and saddened." In an effort to persuade the clergy to lift their interdict she explains her philosophy of music in detail: "I heard a voice coming from the Living Light concerning the various kinds of praises, about which David speaks in the psalm: 'Praise Him with sound of trumpet: praise Him with psaltery and harp,' " Hildegard begins. "These words use outward, visible things to teach us about inward things. Thus the material composition and the quality of these instruments instruct us how we ought to give form to the praise of the Creator and turn all the convictions of our inner being to the same." Adam lost this voice when he sinned in the Garden, so the prophets were called upon to restore it and "not only to compose psalms and canticles (by which the hearts of listeners would be inflamed) but also to construct various kinds of musical instruments to enhance these songs of praise with melodic strains. Thereby, both through the form and quality of the instruments, as well as through the meaning of the words which accompany them, those who hear might be taught, as we said above, about inward things." People who have followed the example of the prophets "have themselves, with human skill, invented several kinds of musical instruments, so that they might be able to sing for the delight of their souls" and, like the prophets, "recall to mind that divine melody of praise" that resounded in the Garden before the Fall. "And because sometimes a person sighs and groans at the sound of singing, remembering, as it were, the nature of celestial harmony, the prophet, aware that the soul is symphonic and thoughtfully reflecting on the profound nature of the spirit, urges us in the psalm [cf. Ps 32.2, 91.4] to confess to the Lord with the harp and to sing a psalm to Him with the ten-stringed psaltery. His meaning is that the harp, which is plucked from below, relates to the discipline of the body; the psaltery, which is plucked from above, pertains to the exertion of the spirit; the ten chords, to the fulfillment of the law."[248]

These thoughts on music were present in nascent form even in her earliest work, *Scivias*. There Hildegard attaches a brief commentary on the role of music in creation which foreshadow the theses developed more fully in her letter to Mainz clergy: "So the words symbolize the body, and the jubilant music indicates the spirit; and the celestial harmony shows the Divinity, and the words the Humanity of the Son of God."[249] It is in this letter written in the waning days of her long life that we see the thoughts on music developed over a lifetime brought to fruition. Music is not merely harmony; it is Harmony capable of reconciling the inherent differences between the macrocosm and microcosm.

Given her philosophical underpinnings, it is not surprising she appreciated music and developed an elaborate theory of music, but "who would not marvel that she composed chant of the sweetest melody with a wonderful harmony," her hagiographer queries.[250] Her musical skill is gaining increased recognition of late, as is the poetry which accompanied her compositions. Music historian Barbara Jeskalían reminds us that "musicologically, Hildegard broke new ground,"[251] while Dronke tells us her songs "contain some of the most unusual, subtle, and exciting poetry of the twelfth century."[252] Hildegard's musical compositions consists of some seventy liturgical songs collected in a lyrical cycle, called *Symphony of the Harmony of Heavenly Revelations,* a title which in itself tells us much about Hildegard's approach to music. All were intended to be performed within the Divine Office as antiphons, responsories, sequences, or hymns. While Hildegard built on the ecclesiastical tradition of Gregorian chant, her music varies from earlier styles by her unique use of melismas (many notes provided for one syllable) and neums (one syllable for many notes) and her individualized inflection.[253] Her melodies demand a taxing control over as much as two and one-half octaves, much more than is typically found in medieval liturgical books,[254] and she does not rely solely on the traditional eight modes of chant that dominated the day. Indeed, her modal system is distinct enough to be dubbed original.[255]

Like most artists of the Gothic era, Hildegard's artistic musical creations were grounded in mathematics. Otto von Simpson long ago reminded us in his influential book, *The Gothic Cathedral,* that geometry was the basis of the Gothic cathedral. He also reminded us how prevalent some of Hildegard's fundamental premises were during this period. Medieval society's approach was build upon Platonic, Augustinian theory, that architecture mirrors eternal harmony and music echoes it, and that both geometry and music have the ability to lead one from this world to the next. Both are based on number—good music is expressed in simple ratios—and numbers were the link between the finite and infinite.[256] Many Hildegardian scholars argue that in these respects she is typical of her day.[257] Hildegard's music is built upon geometric proportions, as are Gothic art and architecture. It is in her particular use of proportion that her creativity enters into the music.

What Dronke admires about the songs is their vivid imagery and the way Hildegard is able to reflect her musical pattern of echo and modification in her poetic text. "Ecclesia, your eyes are sapphire-like, your ears are as the mountain of Bethel, your nose is as a mountain of myrrh and incense, and your mouth is like the roar of many waters,"[258] are the images with which Hildegard opens her sequence for St. Ursula. In an antiphon for the same feast Dronke points out Hildegard's use of imagery that anticipates Marlowe centuries later:

> Redness of blood
> which flowed from that high place
> touched by divinity,
> you are a flower
> that winter with its serpent blast
> has never harmed.[259]

Hildegard's poetic talent is not restricted to her music, either, for all her written works without exception are filled with poetic imagery and cadence, albeit not of the highest quality. Her literary talent bears its fullest fruit in one particular work, not yet mentioned, but one that must be discussed before we end this section on Hildegard. The work, *Ordo virtutum* (*Play of Virtues*) is one of her earliest, composed sometime between 1141 and 1151; Dronke maintains that the play was written before *Scivias* was completed and was independent of *Scivias* even though a proportion of the play is presented in Book Three.[260] If Hildegard had left us with no other work *Ordo virtutum* would mandate her inclusion in intellectual history, because with this play a new literary genre comes into existence, the morality play.

Prior to recent Hildegardian research standard works in drama history dated the origin of the morality play in the fourteenth century,[261] simply by failing to identify the genre of Hildegard's play properly. During Hildegard's life, drama was beginning to sprout wings. With the very important exception of Hrotsvitha, the earliest expressions of this new interest in drama were found in liturgical settings. The oldest known trope (an elaboration of the words of the liturgy) is the famous *Quem quaeritis?* (*Whom do you seek?*), which was a series of questions and answers sung before the Introit during Easter liturgy. By the late tenth century this trope was performed with music, and by the eleventh century the trope *Quem quaeritis?* was transformed into a liturgical drama known as *Visitatio sepulchre* (*The Visit to the Sepulchre*).[262] Variations of liturgical dramas like the *Visitatio sepulchre* were developed by the next generations, and by Hildegard's time two other dramatic forms were popular, the scriptural drama and one of Hrotsvitha's dramatic forms, dramatic legends of the saints. To these three types Hildegard added a fourth, the morality play. This is an innovation worthy of note, since the morality play is an essential step along the road to modern drama. Morality plays differ from their predecessors in the amount of freedom the author had in constructing the plot and dialogue and in the dominant use of the personification of concepts instead of human characters. The dramas were message-driven, that is, vehicles for the author to communicate her beliefs. Consequently, the action of the play takes place in the mind, as does the development of the personified character.[263] Just as Hrotsvitha was the first to realize the potential dramatic element in saints' legends, Hildegard was the first to discern the possibilities of psychological drama.[264] In *Ordo virtutum* patriarchs, prophets, virtues, and Anima (a soul), battle the devil in unpredictable dramatic tension for the triumph of good. In language that Dronke says "achieves a visionary concentration and an evocative and associative richness that set it apart from nearly all other religious poetry of its age,"[265] Hildegard stages a psychological and cosmic struggle in which Virtues and Anima sing and dance and the devil speaks and shouts. Anima is torn between the joys of heaven "which I lost in my first manifestation"[266] and the attraction to the world, for "God created the world: I'm doing him no injury—I only want to enjoy it!"[267] Much to the disappointment of the Virtues, Anima enters the world, and the devil taunts the Virtues for their failure to keep Anima safe.[268] The Virtues eventually save Anima and Chastity proclaims to the devil how the inner and outer worlds are harmoniously reconciled in the Incarnation: "In the mind of the highest, Satan, I trod on your head,/and in virgin form I nurtured a sweet miracle/when the son of God came into the world."[269] In *Ordo virtutum* we have many of Hildegard's major themes reiterated and brought center stage, but in strikingly forceful, exuberant language. In *Scivias* she describes her visions; in her music and her play she paints her visions.

It is hard to disagree with Dronke's observation that "there is scarcely a field to which [Hildegard] did not bring her individual contribution."[270] She possessed a comprehensive intellect and an unquenchable thirst for knowledge. She also had something else, something that, unfortunately, Dhuoda and Hrotsvitha were lacking: influence. While it has taken modern scholars many decades of research to appreciate fully the contributions and impact Hildegard had on the intellectual culture of her day, her contemporaries appreciated her during her lifetime. Only Bernard of Clairvaux comes to mind as a contemporary equal in renown. As she sought his advice as to whether she "should speak those things openly or keep my silence"[271] before she made her visionary knowledge public, so too would many turn to her for similar advice after her disclosures made her famous. Monks, nuns, laity, abbots, abbesses, popes, bishops, archbishops, visionaries, cardinals, nobility, kings, a queen, an empress, and an emperor all corresponded with Hildegard because, as Hermann, Bishop of Constance, wrote her, "the fame of your wisdom has spread far and wide and has been reported to me by a number of truthful people."[272] The vast majority of correspondents sought spiritual direction from Hildegard,[273] but what is of interest here is the distance Hildegard's reputation spread: Rome, Paris, Constantinople, Jerusalem, and all the corners of the Holy Roman Empire knew of Hildegard's wisdom. One of the most interesting letters is that of Odo of Soissons, famed teacher at the University of Paris, who wrote Hildegard ca. 1148 thus: "It is reported that, exalted you see many things in the heavens and record them in your writing, and that you bring forth the melody of a new song," indicating that her musical talent was already known as far away as Paris even before *Scivias* was completed. "Despite the fact that we live far away, we have utmost confidence in you, and, therefore, we would like for you to resolve a certain problem for us. Many contend that God is not both paternity and divinity. Would you please explain to us in a letter what you perceive in the heavens about this matter."[274] The problem Odo was referring to concerned one of Gilbert of Porrée's theses which many believed to be heretical and which was debated at the Council of Reims later in 1148. That a master of Paris should consult Hildegard for her learned opinion of the matter before the council met is an impressive indication of the esteem Hildegard was held in by her contemporary intellectuals.[275] In both her *vita* and the liturgical readings proposed for Hildegard's projected feast by Theodoric there is mention of "a philosopher of Mainz" who "scorned her, sharply opposing her in what she said and wrote,"[276] but after continued examination of her works "in the end he came around to our cause."[277] In the 1150s Hildegard's reputation earned her an invitation to visit Frederick Barbarossa. From the late 1150s until 1170 Hildegard undertook four preaching tours, a significant fact in and of itself, given how sensitive many male ecclesiastics were concerning the exclusiveness of the preaching domain.[278] There is no evidence that Hildegard's preaching tours ignited any controversy. They were well received and did much to extend her influence. The map of her visits is impressive in its extent. Her biographer reports thus: "Amidst all this it is remarkable of her that she, not so much led as driven by the Divine Spirit, came to Cologne, Trier, Metz, Würzburg and Bamberg. . . . She also made known whatever was for the benefit of souls, as God had revealed it to her, in Disibodenberg, Sieberg, Eberbach, Hirsau, Zwiefalten, Maulbronn, Rothenkirchen, Kitzinger, Krauftal, Herde, Hönningen, Werden, Andernach, Marienberg, Elsen, and Winkel."[279]

Despite the highly influential status Hildegard attained during her lifetime it was greatly diminished after her death. Her monastery at Bingen was not able (or did not choose) to build upon Hildegard's intellectual contributions and establish itself as a center of study. The only disciple of note was a young woman, Elizabeth of Schönau, and their link was more because of their prophetic roles than any intellectual parallel. As an aspiring nun Elizabeth wrote to Hildegard for assurance and direction after receiving her first visions, much as Hildegard had written to Bernard of Clairvaux. Clearly, Elizabeth's account of her own spirituality, *Liber viarum Dei* (*The Book of Divine Works*) was modeled on Hildegard's *Scivias,*[280] and thus both works can be considered to pioneer new literary genres to accommodate their visions.[281] The little that Elizabeth does discuss philosophical underpinnings reveals disagreement rather than imitation of Hildegard's Platonism.[282] In this Elizabeth was typical of the next generation's attitude toward Hildegard. In an intellectual world increasingly Aristotelian and scholastic, thirteenth-century intellectuals saw little that attracted them to Hildegard. We can wonder why Hildegard's medical, musical, and scientific work did not inspire a following, but it is no mystery why her more speculative works decreased steadily over the decades in importance.

The question of Hildegard's influence is a field that needs more attention before definitive conclusions can be reached. Her prophetic thought was kept alive by the circulation of Jebeno of Eberbach's 1220 anthology of her apocalyptic writings. Until the recent research of Kathryn Kerby-Fulton scholars believed that because this was the only way Hildegard's thought was kept alive until humanists Trithemus and Jacques Lefèvre d'Etaples resurrected interest in the sixteenth century,[283] Hildegard's influence was historically negligible in early modern society. Kerby-Fulton, however, has negated these hastily drawn conclusions by tracing the presence of Hildegardian manuscripts during the period which is quite impressive (Matthew Paris, John Pecham, Henry d'Avranches, Langland, Gower, Wycliff, and many more[284]) and then analyzing the role her thought played in the radical politics of the day. Throughout the late Middle Ages "Hildegard's writings, bucking all trends, still found a serious male audience" and in some form were "now regularly reaching lay audiences concerned with lay political matters."[285] Kerby-Fulton's research reinforces to all how much more has to be done before Hildegard's influence is properly assessed.

3

The Coming of the Vernacular

In every example discussed so far the text focused on was written in Latin. Latin remained the chief language of the Western intellectual through the Italian and northern renaissances (the sophistication of one's Latin even becomes a criterion for judging one's credentials as an intellectual), but only with the coming of the vernacular does the West establish its own distinctive nature. The retrieval of ancient Latin classics during the Carolingian and Ottonian renaissances was an essential first step in the development of its own intellectual tradition. The second step was the establishment of a vernacular culture. Even historian Charles Homer Haskins recognized this in his classic, *The Renaissance of the Twelfth Century*.[1] If the Western societies had pursued only ancient Greek and Roman cultures then they might have proven to be only a reinvention of the past. They chose otherwise; as Colish says, they chose to use the classical past, particularly Latin, as "the medium through which other writers gained access to a vernacular tradition not originally their own." The medieval Westerners decided not simply to repeat and reverence the classical past but to empower "vernacular languages and literatures, enabling them to become the means by which late medieval writers and their audiences appropriated, not only their Christian and classical inheritance but also their earlier vernacular legacies, achieving cultural self-definition by their own selection from and re-expression of these sources."[2] We shall proceed in this chapter and Chapter 4 to identify those women who contributed to the establishment of this key aspect of the Western intellectual tradition.

The function of the vernacular in the rise of Western intellectual traditions is beginning to get the attention it deserves, thanks to recent interest in linguistic theory, especially in the late Middle Ages.[3] Scholars have long shared a general sense of its importance but the topic awaited historical theorists to piece together isolated acknowledgements into a comprehensive, cohesive whole. The text of the Strasbourg oaths of 842 taken by Charles the Bald and Louis the German marks the first written record of a Romance vernacular language being used within the area of the then defunct Roman Empire. Most historians have noted that during the next three centuries the use of vernacular languages increased proportionately to the growth of nations and the demise of a single continental empire.[4] Iceland provides excellent evidence for this thesis. First settled by Irish monks in 795 and then by various Norse during the ninth century, by 930 the settlers were organized enough to meet in a central assembly called *Althing*. During the next one hundred years, referred to as the

Saga Age, Iceland developed slowly into a nation, and these events were captured first in oral sagas and then recorded in the vernacular by the thirteenth century. What is extraordinary is that even after Christianity was accepted as the national religion in 1000, Latin did not threaten the monopoly of Icelandic language in written documents. All the literary masterpieces of the medieval period were composed or preserved in the vernacular. *Prose Edda, Poeta Edda,* court poetry, skaldic poems, *Book of Icelanders, Book of Settlements,* the great sagas, laws, annals, and just about every extant manuscript were written in Icelandic, not Latin. That Iceland developed the earliest central assembly and the earliest extensive vernacular literature of any Western nation, in particular a vernacular prose "on historical subjects which had no rival in medieval Europe,"[5] are interrelated realities. The rise of national consciousness of Icelanders fed their desire to preserve their own distinct language, and the dominance of their own distinct language contributed to Icelanders' sense of being a distinct nation. It is a relationship that Icelanders have jealously preserved throughout the centuries. Despite their long political domination first by Norway and then Denmark, Icelanders maintained their identity in large part by jealously guarding the purity of their language. Even today Icelandic nationalism enjoys an extremely strong tie to Icelandic language and the literary vernacular masterpieces that define its identity.[6]

Similar developments followed in most Western societies. Latin was an international language; the vernacular was national. As historian Friedrich Heer observed, "the growth of language implies the growth of nations,"[7] although such an observation should not lead us to conclude that the development of vernacular literature is an inevitable stage in every society's political or literary history, any more than literacy is inevitable. Society's choice to communicate in a vernacular when a scholarly language is readily available is a conscious choice, sometimes articulated and often for a set purpose, as various historians point out. Gabrielle Spiegel points out, for instance, that French vernacular historiography was created in a deliberate attempt to bolster the claims of the aristocracy whose patronage supported the work of designated authors.[8] Katherine Gill and Carlo Delcorno attribute the rise of vernacular translations of Latin religious classics to mendicant pedagogy.[9] Herbert Grundmann ascribes the birth of vernacular religious prose literature to the lay community's new relationship to the clergy, specifically, between lay women in the Low Countries and Germany and their male spiritual directors. He also traces the development of vernacular poetry to women.[10] Colish maintains that vernacular drama was rooted in the growing need within burgeoning medieval towns to form a cohesive whole,[11] and that vernacular *fabliaux* were born out of love of entertainment and a desire among the non-nobility to critique and ridicule courtly behavior.[12] Vernacular devotional literature, especially mystical and revelatory, resulted from the vita apostolica movement of the twelfth century.

Marie de France

When we study the work of Marie de France, a major contributor to the development of vernacular literature, we can easily find her reasons for choosing to write in the vernacular. Marie flourished in twelfth-century northern France, and her compositions are written in three different genres. Her *Lais* are short love narratives, twelve in number; *Isopet* (*Fables*) are 102 fables based on Aesop's works; and *Espurgatoire Seint Patriz* (*Saint Patrick's Purgatory*) is a translation of Henry of Saltry's tale of a journey to the underworld. All are in the vernacular. Her works enjoyed much fame and were, in turn, translated into other vernaculars during the Middle Ages: Italian, German, Old Norse, English—and even Latin.[13] Little is known about Marie beyond what she tells us in her work, which, unfortunately, is not much. Basically she tells us only her name and her country: "I am from France, my name's Marie."[14] Generations of scholars have puzzled over her identity. There are only two clues hidden in her writings to help scholars in their search: Marie's mention in *Fables* of "earl William," and her dedication of the *Lais* to a "noble king."[15] Speculation has led some to suppose these refer to the English king Henry II and to the earl of Essex, William of Mandeville, or William Longsword,[16] and then to infer that Marie de France is one and the same as Marie de Champagne, daughter of Eleanor of Aquitaine and Louis VII of France. Others conclude it is Marie de Boulogne, Marie de Meulan, or a nun named Marie from Reading Monastery. Unless further manuscript evidence is found in the future, Marie's identity will remain undecided. She is, however, clearer about other aspects of herself. Unlike the anonymous artists busily working on the construction of cathedrals at the same time she is aware that she is constructing her personal literary legacy and openly admits that she desires recognition: "I'll give my name, for memory." Contrary to most medieval writers, male and female, Marie does not employ humility topos. Instead, she declares herself quite intent upon receiving all the praise due her and her alone for her work. She even goes so far as to argue that those who do not fight for credit they have earned are in the wrong: "And it may hap that many a clerk/Will claim as his what is my work./But such pronouncements I want not!/It's folly to become forgot!"[17] We are surely meeting a self-confident, proud, independent individual when we approach Marie de France. Her writing skills and her creativity give her power in her world, and she likes it very much. Beware of any contemporary who thinks differently. In the lai *Guigemar* she reveals her state of mind without equivocation: "When there is a man or woman of distinguished reputation living in an area, people who envy their gifts often spread hateful gossip about them in order to demean them. They start behaving like malicious dogs, base cowards who nip spitefully at others. I don't ever plan to give up because of that. If chatterboxes and slanderers want to do me an evil turn, it's their right. Let them carp!"[18]

Marie also tells us who she wants to be remembered by. In the epilogue of *Saint Patrick's Purgatory* she identifies her intended audience: "I, Marie, have put/The Book of Purgatory into French,/As a record, so that it might be intelligible/And suited to lay folk."[19] Here we have Marie's explicit reason for writing in the vernacular. She wants to provide the Latin-less laity access into Latin culture. She demands respect from the educated literate clerical world of Latin scholarship, but her chief interest lies elsewhere, with lay people. To fulfill her goal the vernacular is the surest means available to her. One of her contemporaries unwittingly tells us how successful she was in attaining her goal. When attacking Marie's lais as "patently untrue in content" (an inconsequential criticism given the nature of the genre),[20] her contemporary Dennis Piramus concedes that they are nevertheless "artfully composed. Court audiences love them." Marie's audience loved them because her stories "dismiss and thrust aside sadness, tedium, and weariness of heart. They make people forget their anger and banish irksome thoughts."[21] By emphasizing their welcome reception and their ability to affect people, Dennis Piramus allows us to contemplate more fully the function vernacular literature fulfilled in the high Middle Ages and its contribution to Western intellectual tradition. Vernacular literature was a bridge medieval society built between the learned Latin culture dominated by a few religious men and women and the less educated but increasingly literate culture of the secular towns and courts. This bridge is most crucial in the development of Western intellectual tradition, for the tradition's non-elite nature is one of its chief characteristics. Accepting vernacular literature as an equal to Latin literature took centuries, but eventually it was. Well into the modern era Latin held on to its monopoly in education, perhaps as it well should have. Latin was, after all, a universal tool one used to gain access to all the diverse societies, past and contemporaneous, that increasingly spread throughout the continent. Latin, in other words, had its functions too.

With the coming of vernacular literature, however, certain areas of culture had the ability to develop further which were limited by Latin literature. Vernacular languages had long dominated all pragmatic communication, oral and written, and as societies continued to form apparatus appropriate to nation building they employed the vernacular to help them.[22] Most legal and financial business was conducted in the vernacular. Hence, the vernacular began its journey toward its modern status as the official language of each state. This, in turn, had wide ramifications on class structure. During the early Middle Ages education was conducted predominately within an ecclesiastical setting. Latin was the language of the church, and thus monks, nuns, and priests were educated in Latin. To be literate was to know Latin. When political expediencies arose which mandated literacy it was to the religious that politicians first turned. Soon two factors changed this. First, the demand outgrew the supply. Second. since the nature of much political business was across classes, the ruling class had to find a language common and accessible to all classes. Court proceedings, for instance, were conducted in the vernacular, and it was just a matter of time before the records of such proceedings were likewise in the vernacular. Both these processes resulted in a secularization and laicization of Western societies. Without the vernacular this process would have greatly stymied. Western society's love affair with Latin would have its last fling during the Italian renaissance, but the future of Western intellectual culture lay with the vernacular. It was the pioneering work of writers like Marie de France who plotted the first steps toward the future.

The change to vernacular and the gradual breakdown of clerical monopoly over written texts may have had another important effect upon the intellectual world. It gave the reader greater freedom to interpret a text.[23] In a culture dominated by an ecclesiastical language revered as almost sacred, there was little encouragement given to individualized interpretation of that language. The bible was the basis of all education,[24] and Christianity had long adhered to the rather strict fourfold method of scriptural reading (the historical or literal, the allegorical, the tropological or moral, and the anagogical[25]). Since Latin was the language in which medieval people encountered the bible,[26] the religious aura of the language was perceived to pertain to all things Latin. There was no association of sacredness to the vernacular, hence the reader entered into a vernacular text with more freedom to interpret outside the four senses. We must also remember, though, that the church never enjoyed full monolithic control over literature and that from the age of the apostolic fathers onward, competing voices of interpretation were heard.[27] Still, the freedom, real and imagined, for the reader of a vernacular text was greater than the reader of a religious text.

There is a final aspect of the advent of the vernacular that should be noted; it allowed people to think in different ways. Such a generalization is hard to substantiate objectively, but what evidence we have is persuasive. This thesis is based on the belief that, as theorist Mikhail Bakhtin says, "form and content in discourse are one, once we understand that verbal discourse is a social phenomenon—social throughout its entire range and in each and every of its factors."[28] The new social realities of the high Middle Ages produced the content of the discourse, while the new literary language shaped its form. Latin encapsulated the essence of ancient culture, so much so that when Italian humanists tried to recreate and continue classical culture they did so by resurrecting Latin. Yet, the high Middle Ages was not identical to the ancient world, and medieval intellectuals realized this. Society was distinctly different and its people experienced a distinctly different reality religiously, politically, socially, and economically. To best symbolize these realities the vernacular languages that were born of these experiences proved to be the proper vehicles. Over time they proved to be the best vehicles. For many artists of the high Middle Ages they were already the best vehicles, because the vernacular allowed the author to approach new realities in new ways; it provided them with the means to think differently about life. As Grundmann says in reference to the religious vernacular of the high Middle Ages, "Language was given new tasks to perform, opening new possibilities which permanently marked its vocabulary and forms of expression, immensely enriching them."[29] The speculative thought of scholasticism which owed so much to the ancient world did fine relying on the ancient world's language, but the vernacular gave other areas of intellectual development which were unique to the medieval world the means to express these new experiences.

Further analysis of Marie de France's work supports this stance. She writes in three different genres, and her use of the vernacular provides her with the means to offer innovation and new conclusions in each genre. First of all, we should remember that prior to the twelfth century, French literature hardly existed. Within a few generations, though, French vernacular literature rivaled Latin for attention among the literate. This is in no small part due to the high quality of literature produced in the vernacular. As a pioneer Marie de France must be given some of the credit for that. She is the first woman to write in the vernacular, the first French woman poet, and probably the creator of the lai. While in none of her work do we detect brilliance, in all of her texts we can identify originality and a high quality of literary style.

We will start with *Saint Patrick's Purgatory,* because critics have routinely dismissed this translated poem as possessing little quality to warrant serious attention other than control of Latin and French languages. Literary historian Michael Curley, however, challenges us to look at the poem anew and discover within many significant contributions.[30] Marie takes a Latin text and in translating it into the vernacular turns a theological treatise written for theological reasons into a secular adventure with didactic moralistic purposes but not theological ones. Sometime before the end of the twelfth century the English Cistercian Henry of Saltrey recorded the story of the revelations of a knight named Owen while on a pilgrimage to a remote cave or pit on an island on Lough Derg in County Donnegal. His visions were primarily of the torments of souls by demons in purgatory. The work, *Tractatus de Purgatorio Sancto Patricii* (*Treatise of St. Patrick's Purgatory*)[31] caused quite a stir, and during the course of the Middle Ages it was repeatedly translated. Marie's was the first of six poetic translations in French alone. The reason for its interest lay chiefly in the topic. Purgatory was a concept and a doctrine much discussed during the high Middle Ages. Even if one rejects the main thesis of historian Jacques Le Goff's *The Birth of Purgatory* as too extreme in its claims, his comment that Henry of Saltry's description of purgatory provided medieval society with "the vision of the genuine Purgatory" rings true.[32] Marie translated the treatise specifically so this vision of purgatory "might be intelligible/And suited to lay folk."[33]

Unlike Henry, Marie does not write for a monastic audience. Her interest rests in a new class, the courtly class which soon was to become the backbone of the French nation state. Henry's prologue and dedication, typical within monastic writings, is to "your paternity" who gave him the task of writing, and "to his father chosen in Christ, Lord .H. abbot of Sartis, brother .H. the least of the monks of Saltrey presents this offering of obedience, as a son should to his father, with his unceasing compliments."[34] Marie does not translate Henry's prologue or dedication but instead substitutes her own. In her prologue she tells us her desire to write is not rooted in monastic obedience or even in the paternalistic structure of society:

> I wish to put into writing in French,
> The Pains of Purgatory,
> Just as the book tells us about them,
> As a recollection and record.[35]

In the dedication she firmly rejects any thought that obedience was compelling her to write. She clearly wants the reader to know that it was her decision and that she is ultimately in charge, even if the idea for the translation originated elsewhere:

> A good man a while ago made a request of me,
> Which I have now undertaken
> By putting myself to the present task.
> I do this out of reverence and honor to him.[36]

She then mentions the secondary motives which persuaded her to accept the task:

> To cause many people
> To come to great profit,
> To amend their ways
> To fear God and serve him better.[37]

The tale affected her in those ways, so she believes it would likewise affect her audience:

> I have heard and seen little of this subject,
> Yet, through what I have learned of it,
> I have greater love for God,

And desire to serve him, my Creator.
For these reasons, I want to open up this writing
For you, and reveal its contents.[38]

We can conclude from all these differences that while Marie is intent upon spreading the visions of purgatory, she is not interested in spreading it among the monastic, clerical Latin world of traditional dimensions. No, she wrote and created for a new world of the French court, thus helping validate that world, educate it and establish its own intellectual culture. In Henry's original tract, after the initial introduction the protagonist Owen is referred to as *miles* or *vir*.[39] In Marie's translation Owen is referred to by his name, thus emphasizing the lasting individuality of this new knightly class. In Henry's version Owen the sinner takes a journey to the underworld to repent; in Marie's version Owen the knight undertakes an adventure filled with fantastic challenges to prove his worthiness as a knight. A subtle emphasis in Marie's tale is on the superior nature of the life of a chivalrous knight who combines the religious and the military life into one. After returning from his journey Owen went to a monastery where he remained:

. . . for fifteen days,
Fasting, praying, keeping vigils,
And performing acts of mortification.
Then he [the knight] recounted what he had seen,
And they set it down in writing.
He then became a crusader out of love
And honor for God his Creator.

Owen proceeds to Jerusalem, returns, and in an audience with the king asks "whether he should become a monk." In Henry's tract the king never answers Owen. In Marie's story the king's answer reveals sentiments that identify where Marie's heart lies and why she is desirous of having the tale made accessible to the courtly class. The answer was in essence a justification of the courtly class. One might even see in it a claim of superiority of the life of a knight over the life of a monk. The monopoly over the worthiest vocation, held for so many centuries by religious, was being challenged directly by the Christian knight. By thus placing a secular vocation on par with a religious vocation, Marie is contributing to the laicization and secularization of medieval society:

The king answered
That he should remain as he was, a knight.
He counseled him to retain this station
So that he might serve God well.
And so he did for the rest of his life,
Never changing his station for another.[40]

Curley discusses a number of other differences between Henry's and Marie's versions to support his thesis concerning Marie's originality. Henry betrays a deep bias against Irish people, calling them "the savage souls" (*bestiales animas*),[41] and quoting Gilbert of Louth who claims "a true expert knowledge of how savage [the Irish] are."[42] Even though critics of Marie de France have often dismissed her work as being simply a literal translation, Curley points out that here is an example of Marie's independence of mind. Not only does she nullify Henry's bigotry by positing that the Irish possessed "fickle and savage hearts"[43] prior to their conversion but not after and by omitting the quote which claimed direct knowledge of Irish savagery, but Marie also resists being inculcated herself by the pervasive prejudice of the day against the Irish. Whereas Gilbert and Henry discuss evil and the intensity of Irish repentance as a defect in their very nature ("the men of this country have the kind of natural disposition" that makes them "more prone to evil"[44]), Marie changes that conclusion drastically. She ignores the claim that the Irish have a natural disposition to do evil, above and beyond other humans. Furthermore, it is not by nature but by custom that the Irish repent:

> It is the custom of that land/
> That those who do the greatest evil,
> When they attain old age
> Are the most proud and steadfast in their resolve
> To suffer harsh penance,
> In order to merit the grace of God.[45]

By thus repudiating "the entire *a priori* epistemology of Gilbert's musings," Curley argues that Marie successfully "subverts the ideological foundation which they support."[46] Too often the intellectual underpinnings of prejudice have been ignored by intellectual historians, sometimes with catastrophic results, as, for example, in our own time with German anti-Semitism. They should be addressed, however, vigorously, and those who present arguments in the intellectual discourse of their day which repudiate prejudice should be properly cited for their efforts. Marie de France addresses a dominant prejudice of her society by presenting an alternative rational explanation that reveals the intellectual bankruptcy of that prejudice.

Marie alters other aspects of Henry's poem in small ways, but taken together they firmly establish Marie's intellectual independence and originality. Henry talks repeatedly about "both sexes and all ages" being tormented in purgatory.[47] Marie omits that formula every time and substitutes phrases like "of every age" and "of every order;" Curley argues that she does so because her sense of decorum made the mixing of genders distasteful to her.[48] I would argue that she does so because she has a greater sense of the commonality of the human condition than does Henry. Curley also argues that Marie reversed the epistemological order of Henry's treatise when she used Owen's *aventure* to confirm Christian theology. The experience of truth trumps the articulation of truth:

> Indeed, who would believe this
> If he did not have proof
> That what we have described here
> Were the truth? [49]

Finally, Curley points out that Marie changes Henry's fear and condemnation of carnal desires to a more benign generalization that after contemplating "the pains, suffering, and torment of hell":

> Anyone who thinks often about this,
> Will find no joy

In the vanity of the world
Or the delights which are in it.[50]

Marie's *Fables* were probably the most well known of her works during the Middle Ages. There are twenty-three extant manuscripts from the thirteenth to fifteenth centuries, as compared to five known manuscripts of the *Lais* and one of the *Saint Patrick's Purgatory.*[51] *Fables* did not continue its popularity beyond the fifteenth century, possibly because of the loss of popularity of the fable tradition after that time. Modern critics are slowly rising above this qualification to judge the work in its own right. Fables are by definition didactic, and throughout antiquity and early medieval society they also functioned as rhetorical models.[52] Rather than being merely children's stories, fables were often the vehicle of choice to teach adults. As Marie states in her prologue:

Yet there's no fable so inane
That folks cannot some knowledge gain
From lessons that come subsequent
To make each tale significant.[53]

Because of their didactic purpose they are potent sources to examine for the author's philosophy and mores:

Those persons, all, who are well-read,
Should study and pay careful heed
To fine accounts in worthy tomes.
To models and to axioms:
That which philosophers did find
And wrote about and kept in mind.
The sayings which they heard, they wrote,
So that the morals we would note;
Thus those who wish to mend their ways
Can think about what wisdom says.[54]

In Marie's case examination proves to be fruitful. This is in spite of the charge that many critics level against *Fables* as being only a translation of a previous collection of fables.[55] Such a charge is faulty on three counts. First, we have identified those areas where Marie's poem differed from Henry's, thus establishing the impossibility of Marie's being a literal translation of Henry's. Secondly, recent theories of translation are reminding us that we must learn to appreciate translations in ways similar to how medieval scholars did. The Russian critic Kornei Chukovsky calls translation a high art, and says that in the end "everything depends on the translator's own originality—his honesty, his tact, his sensitivity, and sense of proportion, his common sense and his knowledge of both his subject and his subject's language."[56] This is consistent with medieval intellectuals who did not denigrate translation or translator, but granted translators, along with scribes, commentators, compilers, and authors, a significant role in the production of a literary culture.[57] Thus, as translator Marie's contribution is significant. In fact, *Fables* is an excellent example of the way translators make contributions of consequence to literary culture. Marie is proud of her role as translator and wants everyone to know and remember it: "To end these tales I'm here narrated/And into Romance tongue translated."[58] If the role of translator did not bestow status on a person, then Marie would have had no reason to worry that another would claim her work. Moreover, in the prologue and epilogue Marie states her belief that the fables come to her from a long list of translations:

This book's called Aesop for this reason:
He translated and had it written
In Latin from the Greek, to wit.
King Alfred, who was fond of it,
Translated it to English hence,
And I have rhymed it now in French
As well as I was competent.[59]

This brings us to the third argument against too hasty a dismissal of *Fables* as "only" being a translation, and that is the question of Marie's sources. Only the first forty of Marie's 103 fables are traceable to a direct source, probably from a part of the fable tradition called *Romulus Nilantii.*[60] Because there is no known source for the remaining fables, literary historian Harriet Spiegel convincingly argues "that Marie herself could have gathered and recorded these fables for the first time."[61] Whether future studies uphold the full extent of Spiegel's claim remains to be seen, especially since she hints she used King Alfred's collection as her source, but there can be no debate that whatever her source, Marie radically altered its nature when she translated it into poetry. Changing a prose narrative into verse cannot be done without imposing another personality unto the work, and *Fables* is no exception. Common sense would almost dictate that we judge the versification an original work. In Marie's case, this is undoubtedly true, for in Spiegel's words, when Marie versified the fables "she medievalizes her classical fables," making them "manifestly a product of the twelfth century, providing commentary on contemporary life, particularly on feudal social structure and questions of justice—the obligation of a ruler to be aware of his people's needs and to respond to them, and the people's awareness of what constitutes a beneficent kingship and their obligation of loyalty to a good ruler."[62]

Thus, in the fable of the Wolf King, despite the fact that the retiring lion king told the beasts "to find the one who'd govern best," the beasts "chose the wolf,/For no one else was bold enough/To dare take anyone but him." When the wolf turned out to be a terrible king who ate them one by one, Marie moralizes:

Thus by the wise man we are taught
That we, no matter what, must not
A wicked man e'er make seignior,
Nor show to such a one honour.
His loyalty's as much pretence
With strangers as with his close friends.
And toward his people he will act
As did the wolf, with his sworn pact.[63]

When the birds "did hold a meeting and conclude/That they should have a king,/one who would govern and be wise and true," they first mistakenly thought the cuckoo would be a good choice. When the titmouse put the cuckoo to the test and it failed, the titmouse advised the following basis for choosing a king:

> We ought to choose one stout of heart,
> Who's noble, valorous, and smart
> A king should be one very righteous
> Who's firm and stern in dealing justice.

After some deliberation they decided upon the eagle, because he was mighty and yet "does not lust too much for prey." Then Marie draws her lesson:

> A prince should be well-rested, too;
> In his delights not overdo;
> Nor shame himself or his domain,
> Nor cause the poor folk undue pain.
> The birds did what I said they'd do.
> And so this lesson's shown to you:
> Do not have as your lord someone
> Who's wicked and a charlatan.[64]

Marie often advocates behavior and values that reflect not traditional Christian values but the changing demands of new circumstances. In the fable "The Peasant and His Horse," for instance, Marie discusses appropriate behavior in the marketplace. When a peasant gets himself into a dilemma while trying to establish a just price to sell his horse, the matter ends up before a judge. The peasant argued his way through the dispute successfully and Marie then concludes:

> Then off the man and horse did walk;
> He'd saved himself through fancy talk.
> This story serves to educate,
> To show us well and demonstrate
> That if one finds he's in a snare
> And none of his good friends is there
> Who could provide some wise direction,
> He'd better act with circumspection
> When he should speak before the court,
> And make quite cunning his report—
> So what he's done, however awful,
> Should thereby seem both right and lawful.
> The wise man in dreadful plight
> Can often turn his wrong to right.[65]

We see in Marie's fable here the types of rationalizations employed by medieval people as they began to confront the demands of the commercial revolution.

Of all Marie's works the *Lais* have always been the most appreciated. It is mostly on the basis of these romances that literary historians Robert Hanning and

Joan Ferrante claim that "Marie de France was perhaps the greatest woman author of the Middle Ages and certainly the creator of the finest medieval short fiction before Boccaccio and Chaucer;" the *Lais* themselves are "a major achievement of the first age of French literature and of the 'Renaissance of the Twelfth Century.'"[66] The *Lais* are Marie's most original work, both in form and content. In *Fables* and *Purgatory* Marie tells us of her reliance on specific written sources for her works, but in *Lais* she tells us that the sources are varied. They are tales "that I heard,"[67] ones which "many have told and recited it to me and I have found it in writing,"[68] or ones which she writes "according to the story as I know it."[69] In the prologue she confesses a near obsession with the tales that often made her an insomniac:

> I have heard many told;
> And I don't want to neglect or forget them.
> To put them into word and rhyme
> I've often stayed awake.

Clearly she is the editor of the fresh, new collection of stories undertaken "to assemble these *lais*/to compose and recount them in rhyme."[70] They are written in vernacular verse, as is all her work, and they likewise reflect the major preoccupations of the day, even while helping to form a new literate culture among the emerging courtly class, just as *Saint Patrick's Purgatory* and *Fables* did. She is also just as insistent in the *Lais* as in *Fables* and *Purgatory* that she, Marie, be given credit for her work. Indeed, she turned to the lais after her previous work failed to gain her fame:

> That's why I began to think
> about composing some good stories
> and translating from Latin to Romance;
> but that was not to bring me fame:
> too many others have done it.
> Then I thought of the lais I'd heard.[71]

This desire for fame is not rooted in a prideful self-centerness but rather in the new individualism of the twelfth-century renaissance.[72]

The strong sense of individualism Marie displays in the prologue is coupled with a deep sense of responsibility for her intellectual gifts:

> Whoever has received knowledge
> and eloquence in speech from God
> should not be silent or secretive
> but demonstrate it willingly.
> When a great good is widely heard of,
> then, and only then, does it bloom,
> and when that good is praised by many,
> it has spread its blossoms.[73]

We have observed this same sense of obligation to one's gifts in Hildegard. Marie de France is perhaps even more consciously aware that her talent will lead her to break new ground. She deliberately deviates from ancient tradition in order to enter into new territory. We heard her admit as much in her rationale for using the vernacular; it was to create a new literate class among the laity.[74] In *Lais* she tells us that this motive forces her to abandon more than just the language of the ancients; she also abandons their methodology:

> The custom among the ancients—
> As Priscian tesifies—
> Was to speak quite obscurely
> In the books they wrote,
> So that those who were to come after
> And study them
> Might gloss the letter
> And supply its significance from their own wisdom.
> Philosophers knew this,
> They understood among themselves
> That the more time they spent,
> The more subtle their minds would become.[75]

She wanted to find a new way to achieve that goal, a way different from the ancients and philosophers and yet compatible with the abilities and opportunities of the new courtly class.

For this reason she set out to write didactic vernacular poetry filled with the symbols and images of that class. Bisclavret is an excellent example of how she hoped to educate the laity. While the educated elite of Marie's day were busy explaining the contingencies of life through the little-known terminology of Greek philosophy, Marie explained the same contingencies by utilizing the folklore traditions well known to the class she was addressing. Bisclavret is a werewolf who is "betrayed, ruined by his own wife"[76] and left in the woods until discovered by the king and his hunting party. Bisclavret's life changes when he humbles himself before the king's authority and asks for mercy. The king's attitude toward the beast changes radically when he realizes that "this beast is rational—he has a mind." Thereafter the beast accompanied the king "to his castle" where "everyone was fond of him;/he was so noble and well behaved/that he never wished to do anything wrong."[77] Eventually the wife's betrayal is discovered, and Bisclavret turns back into a man who then serves his king well. The precarious nature of existence, the need to retain nobility of character even under the most stressful of situations, the final rewards for good behavior and punishments for bad, the triumph of justice for those who persevere, and the ability of humans to transcend their baser, more "animal" aspects of their nature by love and service are all aspects of Marie's didactic lesson.

Taken together, these elements present a rather sophisticated philosophy of human life consistent with many scholastic philosophers of her day, in addition to Heloise and Hildegard. Sin's origin is in the intellect, not in passion or perverse love, just as goodness begins in one's mind. According to Abelard, for example, the intellect is where judgments of free will are made.[78] According to Peter Lombard, the first sin was an intellectual sin, for when Adam and Eve fell in the Garden of Eden it was because they were tempted by the desire to become omniscient.[79] Furthermore, God does not intervene directly in human life but gives humans the freedom to develop naturally. Marie's lai teaches both philosophers' theses, but in a more accessible and entertaining way. In this instance Marie's content is as truthful and valuable as Abelard's and Peter Lombard's, albeit not as original. However, credit should be given to Marie for creating a new way to communicate these truths to a new and less educated audience. While the composition of an audience helps determine the shape and even the content of a text,[80] the social status of the audience does not have a bearing on the veracity of the text or its value.

The Trobairitz

While Marie is the first documented vernacular woman poet in the West, she is not the only one. Contemporaneous to Marie (whose exact dates are unknown) was a group of women poets from the Provençal region who also participated in the creation of courtly vernacular literature. That so few women poets' work has survived the Middle Ages makes the appearance and the survival of twenty-three women poets from one small, contained area and one century quite curious. Given the odds for any manuscript surviving the centuries we can speculate that perhaps more women poets existed there, elsewhere, and at other times whose works are not extant, but that remains speculation. What is more probable, though, is that these Provençal women wrote much more than has survived, since their contemporary *vidas* which accompany their poems identify almost half of them as poets;[81] that any person would have a reputation as a poet on the basis of one poem seems unlikely. Lombarda, for example, only has one extant lyric, yet one could conclude from her vida that she was a prolific poet: "Na Lombarda was a lady of Toulouse, noble and beautiful, gracious of person, and learned. She knew very well how to write poetry, and composed beautiful stanzas on amatory subjects."[82] This and other similar *vidas* lead one to conclude that these women were known as poets even during their own lifetime.

The themes and literary styles of these trobairitz contributed significantly to the development of the highly influential courtly love literature born during the twelfth century. The poetry of troubadour William of Poitou (grandfather of literary patron Eleanor of Aquitaine and great-grandfather of patron Marie de Champagne) is the first poetry we know of that can be classified this way, and it was so influential that within a generation of his death (ca. 1125) troubadours were found throughout most of southern France. The trobairitz whose works survive thrived after the second generation of troubadours, ca. 1170–1260, but are absent during the last generation. Many different genres of lyric poetry developed within the movement, but the women's extant poetry is found in only three types: the canso, or love song; the tenso, or debate; and the sirventes, or political song.[83] Only Gormonda of Montpellier wrote a sirventes; the rest are cansos and tensos. The appeal of troubadour poetry was near universal in the West, and by the thirteenth century it had spread to French trouvères and German minnesingers and south into Italy and Catalan, and even into Moorish strongholds in the Iberian peninsula. Its influence and appeal has also stood the test of time, extending into the early modern period with the poetry of Christine de Pisan (1364–1429/34), Eustache Deschamps (ca. 1346–1406), William of Machaut (ca. 1300–1377), and even Dante.

It is clear from the poems themselves and their *vidas* that the trobairitz knew the troubadours and debated with them, and that many of the women (Clare d'Anduza, Almucs de Castelnau, Tibors, Maria, and Garsenda) were patrons of troubadours. They were members of the same society. Scholars have identified some differences between the poetry of the men and women, but given the sparsity of women's poetry that have survived and the inability to know if the poetry we do have is representative, the differences are hard to identify with certainty. Some appear to be insignificant; women use more negatives and discuss more negative feelings, for example.[84] Other differences are worthy of more attention; the women's use of first person has perhaps not been noted enough.[85] Another area where differences are seen is highlighted by the structure of this particular poetry. Its tensos juxtapose a woman's opinion to a man's as part of the debate format of the poem, so the differences between the two main characters' way of judging matters is highlighted more in this genre. In the poetry of the Countess of Dia, the only woman who has four poems survive, the different value system she has in matters of love from her beloved forms the essence of the poem's narrative content. "Now I see I've been betrayed/because I wouldn't sleep with him,"[86] the Countess laments, revealing the heart of the matter. She is not content with silent resignation, but she wants her beloved to engage in a debate over his behavior:

> So I send you, there on your estate,
> This song as messenger and delegate.
> I want to know, my handsome noble friend,
> Why I deserve so savage and so cruel a fate.[87]

Such debates may in reality reflect actual discussions the women poets had with the men in court. This is indicated in the razo (prose commentary) accompanying Maria de Ventaforn's poem, which describes Maria as the consummate literary patron who drew Gui d'Ussels back to a full life after a love loss by debating with him. "And the Count of the Marche, who was saying that every true lover, if a lady gives him her love and takes him as her knight and friend, and if he's loyal and chivalrous with her, should have as much seigneury and authority over her as she over him; and my lady Maria held the view that the lover should have neither seigneury nor authority. En Gui d'Ussels was in the court of my lady Maria, and she, to draw him back into singing and happiness, composed a couplet in which she asked him whether it was right that the lover should have as much authority over the lady as the lady over him."[88] Maria starts her poem thus:

> Gui d'Ussel, because of you I'm quite distraught,
> For you've given up your song,
> And since I wish you'd take it up again,
> And since you know about such things,
> I'll ask you this: when a lady
> Freely loves a man, should she do
> As much for him as he for her,
> According to the rules of courtly love?

Gui answers Maria's challenge directly:

Lady Maria, tensons
And all manner of song
I thought I'd given up,
But when you summon, how can I refuse to sing?[89]

Perhaps one of the more striking differences between the men and women was the personal conviction with which the women composed. From what is known about the man, singing courtly love songs was a profession for many, not so with the women. There are no known instances of professional trobairitz. They were motivated to write for other reasons than professional. We can also detect a greater degree of personal experience reflected in their poetry and motivating them to write it:

Lady Carenza of the lovely, gracious body,
Give some advice to us two sisters,
And since you know best how to tell what's best,
Counsel me according to your own experience:
Shall I marry someone both know?
Or shall I stay unwed? that would please me,
For making babies doesn't seem so good,
And it's too anguishing to be a wife.[90]

There is an immediacy in the women's poetry that is not found in the men's, and hence the women's is often a "vehicle of self-expression."[91] Taken together these characteristics produced a sense of individualism, albeit limited and peculiar to each trobairitz.

The most unique poem of the group is the sirventes written by Gormonda de Montpellier. It is too frequently ignored by literary scholars who bypass it because of its political nature and the subsequent absence of the courtly love theme therein.[92] Given our focus here, these characteristics actually make it more, not less, interesting for us. Gormonda is a woman participating in a key political debate of the day, the Albigensian Crusade, and articulating her participation in an *avante garde* literary genre. Although it has been suggested that two other anonymous sirventes were written by women,[93] in all likelihood Gormonda's sirventes is the only extant example, thus making it the first French vernacular political poem written by a woman.[94] The structure of her poem is intriguing, for it corresponds exactly in stanza formation and rhyme scheme with the poem she was responding to, Guilhem Figueira's sirventes. The correspondence is exact enough for some to wonder whether Gormonda had a copy of Guilhem's poem in front of her or whether it was recited to her as she composed her response. On the other hand, the immediate responsorial nature of the two poems together build up enough dramatic tension to consider the possibility that the two poems were performed together in a staged debate.[95]

Her knowledge of the theological and political issues of the day is thorough and impressive, as is the logic of her arguments, indicating that she was an educated, and, of course, literate woman of the court. She is also well informed and current on even mundane political conflicts, as is evident in her comment that "I am pleased to know, Rome, that for those from Avignon you lowered the evil toll, which was a great mercy," referring to the road tolls of Avignon.[96] She offers her own judgment of the ongoing disputes between Rome and two rulers, Count Raymond VII of Toulouse and Emperor Frederick II. Gormonda proclaims thus:

> Rome, I am well pleased
> That the count and the emperor
> Having turned away from you,
> Have lost their strength,
> For their foolish behavior and their wicked opinions
> Make them [both] fall according to your will.[97]

Her political alliance rests with Rome and the king of France opposes those who challenge either of them. Guilhem blames Rome for losing Damiette in 1221 during the Fifth Crusade, while Gormonda argues that "the folly of the fools caused the loss of Damiette." Guilhem also blames Rome for Louis VIII's death after he responded to the erroneous preaching of the Crusade; Gormonda argues that not only is Rome not responsible for the French king's death but that the king died because of "what Merlin prophesied of the good King Louis that he would die in Pansa." Her adherence to Rome is total: "Rome, I truly know and believe without doubt that you shall lead all France to true salvation."[98] When Guilhem complains that Rome has not defeated the Saracens, politically or militarily, Gormonda believes that because theologically they are less of a threat than heretics—"worse than the Saracens and of more deceitful mind are the pitiful heretics"[99]—military defeat must come after the more pressing problem the heretics present is addressed. "Rome, may the great king [Louis VIII] who is lord of justice bring great misfortune upon the false people of Toulouse,"[100] for remaining loyal to Count Raymond. Instead of reconciling to Rome by complying with the demand "to satisfy all the grievances of the clergy and restore everything that he was accused of taking from the church; heresy would be uprooted from his dominions, and the authority of the church re-established everywhere," as the Council of Bourges in 1225 had mandated,[101] the people of the town resisted.

Gormonda also backs the political power of France and Rome, because she sees in it the ability to suppress heresy which she believes leads to an unjust life, "heresy must be fought with real political power." "Rome, I hope that your dominion and France," she begins, "will bring to destruction the pride and the heresy: the false, secret heretics, who neither fear prohibitions nor believe in mysteries, they are so full of treachery and wicked thoughts."[102] In her reliance on her aggression and violence as a solution for heresy she differs little from her male contemporaries, wishing in her concluding stanza that Guilhem "die, him and his possessions and his wicked heart, in the same way and with the same pain as when a heretic dies."[103] As far as Frederick II goes, "I say that if he does not unite with you, his crown will fall into great dishonor—and that will be just."[104]

Gormonda chose to debate the politics of the day chiefly within the environment of the court, either through vernacular troubadour poetry or actual debates. We have already seen other women who contributed to the political life by participating in varying degrees and ways in the production of Latin history written at least in part to justify and defend dynastic, political claims. Besides Hrotsvitha's histories already discussed we know of one other woman and probably three more, who authored histories prior to the advent of the vernacular. Matilda of Quedlinburg commissioned members of her community to write the *Annales Quedlinburgenses.* In all likelihood Gisla of Chelles (Charlemagne's sister) directed her community to write *Annales Mettenses Priores,* Otto II commissioned an anonymous nun from Nordhausen (maybe Abbess Richburga) to compose the first life of Queen Matilda (*Vita Mathildus reginae antiquior*) and Holy Roman Emperor Henry II later requested another nun from the same community to compose a second life (*Vita Mathildus reginae posterior*).[105] Many scholars today argue that a much greater number of women should be included in group categorized as historians, because women often kept genealogical records of ruling families, particularly in tenth-century Germany.[106] One of the chief functions monasteries fulfilled for society at the millennium was to pray for the dead.[107] This necessitated record-keeping, which in turn resulted in genealogies of those families who turned to the monasteries to preserve the memory of their dead. Women's German monasteries were in the forefront of this work.[108] Saxon women, such as Abbess Matilda of Essen, participated in the preservation of the past also by commissioning works; Matilda commissioned her cousin Aethelred to write a Latin version of the Anglo-Saxon Chronicle. Aethelred's dedication to Matilda includes a recitation of their lineage back six generations, hinting that he was writing thus after having "received your letter, for which I longed, and having embraced with my spirit what you wrote."[109]

Anglo-Saxon women also commissioned work. Royal women like Emma, Edith, Matilda, and Adela commissioned or were the dedicatees of such important historical Latin works as William of Malmesbury's *De gestis regum Anglorum,* Hugh of Fleury's *Historia ecclesiastica,* and vitae of Edward the Confessor, Queen St. Margaret of Scotland, Henry I, and Cnut (*Encomium Emmae Reginae*).[110] Ferrante vigorously argues that those historical works which were written by women, commissioned by them, or written for them, contain portraits of women much more powerful and actively involved in politics than male produced histories, and, most significantly, accept these powerful women "as a normal, and indeed essential, part of history." Ferrante concludes that "the women for whom the histories and lives were written did influence the content of these works by their position or political needs and did thereby influence our sense of that history."[111] I propose we take her conclusion a step further and note that since this history is at the matrix of the Western historical and political traditions we must acknowledge women's contributions to their development. Western historiography began its journey toward secularization during the high Middle Ages by politicizing history and in this task women actively participated. As Spiegel observes, "As long as meaning in history was generated and guaranteed by divine intervention and transcendent significance, the medieval nobility could scarcely have hoped to take control of the past, to make *its* history *the* history. The secularization and laicization of historical writing in the thirteenth century, by removing from view God's active participation in human affairs, brought history squarely into the realm of human contest and historiographical contestation."[112]

Thus, when the English queen Emma, mother of Edward the Confessor, commissioned the writing of the *Encomium* to defend her continued involvement in politics after her husbands Aethelred and Cnut had died, and Edith, wife of Edward the Confessor, had the life of Edward written to further the claims to power of her family, they were both helping break new historiographical ground. God's will is still present in their histories, but by purpose and goal they were distinctly different from earlier histories. The adoption of the vernacular during the twelfth century as the vehicle for political histories was but a continuation of what these women helped create. As the population of the West became more laicized more people were in a position to read, but they had decreasing incentives to learn Latin.[113] Some of the educated upper class perceived this potential vernacular audience and saw in vernacular historiography a way of politically influencing them. In the forefront of this small but instrumental movement which began in England in the twelfth century were noble women. Recent research has established just how important the royal women were in the spread of vernacular literature in general, beyond even vernacular history. Women were also involved in vernacular hagiography. The author of the thirteenth-century *Life of Saint Aubrey* identifies herself as Marie[114] (probably Marie of Chatteris); it is a hagiographical work with strong political overtones.[115] Two vernacular vitae from the women's monastery at Barking, *Life of Edward the Confessor* and *Life of Saint Catherine,* were written by a woman during the twelfth century, probably the woman Guernes de Pont-Ste.-Maxence refers to in his own vita of Thomas Becket when he mentions "vernacular lives which have been composed about the martyr by clerics or lay people, monks or a woman."[116] This would be Clemence of Barking, discussed at length in Chapter 4. The abbesses of Barking had a long history of patronizing and commissioning Latin works, so it is not surprising that they should be in the forefront of patronizing vernacular works, or even encouraging their own members to write.[117] While both vitae are important as vernacular religious literature, *Life of Edward the Confessor* is definitely written with the political concerns of the court in mind. Edward's marriage and the succession to the English throne are the main themes in the vita, but unlike the thirteenth-century vita of Edward by Matthew Paris, the Barking vita provides Edward's queen Edith's perspective on matters.

Queens Matilda, Adeliza, Eleanor of Aquitaine, Eleanor of Provence, and Eleanor of Castile either commissioned or received vernacular works during their reigns. Eleanor of Aquitaine's direct patronage of a vernacular adaptation of Geoffrey of Monmouth's popular *History of Kings of Britain* by Wace in his *Le Roman de Brut* is questionable, but her role in creating a court conducive to the production of vernacular literature is not in doubt.[118] Eleanor of Castile, wife of Edward I, had Guard d'Amiens write the romantic work *Escanor* and John Peckam write a vernacular adaptation of *Jerarchie* for her, while Eleanor of Provence, Henry III's wife had Aelred's Latin vita of Edward the Confessor translated into French for her.[119] Adeliza, wife of Henry I, commissioned a man we know only by the name David to write a vernacular biography of her husband. The manuscript did not survive, but our knowledge of it comes from Geoffrey Gaimar, who discusses it in his own vernacular work, *Estoire des Engleis*. Besides telling us about Adeliza's commission he also tells us that his own patron was a woman, Constance Fitzgilbert. Constance was not royalty but a wife of the gentry class. For some unknown reason she commissioned Geoffrey Gaimer to write a vernacular history of England from 495 to 1100. Since her motive was obviously not to strengthen her political line, we can only surmise that after reading David's history of Henry I (which Geoffrey tells us she read often in her room[120]) she was inspired to have her own history simply because she desired to be informed and educated.[121]

Constance was not unique. We know of other non-royal, lay women who were patrons or who commissioned works. Curiously, the popular *Pseudo-Turpin-Chronicle,* an account of Charlemagne's miltary foray into Spain, was translated into French when commissioned by two women in two different lands. Alice de Curcy and husband Warin Fitzgerald commissioned William de Briane to translate the chronicle into the vernacular sometime in the second decade of the thirteenth century.[122] At almost the same time the Flemish Yolande, countess of Saint-Pol, and her husband Hugh IV requested a vernacular translation be made of the work for them.[123] Analysis of the text for a reason why two wives and their husbands desired translations of the same work at nearly the same time has yet to be undertaken, so we are left only to our own speculations. In that vein I would suggest that it indicates that, given the topic and the need for translation, women shared greater feudal, quasi-historical interests and educational levels with their husbands in the Anglo-Saxon cultural world of the thirteenth century than was previously thought.

This is certainly true in France. "When the sources are allowed to speak," historian Kimberly Lo Prete argues, we "discover that women exercised more acknowledged power than has been assumed and that accounts of medieval politics are incomplete if they ignore the deeds of female lords."[124] Contrary to the theses of George Duby, JoAnn MacNamara, and Suzanne Wemple,[125] Lo Prete's study of Adela of Blois proves her point, as do the studies of aristocratic women in the counties of Blois, Chartres, Champagne and Flanders, and in Occitania.[126] In each instance the sources show conclusively that medieval French women were allowed to exercise "the same lordly powers as their male peers, even though they did so less frequently" and that they had a whole "range of social and political roles open to them."[127] One of these roles was in constructing a new historical tradition. Review of the active role women played in establishing a new vernacular historical tradition serves to reinforce Ferrante's conclusion that women were indeed "at the center of public life."[128]

4

The Vernacular Mothers

While the courtly and royal classes' desire for its own poetry and history did much to popularize vernacular texts,[1] the greater responsibility for the creation of vernacular cultures in the medieval West lay with another group and another genre. One of the first scholars to address the issue of the coming of vernacular literature was Herbert Grundmann, and he identifies religious women as the leading group and religious literature as the most popular genre, especially religious mystical literature.[2] Grundmann traces the origin of vernacular religious literature to Lambert (d. 1177), a priest from Liege, who translated two works, the Acts of the Apostle and *The Legend of St. Agnes,* for the laity. He embarked upon this endeavor when he found himself ministering to "a lay community desiring to read and use religious writings itself, but with inadequate Latin to use the existing literature."[3] The laity had always prayed and been preached to in the vernacular,[4] but now they wanted more. They wanted both translations of past Latin works and accessible contemporary literature that expressed their own religious world. While numerous clergy provided translations, it was religious women who responded to the latter desire. The earliest known extant vernacular Dutch prose, for example, is Beatrice of Nazareth's *Seven Manieren van Minne* (*Seven Manners of Loving*).

One of the more remarkable features of the vernacular religious works of such women as Beatrice, Hadewijch, and Methtild of Magdeburg is the common ground they share with vernacular secular works of the troubadours. Troubadour literature's chief theme, its raison d'être, is love; for these three women *Minne,* Love Itself, is their main theme. The vocabulary of courtly love is found throughout both groups' works. The trobairitz tended to write from personal experience, and the women religious did too. Both groups used their writing as a form of self-expression and individuality. Hadewijch skillfully adapts troubadour imagery and settings to communicate her religious message. The Countess of Dia complains about "a courteous and worthy knight" she pledged her love to:

> So bitter do I feel toward him
> whom I love more than anything.
> With him my mercy and fine manners are in vain,
> my beauty, virtue and intelligence.
> For I've been tricked and cheated
> as if I were completely loathesome.[5]

Hadewijch's imagery is so similar that the unsuspecting might believe some random passages of her poetry belong within the secular courtly love genre:

If in love
I cannot win,
What will become of me?
I am small now; then I would be nothing.
I am disconsolate unless Love provides a remedy.
I see no deliverance; she must give me
Enough to live on freely.[6]

In some of her poems she borrows analogies from the courtly world to understand Divine Love:

I know brave knights, strong of hand,
In whom I place my fullest trust.
They ever serve in the chains of Love,
And they fear no pain, grief, or vicissitudes,
But they wish to fare through all the land
Which the loving soul ever found with Love in Love;
Their noble heart is of lordly turn:
They know what Love teaches with Love,
And how Love honors the loyal lover with love.[7]

We know, for example, loyalty, fidelity, honor, justice, charming appearance, public generosity, truthfulness, courage, beauty, suffering, and exile are favorite themes in troubadour poetry, and Hadewijch manages to present every one of them in just this one poem (the modern appellation is "The Knight of Love").[8] However, she uses them for an entirely different purpose than they serve in courtly love poetry.

In Hadewijch's hand chivalric virtues are used to bring the audience to "gain knowledge of the Beloved with love/That nothing else be known by it/Except: 'I am love conquered by Love.' "[9] Hadewijch's Love is a demanding mistress, and anyone who wishes to serve Love "must resign himself to all things,/Not only easy but hard,/Exactly as if he were her serf."[10] Hadewijch's Love is metaphysical, and her unique ability to capture its essence in lyric poetry earns her a place in the pantheon of great Western vernacular poets. Not only does she possess what "only can be termed lyric genius,"[11] but she played a key role in the next stage of development in Western poetry. As literary critic Theodoor Weevers says, Hadewjich belongs with "Dante and the other poets of the *dolce stil nuovo* as one of the great masters who, toward the close of the era of courtly chivalry, transformed the troubadour lyric with its rigidly circumscribed conventions into a form capable of expressing the highest aspirations of the human soul."[12] The power of Hadewijch's poetry is not lost even in translation, as in "Love's Great Power" where she expresses her deeply held belief in human potential:

Love wills that the loving soul lovingly demand total love.
She has set up her highest banner.
From this we learn what kind of works she requires

> With clear truth and without doubt.
> O noble souls! Apply yourselves to the exercise of love,
> And adorn yourselves with the light of truth,
> So that no darkness may assail you,
> But you may consort with your Beloved according to the law of love.[13]

In writing such verse Hadewijch was in actuality creating a new genre, the mystical love lyric, a genre that was well appreciated by Renaissance humanists.

Since the genius of Hadewijch is easily identified in her poetry, one might make the mistake of supposing that therein lies her main contribution to Western intellectual culture. Her poetry is only a part of her contribution, though, for her vernacular prose is of equal importance. Her prose and poetry together are the vehicles she uses to develop and disseminate what historical theologian Bernard McGinn astutely identifies as "vernacular theology." In a study of beguine mystics and Meister Eckhart McGinn makes the case for the need for historians and theologians alike to acknowledge the existence of vernacular theology and to analysis and assess it accordingly. Scholars have always recognized the presence of scholastic theology in the Middle Ages, and since the mid-twentieth century they have acknowledged monastic theology as a major component of theology, co-existent with scholasticism. Now it is time to give a third type of theology its due, a theology that developed among intellectuals after the twelfth century and one McGinn calls vernacular "to indicate its primary distinguishing mark—linguistic expression in the medieval vernacular tongues." McGinn realizes that "it is in this tradition that women, for the first time in the history of Christianity, took on an important, perhaps even a preponderant role," mainly because the vernacular put laywomen on equal footing with laymen. Latin was the language of the church, and thus only women religious had traditionally had access to it, but in much smaller numbers than clerics and monks. When the vernacular opened up the literate, educated world to the laity, it opened for greater numbers and for both sexes.[14] As Grundmann points out, when "language was given new tasks to perform"[15] by those writing vernacular religious literature, it created new possibilities in that language which, I would add, provided people with tools for new studies. Once we recognize vernacular theology as a valid, separate intellectual field that played an essential role in the development of Western culture, then we are able to position many women vernacular writers more precisely in their rightful niche in intellectual history.

Vitae from Barking Monastery

Some time in the second half of the twelfth century two French vernacular *vitae* emanated from the women's monastery of Barking, the *Life of Edward the Confessor* and the *Life of St. Catherine*. Barking was the pre-eminent women's monastery in England. Its abbess was appointed by the king, and she took precedence over all other abbesses in the king's domain. Many of the twelfth-century abbesses were connected to the royal family,[16] and all were well educated. Given these circumstances it is not particularly surprising that the monastery had a reputation as an intellectual center or that two vernacular *vitae* were written by one (or two[17]) of its members during this period. The woman author of Edward the Confessor's *vita,* written ca. 1163, refuses to give her name beyond being a nun at Barking, "for she knows very well that she is not yet worthy that it should be heard or read in a book where she has written such a holy name" [as Edward the Confessor].[18] The author of St. Catherine's *vita,* written well after Edward's, has no such qualms. In her concluding remarks she confidently tells us that "I who have translated her life am called Clemence. I am a nun of Barking."[19] In all probability Edward's *vita* was written early in Clemence's career when she was still unsure of herself.

The two poems are of interest because they are in many ways transitional pieces, from the Latin clerical world of literature to the vernacular lay world of literature. They are both based on Latin works; Clemence considers it her task to be that of revision and translation, but scholars have long recognized that the vernacular versions of the *vitae* differ greatly from the Latin. Far from being a literal translation Clemence's works, particularly the *vita* of St. Catherine, are dominated by her own agenda. Thus in St. Catherine's *vita* Clemence follows the basic narrative of the Latin poem but digresses frequently to offer her own commentary on the matter at hand or to make some general observations on the human condition.[20] Sometimes she simply retells things in the vernacular, because she apparently believes she can do it better. In Edward the Confessor's *vita* she reconstructs her own version of a miracle story, either because she believed that her primary source was better, or that she could be more effective: "Later on there heard tell of this marvel a lady of our abbey, which is called Barking," the author explains, "and from her I have heard this miracle about which I shall now tell you—and yet he who made the Life in Latin wrote about it before."[21] The author remains faithful to the shell of the story but uses the vernacular to paint a version that opens up new worlds to the lay reader, the world of romance. She seems acutely aware of the responsibility that comes with the introduction of the vernacular and defends her pioneering attempt this way: "If I do not keep the order of cases, or join part to the right part, indeed, I ought not to be taken to task, for I cannot do it in any way. What is nominative in Latin, I shall make accusative in Romance. I know a false French of England, for I have not gone to seek it elsewhere. But you, who have learnt it elsewhere, must amend it where there is need."[22]

So strongly does she believe in the benefits of presenting the less accessible Latin *vitae* in the more accessible vernacular that she calls upon her audience to participate in the task as need warrants. Her concluding remarks reiterate this theme, this time emphasizing the pioneering aspect of her work by reminding the reader of the uniqueness of someone of her sex attempting this: "So she requires all who hear, all who will ever hear, this romance of hers, that it should not be despised for this reason, that a woman has thus translated it. For this alone one should not be contemptuous of it, nor condemn the good to be found there. She cries mercy, and asks pardon for her presumption in undertaking to translate this Life. That it has not been better accomplished, blame her lack of power, for her wish she has performed."[23] In St. Catherine's *vita* Clemence reveals herself to be aware not only of the importance of vernacular literature, but also that it be good and be able to reach the people effectively, as in Edward the Confessor's *vita.* Clemence explains in detail: "It [the *Life of*

St. Catherine] was translated before, well-ordered according to the time. But men were not then so wicked or so envious as they are at the present time, and as they will be still more after us. Because times have changed, and the quality of men has altered, the rhyme is esteemed vile, because it has become somewhat corrupted. Therefore it has to be amended and the time passed suitably to the people."[24]

The additions found in *Life of St. Catherine* are pronouncedly more transitional in subject matter than in Edward's *vita,* for here the additions made to the Latin source change the genre of the poem from hagiography to courtly love literature. This is indeed a significant fact, for as literary historian M. Dominica Legge proclaims, "nowhere else save in this text do such courtly passages occur in a saint's Life."[25] Clemence's plaintive laments could easily be the words in a trobairitz song of a jilted lover who loses her knight in battle: "My life will be nothing but death without you. How can you die without me? How can I live without you? . . . I will thus lead my life in total sadness when I lose you, good friend."[26] The emotion of courtly love literature is also present throughout the *vita.* "On a Wednesday she departed this life, she lost life, she found life," Clemence dramatically observes.[27] When the queen is killed Clemence adds to her Latin source an emphasis on the grief of the queen's women, commenting that "if you have loved a woman you might well be able to pity" the queen's friends,[28] and reminding the reader that "against grief there is comfort, and against vexation joyful pleasure."[29] Clemence's characters are mindful of feudal etiquette, even pagan characters, thus indicating feudal values should be peculiar to all rulers, not simply Christian ones. When the Emperor is trying his hardest to make Catherine abandon her faith, he promises her. "You will be granted great honor and will be second in my palace if you sacrifice to our god. You will come after the queen of my whole kingdom, and have anything except her dowry because I do not wish to be unfair to her."[30] Such feudal consideration is not present in the Latin source but added by Clemence.

Clemence also adds more intellectual strength to her women characters, including St. Catherine. The most fascinating aspect present in all the St. Catherine legends is her intellectual acumen. Clemence is the first to introduce extraordinary intellectual talent as part of the model saint and feudal heroine's makeup. For Clemence, Catherine personified the ideal woman, a saint, yes, but also a very smart woman who "could comprehend Scripture and could defend herself in opposition to all other dialecticians in the world."[31] When Catherine seeks out the Emperor—not waiting to be summoned as most early Christian martyrs did—to debate the validity of his laws demanding pagan sacrifice, he arranges her to debate not one but "fifty of the best debaters in his court."[32] Rather than being intimated she engages them with gusto until they acknowledge that "never since our mothers bore us have we heard a woman speak so or dispute so wisely."[33] She converts the fifty men of the Emperor's court by the strength of her intellectual arguments. Women, nobility, and intelligence are intertwined in Clemence's heroine, and this model is indeed part of the new vernacular Catherine that Clemence introduces to her audience, both in the monastery and the court. Given the history of Barking's intelligent and holy abbesses during Clemence's life, the creation of a literary model that possesses these traits is understandable, welcome, and influential. Thus, even Gui's thirteenth-century version, which seems intent upon reducing Catherine's stature throughout the poem, has to admit thus:

Her mind was so enlightened
And her intelligence so keen,
That there was no cleric, learned as he might be,
Expert in the art of the dialectic,
In poetry, or in rhetoric,
Who would dare speak in front of her.
She had paid heed to the teaching
Of all the Arts, and knew them all.
She surpassed all the masters
Who were in the city
By her ability to reason and to argue.[34]

Clemence's *vita* of Catherine is not all romance, though; it is also hagiography. Clemence emphasizes this point when she introduces Catherine to her audience and tells us immediately that despite her attractive looks, despite her unmatched intellectual prowess, Catherine's priorities are implacable: "She knows much about the things of the world but her desire rests elsewhere: In God."[35] As a transitional writer Clemence walks the line between the church and the court, and while her poems never reach the level of theology, they do prepare the way for vernacular theology to follow. In *Edward the Confessor* the author discusses the sin of envy, injustice, the boundless love of God, and the role of miracles in human lives;[36] in *St. Catherine* Clemence concerns herself with righteousness, the soul, the effects of original sin, and the goodness of God to humanity.[37] "Our Jesus, our lord, our comfort, our strength," Edward prays, while Catherine prays in vain: "my honor," "my strength," "my comfort," "my pleasure."[38] None of these topics or titles are developed theologically, but again, they prepare the way for women vernacular writers of theology in the thirteenth century and beyond.

When we look for these writers we find that they are familiar to us as mystics. Our challenge now is only minor; we must examine the writings of these women mystics anew for their theological and intellectual content. Among the mystics who are particularly pertinent to us here are two Flemish women already mentioned, Beatrice of Nazareth and Hadewijch, Mechthild of Magdeburg, a German woman from the famed intellectual monastery at Helfta, and a French heretic, Marguerite Porete. These women's use of the vernacular in their presentation of metaphysical, epistemological, and ethical issues was innovative, creative, and among the earliest examples. Beatrice's *Seven Manners of Loving* is the earliest Dutch prose, Hadewijch's poetry helped mold medieval Dutch,[39] and Mechthild's *Flowing Light of the Godhead* is the earliest middle low German prose written in a genre that has "no obvious antecedents or descendents" and defies "all attempts to categorize it."[40] All the women were familiar with vernacular secular literature, and they adapt, amend, and alter the forms and images of courtly love literature to better communicate their ideas to a wider audience than Latin theological writers were able to do. No one had ever explained the role of reason in the human quest for God the way that Beatrice did in *Seven Manners,* because no one had ever explained it in Dutch before.

We can almost feel Hadewijch's frustration when she ruminates over her use of the vernacular and the role of languages in human communication: "For earth cannot understand heavenly wisdom. Words enough and Dutch enough can be found for all things on earth, but I do not know any Dutch or any words that answer my purpose. Although I can express everything insofar as this is possible for a human being, no Dutch can be found for all I have said to you, since none exists to express these things, so far as I know."[41] Thus acutely aware of the problems inherent in the use of any language, she searches for new ways to express her innermost thoughts and experiences. She knew Latin and was proficient in French,[42] yet she chose her vernacular as the best means available to overcome the limits of language and to allow others to share in her ideas. We have always acknowledged the importance in intellectual history of the Latin Fathers, in part because their articulation of the Christian message in their vernacular opened up new areas for speculation and admitted new spectators. We must now do the same for these Vernacular Mothers, for many lay and religious women played the same role in the thirteenth century that clerical and monastic men played in early Christianity. In both instances these Fathers and Mothers challenged their contemporaries to ponder the meaning of life with renewed energy by reflecting on the essential matters of the human condition in a new linguistic field. There are many women mystics who wrote in Latin and whose theology is highly significant—Birgitta of Sweden, for example—and we will discuss them below. For now it is important that we focus on the contributions the Vernacular Mothers made to Western intellectual history, because their work formed a bridge between the Latin intellectual world of clerics involved chiefly in scholastic and dogmatic theology, and the vernacular lay world of literate men and women interested in a more pragmatic theology.

That these women wrote in the vernacular is important and deserves emphasis, but it is the content of their theology that mandates their inclusion in intellectual history. They used the vernacular because they intuitively recognized it as the vehicle most compatible with their goal. That goal was to present a new type of theology to a new audience. They wanted to bring the reader to a genuine understanding and a full acceptance of ultimate truths. Hence, they shared their deepest convictions concerning Truth. The method they used was not deductive or inductive but descriptive, a method better suited to address an audience wider that the intellegensia. Their intention was not to prove anything to the readers but rather to allow the readers to see the reality for themselves. Their approach was more existential than rational but never anti-rational; they relied heavily on the readers' ability to apply their reasoning powers to the experience described. Their theology was of a type theologian John Macquarrie labels "philosophical theology." It is theology that "will provide a bridge between our everyday thinking and experience and the matters about which the theologian talks: it will relate religious discourse to all the other areas of discourse. It will do this by setting out from ordinary situations that can be described in secular language, and will seek to move from them into the situations of the life of faith." The Vernacular Mothers provided such a bridge, placed their religious discourse within reach of the new lay literate class, and did so in the language of the audience they were addressing. Macquarrie adds that an important task of philosophical theology is to show how traditional religious words "find their places on the map of meaning" for those not formally educated in theology.[43] Here again we see how well the writings of the Vernacular Mothers fulfill the conditions of philosophical theology, specifically by choosing to communicate in the vernacular.[44] The theology of the Vernacular Mothers was quite distinct from that of their contemporary scholastic theologians, but no more than the requirements of philosophical theology demanded. More to the point, it was just as valuable a contribution and needs to be seen as such.

Beatrice of Nazareth

Approximately seven years after Beatrice's death in 1268 a brother of one of the nuns at Nazareth wrote Beatrice's *vita,* claiming though "that I am only the translator of this work, not the author. Of my own I have added or changed little; rather I have only given a latin coloring to the vernacular words as they were given to me in [Beatrice's] diary-notes. She who is served by our work of translation rightly claims its authorship."[45] Thus we know that Beatrice wrote a vernacular autobiography, which indeed would have been highly significant if it had survived, but the mere fact that she wrote one is worthy of attention. It indicates that she was intent upon self-reflection and eager to educate others by sharing her insights and experiences. It also means that she was committed to the vernacular as the best means available for religious discourse to be accessible to other areas of discourse and that she wanted to describe her ordinary life in a language that would help people understand her spiritual life. Given what her biographer tells us was in her autobiography we have every reason to believe that she used the genre to expound her own philosophical theology. Unfortunately, only one of her works has survived,[46] a short treatise on love, yet it and the summaries of her work in her *vita* provide us with at least a minimum appreciation of her work as a Vernacular Mother.

Beatrice's first mode sets the tone for all that will follow: "The first manner is an active longing, which proceeds from love, and must rule a long time in the heart before it can conquer all opposition, and can work with its power and judgment, and grow within us in holiness," Beatrice begins, "and the soul longs to lead its whole life so, and to act so and to grow and to climb to still greater heights of love and nearer knowledge of God, to that perfection for which it was made and is called by its Creator." She continues, describing her metaphysical concerns thus: "Always such a soul ponders what it is and what it ought to be, what it possesses and what it lacks; with its whole attention and with great longing and with all its powers it strives to preserve itself and to shun everything which could burden or hinder it as it works to this end. Its heart never ceases, its will never falters in seeking, entreating, learning, gaining and keeping everything which can help it and bring it to love."[47] The effectiveness of her existential description is hardly diminished even in the English translation. She challenges her audience to contemplate the ultimate goal for all humanity, perfection. She subtly dares them to see for themselves that her description of the soul ever acting, growing, climbing, longing, and the heart ever entreating, learning, gaining, and keeping everything which can bring it to that goal is indeed their own personal experience. There is no syllogism, no formal argument, no deductive reasoning in the passage, for Beatrice persuades by description. The power of her words evokes a response within her audience and an acknowledgment that her personal experience is universal. There is such movement in her conception of life, constant, active engagement in life. In contrast to popular contemporary trends within scholastic thought that prized the Greek legacy of reverence for stability and equated motion with instability, hence, imperfection, Beatrice rejected stability and embraced motion. Motion is being. "Always" a soul must be thinking, judging what is right and wrong, avoiding that which detracts from its goal. Written in an age deeply involved in creating new forms of secular life, Beatrice's philosophy reflects that movement and at the same time attempts to guide it properly. Her approach is rooted in neoplatonic principles and somewhat reminiscent of Pseudo-Dionysius' thought, if not directly influenced by it. Her opening statement is one of process: "There are seven manners of loving, which come down from the heights and go back again far above."[48] This theme of cyclical return is maintained throughout the treatise. She believes that "the soul always wishes to follow after love, to see love, to delight in love, and this cannot come to the soul here in this exile. So it longs to leave this life and find its home, where already it has established its dwelling, where it directs its longings that it may in love find rest."[49]

There is also a raw hunger present in Beatrice's writing that contributes much to the power of her argument. Beatrice believes that her own experience of this hunger is universal and that by describing it she will strike a responsive chord in the audience which will lead to acceptance of her thesis:

> For the soul longs single-handed to do as much as all the men upon the earth, as all the spirits in heaven, as every creature that ever is, to do more beyond all telling than they do, serving, loving, glorifying love as is love's due. And because the soul comes so short in what it does, it wants with all its will and with great longing to do yet better. Yet this cannot satisfy the soul. It knows well that to achieve what it longs for is far above its powers, beyond human reason and all the senses; yet it cannot moderate or restrain or calm itself. It does everything that it can. . . . But none of this gives the soul any rest, and it is a great torment to long for what it cannot attain. And so the soul must stay in sorrow and longing, and it will seem that living, it dies, and dying, it feels the pain of hell, and its whole life is torment and rejection and refusal, racked as it is with these desires which it can never appease or quicken or satisfy.[50]

The movement within the soul being driven by this hunger for perfection is frustrating, driving the soul to even more movement. "Always the soul will be driven and goaded on, never will it be satisfied and at rest," she observes.[51] "The soul feels itself so greatly stirred from within," Beatrice reports in the fifth manner, "so mightily and violently moved in the heart, that it seems to the soul that the heart is wounded again and again." The pain is real and takes on the appearance of physical pain; "it seems to the soul that the veins are bursting, the blood spilling, the marrow withering, the bones softening, the heart burning, the throat parching."[52] Thus Beatrice prods the audience to think beyond the traditional arguments of logic to the existential reality they experience. The strength of Beatrice's words almost force the complacent and the passive person to participate in the intense experience of life then and there, something that can be done simply by becoming conscious of the hunger within.

The hunger is described by Beatrice as love, thus forming a bridge between two elements in society not frequently joined in her day, the academic world and the court. Love is the cornerstone of courtly literature, and it is not by coincidence that it is Beatrice's cornerstone also. She openly courts the feudal world, using the imagery of that world to help attract its people to her message. "The soul is like a maiden who serves her master only for her great love of him, not for any payment, satisfied that she may serve him and that he suffers her to serve," Beatrice writes. She continues, unabashedly using her metaphor to urge her audience to rely on more than human reason. "So the soul longs to serve love with love, without measure, beyond measure, and beyond human sense and reason, faithfully performing every service."[53] She repeatedly draws upon the same understanding and vocabulary of courtly love that the troubadours had to communicate her own theology. Love is "exalted so high," it is "above the soul's comprehension, above all the soul can do or suffer." Just as the knight is driven to distraction by the love of his lady, so is human reason overwhelmed by love: "The soul is so fettered with the bond of love, so conquered by the boundlessness of love, that it cannot rule itself by reason, cannot reason through understanding, cannot spare itself this weariness, cannot hold fast to human wisdom."[54] Just as the knight must prove his love by hardship and ordeal, so too must the soul: "All who want to attain to love must seek it in fear and pursue it in faith, exercising themselves in longing, not sparing themselves in great labours, in many sufferings, undergoing many sorrows and enduring much contempt." The rewards for the knight and the soul are the same; they will eventually reach "the state where love rules in it and performs its own mighty works, making great small, labour easy, suffering sweet, and all debts paid. This is freedom of conscience, sweetness of heart, subjection of the senses, the soul's excellence, the spirit's exaltation, and the beginning of everlasting life."[55]

Macquarrie notes that while philosophical theology does not prove theses but rather illuminates them so the audience can see its claims, it may, in fact, be more persuasive than logic, because participation leads to a genuine understanding in ways that theoretical argument does not.[56] We will never know how effective Beatrice's approach was, whether the audience did look within as she bid them or whether her vernacular theology gained more adherents than those who read scholastic theology. We do know, however, the vernacular theology reached a different audience, one that scholastic theology did not address. We also know that Beatrice was a harbinger of a type of theology that remains dominant today, vernacular philosophical theology. Her use of the vernacular and her choice of philosophical theology to express her understanding of reality are both deliberate and wise. By choosing to describe rather than demonstrate, and by describing in the vocabulary and setting of the new courts of the high Middle Ages, she introduced a whole new world of thought to a whole new world of intellectuals.

Hadewijch

What Beatrice accomplished in her one small treatise Hadewijch expanded and nearly perfected in her many poems. While judging the aesthetic value of poetry is surely subjective, it is hard to imagine any reader being oblivious to the beauty of Hadewijch's writings, as we have already seen above. They are strikingly vivid expressions of the same Love that Beatrice wrote about, even sometimes in strikingly similar expressions. There is no evidence that either woman was familiar with the work of the other, but Beatrice's and Hadewijch's use of the memorable phrase "love with love"[57] indicates that they were drawing upon the same courtly love culture. Their works also share a common love of nature. In one of her most poetic passages Beatrice describes the free spirit in metaphors taken from nature: "And like the fish, swimming in the vast sea and resting in its deeps, and like the bird, boldly mounting high in the sky, so the soul feels its spirit freely moving through the vastness and the depth and the unutterable richness of love."[58] Hadewijch's love of nature pervades almost every one of her stanzaic poems. She talks about birds, meadows, plants, mountains and valleys, fruit, flower buds, and so on, with deep seated respect, but most of her admiration focuses on the seasons.[59] To Hadewijch the experience of nature is a spiritual experience, and the cyclical return of spring is but nature's imitation of the soul's return to God. Of her forty-five stanzaic poems only four do not refer to the seasons and the passing of time in the introductory stanza; three of those four refer to the seasons in the body of the text. Only Hadewijch's poems on Mary contain no mention of the seasons, but even this one employs imagery from nature.[60] This characteristic of Hadewijch's stanzaic poems is second only to her preoccupation with Love, and it may be understood as Hadewijch's way of gaining access to that Love, both in literary terms and experientially:

> As this new year begins for us,
> We hope for the rapid coming
> Of the season many await,
> Which causes mountain and valley to burgeon,
> Although the joy is not yet ripe.
> So is it, likewise, with him who gives his all
> At high Love's alluring promise,
> Before he measures the remoteness of Love.[61]

The temporal return of spring and life is but a preparation for the Eternal Return of souls and love:

> When March begins, we see
> all beings live again,
> And all plants spring up
> And in a short time turn green.
> It is the same with longing,
> Particularly that of the true lover.[62]

Winter, on the other hand, is "the sad season," "dark and cold," the "harsh" season "which makes many a heart heavy" and fearful of one trouble "above all: How shall I attain to Love."[63] Winter need not be so sad though, if one accepts Hadewijch's theology of Love:

> However, it may be with the season,
> Anyone who is accompanied by works in truth
> Finds himself ever face to face
> With blossoms, joy, summer, and daylight.
> He is always new and afire with longing;
> Winter no longer molests him.[64]

Hadewijch's prose writings incorporate Love and nature into her philosophical theology, but not to the same degree that her poetry does. Her prose consists of a collection of letters chiefly on spiritual direction, six in the form of short treatises, and a book of visions, perhaps also compiled for spiritual direction.[65] Given the nature of her writings, we must examine their intellectual components within the expectations of that genre.[66] This is actually easier than might be expected, because much of medieval spiritual direction was grounded in what future generations called Christian philosophy. Surprisingly, quite often the content of medieval spiritual direction was more rational than pietistic. Hadewijch's direction is an example of the former. Her spiritual direction is rooted in a rational definition of the human condition and is focused on analysis of that condition and the means available to attain happiness within that condition. She realizes the limits of direction, acknowledging that while "there were persons I delivered from sins, persons I delivered from despair,"[67] there are many more people she could not reach because of the fundamentally incommunicable nature of human experience:

> Nobody who has loved Love with love
> Could explain to others,
> Or write, or bring to their understanding,
> All the wonders she finds in Love's sublimity.[68]

Still, she believed that by teaching others in an analytical way, the proper order and relationships of body and soul, this world and the next, she could "lead all the unled"[69] to happiness.

At the basis of her philosophy is the Socratic moral imperative, "Know thyself." Like Socrates she advocates self-reflection and criticism as the means to happiness. Knowledge is the key. "And this Angel said: 'Human nature, understand and know what this tree is!' " Hadewijch is told in her vision of the garden of perfection. "And I understood ... that the tree was the knowledge of ourselves":[70]

> If you wish to experience this perfection, you must first of all learn to know yourselves: in all your conduct, in your attraction or aversion, in your behavior, in love, in hate, in fidelity, in mistrust, and in all things that befall you. You must examine yourselves as to how you can endure everything disagreeable that happens to you, and how you can bear the loss of what gives you pleasure; for to be

> robbed of what it gladly receives is indeed the greatest sorrow a young heart can bear. And in everything pleasant that happens to you, examine yourselves as to how you make use of it, and how wise and how moderate you are with regard to it. In all that befalls you, preserve your equanimity in response or in pain. Continually contemplate with wisdom our Lord's works; from them you will learn perfection.[71]

This maxim places a huge responsibility on the individual. While never denying the Christian doctrine of grace and election Hadewijch places great emphasis on personal responsibility and effort in attaining knowledge. She tells her directees "for each revelation I had seen partly according to what I was myself, and partly according to my having been chosen," and the Voice in her visions confirms the importance of her own efforts. "The Voice said to me: 'O strongest of all warriors! You have conquered everything and opened the closed totality, which never was opened by creatures who did not know, with painfully won and distressed Love, how I am God and Man! O heroine, since you are so heroic, and since you never yield, you are called the greatest heroine! It is right, therefore, that you should know me perfectly.' "[72] The role reason plays in the quest for self-knowledge and knowledge of God is central, for it is "Reason [that] well knows that God must be feared, and that God is great and man is small."[73] If we are not careful and we allow reason to err, "the will grows weak and powerless and feels an aversion to effort, because reason does not enlighten it."[74] Reason is a special and unique faculty that must be treated accordingly; we are "strong as a result of possessing right reason," we must hold on to it and "not let [it] slacken through inactivity."[75] Human reason is most powerful and at the same time most humbling, for "he who wishes all things to be subject to him must himself be subject to his reason, above whatever he wills or whatever anyone else wills of him. For no one can become perfect in Love unless he is subject to his reason."[76] In her visionary work Hadewijch explains that the process of subjection begins by recognizing that three virtues must always accompany Reason: Holy Fear, Discernment, and Wisdom. Reason "ordered me to acknowledge the whole number of my company; and I truly acknowledged it." This leads to a paradoxical situation. Once Reason is fully and properly utilized it ceases to be needed. Reason has done its job and shown the person the way to the ultimate goal, Love: "Then Reason became subject to me, and I left her. But Love came and embraced me."[77] Sometimes we become too enamored with reason, place too much value it in, and forget it is not the ultimate goal, "but if rational man's noble reason would recognize its just debt and follow Love's leading into her land—that is, follow Love according to her due—then he would be capable of attaining that great object."[78] Reason is, after all, limited. "We shall reach our full growth" only after reason is merged and subsumed in love.[79] There is a precarious balance between the two, though, and one must learn how to safeguard that balance existentially, for "when reason abandons itself to love's wish, and love consents to be forced and held with in the bounds of reason, they can accomplish a very great work. This no one can learn except by experience."[80]

The actualization of human potential is, after all, the ideal goal of life, Hadewijch instructs her directees. Human nature is flawed but eminently redeemable, "and even if you do the best you can in all things, your human nature must often fall short."[81] Human nature also entails sacrifice as well as failure. Hadewijch reminds her directees that "we must be continually aware that noble service and suffering in exile are proper to man's condition."[82] Because of this weak human nature they must always do "your utmost to examine your thoughts strictly, in order to know yourself in all things."[83] Self-knowledge leads to the realization that only "if you abandon yourself to Love, you will soon attain full growth."[84] Love and only "Love rewards to the full."[85] Hadewijch is very careful, however, to make sure her directees do not confuse her conception of Love[86] with limited emotional love, even as she describes it in the imagery of courtly love. "You are still young, and you must grow a good deal, and it is much better for you, if you wish to walk the way of Love, that you seek difficulty and that you suffer for the honor of Love, rather than wish to feel love."[87] True knowledge of love begins, as always, in self-knowledge. By realizing the limits of human love, we come to know about divine love. "The being of love," that is, God, "is in the height of his fruition, and we are in the abyss of our privation. I mean you and I, who have not yet become what we are, and have not grasped what we have, and still remain so far from what is ours. We must, without sparing, lose all for all; and learn uniquely and intrepidly the perfect life of Love, who has urged on both of us to her work,"[88] remembering always that "where Love is, there are always great labors and burdensome pains."[89] Hadewijch's directees must also remember because "we must do without the satisfaction of Love in order to satisfy Love," life becomes "miserable beyond all that the human heart can bear. For nothing in their life satisfies them—either their gifts, or their service, or consolations, or all they can accomplish." The only thing they experience is "pleasure in proportion as Love was advanced or grew in themselves and in others; pain, in proportion as Love was hindered or harmed in those who love."[90]

Suffering has always been a stumbling block for humans who believe in a good God, and given the amount of writing Hadewijch does on this phenomena, it apparently was one for herself and her directees. In Hadewijch's philosophical theology we have her resolution of the matter. Suffering, we have heard her say, is proper to human nature. The experience of suffering is positive, not negative, because it provides us with the means of participating in divinity by likeness. "Moreover 'I give you a new commandment' (John 13:34): If you wish to be like me in my Humanity, as you desire to possess wholly in my Divinity and Humanity, you shall desire to be poor, miserable, and despised by all men,"[91] God tells her in a vision, and she relays the message to her directees. "We all indeed wish to be God with God, but God knows there are few of us who want to live as men with his Humanity, or want to carry his cross with him, or want to hang on the cross with him and pay humanity's debt to the full."[92] Despite this natural aversion they must "suffer gladly, in all its extent, the pain God sends you."[93] As Jesus "lived merely as Man" and experienced "all the suffering that belongs to the human race," so must they "feel yourself as man in all the hardships proper to the human condition."[94] They must embrace the human condition, because it is through one's humanity and suffering that God is encountered. To suffer is to imitate the Divine Exemplar and actually participate in that divinity. "The Godhead has engulfed human nature wholly in itself," so the more one embraces human nature, the easier it is to be "taken up into a fuller participation in the Divine Nature."[95]

We hear these same themes in another vision where she was given a new power, "the strength of his own Being, to be God with my sufferings according to his example and in union with him, as he was for me when he lived for me as Man."[96] Contemporaneous to Hadewijch instructing her directees in a qualified and restrictive doctrine of divine exemplarism, Thomas Aquinas was also writing about the matter. Hadewijch and Thomas reject the Platonic exemplarism of archetypes and demiurge and the neoplatonic notion that the One produced creation from necessity, but they both adapt elements of exemplarism, particularly neoplatonic exemplarism, to suit their own philosophy.[97] "The order of the universe is properly intended by God, and is not the accidental result of a succession of agents, as has been supposed by those who have taught that God created only the first creature, and that this creature created the second creature, and so on," Thomas argues. "Inasmuch as He knows His own essence perfectly, He knows it according to every mode in which it can be known. Now it can be known not only as it is in itself, but as it can be participated in by creatures according to some degree of likeness. But every creature has its own proper species, according to which it participates in some degree of likeness to the divine essence."[98] What Thomas demonstrates through syllogism Hadewijch describes existentially. "For when the soul has nothing else but God, and when it retains no will but lives exclusively according to his will alone; and when the soul is brought to nought and with God's will wills all that he wills, and is engulfed in him, and is brought to nought—then he is exalted above the earth, and then he draws all things to him, and so the soul becomes with him all that he himself is."[99] Her description was effective and probably influential, for Eckhart and Ruusbroec promoted much the same doctrine in their own writings.[100]

There are other neoplatonic elements in Hadewijch's thought that are of interest. Although her approach to God is overwhelmingly through the via affirmativa, sometimes she does direct her charges through the via negativa, as did Pseudo-Dionysius and John Scotus Erigena before her. God is Love, but occasionally Hadewijch describes Love via negativa, as when she tells us that "no mercy can dwell in Love, no graciousness, humility, reason, fear; no parsimony, no measure, nothing. But Love dwells in all these, and they are all nourished on Love."[101] Hadewijch continually promotes reason as a guide to knowledge, but she reminds her directees of the ability of reason to find knowledge of God via negativa, and she juxtaposes that approach to love's via affirmativa to emphasize that the two ways are mutually dependent, not mutually exclusive. "This power of sight has two eyes, love and reason. Reason cannot see God except in what he is not; love rests not except in what he is," Hadewijch explains. "Reason advances toward what God is, by means of what God is not. Love sets aside what God is not and rejoices that it fails in what God is. Reason has more satisfaction than love, but love has more sweetness of bliss than reason. These two, however, are of great mutual help one to the other."[102] In one of her visions she tells us that she saw two heavens, Christ and the soul "each of them equally powerful, in the same service , the same glory, the same omnipotence, and the same long-suffering mercy in all eternal being." The Lord tells her "how it might come to pass, and through what works, that she [the soul] should attain full growth so as to be like me;" the description of the fourth work enunciates a theme that becomes the mainstay of many future mystics, that of all-darkness: "Her fourth work and the greatest of all, which she shall lead to the end in us, is the privation—which each of us feels from the other—of our sweet nature, and the knowledge and the perception of it that we have twofold in ourselves while she, not full-grown, must do without him, whom she must love above all, and must consequently experience as all-darkness."[103] Through this experience of negativity, though, knowledge of God is attained. "Your great privation of Love has given you the highest way in the fruition of me," God told Hadewijch in a vision. "This privation of what you desire above all, and this reaching out to me who am unreachable: This is the short hour that outvies all long hours."[104]

Hadewijch's call for renewal and return is present in every one of her stanzaic poems, particularly through her spring imagery, and while those themes are not as pervasive in her letters and visions, they still are indicative of the neoplatonic foundation upon which she writes. She tells us that one Easter Sunday God "embraced me in my interior senses and took me away in spirit" where "I received all understanding." There a Voice told her that "when you fully bring me yourself, as pure humanity in myself, through all the ways of perfect Love, you shall have fruition of me as the Love who I am. Until that day you shall love what I, Love, am. And then you will be love, as I am Love." The Voice concludes by commanding her to "go forth, and live what I am; and return bringing me full divinity, and have fruition of me as who I am."[105] In her vision of "the noble mountain," with its five paths to the zenith, God ends the visionary instruction by emphasizing the element of return: "And he continued, 'Return again into your material being, and let your works blossom forth. The blows of enmity are drawing near you. But you return as victor over all, for you have conquered all.' "[106]

One final dimension of Hadewijch's intellectual analysis of life still needs to be discussed, her anthropology. Without denying the limitations of the human condition she has a somewhat exalted opinion of human life that is rarely tinged by pessimism or despair. She defends her optimistic interpretation with many arguments. First, she is an advocate of human freedom and dignity. She believes strongly in the inherent freedom of every human, a freedom that makes us all equal. After a vision in which she was united with Augustine she tells us that "I reflected on this union with Saint Augustine to which I had attained" and decides to ask "my Beloved to deliver me from it. For I wished to remain in his deepest abyss, alone in fruition." She has "no doubt [that] I continued to belong to God alone while being united in Love to this creature," but she believes it threatened her liberty which "was given me moreover for reasons of my own, which neither Augustine nor many others had." She explains in greater detail, revealing as she does how deeply held her belief in human freedom was. Her identity appears to be vested in this freedom: "For I am a free human creature, and also pure as to one part, and I can desire freely with my will, and I can will as highly as I wish, and seize and receive from God all that he is." The freedom of each human is also the basis for humanity's unity, or, in theological terms, for the communion of saints: "In this wonderful way I belong to God alone in pure love, and to my saint in love, and then to all the saints, each one according to his dignity, and to men according to what each one loved and also according to what he was and still is."[107] Because of the gift of free will, then, humans have many dear possessions; they have liberty, equality, and dignity.

Second, as free and equal agents humans have the ability to "wish to be God with God,"[108] to be perfect with God. They are able to fulfill their wish because of the Incarnation. Humans have, in other words, the potential for perfection. God's full and complete acceptance of all aspects and restrictions of the human condition ("we do not find it written anywhere that Christ ever, in his entire life, had recourse to his Father or his omnipotent Nature to obtain joy and repose"[109]) means that when humans are united with God they are most fully human. The more we are one with the divine, the more human we are, and the more perfect. This comes with a price, however, for being human means being subject to limitations. In Hadewijch's thought these limitations take on new meaning. They become vehicles through which a person can meet God in a shared experience. Jesus experienced every aspect of the human condition, good and bad "*except sin* alone," and, He tells Hadewijch in a vision, "never for a single instant did I call upon my power to give myself relief when I was in need, and never did I seek to profit from the gifts of my Spirit, but I won them at the price of sufferings." Jesus did not resort to his Divine nature to make his human nature more palatable; "never did I dispel my griefs or my pain with the aid of my omnipotence." His advice to humanity is simple: embrace humanity to the fullest. "Feel yourself as man in all hardships proper to the human condition, except sin alone," he urges. "Since, then, you are a human being, live in misery as men."[110]

The sting of suffering disappears under Hadewijch's premise, for to suffer is to be human, and to be human is to be one with the divine. This was a personal lesson Hadewijch learned when, through "great desire and in the madness of love," she gained "the strength of his own Being, to be God with my sufferings according to his example and in union with him, as he was for me when he lived for me as Man." God's embrace of humanity meant that all human experiences were now potential channels people could utilize "to content him and to live as a perfect human being."[111] Knowledge of the union of the divine and the human is the key to human happiness, as the Voice tells her in a vision: "O strongest of all warriors! You have conquered everything and opened the closed totality which never was opened by creatures who did not know, with painfully won and distressed Love, how I am God and Man!"[112]

Hadewijch also argues that the purpose of humanity's creation is reason enough to revere its life, because its purpose gives it dignity. "It is man's obligation to practice virtues," Hadewijch explains, "solely out of homage to the incomparable sublimity of God, who created our nature to this end and made it for his own honor and praise, and for our bliss in eternal glory."[113] As Hadewijch continues to explain she calls upon her basic philosophical theology with its emanation, exemplarism, and perception of the human condition as limited and painful but free, with dignity, and capable of perfection to support her anthropology:

> This is the way on which the Son of God took the lead, and of which he himself gave us knowledge and understanding when he lived as Man. For from the

> beginning to the end of time he spent on earth, he did and perfectly accomplished, amid multiplicity, the will of the Father in all things and at all times, with all that he was, and with all the service he could perform (Matt 20:28), in words and works, in joy and pain, in grandeur and abasement, in miracles, and in the distress of bitter death. With his whole heart and his whole soul, and with all his strength (Deut 6:5) in each and every circumstance, he was ready to perfect what was wanting on our part. And thus he uplifted us and drew us up by his divine power and his human justice to our first dignity and to our liberty (Gal 4:31), in which we were created and loved, and to which we are now called (Gal 5:13) and chosen in his predestination (Eph 1:4–5), in which he had forseen us from all eternity.[114]

Humanity is good for the simple reason that "he who loves God loves his works," and humans are God's work. That humans can love God is in itself evidence of the dignity of humanity. Hadewijch is careful to remind her directees that the capacity to love is part of human nature, not something given through grace. Love "is not wholly divine, for it wells up from the experience of the senses rather than from grace, and from nature rather than from the spirit."[115] In Hadewijch's anthropology human nature is the way to divine nature, hence she wants to "taste Man and God in one knowledge,"[116] Love "touches [humans] with herself,"[117] and Hadewijch "can taste and feel" Love.[118] The more one shares in the experiences of humanity the closer one is to divinity.

This premise reaches its fullest expression in Vision Twelve, when Hadewijch invites us to share in the deepest experiences of Jesus' humanity, the Incarnation, so that we can know the "Father as Father," the Son as Son, "the Holy Spirit as Holy Spirit," and know them all "as One, and the Essence in which they are One." Humanity is good, because it can participate in the fullness of being by way of likeness. Hadewijch then describes how peacefulness, the symbolic human soul in her vision, participated thus in Jesus' life, "that she had been announced and born with him, and that her body was born from the other; and that she grew up with him and lived together with him as man in all like pains, in poverty, in ignominy, and in compassion for all those with whom justice was angry; and that her body was nourished interiorly and exteriorly from the other, and never received alien consolation; and that she died with him, and freed all the prisoners with him, and bound what he bound, and with him rose again, and one with him ascended to his Father."[119] Humanity that can share so intimately with Divinity, be announced by God, be born with God, grow up with God, live and suffer with God, and die with God is surely a blessed creation. Yes, there are unpleasant even harsh realities that are part of humanity, and "God knows there are few of us who want to live as men with his Humanity, or want to carry his cross with him," but that is what we must do if "we all indeed wish to be God with God."[120]

What is amazing about Hadewijch is her ability to communicate in such effective, persuasive and yet elegant manner. There is a grace and comeliness of expression in her work that still has the power to move through the centuries and across the barriers of translation. While her intellectual thought is rigorous and solid enough to deserve inclusion in intellectual history, her genius of expression and her profound understanding of the uses of language demands inclusion. Hadewijch established new parameters for vernacular language in her work as she shaped Dutch to fit the concepts of Latin, but she also established new standards for intellectual prose and poetry as well. Although we are unsure of how well known her writings were in the centuries following her death, we do know that very few intellectuals since Hadewijch have ever been able to marry language with intellectual discourse as exquisitely as she did. To this day her prose and poetry and her philosophical theology retains the power to convert and to teach. It is a rare twenty-first-century reader who does not respond to her message, rationally, emotionally, and even spiritually.

Mechthild of Magdeburg

Some scholars would argue that the nearest rival Hadewijch has is Mechthild of Magdeburg. Mechthild produced a work that many claim is unique in world literature; her *The Flowing Light of the Godhead* has no antecedents, no descendents, and does not belong to a particular genre.[121] Critic Wolfgang Mohr claims it possesses characteristics of a vast number of genres: prophetic literature, hymn, sermon, courtly love poetry, allegorical dialogue, autobiography, drama, epigrammatic poetry, wisdom literature, letter, nursery rhyme, polemics, parody, litany, and spiritual tract, to name just the major ones.[122] In her creativity she constructed a genre specific to fit her message, because available genres did not do it justice. We have seen such originality before, in Hugeberc, Hrotsvitha, Hildegard, Beatrice, and Hadewijch, an impressive number when we remember how few women writers' works we know about. In each instance these women constructed new forms or utilized new language fields to communicate their thought. The characteristic is predominant enough in medieval women writers for us to wonder if or why women intellectuals were prone to create new literary forms. At the very least we can conclude that while few women wrote, when they did, for whatever reason, once they sat down to write they exercised great creative freedom. Mechthild's *The Flowing Light of the Godhead* is an example par excellence of such creative freedom.

A contemporary of Beatrice of Nazareth and Hadewijch, Mechthild (ca. 1207–ca. 1282–1294) spent nearly forty years of her life as a beguine in Magdeburg. Sometime around 1250 she tells us that she "went to my confessor, told him the whole story" of her daily visionary experiences "and begged him for advice. He said I should boldly go forward with a light heart," and then "he commanded me, a frail woman, to write this book out of God's heart and mouth."[123] During the next ten years she completed the first five books of her work, and during the next ten years she wrote one more.[124] These circulated among her contemporaries under its current title. After exchanging her life as a beguine for life as a Cistercian nun at Helfta ca. 1270 Mechthild dictated a seventh and final book for inclusion in *Flowing Light.* She wrote in middle low German and used it to explore uncharted visionary experiences and communicate those experiences in new and different imagery. The cosmic, sensual, erotic, theological, and spiritual imagery she employs results in an unharnessed energy that reaches up from the text to affect the reader in ways similar to those associated with ritual or liturgical chant.[125] One experiences her writing as well as learns from it. However, because the ultimate goal is knowledge, Mechthild reminds us that the whole person must be involved in the experience. "I do not know how to write, nor can I, unless I see with the eyes of my soul and hear with the ears of my eternal spirit and feel in all the parts of my body the power of the Holy Spirit,"[126] Mechthild proclaims, thus reinforcing one of her chief premises. Mechthild perceives sensual, intellectual, and spiritual knowledge to be interdependent[127] and unified. While she maintains that "one cannot grasp divine gifts with merely human understanding,"[128] she also argues that sensual knowledge is the beginning of ultimate spiritual knowledge. Thus in her vision Knowledge describes three heavens, the second of which "was created by the longing of the senses" where "the soul does not see God there./Rather, she tastes an indescribable sweetness/that permeates all her members." Here, even though "she is still joined to her earthly senses," the soul "shall travel on to the third heaven/Where the true light is given to her" if she possesses "perfect humility."[129]

Sensory knowledge plays an indispensable function in Mechthild's epistemology, a somewhat unusually high position for a medieval schema and makes it very clear that such knowledge is available to all people, not only the educated elite. "One finds many a professor learned in scripture who actually is a fool in my eyes," God replied to her after she was "warned against writing this book." Mechthild wondered whether she was truly capable of attaining and communicating knowledge, because she lacked formal training. "And I'll tell you something else," he comforted. "It is a great honor for me with regard to them, and it very much strengthens Holy Christianity,/That the unlearned mouth, aided by my Holy Spirit, teaches the learned tongue."[130] The reason Mechthild values the senses to the extent she does is due to the centrality of the Incarnation in her intellectual framework. Union with Truth is through the Godhead, and this is possible only because the Godhead assumed human nature in the person of the Son. We encounter the Son as human first, and only afterwards as the divine: "The humanity of our Lord is an intelligible image of his eternal Godhead, so that we can grasp the Godhead with the humanity and, like the Holy Trinity, enjoy, hug, kiss, and embrace God in an incomprehensible manner." Human nature is thus not to be scorned but, thanks to the Incarnation, is elevated to new heights. "The eternal Godhead shines forth, lighting up all the blessed who are in its presence and making them ready for love," Mechthild continues. "The humanity of our Lord greets, rejoices, and loves his flesh and his blood without ceasing."[131] This reality is a never-ceasing source of happiness for Mechthild, for "when I reflect that divine nature now includes bone and flesh, body and soul, then I become elated in great joy,"[132] and respect the body and its sensory knowledge for what it is. Without sensory knowledge, knowledge of the eternal is impossible, since it is only "through the senses [that Love of God] storms the soul with all its might."[133] Access to the soul, which alone is capable of the highest form of wisdom, occurs through the senses, as Mechthild explains in a dialogue between Knowledge and the senses:

> Then the senses say: "Our lady, the soul, has slept since childhood.
> Now she has awakened in the light of open love."

In this light she looks around herself to discover
Who that is who reveals himself to her,
And what that is that one is saying to her.
Thus does she see truly and understand
How God is all things in all things.[134]

By virtue of this function the body is indispensable in the search for knowledge and happiness: "The soul alone with its flesh is mistress of the house in heaven, sits next to the eternal Master of the house, and is most like him. There eye reflects in eye, there spirit flows in spirit, there hand touches hand, there mouth speaks to mouth, and there heart greets heart. Thus does the Lord and Master honor the mistress at his side."[135]

Theologian Ulrike Wiethaus points out that Mechthild's choice of imagery here is reminiscent of Platonic and Augustinian metaphors for the three processes by which knowledge is attained: " 'eye of the mind,' 'eye of the body,' and 'eye of the soul.' " These, in turn, refer to the distinctly different operations of a rational, empirical, or spiritual approach, and "only the knowledge accessible to its particular radius of 'vision' or awareness" is valid for each approach.[136] When applied to Mechthild's epistemology this analysis helps explain how she accepts rational and empirical knowledge as valid sources of wisdom but still remains frustrated that her mind cannot fully grasp spiritual truths. Even after years of reflection she confesses that "I am surprised in my human way of thinking that my soul is so surprising."[137] Advocating this tripartite division of epistemology Mechthild reiterates throughout her work the basic premise that "one cannot grasp divine gifts with merely human understanding" and that "what one is able to see with the eyes of the flesh, hear with the ears of the flesh, and say with one's fleshly mouth is as utterly different from the open truth of the loving soul as light from wax is from the bright sun."[138] Whereas Hadewijch extols Queen Reason Mechthild acknowledges its value and function but places irrationality—that is, wonder—above rationality;[139] when identifying the three places God imparts knowledge to the soul (in the senses, the soul, and heaven), Mechthild portrays heaven simply as the place where "God raises up the soul in the pleasure of his will and suspends her there where she may take pleasure in the wonder of him."[140] She describes bliss as "the heights where I was so lost in wonder/That I could not find the boundaries of things."[141] She describes the knowledge gained in such non-rational, non-sensory ways[142] as coming to her through "the eyes of my soul" which saw "the indescribable order and recognized the inexpressible glory, the incomprehensible marvel, the special intimacy with separation, complete fulfillment, the greatest concentration in knowledge, bliss with interruption in proportion to the capacities of the faculties, unadulterated joy in the common union, and the ever vibrant life in eternity as it is now and ever shall be."[143] Mechthild communicates her understanding of the higher level of knowledge gained through non-abstract thought in part by repeatedly referring to secrecy. Statements such as "God gave them true knowledge in secret"; "God has secretly saved many a soul"[144]; "my eternal Godhead shall make you radiant with the secret wonder of my attractiveness"[145]; "how admirable do they proclaim my personal secrets"[146] are interspersed throughout. Whereas discussion of secret knowledge in Christian theology has often indicated an embrace of gnosticism, Mechthild uses it to elevate the status of the communication to indicate the private, individualized nature of that communication.

Because Mechthild argues that "the body receives its value from its relationship as brother of the Son,"[147] she places great emphasis on personal responsibility. The foundation for this is God's proclamation that "I give you free will in abundance."[148] She makes her case for individual accountability in a discussion concerning nature versus grace. She begins strongly: "Now listen here: Virtues are half gifts from God and half our own doing."[149] Early in her writing (Book One) she makes a statement that stirred controversy: "I must go from all things to God,/Who is my Father by nature";[150] when she writes Book Six some years later she addresses the issue at length:

> I said in one passage in this book that the Godhead is my Father by nature. You do not understand this, and say: "Everything that God has done with us is completely a matter of grace and not of nature." You are right, but I am right, too. Consider this analogy. No matter how good a person's eyes are, he can't see farther than a league. No matter how acute a person's mind is, he cannot grasp nonphysical things except with faith, and he gropes around like a blind man in the darkness. The loving soul that loves everything that God loves and hates everything that God hates has one eye that God has illuminated. With it she peers into the eternal Godhead and sees how the Godhead has labored in the soul with her nature. He formed her according to himself. He planted her in himself. With her, most of all among all creatures, he united himself.[151]

Granted, Mechthild admits that while "I shall certainly need his grace," works must accompany grace. Mechthild's Knowledge tells Lady Conscience, the pinnacle of love "is a love that toils. One cannot do without it if one waits to possess with God the highest honor."[152] Indeed, "to the degree that we perform good works here, God's holy toil shall light up and shine into our holy toil."[153]

Mechthild does not have a developed social or political ethical system beyond this principle of personal responsibility for one's own destiny, but she does occasionally draw out the implications of the principle in regards to behavior toward others, as in Book Five. There she presents seven situations from everyday life and provides guidelines for proper conduct. For example, her fourth lesson is "to be ready to help in secret. Explanation: that one search out and inquire where the lonely, sick, and prisoners are; and that one soothe them with words and bid them tell you their secret distress, so that you might be able to come to their aid."[154] Mechthild's commitment to her neighbor is rooted in and through Christ, who instructs Mechthild accordingly: "Those who know and love the nobility of my liberty cannot bear to love me only for my own sake. They must also love me in creatures."[155] Love of fellow creatures extends beyond the grave, though, and Mechthild informs us that "a person should pray very simply and with great intensity to God in heaven for the poor souls" in purgatory.[156] Her attitude toward Jews is less than generous, however, and she counsels her audience to keep their distance from them: "One should not observe their law. One should not reside with them. One should not spend the night in their dwelling. One should buy and sell from them without acting too friendly and without cunning or greed."[157]

Like Beatrice and Hadewijch, Mechthild's basic acceptance of the secular world and its courtly culture is demonstrated in her use of its imagery to communicate her thought. Lady Love (the vernacular *Minne*) is present throughout Mechthild's work, although perhaps it does not play as central a role as in the other two Vernacular Mothers' writings. The image allows her access to the meanings and symbols of two popular literary traditions, that of the spiritual Song of Songs, reinvigorated by Cistercians Bernard of Clairvaux and William of St. Thierry during the preceding century, and the secular *Minnesang,* Germany's courtly love literature. She does not limit herself only to the nuptial, spiritual, and erotic imagery of these traditions but burrows deep into their traditions for images that embraces all aspects of life. The tavern, wine cellar, and innkeeper are called upon to help her "become so drunk,"[158] and violent, vivid images of being "buffeted and beaten with severe blows," slapped, and "stripped of all things" are elements in her participation in Christ's passion.[159] She describes how Love has "hunted me, trapped me, bound me and wounded me," how God is "my softest pillow, my most lovely bed, my most intimate repose," and how she "cannot dance, Lord, unless you lead me."[160] She characterizes her visionary people graphically as "a virile vassal in battle," "a finely attired maiden," and "a professor learned in scriptures who actually is a fool."[161] In addition to tapping into the metaphors in these two literary traditions she utilizes themes within the philosophical tradition of neo-Platonism, specifically emanation and return. "Love above all loves, draw me back into you," she demands again and again, "that I might flow spotless into you," while God "pours forth from the flowing God into the poor, parched soul unceasingly with new knowledge."[162] Redemption is but a return to the primordial garden where "we were and still are able to return," because God still wants "to restore us with his own feet and his own hands so that we would have great oneness with him."[163] In almost every passage "angels return" or "she ascends in love and joyfully comes back again,"[164] or similar movement is noted. Imagery drawn from classical cosmic elementary theory also permeates her poetry and prose. Her spirit travels "between heaven and the air;" she "cannot rest;" she knows that "the kingdom of earth is, alas, quite changeable;" and that "a fish in water does not drown. A bird in the air does not plummet. Gold in fire does not perish."[165]

Mechthild's anthropology is of interest, both because it breaks with certain hagiographic and ascetic traditions of the near and distant past, and because it is part of a new tradition which becomes very popular within German female piety and among late medieval mystics, particularly Meister Eckhart.[166] Mechthild minimizes the duality of body and soul by emphasizing the role of the will. Sin does not arise from the body but from the will as the devil himself tells her about the origin of evil: "And the devil said: 'Nothing other than this person's own selfish will gave me this power.' "[167] Reciprocally goodness also originates in the will, as the Lord tells her: "With good will and with holy desire you can make good whatever you want."[168] The will is indeed the source of human power, for it carries with it the ability to determine its future, as again the devil explains when Mechthild asks him about a woman in her community: "The devil, under compulsion from God, said: 'No one can help her but her own free will, for God has given her the power to change. If she does that, I will be forced to scurry off.' "[169] Mechthild's faith in the will is supreme, for when

Mechthild confesses that "I have often been much saddened/That I could never turn good intentions into good works," God told her "that all good will shall/Out of abundance of a good life/Become blossoms of eternal bliss."[170] The body is essential, because of the access it offers to God through Jesus' humanity, but it is not the source of sin or sanctity. Mechthild addresses the issue directly, challenging "some people who are learned [who] say it is human to sin." To the contrary, sin comes "through our selfish free will that is much more harmful to us than our whole human nature. This is human: hunger, thirst, frost, pain, grief, temptation, sleep, weariness"—not sin. The ultimate proof she offers is Jesus' humanity, for "indeed, if sin were purely human, then he should have sinned, too. For he was true man in the flesh," and yet did not sin.[171] It is the will that chooses sin freely, not a body with no options. Again, Mechthild emphasizes that the body is far from superfluous. Its harnessing is necessary for salvation, but without the surrender of the will it can accomplish little. "The well-intentioned high and mighty in the world offer up to God their possessions and their alms," hoping that the physical road alone will bring them to heaven, but "religious people offer their flesh and blood in his service, offering up to God, above all things, their own will in obedience. That weighs more, that has greater value." Happiness rests in the will, because at all times people retain the "freedom of choice to go to heaven or to hell or to a long stay in purgatory."[172]

Marguerite Porete

The fourth Vernacular Mother we will discuss here is Marguerite Porete. She has rarely if ever been considered in intellectual histories, because, first, her authorship of *The Mirror of Simple Annihilated Souls and Those Who Only Remain In Will and Desire of Love* was established only in 1946;[173] second, the first critical edition was not published until 1965;[174] and, third, the work was condemned as heretical. Current scholarship is trying to make up for lost time, with six major editions or translations published since 1965.[175] Accessibility to the work has in turn led to analysis of Marguerite's thought and to the realization that she is indeed significant in Western intellectual history. That she possesses lyrical genius of expression is accepted by all critics, as well as the assessment that her language, with all its "annihilation," "oblivion," and dramatic imagery is, in Dronke's words, "provocative and deliberately shocking."[176] A good portion of the reason why she is important is because she wrote heresy[177] and did it in the vernacular.[178] Stock contends that the development of heresy during the high Middle Ages was an intellectual achievement of sorts, because at its heart it was the "free circulation of ideas," a necessary condition for "developing a skeptical scientifically oriented view of the world," so characteristic of modern Western culture.[179] The use of the vernacular was in and of itself an exercise in freedom from the ecclesiastical, monastic, and scholastic thought categories and strictures of Latin.[180] That Marguerite wrote vernacular heresy is thus noteworthy, a fact that Marguerite herself seems aware of:

> O my Lover, what will beguines say and religious types,
> When they hear the excellence of your divine song?

Beguines say I err, priests, clerics, and Preachers,
Augustinians, Carmelites, and the Friars Minor,
Because I wrote about the being of the one purified by Love.[181]

Little is known about Marguerite's life other than that she was "a beguine very capable of theology," as John of Paris describes her.[182] Born somewhere in Hainaut, her existence is first noted in the sources in 1296 when Guy II, bishop of Cambria, condemned a manuscript written by her, *A Mirror of Simple Souls,* and ordered it burned publicly and in her presence in Valenciennes. Undeterred by the commandment to cease disseminating her heretical ideas, she managed to save a copy (or copies) of her work and even tried to promote it by getting reputable scholars to approve it. She was accused of heresy again in 1306 or 1307, and in 1308 she was imprisoned and interrogated by Philip the Fair's confessor and papal inquisitor in Paris, William Humbert. Eventually twenty-one theological regents examined her book and unanimously declared fifteen of the articles to be heresy. Because this was her second offense she was executed on May 31, 1310, as a relapsed heretic. That she wrote her treatise in the vernacular may or may not be relevant to her fate; translator Ellen Babinsky believes it is.[183]

When we do turn to her work we see that she was quite deliberate about her intent and conscious of the challenge her ideas poised in the intellectual establishment. She wanted her probing to break new ground. She dared old-school intellectuals to meet her on her own terms and, in fact, declared to them that unless they did, her work would remain incomprehensible to them. She announces without apology:

You who would read this book,
If you indeed wish to grasp it,
Think about what you say,
For it is very difficult to comprehend;
Humility, who is the keeper of the treasury of Knowledge
And the mother of the other Virtues
Must overtake you.
Theologians and other clerks,
You will not have the intellect for it,
No matter how brilliant your abilities,
If you do not proceed humbly.

The key to understanding her thought is not the method of the scholastic but the willingness to "place all your fidelity/In those things which are given/By Love, illuminated through Faith./And thus you will understand this book."[184] She concludes with the same reminder:

There is not so great a cleric in the world who knows how to speak to you about [the secrets which you know].
"You have been at my table, and I have given you my feast,
And you are so very well taught," the Trinity tells her that "no one but you knows how to speak of it."[185]

In addition to implying her thought was beyond the comprehension of her contemporary intellectuals, Marguerite further antagonized the community by proclaiming that even given that the "Simple Souls," that is, the laity, may find her words "hard to grasp with their intellect" they will still "be able perchance to come to this stage."[186] She knows that through her unorthodox and bold analysis "I do not make Reason safe for them," the intellectual elite.[187] Her use of the terms "Church the Great" (*l'eglise la grande*) and "Church the Little" (*l'eglise la petite*) is also an overt attack on that community; the lesser church of clerics and hierarchy is "the Church who is governed by Reason, and not the Holy Church the Great, says Divine Love, who is governed by us."[188] In other words, her way is superior to theirs. This is the reason why she wrote the book. "As for you little ones of Holy Church, says Love, I have made this book for you, so that you might hear in order to be more worthy of the perfection of life and the being of peace," she explains, "which gift you will hear explained in this book through the Intellect of Love and following the questions of Reason."[189] What is most paradoxical, however, is that while Marguerite directly challenges academics, with their scholastic categories and disputational methodology,[190] central to her whole treatise is the dialectic of all and nothing, as, for instance, in this description of the essence of the soul as one that "possesses all and possesses nothing, she knows all and knows nothing, she wills all and wills nothing."[191] This, and the fact that Marguerite's presentation is in the format of a Boethian dialogue among Reason, Love, and the Soul, and that the work is filled with Pseudo-Dionysian themes, renders *Mirror* more philosophical in tone than the other Vernacular Mother writings. For example, Marguerite's adroit use of her philosophical and theological training is evident in the Soul's explanation for why she is a model of salvation for all humans:

> For the salvation of every creature is nothing other than the understanding of the goodness of God. Thus, since all will have understanding through me of the goodness of God, which goodness of God creates such goodness in me, this goodness will be understood by them through me. Nothing was ever understood if not my wretchedness. Since the divine goodness is understood by them through my wretchedness, and their salvation is nothing other than understanding the divine goodness, therefore I am the cause of the salvation of every creature, for the goodness of God is understood by them through me.... For the goodness of His pure nature is understood through the wretchedness of my crude nature. I have no possibility of possessing His goodness other than by reason of my wretchedness. This I can never lose His goodness, for I cannot lose my wretchedness, and in this point He has assured me about His goodness.[192]

The gist of *Mirror* is Marguerite's identification of seven stages that the soul travels through in its pursuit of perfection. She is preoccupied with the nature of the journeying soul and has much to say about the soul's faculties of ability, intellect, and understanding. Its "ability is the substance of the Soul; and the intellect is the operation of the soul; and the understanding is the height of the Soul; and such understanding is from substance and from intellect," thus mirroring the Trinity.[193] Likewise, Marguerite's analysis of knowledge is trinitarian: to know (*savoir*), to perceive (*entendre*), and to understand (*connaître*).[194] Reason begins the soul's journey, but its ability is limited; reason proclaims to Love "that none will grasp this book with my intellect unless they grasp it by the virtue of Faith, and by the power of Love, who are my mistresses."[195]

Marguerite's treatment of the will, though, is probably the most controversial, for she renders it impassive and non-contributory in pursuit of perfection.[196] This, in turn, led to bypassing the ministry of the sacramental church, for a person dependent wholly on grace is not in need of works. The perfect soul is one which "neither desires nor despises poverty nor tribulation, neither Mass nor sermon, neither fast nor prayers, and gives to Nature all that is necessary." Marguerite is so confident in the power of Love that she claims that a soul "so well ordered through the transformation by unity of Love, to whom the will of this Soul is conjoined" would never demand anything "which is prohibited."[197] The soul absent a will is most noble. She summarizes her analysis most pointedly in Chapter Five:

1. A Soul
2. who is saved by faith without works
3. who is only in love
4. who does nothing for God
5. who leaves nothing to do for God
6. to whom nothing can be taught
7. from whom nothing can be taken
8. nor given
9. and who possesses no will.[198]

Despite protests from Church the Little which demands to know "what [does she will] for God's sake?" Love answers again and again, "Nothing, says Love, she wills nothing."[199] Marguerite reinforces this annihilation of will within the annihilation of the soul by repeatedly emphasizing the lack of willful motivation in goodness. The Soul "has given all freely without a why;" "one has the why within him;" and the Trinity "wills the return of His beloved nakedly and freely, without a why for her sake."[200] Such absence of motivation was present in the soul's pre-creation stage of union with God, and a return to that stage is a return to union with God: "Now He possesses [the will] without a why in the same way that He possessed it before she was made a lady by it."[201]

While Marguerite's thought shares many characteristics with her fellow Vernacular Mothers, there are striking differences, too. Beatrice, Hadewijch, and Mechthild wrote as visionaries; Marguerite does not. Her mysticism is more speculative than theirs, and much more apophatic and negative. While all four mothers are intent upon addressing the conflicts brought to light in the dialectic of all and nothing, Marguerite is the more extreme in her conclusions. Hadewijch and Mechthild believe perfection is through the Incarnation,[202] but Marguerite bypasses the Incarnation and humanity with all its sufferings and works as a way to happiness. Marguerite also confronted her contemporaries and their intellectual edifices more than Beatrice, Hadewijch, and Mechthild did, and this may be the reason why her ending is so difference from the other women. Regardless of her condemnation, though, her thought exerted influence on future generations, and her literary skills still impress today's readers.

5

Scholastics, Mystics, and Secondary Intellectuals

When scholars try to evaluate the merits of particular works in intellectual history it is helpful to remember the goal of such history. That goal may be expressed in various ways and with innumerable different emphases, but ultimately the goal is simply to discover those elements in the past that contribute to the making of that society's intellectual culture. The easiest path to follow in so doing is to identify and assess those writings that deal explicitly with intellectual themes. This explains the dominance of philosophy in intellectual histories. Philosophy confronts rational and speculative thought head-on; there is no mistaking its relationship to intellectual history. We have repeatedly seen that women rarely approached intellectual matters in the same manner that men did and that they did not often explicitly or self-consciously engage in speculative thought. For too long this lack of direct philosophical engagement has contributed to scholarly neglect of women's intellectual contributions. This need not be, and thus we ask here, along with Dorothy Koenigsberger, why the historical contributions of any group should "be confined only to an assessment of the self-conscious goals or activities of that group."[1] It may be that the way women's ideas are presented accounts for the greatest difference between women's intellectual contributions and men's. Medieval women intellectuals present their thoughts overwhelmingly through description and narration. They rely more on the authority of their personal experiences and their imagination than on the authority of past masters. This too has contributed to scholarly neglect of women's thought, for given Western historians' long tradition of favoring reason over imagination,[2] it is not surprising to see women's experiential, imaginative approaches to issues not fully appreciated. Medieval male intellectuals overwhelmingly present their thought in philosophical terms and methods, and since intellectual historians have traditionally approached their subjects in the same manner, it is easy to see why men's writings dominate intellectual history to the point of virtual exclusion of women's. For all these differences, however, when the two groups are carefully analyzed they are actually closer in substance than often assumed. At their extreme expressions, men and women intellectuals may appear to have little in common, but there are also men and women intellectuals in between the extremes who share many characteristics. By briefly comparing the two moderate groups before proceeding further, we will be able to see that women's thought, particularly their mysticism, has much in common with major male writers whose thought we readily include in intellectual history. It will also reinforce the chief thesis of this study that women's intellectual contributions were real and substantive. Women's role in the development of Western intellectual tradition differs to some degree from men's but is just as essential.

Bonaventure and the Mystics

Even though we all know that medieval intellectual thought consists of more than Thomistic and Aristotelian philosophy, some stereotypes are harder to exterminate than others. When the Vernacular Mothers are compared to members of the Thomistic school there appears at first sight to be little or no overlap. When the Vernacular Mothers are studied alongside neoplatonic scholars, however, their similarities are more easily identified. It is especially true that when the Mothers are studied within the context of the Franciscan school and its chief spokeman, Bonaventure, more overlap appears.

Born in Tuscany in 1221 just as Francis of Assisi's group of mendicants were sweeping across Italy, Bonaventure (John of Fidanza) joined the Franciscans, studied at Paris under Alexander of Hales, befriended Thomas Aquinas, and by 1257 was named General of the Franciscans. His thought, articulated in three principal works—*Commentaries in Four Books on the Sentences of Peter Lombard, Breviloquium,* and *Itinerarium mentis in Deum* (*The Mind's Road to God*)—is representative of medieval thought in general, because Bonaventure includes all the major trends of the thirteenth-century world in his work. He embraces Plato, Augustine, and the neoplatonists, but at the same time he engages in Aristotelian debates and problems such as the eternity of the world and the Averroist doctrine of the oneness of humanity's intellect.[3] While he claims that "I do not intend to put forth new opinions, but to renew commonly held and approved ones,"[4] he often falls short of that intention. At first glance Bonaventure presents us with a paradox, if not a contradiction. He claims to offer no new opinions, but he does. He is an avowed Augustinian thinker, yet he is heavily influenced by Aristotle. He immerses himself in philosophy, explicitly discusses philosophical issues, and uses traditional philosophical methods to argue his point, but at all times he is "first and foremost a theologian."[5] He is also a mystic who maintains that truth is accessible through reason as well as revelation. Rather than being negative factors, however, these opposing stances render Bonaventure's thought more representative than Thomas' because of their inclusive nature. Philosophical historian Julián Marías argues that while the study of Thomas is absolutely essential to our knowledge of medieval scholasticism, study of Bonaventure is as essential to our comprehension of "the entire current of medieval speculation."[6] I concur and also believe that when we review Bonaventure's main themes it is easier for us to appreciate where and why women's intellectual contributions fit into medieval speculation.

At the heart of Bonaventure's thought is a Franciscan worldview, which, in turn, is a conception of life developed, promoted, and adopted by various vita apostolica groups during the eleventh and twelfth centuries. It is a worldview that reveres nature and "earthly things" as created, in Bonaventure's words, "after the fashion of an imprint [*vestigium*]," and humans "as a vestige of the Creator" created *imago Dei.*[7] It is a sacramentalized world where the humanity of the Word shares equally with the Word's divinity. Key to these apostolic movements was the belief that, in Bonaventure's words, the Creator "produced creatures bearing not only the nature of His *vestige* but also of His *image* so that through knowledge and love, they might be united to Him."[8] *Imitatio Christi* became the rallying call for people who, as *imago Dei,* believed only imitation of Christ would save the world, their neighbors, and themselves. The next step was the demand for church reform, the formulation of new spiritualities and pietistic devotions, and the establishment of new religious orders that encapsulated this ideal. Beatrice, Hadewijch, Mechthild, and Marguerite were each beguines—religious women self-consciously dedicated to the vita apostolica through the imitation of Christ as *imago Dei.* With innovation came the predicable problems of adjustment to change, and many intellectuals responded to the dilemma by reformulating the ideology of the movement philosophically for greater scrutiny among the intellectuals. Others responded by popularizing it, particularly among the laity.[9] In varying degrees through diverse methods Bonaventure and the Vernacular Mothers did both. For example, the most compatible philosophy in the medieval world with Christian doctrine of *imago Dei* was platonism and neoplatonism. We have seen the neoplatonism of the Vernacular Mothers; Bonaventure was also a platonist. Bonaventure wrote *Collationes in Hexaemeron* (*Conferences in the Hexaemeron*) as a structured attack on the logic of Aristotle's own attack on Platonic ideas "in his *Ethics* where he says that the highest good cannot be an *Idea.* His arguments do not hold."[10] His intended audience was scholarly, and his method and presentation was scholastic. The same was true of his commentary on Peter Lombard's *Sentences.* Here he tried to prove Aristotle's and Averroes' opinion that the world was eternal was false by using not faith nor revelation but reason to defend his position. He presented "a demonstrative argument" which exposed "the absurdity consequent" of "Aristotle's arguments based on the character of the world itself."[11]

On the other hand, *The Mind's Road to God,* Bonaventure's interpretation of Francis of Assisi's vision at Monte Alvernia, is more descriptive and written with a wider and somewhat different audience in mind. Here Bonaventure relies on Pseudo-Dionysius for structure and philosophical framework for his presentation and reveals his mystical side; philosophy is, after all, at its core *itinerarium mentis in Deum.* This journey to God can begin in the discovery of God through nature, through the *imago Dei* in our souls, or directly through mystical union in "the apex of the mind."[12] In *Retracing the Arts to Theology,* another important work, Bonaventure once again uses scholastic terminology and methodology, but his message is the same as that found in *The Mind's Road,* that "the manifold Wisdom of God, which is clearly revealed in Sacred Scripture, lies hidden in all knowledge and in all nature." The sincere person seeking the Wisdom of God takes "advantage of all sciences" and "makes use of illustrations and terms pertaining to every branch of knowledge."[13] This is because God is "the source of all illumination." Indeed, his is "that Fount of light from which the generous flow of manifold rays issue."[14] Not only should all branches of knowledge be exploited but all kinds of knowledge also. "Indeed, every sense seeks its proper sensible with longing, finds it with delight, and seeks it again without ceasing," Bonaventure writes in a vein reminiscent of Beatrice of Nazareth. "In the same way, our spiritual senses must seek longingly, find joyfully, and seek again without ceasing the beautiful, the harmonious, the fragrant, the sweet, or the delightful to the touch. Behold how the Divine Wisdom lies hidden in sense perception and how wonderful is the contemplation of the five spiritual senses in the light of their conformity to the senses of the body."[15]

When we compare these aspects of Bonaventure's thought with the Vernacular Mothers we see how much they have in common. Beatrice's underlying message, as well as her literary style, of "seeking, entreating, learning, gaining and keeping"[16] is the same as Bonaventure's longing, seeking, and finding; both believe that humans must actively participate in their own salvation and use grammatical structure to communicate that activity. Bonaventure goes to great length to defend the existence of transcendental Ideas; Marguerite Porete dies defending them, and Hadewijch talks of the "One," "Countenance," "that terrifying Being," and "the Essence."[17] In other places Hadewijch allegorizes the platonic ideals in order to analyze them at length, as in her vision where Queen Reason is accompanied by Holy Fear, Discernment, and Wisdom.[18] In her letters Hadewijch adapts a more explicitly philosophical tone, as, for instance, in her exposé on the Trinity. "I have understood all diversity in the pure Unity," she writes. "God is manifold in unity, and he is onefold in manifoldness," and this the soul sees; "It sees a truth—Subsistent, Effusive, Total—which is God himself in eternity."[19] Like Bonaventure, Hadewijch adjusts her vocabulary and style to her audience and subject matter. "He who wishes to understand and know what God is in his name and in his Essence," she instructs her directees in a more explicit manner than that found in her poetry.[20] "Give reason its time, and always observe where you heed it too little and where enough," she advises.[21] Marguerite tries to do both and succeeds. She deals with philosophical realities directly and then addresses the laity. "Now, Love, says Reason, you have condescended to our prayer, that is, to have declared the things said above for the Actives and Contemplatives," Marguerite writes immediately after a prolonged discussion to answer Reason's questions on the human will, but now "I pray again that you declare them for the sake of the common folk, of whom some will be able perchance to come to this stage, for there are several double words which are hard to grasp with their intellect."[22]

Bonaventure emphasizes the role of the senses in the quest for spiritual knowledge and speaks with reverence about the body; Mechthild of Magdeburg tells us that Love "teach[es] the senses," "passes through the senses and storms the soul with all its might," and finally "dissolves through the soul into the senses. Then does the body gain its share, so that it is refined with respect to all things."[23] Beatrice does not speculate about the potential use of the senses in the pursuit of knowledge; she simply uses them. Hence, she describes the sensual experience of the fifth manner of love as the experience of feeling that "the veins are bursting, the blood spilling, the marrow withering, the bones softening, the heart burning, the throat parching, so that the body in its every part feels this inward heat, and this is the fever of love. Sometimes the soul feels that the whole body is transfixed."[24] Hadewijch, Beatrice, and Mechthild find God in earthly things, just as Bonaventure claimed. Beatrice and Mechthild contemplated the fish "swimming in the vast sea and resting in its deeps" and the bird "boldly mounting high in the sky" as they attempted to comprehend "the vastness and the depth and the unutterable richnesses of love."[25] Hadewijch seeks knowledge in the whole of nature. "News is spread by many tokens—/The birds, the flowers, the fields, the daylight—"[26] Hadewijch tells us in her poetry. Her insights into the nature of the human condition arise from her keen observation of the world around her. "When March begins, we see/All beings live again,/And all plants spring up/And in a short time turn green," she observes and then draws an analogy to the intellectual world: "It is the same with longing,/Particularly that of the true lover" of truth. "Moreover he cannot bear flowers and fruit/When the sun is absent—/That sun is veritable Love, who calls forth/Flowers and fruit from the mind."[27]

Bonaventure's writings are steeped in the neoplatonic themes of emanation and exemplarism, and we have already noted the presence of these themes in the Vernacular Mothers. The title of Mechthild's masterpiece, *The Flowing Light of the Godhead,* is but a more succinct summary of Bonaventure's statement concerning the flow of rays issuing forth from the Fount of light quoted above.[28] Marguerite's use of "mirror" in her title is based in *imago Dei* imagery, as is her use of iron "invested with fire which has lost its own semblance because the fire is stronger and thus transforms the iron into itself."[29] Beatrice begins her treatise with emanation and exemplarism. "There are seven manners of loving, which come down from the heights and go back again far above," she states in her opening sentence, and the first manner is a longing of the soul "to follow Him in holiness" because "it was made by its Creator, in His image and likeness, which the soul must love greatly and zealously preserve."[30] In analyzing the paradoxes of God's nature Hadewijch employs knowledge of the "emanation of his name" to know his nature and "his unique name in the properties of the Persons,"[31] while in her visions God tells her to "return again into your material being, and let your works blossom forth."[32] Mechthild echoes this principle, believing that a return is possible because even though "Adam's nature was broken and changed and his inheritance lost forever, God never gave up on Him. Hence we were and still are able to return."[33] Because "we receive these good works from God's holy humanity and perform them through the power of the Holy Spirit. Thus do our works and our life return to the Holy Trinity."[34] Mechthild also employs mirror imagery, using it to emphasize the same point Bonaventure makes, that God can be found in creation and in creatures. "A mirror was seen in heaven before the breast of each soul [and body]. In it shines the mirror of the Holy Trinity, giving truth and knowledge of all the virtues the body ever practiced and of all the gifts the soul had ever received on earth," Mechthild narrates. "From here the glorious reflection of each and every person shines forth back again into the sublime majesty from which it flowed forth."[35]

All the women agree with Bonaventure's belief, albeit in varying degrees of insistence and expression, that knowledge comes from more sources than simply revelation.[36] "He who wishes all things to be subject to him must himself be subject to his reason, above whatever he wills or whatever anyone else wills of him," Hadewijch instructs one of her directees. "For reason loves God on account of his sublimity, noble men because they are loved by God, and ignoble men because they are in want of Love."[37] As mystics, each of the women places ultimate value on unitive knowledge (usually expressed by *minne*), as does Bonaventure in *The Mind's Road to God,* but they also promote the use of reason in all matters, for, as Hadewijch says, "reason by its nature throws light on each of these points."[38] Mechthild analyzes the sources of knowledge thus: "The first is priestly wisdom and Christian teaching, as God revealed them" (Scripture); the second kind "comes from our natural faculties" (reason); and the third "comes from grace" (mysticism).[39] Marguerite places great emphasis on reason and personifies it as the mistress of the soul, but she too holds that unitive knowledge is superior. " 'This no one can grasp with my intellect,' says Reason, 'if he is not taught it by [Love] through your teaching.' " This pertains specifically to Marguerite's teaching, as well as knowledge in general. "Thus I say to all, that none will grasp this book with my intellect," Reason continues, "unless they grasp it by the virtue of Faith, and by the power of Love, who are my mistresses."[40] Marguerite considers this point to be so essential that she reiterates it in the Explicit preceding the prologue:

> Even Reason witnesses
> In the Thirteenth Chapter of this book,
> And with no shame about it,
> That Love and Faith make her live.[41]

All that being said, Marguerite's own writing is rigidly guarded and developed by reason; Babinsky reminds us that *Mirror* penetrates "the relation of the discursive and affective capacities of the soul" in an innovative, critical way.[42]

As important as these similarities arc, noting the significant differences between the women and most scholastic writers is also helpful in any assessment of the women's role in intellectual history. The differences in presentation are the most obvious and thus easiest to recognize. The men's is often systematic, dry, abstract, self-conscious in its analysis and use of logic, and is intended for only an elite, rather homogenous, educated group of men. The women's presentation is experiential, spirited, prosaic and poetic, lacking in self-awareness of its methodology, and is addressed to various groups: men, women, educated, uneducated, monastic, clerical, and lay. The former is written in Latin; the latter is often written in the vernacular. The men predominantly speculated about the abstract world; the women overwhelmingly described the visionary world. The men expanded the mental frontiers inherited from their predecessors; the women created new imaginary worlds for their descendents. Just as the intellectual life of the early modern period was energized, for example, by both aspects of Thomas More's rational contributions, his religious philosophy and his literary imagination, so too was medieval intellectual life informed by two different approaches. Indeed, Western culture has a long history of nurturing these two traditions, although, unfortunately, not a lengthy historiography of the same. Historians need no reminder of Western culture's love affair with the physical world and the solving of its mysteries. They also readily acknowledge that the modern scientific, experimental approach to the physical world, although it took advantage of the progress made in the ancient world, started in earnest during the high Middle Ages.[43] Historians are less likely to remember that Western culture has also been molded by dreamers, those individuals who create imagined ideals that inspire others to turn them into realities. The contributions of medieval scholastics are important in and of themselves, but when they are combined with the contributions of medieval mystics the resultant synthesis becomes invaluable. It is this synthesis that lays at the foundation of Western culture.

The importance of the visionary worlds described by these women in such captivating and enchanting literary forms can also be seen in the world of art. Much of the imagery of these narratives entered into societal imagination and became the standard visualization of things like the crucifixion and the nativity in ways similar to Dante's imagery entered permanently into societal consciousness. Sometimes a written description of a vision was simply made visual, as with a vision recorded in the *vita* of Clare of Montefalco of her acceptance of the sufferings of the crucifixion; in 1333 an artist painted the scene for a chapel dedicated to her.[44] At other times a woman's vision became the sum and substance of a new iconographic tradition, as did Birgitta of Sweden's bucolic narrative of the Nativity. "With [Mary] there was a very dignified old man; and with them they had both an ox and an ass. When they entered the cave, and after the ox and the ass had been tied to the manger, the old man went outside," Birgitta begins. While Joseph was modestly withdrawn from the scene, "in a moment and the twinkling of an eye, she gave birth to a Son" whom she "pressed to her breast, and with cheek and breast she warmed him with great joy and tender maternal compassion." When modesty permits, "the old man entered and prostrating on the earth, he adored him on bended knee, and wept for joy."[45] Birgitta's description of her emotional vision of Jesus' birth is one of the most influential descriptions in Western art, for it radically changed the Nativity representation. Fra Angelico, Niccolo di Tommaso, Turino Vanni, and Lorenzo Monaco soon were visually representing Birgitta's narrative in paintings that posterity has revered as masterpieces; Roger van der Weyden's *Bladelin altarpiece* is a singularly significant representation of Birgitta's vision.[46] That Birgitta's vision captures both the spiritual and the physical dignity of woman so impressively makes her imagery even more important in intellectual history, for it permanently popularized the theme in Western culture.[47]

Birgitta's vision of the crucifixion also influenced its depiction. Her imagery of Jesus' body being "supported by the nails with which his feet had been crucified" and "his fingers and hands and arms were now more extended than before" is found in the work of such artists as Matthias Grünewald, Jan van Eyck, Hans Membling, Albert Dürer, Titian, and El Greco. The depiction of the Pietà, one of the most beloved subjects in Western art, was likewise influenced by Birgitta's description of Jesus "all torn as he was and wounded and black and blue" being laid across Mary's knee, particularly within the Avignon School. Johann Sebastian Bach's *The Passion According to Saint John* follows Birgitta's *Revelations*.[48] Angela of Foligno's vision of "the image of the blessed crucified God and man" was also influential. Her expression is quite vivid and violent: "His blood flowed fresh and crimson as if the wounds had just recently been opened. Then she saw how the joints and tendons of his blessed body were torn and distended by the cruel stretching and pulling of his virginal limbs at the hands of those who had set upon him to kill him on the gibbet of the cross. The bones and sinews of his most holy body seemed completely torn out of their natural position;

and yet his skin was not broken."[49] Clare of Assisi, Hildegard of Bingen, Hadewijch, and Mechthild of Hackeborn all contributed to a new devotion to the Sacred Heart, and their vivid descriptions are still portrayed in modern illustrations.[50] Perhaps the most influential descriptions of the Sacred Heart and the sacred wounds come from Gertrude the Great of Helfta, who had "imprinted in the depth of my heart the adorable marks of Thy sacred Wounds, even as they are on Thy body" and had friends pray daily that God would "by Thy pierced Heart, pierce her heart with the arrow of Thy love, so that nothing earthly may remain therein."[51]

The imagery of Corpus Christi comes almost entirely from women responsible for the foundation of this devotion and of its extremely popular feast. Juliana of Mont-Cornillon received a vision of "the full moon in its splendour, yet with a little breach in its spherical body," symbolizing "the absence of a feast" honoring "the institution of the Sacrament of his Body and Blood." For some twenty years Juliana begged Christ to "release me, and give the task you have assigned me to great scholars shining with the light of knowledge," thus revealing an awareness of the existence of two influential groups within her society capable of shaping culture. At this point she believes visionaries are inferior to scholars, for while scholars "would know how to promote such a great affair," she "could not understand it, nor could I fulfill it."[52] Gradually she realizes the power of the visionary and not only accepts the task of promoting a new cultural phenomenon but also endured the abuse of people who opposed her and "called Christ's virgin a dreamer." Soon "the name 'Juliana the dreamer' was constantly slandered and maligned" and "she became a laughing-stock."[53] But the dreamer had her way, and within decades of her death the feast was formally established in 1261. Western drama owes much to the feast, for early in the fourteenth century (ca. 1335) the first Corpus Christi play was performed, and within years cycles of Corpus Christi plays were being produced by a variety of communal organizations throughout the continent and England.[54] These plays have long been recognized as being an essential part of the foundation of modern Western drama.

Intellectuals eventually constructed a whole new field of sacramental theology to explain the significance of the feast and to justify Juliana the dreamer's interpretation. When we remember that the Eucharist became, in Miri Rubin's words, "the central symbol of a culture"[55] and that the feast of Corpus Christi was the chief communal celebration of late medieval society, its visionary origins take on a new significance. All of this is not to argue that in any of these examples only dreamers construct visual, literate, or social culture. Rather, it is to emphasize the creative force and active role visionaries in general and women visionaries in particular played in the formation of Western intellectual traditions. The imagination is as much an activity of the mind[56] as is logical analysis. It is to society's advantage to have people who can master an entire field of knowledge and to have other people who can expand the frontier of that field by creating imaginary worlds where all things are possible. It is often the combination of logic and imagination that produces change and improvement in standards of living in the West. The plays, processions and town celebrations that were organized around the feast of Corpus Christi had to be produced by the more practical and pragmatic members of society before they were to prove successful. Successful they were, and that success is usually related to the degree to which the two approaches and groups collaborate.[57] One of the most admired achievements of Western culture is its development and application of science to the betterment of human existence, yet too infrequently is it acknowledged that Western science is a synthesis of these two approaches.

Secondary Intellectuals

When contemplating the magnitude of the differences between women and men intellectuals we are drawn to the realization that these differences sometimes existed because of an even more fundamental disparity between the two groups. Sometimes the groups fulfilled different functions in the intellectual world. The men most often functioned as the primary intellectuals in society, while the women did so much less frequently. More usually they functioned as secondary or "middle class" intellectuals who bridged the gap between the masses and the intellectual elite. They were the ones who popularized complex intellectual developments by making them simpler and thus more accessible. The vernacular helped the women accomplish the latter, while their own genius many times provided the means for the former. Obviously, not all intellectual endeavors are pursued by geniuses, male or female, and the medieval world provided plenty of opportunity for lesser skilled intellectuals. Henry of Ghent, revered thirteenth-century master at the University of Paris, talked about "rural intellectuals and preachers who frequently preached and taught while ignorant of the basis for their rational principles but still taught with confidence, because they knew that what they taught had been found acceptable by the masters."[58] In recent years sociologists and historians have renewed interest in this class, particularly during the late Middle Ages,[59] but scholars have been amiss in not recognizing how apt this category is for women. Many women flourished as secondary intellectuals after scholasticism crested in the high Middle Ages, and their contributions are critical to the way the West developed politically and socially, as well as intellectually. They provided the groundwork for a more democratized intellectual tradition upon which the West wrote a new chapter in human freedom. Key to Western people desiring, accepting, and preserving a sense of equality among themselves was their participation in a reservoir of ideas that fostered that sense. If Western intellectuals had remained an elite clique inhabiting the stratosphere, its intellectual traditions would have developed quite differently. It is at this pivotal point in the Middle Ages that the West began to break down the exclusionary barriers that had separated intellectuals from the larger population since the time of the ancient Greeks. This was especially true among those who intellectualized religious issues; the spiritual elite were no longer the chief articulators of doctrine. A new appreciation for "learned ignorance" among the masses was common by the fourteenth century.[60] The spread of literacy, the advent of the written vernacular, and then the transformation of the complex into the simple and its dissemination in the vernacular to the new literary classes are very important factors responsible for the particular shape Western intellectual history took. Women participated in all stages of that development.

Angela of Foligno (1248–1309) is an example of this type of intellectual. The author of the epilogue to her *Instructions* (part two of *The Book of Blessed Angela of*

Foligno, the first part being *Memorial*) describes her as "a woman of lay state, who was bound to worldly obligations, a husband and sons, possessions and wealth, who was unlearned and frail."[61] She suffered the loss of her family when they died, for reasons unknown to us, around 1288. Three years later she became a Franciscan tertiary. Despite the claim that she was uneducated, she certainly was educated to a degree by modern standards. In *Instructions* she mentions that she has "not been able to write to you or to any others" because of her other duties, and that, moreover, "I do not see that my letters or my words should or could console you."[62] These comments indicate that she knew how to read and write. She did not, however, write *Book* herself but dictated it to her confessor, "a certain trustworthy Friar Minor" who also calls himself "brother scribe."[63] The scribe claims that he was most scrupulous about being faithful to Angela's narrative. "I wrote everything as well as I could, while she was present, not adding anything of my own from the beginning to the end," and then he even "requested Christ's faithful one to beseech God and pray that if I had written anything false or superfluous he would, in his mercy, reveal it and show it to her, so that we would both know the truth from God himself."[64] Scholarly opinion varies concerning how successful the friar was in presenting only Angela's thought, but the general consensus is that Angela is the primary author of *Book.*[65] Her contemporaries thought highly of her and often traveled far and wide to hear her expound her teachings and gain her spiritual guidance. Ubertino of Casale, the leader of the radical wing of the Franciscans, the Spiritualists, considered her his spiritual mother who "changed the whole tenor of my life;[66] Giovanni Targarioni Olorini (d. 1348) calls her "a tertiary of great sanctity and fame";[67] and the reform-minded branch of the Franciscans, the Observants, revered her as one of their saints.[68] By the sixteenth century she was an established authority, with her manuscript circulating in the Low Countries, France, Germany, Italy, and Spain. In Spain Angela enjoyed particular attention; Cardinal Jimenez de Cisneros Ximenes ordered it printed in Latin in 1505 and in Spanish in 1510 as part of his reform program.[69] Her writing exerted much influence upon the great Carmelite women of that century. Teresa of Avila was inspired by it, and María de San José acknowledged her debt to Angela's thought and claimed Angela, along with other women saints, helped posterity learn about the accomplishments of "so many sainted women."[70] In the seventeenth century the great editor of hagiography, J. Bollandus, included a contemporary's appellation for Angela, "the teacher of theologians," a variation of the sentiments of the author of *Instructions*' epilogue: "It is not against the order of providence that God, to men's shame, made a woman a teacher—and one that to my knowledge has no match on earth."[71]

Modern accolades for Angela seem to increase as her work is disseminated more widely. She belongs in many categories rarely represented in intellectual history. As a non-noble, informally educated, lay woman pursuing a life of service to the poor, Angela fits well into our group of secondary intellectuals. As Colish summarizes, this "leading Franciscan mystic of the late thirteenth and early fourteenth centuries" is an excellent example of "how relatively unlearned people, including women, could gain a good theological education" and overcome all "impediments to [the] acquisition of considerable religious authority as well as religious knowledge."[72] She used this authority and knowledge to communicate to her world and posterity a construct of unique dimensions.[73] If Bonaventure's task was to philosophize the Franciscan ideology, Angela's was to popularize it. "I cannot think of any saint who demonstrates to me more remarkably than [Francis of Assisi] did the way found in the Book of Life," Angela proclaimed, "and because he set himself with such total determination to follow this path he was filled to overflowing with the highest wisdom." Angela tells us that the first lesson Francis teaches us "is to recollect ourselves in God," a theme upon which Angela elaborates at length.[74] Self-knowledge is the beginning of all knowledge and leads to ultimate truth. "Knowledge of God presupposes knowledge of self," she reminds us, and only after this is attained does "one begin[s] to attain knowledge of God"[75] or know God in truth. "By 'to know God in truth' I mean to know him not just from the externals—such as the tone conveyed by writing, words, signs, images, or resemblances to anything created—for this way of knowing something according to the way we speak about it gives a kind of simple knowledge about God. To know God in truth is to know him as he is in himself, to understand his worth, beauty, sweetness, sublimity, power, and goodness," she continues, "for the way in which a wise person knows something in truth differs from the way a simple person knows only the appearance of truth." Addressing a non-academic audience, Angela uses the following analogy to explain: "To illustrate this, perhaps the following example or comparison might be useful. Suppose two florins, one of gold and one of lead, were lying in the road. A simple person might pick up the gold florin because it was beautiful and shiny, but would not know about the value of gold. The wise person, knowing the truth about gold and lead, would avidly go for the gold florin and pay little attention to the lead one. Similarly, the soul knowing God in truth, is aware and understands him as good, and not only good, but as the supreme and perfect Good."[76]

The content of Angela's epistemological framework is in basic agreement with Bonaventure's presentation in his mystical work, *The Mind's Road to God,* but how differently he presents it. His is systematic and structured. "Enter then into yourselves and see, for your mind loves itself most fervently," Bonaventure writes, but the mind could not do so "unless it knew itself." Self-knowledge comes from the operation of three powers: that of memory for "retention and representation, not only of things present, corporeal, and temporal, but also of past and future things, simple and eternal;" that of the intellect which deals "with the meaning of terms, prepositions, and inferences;" and that of choice "in deliberation, judgment, and desire."[77] According to Bonaventure, this trinity of powers represents the three persons of the Trinity: "The first is divided into metaphysics, mathematics, and physics. The first concerns the essences of things; the second, numbers and figures; the third, natures, powers, and extensive operations. Therefore the first leads to the First Principle, the Father; the second, to His image, the Son; the third, to the gift of the Holy Spirit."[78]

This kind of structure is not present in Angela's work. As a secondary intellectual, though, Angela occasionally talks in the language more common to Bonaventure's formal world of speculation. Employing typical scholastic terminology, she discusses how "every creature has its being from the one who is the supreme Being; how all things and all that exists come to be through the supreme Being; how God is indeed the only one who has being, and that nothing has being unless it comes from him."[79] On the other hand, Bonaventure's writing sometimes displays the characteristics found more frequently in the visionary world of personal experience.[80] Certainly, there is no mistaking the fact that Angela sees her goal to be the same as the scholastics: to find God in truth. To seek God is identical to seeking the truth, because "once the soul is perfectly united to God, it is placed in the seat of truth, for truth is the seat of the soul." Union with God actually increases the soul's capacity for truth, since "God even expands the soul so that it may hold all that he wishes to place in it. The soul then sees the One who is, and it sees that all else is nothing except insofar as it takes its being from him."[81] In many ways she was as confident in her authority as the scholastics were in theirs. Toward the end of her life she reflected on that vocation thus: "I have nothing to do with what I wish to say, for all of it is from God. For it pleased the divine goodness to place in my care, under my solicitude, all his sons and daughters who are in the world, who are on this side of the sea or beyond it. I have kept them in my care," but now, as death approached her vocation was ending, so "I now place them once again in your hands."[82] Elsewhere she writes confidently: "I would have scruples about divulging what I am telling you, were it not for words in which I was told that the more I speak and continue to speak about what is happening to me, the more it will remain with me."[83] However, sometimes she was frustrated by the limitations of the human condition in general and could "in no way find words to express any of this, for it is totally beyond our human capacities to do so."[84] Throughout *Book,* though, it is clear that Angela believes her vocation to be that of the herald of Franciscan ideology to the people.

Angela of Foligno is but one of the more well-known medieval intellectuals who functioned as intermediaries between the university and the people. Umiltà of Faenza (1226–1310) is less famous, but her profile and accomplishments are remarkably similar to Angela's. Married and the mother of several daughters, she received no formal education while young. After her children died and her husband was struck with a debilitating illness, she entered a Vallombrosan monastery where she had access to books. Her biographer tells us that when Umiltà entered the community "she was still illiterate." Despite this fact when she was called upon to read in the refectory she read so well "that she excited the entire convent, who came running to see this spectacle, marveling in wonderment." Apparently her gift disappeared at the conclusion of the reading, and so "from that time on, the convent took care to teach her letters—which she did learn—by getting a woman teacher for her."[85] When she began to write, then, she was literate, but she still chose occasionally to have "with her a nun who was writing down in short form what she was dictating to her—that is, a book about angels, about the soul, and of many very good sayings."[86] Of all her works, only nine prosaic sermons and a few poetic offices survived. The first three sermons are of note, for her intention was to present doctrinal matters in an accessible way. The second sermon, for instance, is *Treatise of the Court of Paradise,* in which she discusses angels "in nine orders, and each order is named for its power, but they also have names among themselves, and each has a personal name of great beauty."[87]

Much of her instruction, though, was oral and has not been preserved. Soon after joining the order of St. Clare Umiltà decided to live the life of a recluse in a "cell next to the church" with "another window facing outside, where she might receive alms and freely give satisfaction to those who had come to see her."[88] After twelve years of providing such informal instruction from her cell, she was called upon to leave her solitude and establish a Benedictine monastery in Malta. Here "very many magnates put their daughters and wives under her direction, and she taught than [*sic*] to observe the aforesaid rule to the very letter."[89]

Umiltà was not unique in her teaching role or in her role as intermediary. As recent scholarship has pointed out, recluses occupied a position "on the borderline"[90] between clergy and laity and between the literate and the illiterate. This thesis is but an expansion of insights Grundmann offered decades ago on the erosion during the twelfth and thirteenth centuries of the distinction between written clerical culture and oral lay culture.[91] Lay recluses became transitional figures between the two cultures, in part because of the high esteem society held the eremitic life and in part because reading was expected of them. Since they lived in solitude, this meant they had to read themselves and not be read to. "Often, beloved sisters, you ought to pray less so as to read more. Reading is good prayer," the author of *Ancrene Wisse*, a rule for women recluses, "so you should read earnestly and long."[92] Most recluses could read in the vernacular, and they formed a ready audience for the vernacular religious literature which soon appeared throughout the West. Aelred of Rievaulx's letter of advice to his recluse sister and "for the young girls who, on your advice, are eager to embrace a life like yours," is typical in its expectations of how the recluse should spend the day. It must be filled with "hours of manual labor, reading, and prayer;" after Vespers "she should quietly read a little of the *Lives of the Fathers,* of their rules, or of their miracles."[93] We have already noted how women often pioneered in the creation of vernacular religious literature; we note here that women also contributed to the process by providing the audience and the demand for such writing.

Women recluses also aided in the transition to a lay literate culture by acting as teachers. Not all recluses were educated; in the introduction to *Ancrene Wisse* the author comments on the need for flexible rules for recluses because of their individual differences: "One is learned, another not and must work more and say her prayers in another way."[94] It was the educated women recluses' task, therefore, to teach those who were uneducated. Thomas Hales sent a poem to a woman recluse who requested one in which he adds this reminder: "Maiden, I send you this poem open and unsealed; I ask you to unroll it and learn it all by heart so that you should become thoroughly familiar with it and teach it well to other maidens."[95] It was also expected that the recluse make herself available at least to some degree to the village at the anchorhold's window for counseling and being counseled. The temptation to always assume the role of teacher in these situations apparently was great, for the author of *Ancrene Wisse* warns against it. "To a priest say first the '*I will confess,*' and then, after the 'Blessed is he' which he ought to say, listen to his words and keep completely quiet—so that when he parts from you he knows neither good nor evil of you, nor knows whether to blame or praise you. Someone, perhaps, is so learned or so wise in speaking that she wants him who sits and speaks with her to know it, and pays him back word for word. And she who should be an anchoress becomes a teacher, and teaches him who has come to teach her. She wants to recognized and known at once for her talk among the wise."[96]

From this admonition against teaching the wrong people we can extrapolate that teaching the appropriate people was acceptable. While there exists a strong tradition within Western Christianity in theory and in fact that frowns upon women teachers, by the high Middle Ages there developed a new attitude toward women's participation in religious education. The right to proclaim scripture in public and to interpret it was still the exclusive domain of the clergy, but by the thirteenth century many intellectuals were arguing for the limited inclusion of women in the education field. Eustache of Arras believed that the practices of early Christian women saints like Mary Magdalene and Catherine of Alexandria bore witness to the presence of a teaching ministry among women in primitive Christianity, while Robert of Sorbon defended the right of women to teach at home what had been taught them in public.[97] Jacques de Vitry, probably the most perceptive male observer of female matters in the thirteenth century, actively encouraged women, especially widows, to become their children's chief educator.[98] The role mothers played in the education of the social elite was accentuated often in their *vitae*; Eadmer wrote of Anselm of Bec's early instruction under his mother's tutelage, as did Guibert of Nogent write in his autobiography: "Put, therefore, to my book, I had learnt the alphabet, but hardly yet to join letters to syllables, when my good mother, eager for my instruction, managed to pass me on to grammar."[99] Royal women were frequently in charge of their son's education. For example, Joinville, Louis IX's biographer, and Charles of Anjou, Louis' brother, both testify to the education Louis received from the hands of Blanche of Castile, his mother. "Child that he was," Joinville reports, "she made him recite all the Hours, and listen to sermons on days of high festival."[100] Overall, the thirteenth century was a time when the complementary roles of women and men in education were more honestly acknowledged than in the past.[101]

Another comment should be made concerning the recluse's role in intellectual history, and that concerns the debate over authorship of anchoritic literature. Much of the extant literature is anonymous and has traditionally been assumed to be written by men. Modern scholars now question that assumption, although without offering any conclusive evidence for female authorship. W. Meredith Thompson believes it possible that the *Wooing of Our Lord* might have been written by a woman recluse but provides no definitive argument to defend the thesis.[102] Still, one must remember in regards to this genre, as in many others, that the assumption of male authorship is only that, an assumption. The reverse sentiment and a warning is colorfully expressed by Bella Millett thus: "But it does not necessarily follow from this that we are entitled to people the gaps in our knowledge with a phantom army of women writers."[103] Whether women wrote vernacular anchoritic literature or not does not diminish the emphasis here, which is on the fact that women as readers of this genre and as intermediaries between an oral lay culture and a written clerical culture made an important contribution in the intellectual history of the West.

Clare of Assisi, often discussed only in the shadows of Francis of Assisi, made a profound contribution of her own as a secondary intellectual when she promoted a sophisticated concept of witness and incorporated it into the Franciscan movement. Witness is a sophisticated concept that demands an understanding of communication, social roles, and personal rights and responsibilities. Deeply embedded in Scripture, witness obligates the individual to communicate to the larger society in a recognizable form, be it through word or example. From Yahweh's command to Israel to be witnesses (Is 43:9–13) to Jesus' last words to the apostles before ascending to heaven "to be my witnesses in Jerusalem, throughout Judea and Samaria, yes, even to the ends of the earth" (Acts 1:8), witness played an essential role in early Christianity but was not reflected upon or analyzed until the high Middle Ages by the founders of the new religious orders of the day.[104] Peter Damian, arguably the most influential thinker of the eleventh century,[105] insisted witness was at the core of the vita apostolica[106] and became the spokesman *par excellence* for the concept. Clare agreed with Damian's understanding of the centrality of witness, and, although we have few extant writings of Clare's, the little we have provide evidence of her grasp of the concept and her promotion of it to her contemporaries.

Clare comprehended its essence and eagerly became a relay in communication of that essence between intellectual elite audiences and less cerebral audiences. Her language is simple and filled with familiar imagery that, as Verger states, allowed the people "to hear an echo, though much diminished, of the scholarly culture of their time and to experience in their everyday lives some repercussions of the practical application."[107] Thus, Clare reminds her women of their basic obligation to bear witness and then explains it further: "For the Lord himself not only has set us as an example and mirror for others, but also for our [own] sisters whom the Lord has called to our life, so that they in turn will be a mirror and example to those living in the world. Since, therefore, the Lord has called us to such great things, that those who are to be models and mirrors for others may behold themselves in us, we are truly bound to bless and praise the Lord."[108] It was Clare's practical application of the concept, however, that had extensive influence, for by insisting that the Second Order of Franciscans bear witness to society even from within their enclosure, she fostered a reconciliation that becomes pivotal in Western society's development of its own culture. That reconciliation is between the needs of the individual and the needs of the community. Clare is arguing here that individual happiness is wholly dependent upon the individual's fulfillment of its obligations to society. These two concepts of individualism and community has a long and twisted history in Western thought, and each society since the Middle Ages has had to discover on its own the relationship between the two. Clare was in the forefront of helping thirteenth-century society do just that.

One of the most overlooked medieval women who completed the tasks of the intermediary intellectual for her society was Herrad of Hohenburg (ca. 1130–1195), abbess of the monastery of Mont-Sainte-Odile in Hohenburg. Little is known about her early life, other than that she received her basic education at Admont, a monastery known throughout the Empire as a renowned center of learning for women. While still young Herrad entered Hohenburg, whose reputation for intellectual culture was dramatically increasing during the capable reign of Abbess Relinda. In 1176 Herrad succeeded Relinda.[109] Herrad's gift to intellectual history came chiefly in the form of an encyclopedic work which she compiled and entitled *Hortus deliciarum* (*Garden of Delights*). In all likelihood the project was initiated under Relinda, for in two instances Relinda and Herrad are artistically portrayed together. In a stone slab still in place at Mont-Sainte-Odile the two women are commemorated along with the monastery's founding abbess, Odilia, and St. Leodegarius. *Hortus deliciarum* itself contains an illuminated miniature of the foundation of the monastery and of the community in which the two women are closely associated.[110] Over the head of Herrad is the following inscription: "Herrad, installed as Abbess of the convent of Hohenburg after Rilindis, who had instructed her by her lessons and examples."[111] While this is not conclusive proof that Relinda was actively involved in the project, it does hint at some sort of influence or even collaboration between the two.[112] There is no doubt, however, that it was Herrad's perceptive intellect that guided the project through its stages to completion.

It was an ambitious undertaking, and it succeeded on all levels. Its original purpose was to provide a single source for the education of the women in the community. Herrad states her purpose thus: "Herrad, who through the grace of God is abbess of the Church of the Hohenburg, here addresses the sweet maidens of Christ who are working as though in the vineyard of the Lord; may He grant grace and glory unto them—I was thinking of your happiness when like a bee guided by the inspiring God I drew from many flowers of sacred and philosophic writing this book called the *Garden of Delights;* and I have put it together to the praise of Christ and the Church, and to your enjoyment, as though into a sweet honeycomb. Therefore you must diligently seek your salvation in it and strengthen your weary spirit with its sweet honey drops."[113] To that end Herrad selected, edited, and compiled a vast number of sources to provide the desired education. Herrad wanted, in other words, to relay the knowledge easily available to the intellectual elite to her own community members. The intention is further evidenced by the presence of vernacular glosses throughout almost the entire Latin text.[114] It is also interesting to note that she obviously believed that education should be enjoyable, a belief explicitly stated in the text and implicitly captured in the manuscript's aesthetic presentation.

The sources are thematically arranged according to the Old Testament, New Testament, and didactic contemporary works. Bede's *On Genesis,* Eusebius of Caesaria's *History of the Church,* pseudo-Clementine's *Recognitiones,* Ivo de Chartres' *Panormie,* Peter Comestor's *Historia scholastica,* Peter Lombard's *Sentences,* Rupert of Deutz's *Commentary on Song of Songs,* numerous works of Honorius Augustodunensis and Augustine, *Aurea gemma,* papal sermons, and the medieval Isidorean encyclopedists *Summarium Heinrici* are just some of the sources that Herrad chose with sophisticated discretion and then wove them into a coherent whole.[115] Art historian Michael Curschmann has noted that modern scholars too often overlook "the process by which these [classical] authorities are popularized and transmitted; *Hortus deliciarum* provides us with an opportunity to do so." Herrad chose her sources judiciously and with purpose, and the result was a manuscript logically developed, highly structured, and pedagogically sound. To quote Curschmann again, "what looks at first like random patchwork is in fact the result of a careful plan carefully executed. The distribution of the source text in this fashion must have required thorough reading, marking of passages as to their desired new purpose, and continuous supervision. The logic that informs the plan, taken on its own terms, bespeaks a perfectly deliberate method."[116] It also speaks of an intellect of no small demeanor as controlling supervisor: Herrad.

Herrad's choice of sources reflects her own philosophical outlook; it is strongly platonic and Augustinian, thus embracing both pagan and Christian wisdom, the secular and the sacred. Her depiction of creation is an example of how effortlessly she blends these approaches together. Inscribed next to God the Creator are the opening words of Genesis. God is portrayed in two scenes as orchestrating the creation of the platonic elements of air and water. To the right the four winds accompany the creation of air, while to the left God extends his hand to create water, represented by the pagan god Pluto. Pluto holds a fish in his hand, and over his head Herrad writes that "water is for bathing, swimming, and washing."[117] Unfortunately, two key texts and illustrations that deal directly with philosophy are missing,[118] but between the texts and the illustrations we have enough evidence to draw a clear, if incomplete, picture of Herrad's intellectual stance. She exhibits no hint of the type of anti-rationalism found in the work of her near contemporary Bernard of Clairvaux. To the contrary, she repeatedly reinforces through the text and illustrations the importance of philosophy and the liberal arts. While she does not actively involve herself in contemporary debates, she seems aware of the current state of the academic world and occasionally uses texts generated within the universities when appropriate to her needs. Without hesitation she baptizes classical wisdom and then employs it to her own use. For example, the nine muses of pagan literature inspired poets, musicians, and dancers. Herrad embraces the muses and illustrates them introducing philosophy and the seven liberal arts, but she also turns them into representations of human intellectual faculties. Clio represents the first engagement in intellectual activity; Euterpe, the desire for knowledge; Melpomene, meditation; Talya, understanding; Polymnia, memory; Eratho, relationships among objects; Terpsichore, instruction and judgment; Urania, heaven; and Calliope, the voice needed to articulate truth. The muses leave all distracting worldly trappings behind and enter into Herrad's work solely as agents of pedagogy. Herrad also openly admirers pagan philosophers, calls Plato and Socrates "the scholars of the world and the clerics of former ages,"[119] and has them listening at the feet of Queen Philosophy. Herrad makes an important distinction, though, for outside the circle of philosophy and the arts are illustrated four anonymous pagan poets and magicians with black birds whispering false wisdom in their ears.[120] Thus, Herrad sees discretion as a major characteristic of a good educator, for the true seekers of knowledge must separate false wisdom from true knowledge for their pupils. Wholesale condemnation of ancient knowledge is as wrong as indiscriminate acceptance of it all. It is philosophy's duty to examine all things human and divine and decide their intrinsic worth.

Even though the text is of superior enough quality as to warrant the rapt attention of intellectual historians—Herrad's reflective selection of sources was a feat of grand order and represents the best of the knowledge available in her day[121]—it is its artistic valuc that usually gets the most praise. This is as it should be, for while Herrad's editorial skills are equal or above any of her contemporaries, her artistic sensibilities belong in a class by themselves. It is hard to disagree with William Turner's assessment that "in almost every instance they [the paintings] show an artistic imagination which is rare in Herrad's contemporaries."[122] The word "unique" is often overused (I am as guilty as the next), but if ever there was an appropriate application it is in reference to *Hortus deliciarum*'s illuminations. The exact number of illuminations contained in the original manuscript, destroyed in 1870, remains elusive, but it was around 336–346.[123] Of these, only slightly more than half were copied in full before the original was destroyed. The rest are recorded in varying degrees of completeness.[124] Illumination in both the Old Testament cycle and the New Testament cycle utilized Byzantine pictorial models to great advantage, but reliance in certain areas of production on these models, as well as Ottonian and other Romanesque iconography, did not preclude the illuminators of *Hortus deliciarum* from being original, imaginative, and creative in other areas. The Lucifer scenes have no precedent, nor does the personification of idolatry and the portrayal of Ezra before Cyrus, Darius, and Artaxerxes.[125] The creation sequence is a novel version of a traditional theme, as are the portraits of the three persons of the Trinity.[126] In the New Testament cycle, the manuscript contains at least twenty scenes that were rarely if ever painted before Herrad's day.[127] Within the scholarly cycle the long Psychomachia is an outstanding achievement, while the three Ulysses scenes, the baptismal font, and the history of the Antichrist "are without any known parallels."[128] The illustration of Ulysses and the Sirens is the earliest known depiction of them in the Middle Ages.[129]

Of particular interest to us here is the depiction of Philosophy, the Liberal Arts, and the Poets,[130] in a design similar to that associated with rose windows. *Philosophia* is represented with a headdress of three heads of *ethica, logica,* and *physics,* indicating Herrad's belief that these three branches of knowledge are essential to philosophy. *Philosophia* is holding a banner in her hands with the following words inscribed: "All wisdom comes from God. Only the wise do what they will."[131] Socrates and Plato are seated beneath her feet, conscientiously recording her words of wisdom. Four streams emit from the right breast and three from the other, symbolizing the seven liberal arts. While the subject matter is traditional, *Hortus deliciarum*'s portraiture is not derivative of Martianus Capella's classic description nor does it derive from any known contemporary source.[132] In its imagery and in its execution it is most ambitious. Taken as a whole, the illuminations reveal much about Herrad's attitude toward secular learning. Her deep appreciation of knowledge, so beautifully captured in the female personification of the liberal arts, could not have been missed by the women Herrad intended the compendium for, her community members. These women were being taught by one who had utmost respect for all knowledge and complete faith in the women's ability to grasp it.[133] Herrad also adamantly believed that knowledge brings pleasure of all kinds. No matter how difficult the task of learning might look, in one of her poems she reminded the women that "delights await you, riches are destined for you." They must become "freed from mental strife" and "not hesitate amidst the doubtful currents of the world." It is because of difficulties that Herrad compiled the book, to aid them and to give them "a garden of delights." Thus she concludes: "May this book prove useful and delightful to you, may you never cease to ponder it in your breast."[134]

The three most well-known illuminations of *Hortus deliciarum* deserve even more attention in today's academic world than they are presently receiving. The Ladder of Virtues, the foundation of Hohenburg, and the Hohenburg community portrait are significant illuminations for numerous reasons. Artistically they are among the most striking and splendid of all medieval illuminations,[135] even though the original coloring is forever lost; by all accounts the coloring was brilliant.[136] Their distinctive style is identifiable to even the novice assessor. In each instance the overall composition is also notable, for it intimately intertwines word and illumination, image and subject matter. Inscriptions explaining the representations are written right onto the picture, thus highlighting the didactic intent of the compendium and establishing its distinctive style.[137] Contrary to almost all other illuminated manuscripts, *Hortus deliciarum* has no painted backgrounds because of these notations. Rosalie Green argues that the sequence in composition was first drawing, then writing, and finally careful painting around the writing.[138] Again, the process underlines the educational intent of Herrad. The foundation illustration and the portrait of the community fill the last two facing folio in the manuscript. They rely to some extent on previous models, but there is enough personal creativity to render it distinctive. Christ stands in the center, with Mary, Peter, and the monastery's secular founder, Duke Eticho, standing to the right; John the Baptist and St. Odilio are to the left. The scenes below these have Odilio leading a group of women to Duke Eticho to accept the key to the monastery, and Relinda, with an inscription over her head, addressing the nuns. On the facing page Herrad stands at the extreme left, with six rows of individual women painted in between Relinda and Herrad with their names printed over each head. Herrad too has her comments to the nuns inscribed over her head, in which she urges them to do "Christ's work" and pursue "always divine ends in knowledge (*theoria*)." Only the names of the first woman and the last are omitted, perhaps representing all those who came before Herrad's community and those who will come after. The only similar group portrait of a women's community is found in the typika in an Oxford, Lincoln College folio,[139] and a comparison of the two makes the superiority of *Hortus deliciarum* immediately evident. It is on all levels one of the masterpieces of medieval art.

The other masterpiece in the manuscript, the Ladder of Virtues (sometimes called Ladder to Perfection) is more engaging on an intellectual level, for it reveals quite a bit about Herrad's rational assessment of matters secular and religious. Caroline Walker Bynum points out that the Ladder of Virtues portrays something new in medieval thought, awareness of different religious groups or orders, and an accompanying desire to define, classify, and evaluate these groups both socially and religiously. This tendency is aptly expressed in the figures and imagery of the illustration. Every rung of the ladder has a person representing a particular profession or group. Bynum notes that even though ladder imagery is Byzantine, Herrad still changes the traditional Byzantine depiction somewhat by having persons, both men and women, representing various social groups and facing temptations offered by other social groups, instead of a ladder transversed by monks attacked and supported by vices and virtues. In Herrad's version soldiers, lay women, nuns, monks, priests, recluses, and hermits find representation. Bynum argues that Herrad's depiction captures the genius of twelfth-century religiosity, a religiosity that was able to express new concerns in new forms. "This creativity was predicated upon optimism about the human being, created in God's image and therefore capable, by nature, of moving Godward," Bynum writes, "And because the God whom the individual dimly mirrored was both judge and lover, creator of rules as well as inspirer of hearts, the men and women moving toward him expressed their progress not just in personal outpourings but also in leadership, in the creation of institutions, in service of neighbor."[140]

The illumination itself is divided in half diagonally by the ladder upon which numerous clerics, monks, nuns, laymen, and laywomen are attempting to ascend. Only one person reaches the top, a woman "who represents all the saints and the elect which the angels have led to heaven." She is a woman identified as "the virtue of Love [*Caritas*] who possesses the necessary virtues to arrive in heaven."[141] Below her, however, the ladder is strewn with those who failed to rise above the temptations peculiar to their situation and thus have fallen off the ladder. The monk, for instance, is bending over to grasp a pile of gold. "He is typical of all false monks whose heart is distracted from the divine office by the sight of money, and to where there is treasure," Herrad has inscribed over the monk's head. Women, too, fail to scale the ladder successfully, and so "the false nun who symbolizes those who are seduced by clerics' flattery and money."[142] Both a man and a woman fall from the ladder as they give in to the temptation of war and the city. The solution for the failures of the religious lie with the vita apostolica, according to Herrad, who laments in a comment typical of twelfth-century advocates of the apostolic movement thus: "How worthy of praise if the spiritual princes of the church (*princeps ecclesiae spirituales*) restored the evangelical teaching of early times in the place of such customs."[143] All the while that human figures are failing to reach perfection, on the opposite side of the ladder a cosmic struggle rages between angelic guardians of those struggling in this world and devils who try to shoot humans off the ladder with bows and arrows. "All those who fall thus dangerously, the Lord, with the remedy of penitence, can make them remount to the summit of Virtues," Herrad wrote on one of the steps of the ladder.[144] Herrad readily admits her personal experience of the struggle for perfection. "Help me who am climbing along a dangerous uncertain path by your fruitful prayer when I pass away from this earth's experience," she beseeches her community. The reality of the struggle for virtue and perfection is also the reason why education is so important. The truth she offers in her book will help the women "complete your best works of ascent," Herrad writes, as long as they do "not leave the way before you have attained it."[145] Salvation can indeed be found in a book.

A similar emphasis on books as the way to perfection is found in striking imagery in the writings of Marguerite d'Oingt. Marguerite (d. 1310) came from an ancient and powerful French family in the Lyonnais province and was elected prioress of an austere Carthusian monastery in 1288. Other than these facts we know only the little that she reveals of herself in her writings. Her work indicates that she was well educated, and she is rare among medieval authors for having written each of her three books in different languages. Immediately preceding her election to prioress she wrote *Pagina meditationum* (*Page of Meditation*) in Latin. Her major work, *Speculum* (*Mirror*), was written next, in French, and completed in 1294, while a *vita* of Beatrice of Ornacieux was completed in Provençal during the final years of her life. In each of these works Marguerite communicates her overall thesis that the mystic is herself a book, a text, upon which the truth is inscribed for all to read. The mystic is a text for education, and mystical experiences are the subject matter of the text.[146] Marguerite offers herself as proof in the validity of her thesis. "This creature," she writes in *Mirror* in the third person, "had inscribed in her heart the holy life that God, Jesus Christ, led on earth, his good example and good teaching. So firmly had she placed sweet Jesus Christ in her heart that it sometimes seemed to her that he was present and that in his hand he held a closed book for teaching." She then proceeds to tell you briefly how this creature applied herself to the study of this book. First, she meditated on Jesus' humanity, and then, "she began to read in the book of her conscience" how she had failed to follow Jesus' example. She continued to learn from the book, reading the "white letters in which was written the behavior of the blessed Son of God," then studying "the red letters in which was written the wounds of Jesus Christ." Thus, "in these letters she learned not only to suffer tribulation with patience, but even to rejoice in it." Finally, she was ready to devote "herself to the study of the letters of gold. There she learned to desire the things of heaven." Being unschooled in the things of heaven and still bound to those earthly elements outside the book, "she was always obligated to return to the beginning of the life that Our Lord Jesus Christ led on earth, until she had thoroughly amended her life according to the pattern of this book." When she next describes the contents of the book, we see how deep was her appreciation of the knowledge contained within books:[147]

> Inside this book there appeared a delightful place, so large that the whole world is only a little thing in comparison. In this place there appeared a very glorious light that was divided into three parts, as into three persons, but the mouth of a man's not capable of speaking of it. From there came all possible good things. From there came the true wisdom by which all things are made and created. There was the power to whose will all things submit. From there came such great charm and such strengthening that the angels and the souls were so satiated that they could desire nothing more. Such a delightful odor came forth from there that it drew to itself all the virtues of the heavens. Such a great kindling of love came from there that all the loves of this world are but sorrow and bitterness in comparison with this love. From there comes a joy so great that there is no human heart capable of imagining it.[148]

Marguerite's book imagery is indeed one of the most extraordinary testimonies to the power of the book during the high Middle Ages. Her appreciation for literacy as a key to happiness is also seen in her attitude toward writing in *Page of Meditation*. Here she insists that writing has the power to influence and to change a person forever and leave an indelible mark on one's inner self. "Sweet Master," she implores, "write in my heart that which you wish me to do; write your laws there; write your commandments so that they can never be erased."[149] Writing is a way of preserving the truth all people search after, a means by which truth could be made readily available to those who wished to comprehend it more fully. Thus she tells us her own personal experience of writing. "And I thought that I would have to either die or waste away, unless I could remove these thoughts from my heart, but I could not find in my heart any way to remove them," she writes, "and so I put down in writing the thoughts that God had arranged in my heart, so that I wouldn't lose them when I removed them from my heart, and so that I might meditate on them occasionally when God should give me his grace."[150] She believed so strongly in the power that the written word exercised over people that her need to record her thoughts which she described as "all written in her heart," was almost an obsession: "She thought that if she were to put these things in writing, as Our Lord had sent them to her in her heart, her heart would be more relieved for it. She began to write down everything [that is] in this book... and as soon as she put a word in the book, it left her heart." She views her near obsession quite seriously: "I firmly believe that if she had not put it in writing she would have died or become crazy."[151]

In her emphasis on writing and the book and the realization of their potential, Marguerite d'Oingt is not the first or the last medieval intellectual to do so, but she may be the most dramatic. As such Marguerite earns her pace in intellectual history as a secondary intellectual, for her communication of the priorities of the academic world to her own non-academic society was well received. Her works circulated in southern France and the demand for them was significant enough to warrant translation in the vernacular of *Page of Meditation* and *Mirror*.[152] Certainly such vivid imagery contributed to an atmosphere within society which encouraged and promoted intellectual pursuits. Margaret Ebner's use of the word "truth" would be another example of how secondary intellectuals served as relays for attitudes first formed among the intellectual elite. Born in 1291 in the imperial city of Donauwörth, Margaret became a Dominican in 1305 when she entered the monastery at Maria Medingen. Seven years later she developed a painful illness at the same time that she began her mystical life in earnest. Two decades later she met Henry of Nördlingen who became her close friend and her spiritual director. As early as his second visit Margaret confesses "that the yearning arose in me to speak with him about all my concerns."[153] It was soon a strong reciprocal friendship, with Henry experiencing similar sentiments: "When I read something from you or when I write to you with a recollected heart, then as usual a gentle flowing foundation springs up in my heart."[154] Even their spiritual direction was reciprocal: "Your sweet, fiery and true words turn and direct my entire life to God," Henry admits in a letter to her.[155] Aware of Margaret's gifts Henry tried to nourish them by directing her to read Mechthild of Magdeburg's masterpiece. "I am sending you a book which is called the *Flowing Light of the Godhead*," he enthusiastically writes to her. "It is the most wonderful German and the most profoundly touching fruit of love that I have ever read of in the German language." As he continues we see an example of the process by which great works were disseminated in the Middle Ages. "Those words that you do not understand you should mark and send to me. For it was handed down to us in a most unfamiliar German so that we had to spend a good two years of hard work and effort before we could put it a little more into our own German." In his closing he adds that "I would also like to lend it to Engelthal."[156]

Under his urgings Margaret began to record her own experiences in the vernacular "reluctantly,"[157] in a book which we know today as *Revelations*. "In the sweet Name of our Lord Jesus Christ and by His truth-filled life," she begins her accounts, thus focusing right from the start on her two main themes, christocentric spirituality and love of Truth. She tells us that a few years after she became ill in 1312 "I took up the *Pater Noster* and reflections on the works of love of our Lord and with these I got better and overcame my illness."[158] This short *Pater Noster* which she composed contains some of her clearest expressions of her regard for truth, expressed in an even more effective style than in *Revelations*.[159] In structure her prayer adopts a Thomistic scholastic schema.[160] Given her Dominican affiliation and the Dominican reverence for *veritas* upon which her community life was based, it is not surprising to find Margaret focused on truth. It is the pervasiveness of the theme and the power of her expression that makes the prayer worthy of note. The word is employed in almost every possible instance, both as the ultimate entity whom she calls "pure Truth" and "Eternal Wisdom and Truth"[161]—and as an attribute of all things worthy of pursuit or possession. Thus she prays for "true innocence," "true love," "true loving desire," "true joy," "true words," "true inner and outer peace, with true humility, and with the true shining light of true Christian belief."[162] What she desires above all else is truth, and her petitions reflect this reverence for truth as the fount of happiness. Thus she prays for "an enlightening of all my senses to recognize the real and only truth" and for the grace to "never harm by evil the pure Truth, O Lord, in whom all truth is seen."[163] She wants to be strengthened "in pure truth" and instructed "in true Christian belief in life and death, in confirmation of real, true hope." Everything important involves truth. "My surest way to you, my Lord, on the way of real truth must be for us the true light of your pure life," she acknowledges, and, of course, "your true words."[164]

Before we dismiss Margaret's use of the principle of truth as interesting but nevertheless un-exceptional, we should recall the medieval history of the principle in order to appreciate its significance in Margaret's work. At the beginning of the second millennium many scholars who found their way to the newly established schools of the West were also drawn to the burgeoning vita apostolica movement. They saw these attractions as incompatible at first, for an academic's role was to search for truth, while a monk's goal was union with God. Bruno of Cologne found himself in that position. In 1080 he, along with six companions "all of which were the most learned men of their time,"[165] decided to retire from his position in the academic world to live as a hermit; eventually they formed the Carthusian order. Robert of Arbrissel, Stephen of Muret, Bernard of Tiron, and Stephen Harding all lived in the academic world before they established popular religious orders that became the backbone of the medieval monastic renewal.[166] These new orders, however, did not scorn the past intellectual activities of their founders. To the contrary, most of these new orders encouraged the academic life. The Carthusians, for example, promoted reading, held books in highest esteem, and maintained an impressive library.[167] Instead of believing that the monastic life demanded the renouncement of intellectual pursuits, Bruno maintained that the monastic life held "the treasures of knowledge and wisdom."[168] Guigo I, prior of the Carthusians shortly after Bruno's death, echoed these sentiments: "Truth is life and eternal salvation, therefore you ought to pity anyone whom it displeases, for to that extent he is dead and lost."[169] Still, they and many other intellectuals realized that society was experiencing conflict that had to be resolved if the intellectual awakening they were part of was to continue. How do sincere Christians justify choosing the academic life over the religious life? The dilemma, simply put, was whether the pursuit of truth detracted from the pursuit of God.

The conflict was resolved by the word truth.[170] The medieval intellectual was keenly aware of the power of language. Hence, the eleventh-century academic world's chief debates centered around the meaning of words, specifically, universals. Inherent in the debates was the realization that language had the power to change lives by influencing behavior and attitudes. Thinkers such as Peter Damian took advantage of the knowledge gained in these debates to solve the dilemma of the Christian intellectual torn between the search for Christ and the search for truth. Peter insisted that the choice was false, for there was no conflict between the search for Christ and the search for truth; Christ was truth. If pursued properly every search for truth, whether in the monasteries or in the schools, leads to salvation, for truth is "found in her essence only in God."[171] This is not a new thesis. It is based in scripture ("I am the way, the truth and the light" Jn 14:6) and enjoys a long tradition in the West. In the eleventh century, however, the situation was such that intellectuals needed to be reassured that intellectual activity, for so long an activity that had been neglected in order to meet more pressing needs, was a worthy occupation. Peter Damian reassured his contemporaries that such was the case, because and only because God and truth are one. Those who pursue truth in any field, secular or sacred, have the blessings of the church "which has united the wise men of this world."[172] He is not blind, though, to the dangers to the religious life when this identity is denied. Thus, he revived Augustine's famous argument that secular learning is subordinate to sacred wisdom. "My grammar is Christ Himself,"[173] Peter proclaims, and "our philosophy is Christ crucified."[174] If seekers of truth acknowledge this reality then they will avoid "the wisdom that blinds" and the church can "leave to the intellectuals of this world the things which are theirs."[175]

Many intellectuals after Peter built upon both his unitive vision of truth and his restatement of the Augustinian formula of the superiority of sacred science. Abelard stated unambiguously that "truth is not opposed to truth."[176] Even his nemesis Bernard of Clairvaux agreed: "Perhaps you consider me unduly severe and narrow in my views on human knowledge, and suppose that I am censuring the learned and condemning the study of letters. God forbid I should do that!"[177] Hugh of St. Victor observed that "the spirit of study sharpens the mental powers, begets a love of learning, preserves knowledge acquired, turns the mind away from vain and useless things, fosters a hatred of sin." It logically follows, Hugh continued, "that all the natural arts serve divine science and the lower knowledge rightly ordered leads to the higher."[178] Roger Bacon justified the pursuit of natural science by pointing out "that one discipline is mistress of the others—namely theology, for which the others are integral necessities and which cannot achieve its ends without them."[179] By the time we get to the fourteenth century and to Margaret Ebner's contemporaries, the eremitic monks' unitive vision of truth is firmly established and adopted within the universities, and all supposed conflicts between religious life and academic pursuits have disappeared there. In fact, the resolution is so complete that by the end of the thirteenth century the academic world is almost entirely peopled with male religious. Bonaventure comments that "truth, assuming human nature in Christ, had become a ladder" for all people to climb to "the Eternal Truth in Itself," and, therefore, that "all kinds of knowledge" are rewarding and direct us to God.[180] By the thirteenth century the thesis was commonplace in the academic world,[181] but the same cannot be said about Margaret's world. Here the new literate class of non-academicians was experiencing conflicts reminiscent of the eremitic monks' earlier conflicts. Margaret's repeated insistence on the identity of Christ and truth is but a continuation of the tradition Peter Damian and his contemporaries resorted to when the monastic world was busy establishing a new academic class. Margaret served her society well by acting as an emissary to her contemporaries busy building a larger literate class.

One can make the case that this was one of the chief functions of all medieval women mystics. They sought the truth with the same determination as the intellectuals did; intellectual curiosity, a major characteristic of the age, was not limited to any one field. A probing mind alone, however, is not enough; people must be intellectually free to pursue answers to their questions in whatever form or matter they appear. Moreover, a healthy society encourages its members to engage in that pursuit. These are two areas where medieval mystics played crucial roles. They created environments where free pursuit of truth was indeed encouraged. For too long scholars have assumed that intellectual curiosity manifest itself in the Middle Ages chiefly in scientific and technological matters, but that conclusion is too narrow. The curious pursued truth in theological matters as well, and these searches often led to advances in other fields. Albertus Magnus explored embryology in addition to creation, and Roger Bacon analyzed optics as well as ancient theological authorities. There existed a unitive vision of knowledge in the medieval period that we no longer possess, so it is somewhat difficult to appreciate the contributions curious religious writers, especially mystics, made to the overall intellectual health of society.[182]

Such obstructed vision often bars us from fully appreciating certain people, activities or institutions that are key in the development of intellectual culture. The monastery of Helfta is an example. Founded originally in 1229 in Mansfeld, the community moved to Helfta in 1258. In 1251 Gertrude of Hackeborn, a respected intellectual in her own right, became abbess and spent her reign fostering the study of liberal arts among the women. Gertrude the Great, Mechthild of Magdeburg (whose genius we have already discussed at length[183]) and her natural sister, Mechthild of Hackeborn, are but the most famous members of the community whose works are extant. These four women are duly recognized today as women who shaped the highly influential German mystical movement, and they are increasingly being afforded the respect they deserve for their individual literary and intellectual achievements. The sum total of the Helfta community, however, was much more than the individual contributions of these four women. The community created an atmosphere in which all kinds of intellectual activity were respected. Central to its creation was the belief in the unitive nature of knowledge.

When we examine the works of Gertrude the Great we see how strongly influenced she was by this belief and how serious she was about its promotion. For Gertrude human activity of every kind is worthy of pursuit if done with God in mind. "Whenever my chosen ones desire some good thing," the Lord tells her, "it is really myself that they desire, since all good things are in me and come from me." It is that simple. "For example, if a man desires health, ease, wisdom, and the like, in order to increase his merit I often consider that it is myself that he desires."[184] In reality, he continues, "it is all the same to me whether you give yourselves to spiritual exercises or to the toil of exterior labor, so long as your will is freely directed toward me."[185]

Religious activity is good, but if that is all God wanted humans to perform then he would have changed human nature. Other activity is good and necessary and worthy of reward:

> For if I took pleasure in spiritual exercises only, surely I would have so reformed human nature after the Fall that there would no longer be any need for either food or clothing, or for any of the other necessities of life that men toil to obtain or construct through their industry. As a powerful emperor likes to have in his palace not only fair and noble maidens but also princes, dukes, soldiers, and others always ready to serve him, each group in its own way in various kinds of business, so I too take pleasure not only in the interior delights of contemplatives. It is also the various kinds of useful employments which are carried out for my honor and love, which draw me to abide and to dwell with delight among the children of men.[186]

Gertrude clearly believes that the merit of human activity extends to intellectual activity as well; human desire for wisdom is specifically included in God's judgment. She also believes that engaging one's mental abilities is inherently good, even though "through his own limitations a man sometimes has difficulty in doing this," that is, meditating, but "the harder he strives to do it," the greater the reward.[187] For Gertrude her desire is uncomplicated. "Move me forward in all these things," she prays. "Bestow upon me a spirit unconquered, a heart sensitive, a rational soul ready." Above all else, "free me, Lord," she prays, "from all blindness and sterility of mind."[188] The monastery of Helfta helped many a person avoid such sterility of mind.

6

The Great Theologians

Much ink and angst have been spent throughout the centuries trying to discern the exact relationship between medieval thought and the origins of experimental science. The topic has been contentious in large measure because of the highly religious nature of medieval thought. Many Enlightenment historians who saw religion and science as fundamentally incompatible projected their perception of hostility between the two onto medieval society. They argued that modern science came into its own only after religion was relegated to a separate, isolated sphere of activity by early modern society, thereby freeing intellectuals to have a scientific revolution in the seventeenth century. According to Voltaire and Condorcet religion was an obstacle to all free inquiry and was responsible for the "general decay and degeneracy" and, specifically, "for the complete decadence of philosophy and the sciences" which marked the intellectual life of the Middle Ages.[1] Jacob Burckhardt accepted the Enlightenment judgment and perhaps drew a deeper line between medieval religion and modern science by his insistence that "in the Middle Ages both sides of human consciousness—that which turned within and that which turned without—lay as though dreaming or half awake beneath a common veil," a veil which "was woven of faith."[2] Some of Buckhardt's students were even more extreme, one claiming that the medieval church "had drawn a thick veil" between "the mind of man and the outer world," leaving it for the Renaissance scholars to liberate "reason from a dungeon."[3]

Such extreme positions begged rebuttal, and they came during the early twentieth century with the work of Pierre Duhem. By proving that modern mechanics and physics "proceed, by an uninterrupted series of scarcely perceptible improvements, from doctrines professed in the heart of the medieval schools,"[4] Duhem's critique began a general assault on the prevailing Enlightenment and Romantic beliefs about, first, the crippling effect religion had on medieval intellectual life and, second, the consequent lack of medieval achievement in intellectual matters, particularly in science. Medievalists have long since ended debate concerning the former; if anything, it is now Renaissance scholars who are on the defensive upholding past claims to uniqueness and grandeur.[5] The debate over medieval contributions to modern science, nevertheless, persists, usually in the form of a debate over continuity: Did medieval society contribute, resemble, or anticipate modern science? Some historians point out that these are the wrong questions, that the historians of science's job is to describe the problems and solutions of a given period, not to assess that period's merit in light of future problems and solutions.[6] Historian David Lindberg argues that a more productive approach than to debate continuity is simply to identify medieval scientific achievements and recognize its legacy. He also argues that the Renaissance conflict model for studying the relationship between medieval church and science should be replaced with an accommodation model.[7]

Roger French and Andrew Cunningham, on the other hand, study medieval natural philosophy and insist that only a more thorough embrace of the religious context of medieval intellectuals will yield further insight into the question of medieval science. They argue that while it made concrete contributions to society's understanding of nature, medieval "natural philosophy was not merely some religious (or religiously motivated) early version of modern science" but that it was "a study in which the central concerns were the detection, admiration, appreciation of God's existence, goodness, providence, munificence, forethought and provision for His creation."[8]

What becomes plain in all this historiography is that as in so many other areas of investigation, historians of the Middle Ages must always start with religion to gain insight into their particular field. Mid-twentieth-century philosopher Frederick Copleston took this approach in his magisterial history of philosophy; he grounded that history in its corresponding religious context. The result was highly successful.[9] Because he thoroughly appreciated how religion helped create the mental environment within which medieval intellectuals functioned, Copleston was able to avoid many of the problems in the debates over science versus religion and modern science's continuity with medieval activity and offer instead some insight worth pursuing. He argued that Ockhamism was an example of how Christian theology shaped the background within which empirical modern science eventually developed, that the Christian acceptance of the value of experience in the pursuit of truth set the stage for science's acceptance of experiments as a way to knowledge, and that "by directing men's minds to the facts or empirical data in the acquisition of knowledge it at the same time directed them away from passive acceptance of the opinions of illustrious thinkers of the past."[10]

As we begin to discuss the works of the major women intellectuals of the late medieval period, I find it advantageous to look to the comments of historians of philosophers such as Copleston for guidance. In the passage just quoted, Copleston was discussing Ockhamism and science, not women. Admittedly, this introductory discussion has focused on science, not women, but I have not done so to introduce previously unidentified women scientists; I know of no such women. Rather, this opening discussion is meant to encourage reflection upon the ways in which women theologians we will discuss in this chapter, Julian of Norwich, Catherine of Siena, and Birgitta of Sweden, contributed to many intellectual currents of their day, including experimental science. Copleston stresses the role of experience in the development of experimental science; we already have established how many women mystic intellectuals promoted the role of experience in the attainment of knowledge. Copleston emphasizes how reliance on experience also lessened dependence on tradition, thus clearing the way for new ideas. We have seen women mystic playwrights, artists, and authors use the authority of their personal experience to override tradition and create new art forms. Lastly, Copleston reminds us of how much theology contributed to the origins of experimental science by forming the intellectual environment within which science would be nourished. Theologians, in other words, played an indirect role in the development of science. Julian, Catherine, and Birgitta are by all accounts major theologians of their time and as such they too shaped society's intellectual culture, just as the women theologians who preceded them contributed to the formation of their society's intellectual environment.

Julián Marías is another historian of philosophy whose generalizations about late medieval thought are helpful in the study of late medieval women's thought. Marías writes at length about the influence the Franciscan love of nature had on Western intellectual traditions, claiming that it "established the basis for nominalist physics and prepared the way for the modern natural science of Galileo and Newton," produced mathematical breakthroughs, and culminated in the idealism of Descartes and Leibniz.[11] There is no doubt that Franciscan influence was extensive in this tradition, but that is not to say it possessed a monopoly here. Women also participated in the medieval love affair with nature. We have seen the strong presence of nature in Hadewijch's beautiful poetic imagery, particularly in her images of the seasons. She is not an exception, for most women mystics of the period described their personal experience of God in terms of nature, especially natural light. Gertrude the Great's description of the mystical union contains imagery that overflows with a love of nature comparable to any Franciscan writing. Her search for God begins when "I watch at daybreak" for his coming; "at noonday," she approaches "the sun of justice" so "that the coal of divine love may burn indistinguishably in her heart;" and her search ends only when "at the sunset of my life" she enters into "eternal life in you."[12] The union itself she describes as a "serene light of my soul, very brightest morning, ah, break into day in me now and begin so to shine for me that by your light I may see light and that through you my night may be turned into day."[13] We have also seen Beatrice of Nazareth's use of nature imagery in her body metaphors and Hildegard of Bingen's interest in nature culminate in her work on natural science, *Physica*.[14] Elizabeth of Schönau, a contemporary and correspondent of Hildegard of Bingen, was a mystic whose work enjoyed a popularity few other writings enjoyed in the Middle Ages; her work has survived in at least 145 manuscripts and were translated into numerous languages, including Icelandic.[15] In *The Book of the Ways of the Lord* Elizabeth uses nature to describe three paths to God "extending from the base of a shining mountain up to its summit." The first path "had the appearance of serene sky or blue stone; the one to my right appeared green, and the one to my left, purple." At the mountain's summit stood a man whose "face was shining like the sun, his eyes beaming like stars, and his hair was like the brightest wool."[16] In the writing of Clare of Assisi themes of nature, rooted either in her mysticism or her Franciscan mindset, are replete throughout. "Cover yourself with the flowers and garments of all the virtues," she writes to Agnes of Prague,[17] while calling herself "the little plant of the holy Father" Francis, whom she calls the "Planter."[18] The vivid imagery and obvious love of nature in Julian of Norwich's masterpiece *Showings* is one of its chief characteristics. One of her key parables, for instance, concerns "a gardener, digging and ditching and sweating and turning the soil over and over."[19] In fact, a detailed examination of Julian's opinion of nature reinforces a variation of Marías' contention that

Franciscan love of nature helped prepare the way for society's engagement in science: Women mystics' love of nature helped introduce various intellectual developments during the late Middle Ages, including science, but also including political thought and humanism.

Julian of Norwich

Julian of Norwich (1342–ca. 1416) was a well-educated woman but where or how she received her education is unknown. Her theological education was particularly deep, for her text reveals knowledge of a wide array of patristic and contemporary theological and spiritual authors. She displays a thorough grasp of the Augustinian synthesis of theology, Platonic philosophy, and classical Latin rhetoric (her modern editors Edmund Colledge and James Walsh call her a pioneer in the adaptation of ancient rhetoric to English prose[20]). She knew Chaucer's translation of Boethius' *Consolation of Philosophy,* John Ruusbroeck's *The Treatise of Perfection of the Sons of God,* and the works of William of St. Thierry, the last being revealing because they circulated only among the intellectual elite.[21] She was, one might say, well read and well rounded in her education. On May 13, 1373, while on what she thought was her deathbed, she received a series of revelations that after recuperating she recorded in what is today called the short text. Some twenty years later she wrote an expanded version, the long text, to offer further interpretations and explanations of those same revelations. Sometime in between she became an anchoress in Norwich where she still resided two decades later when Margery Kempe decided "to go to an anchoress in the same city [Norwich] named Dame Julian" for spiritual direction, "for the anchoress was an expert in such things, and could give good advice."[22] Julian wrote *Showings* in the vernacular.

When describing her visions Julian creates extremely vivid images to communicate her grasp of nature. "The flesh was torn from the skull, falling in pieces until when the bleeding stopped; and then it began to dry again, adhering to the bone," she sensuously writes in her description of Jesus' scourging, but her emphasis on the sensual is deeply rooted in her concept of humanity: "For then the tossing about and writhing, the groaning and the moaning ended, rightly; and our foul mortal flesh, which God's Son took upon him, which was Adam's old tunic, tight fitting, threadbare and short, was then made lovely by our saviour, new, white and bright and forever clear, wide and ample."[23] Nowhere in her text does she warn against the evils of nature or urge custody of the senses.[24] Instead, she sees the senses as instruments to be used to experience God. With death comes not the end of sensual feeling but the beginning of the total sensual experience, for only then will we be "truly seeing and wholly feeling, and hearing him spiritually and delectably smelling him and sweetly tasting him."[25] Much has been made of Julian's recourse to the Christ-as-mother theme as it applies to gender and feminist theology, but note should likewise be made of Julian's positive attitude toward nature contained in the construct. In fact, Julian tells us that the reason why the theme is proper is precisely because the analog flows so naturally. "And so Jesus is our true Mother in nature by our first creation," she tells us,[26] for "the mother's service is nearest, readiest and surest: nearest because it is most natural, readiest because it is most loving and surest because it is truest." It is nature that brings us to God, for contemplation of the wonders of motherhood bring us to wonders of Jesus. "The mother can give her child to suck of her milk, but our precious Mother Jesus can feed us with himself, and does, most courteously and most tenderly.... The mother can lay her child tenderly to her breast, but our tender Mother Jesus can lead us into his blessed breast through his sweet open side, and show us there a part of the godhead," Julian continues. "The kind, loving mother who knows and sees the need of her child guards it very tenderly, as the nature and condition of motherhood will have."[27] Julian's reverence for nature is also found in the cosmos. "God in his goodness, who makes the planets and the elements to function according to their natures" made all things good; "All creatures which God has created for our service"[28] are good, "for everything which exists in nature is of God's creation, so that everything which is done has the property of being God's doing... and therefore the blessed Trinity is always wholly pleased with all its works."[29]As we can see, Julian has some definite ideas about the philosophy of creation. First, God as creator is the primary cause of all things. Second, once created, the elements "function according to their natures," that is, through secondary causality.[30] Acknowledgment of secondary cause is of utmost importance in the Christian theology of work,[31] and so Julian's emphasis on it is significant.

Articulation of Julian's respect for nature is not limited to imagery or analogy. She makes her case explicitly in her discussions of creation. "I know well that heaven and earth and all creation are great, generous and beautiful and good," because "he who created it created everything for love, and by the same love is it preserved, and always will be without end."[32] The implications of these principles were dramatically brought home to Julian when God showed her a tiny, insignificant part of his creation, and she pondered its meaning:

> And in this he showed me something small, no bigger that a hazelnut, lying in the palm of my hand, as it seemed to me, and it was as round as a ball. I looked at it with the eye of my understanding and thought: What can this be? I was amazed that it could last, for I thought that because of its littleness it would suddenly have fallen into nothing. And I was answered in my understanding: It lasts and always will, because God loves it; and thus everything has being through the love of God.
>
> In this little thing I saw three properties. The first is that God made it, the second is that God loves it, the third is that God preserves it. But what did I see in it? It is that God is the Creator and the protector and the lover. For until I am substantially united to him, I can never have perfect rest or true happiness, until, that is, I am so attached to him that there can be no created thing between my God and me.[33]

It is the presence of God's love in creation, then, that renders it lovable and good. This means creatures, too, were made with love, "for before he made us he loved us, and when we were made we loved him." In fact, "he wants us to know that the noblest thing which he ever made is mankind."[34] God's love is without discrimination and showered on all humans equally "for the great endless love that God has for all mankind, he makes no distinction in love between the blessed soul of Christ and the least soul that will be saved."[35] Julian includes herself in this generalization, clearly stating that she is not special by virtue of her visions. "I am not good because of the revelation, but only if I love God better, and so can and so should every man do who sees it and hears it with good will and proper intention. And so it is my desire that it should be to every man the same profit that I asked for myself," she explains, "for truly it was not revealed to me because God loves me better than the humblest soul who is in a state of grace."[36] This presence of God's love in each and every human is the basis that binds the human community together. "What can make me love my fellow Christians more than to see in God that he loves all who will be saved, all of them as it were one soul?"[37] Julian plaintively asks. "That is to say, the love of God creates in us such a unity that when it is truly seen, no man can separate himself from another."[38] Again Julian includes herself in her generalizations in order to emphasize that the fundamental equality of all humans is based on God's indiscriminatory love for all, which, in turn, binds all humans together. "If I pay special attention to myself, I am nothing at all; but in general I am, I hope, in the unity of love with all my fellow Christians," Julian begins. "For it is in this unity that the life of all men consists who will be saved. For God is everything that is good, as I see; and God has made everything that is made, and God loves everything that he has made. And he who has general love for all his fellow Christians in God has love toward everything that is." Her conclusion is succinctly stated: "For God is in man and in God is all."[39] Personally this knowledge motivates Julian to teach others what she has learned for knowledge is not private or individualized but public and universal: "In all this I was greatly moved in love towards my fellow Christians, that they might all see and know the same as I saw, for I wished it to be a comfort to them, for all this vision was shown for all men." Moreover, "everything that I say about me I mean to apply to all my fellow Christians, for I am taught that this is what our Lord intends in this spiritual revelation." She ends with a reminder of her alternative motives: "I counsel you for your own profit."[40]

When these principles are placed within the context of Julian's society their significance increases. Fourteenth-century English society was a tumultuous one dealing with numerous natural and human upheavals. The effect the Black Death had on European society is hard to over-estimate, as is its effect on people's beliefs, both religious and social.[41] The Avignon papacy, the Great Schism, the Hundred Years' War, Wycliff's condemnation, the Merciless Parliament, Richard II's forced abdication and probably murder, the Peasants' rebellion of 1381 were just some of the political events that occurred during Julian's lifetime that had profound effects on her society's self-understanding. It was also the time of Geoffrey Chaucer and William Langland, of bastard feudalism, of the growth of parliamentary power, the rise of the Commons, and the birth of the gentry. Historians remain divided over the general condition the English people found themselves in as a result of these phenomena. Janet Coleman and Christopher Dyer believe that it was a century of fragmentation.[42] Barbara Hanawalt argues that the traumas of the fourteenth century eroded the institutions which regulated village communal life and thus "neighbor became estranged from neighbor,"[43] while Eamon Duffy and Miri Rubin hold that new forms of religious piety such as Corpus Christi celebrations were busy forging new communal bonds.[44] Frederick Bauerschmidt maintains that the cultural matrix of Julian's world was fragmented and that it was to this fragmentation that Julian addressed her theology of a political community. What Julian is doing, according to Bauerschmidt, is rethinking and reformulating the Christian mythos (that is, the metaphysical image) responsible for the political form of her contemporary society.[45]

Given the force with which Julian presents her case for the nature of creation and community, I tend to agree with Bauerschmidt's contention that Julian's theology is addressing a very real political issue in her day. The fact that she did not live among the political hierarchy but rather among the masses increases the probability of this being her intention, for the social fragmentation the scholars above refer to was occurring at the base of society. Julian counters the human condition of estrangement and division by emphasizing community and unity, "for in the sight of God all men are one man, and one man is all men."[46] The human condition is overcome and happiness is complete when God's grace makes "us all at unity with him, and each of us with others in the true, lasting joy which is Jesus."[47] The unifying factor of the community, then, is Christ, and Christ's presence in every human gives them the ability to form community. "Let us all join with God's working in prayer, thanking, trusting, rejoicing,"[48] Julian implores, noting that even the simple things so necessary to communal living are made possible by God's presence in each person. She even claimed that acknowledging the unifying presence of God's love in each individual gives us a way to accept the failings of others. "So I saw how Christ has compassion on us because of sin, and just as I was before filled full of pain and compassion on account of Christ's Passion, so I was now in part filled with compassion for all my fellow Christians because he loves very dearly the people who will be saved," Julian explains. "And then I saw that every natural compassion which one has for one's fellow Christians in love is Christ in us."[49] No matter how grave the human failing "the place which Jesus takes in our soul he will nevermore vacate, for in us is his home of homes and his everlasting dwelling."[50] It should also be noted that Julian quite self-consciously includes herself in the concept of humanity, perhaps in response to misogynistic statements she came in contact with in her reading. After applying the revelation of herself as sinner "merely to my own single self," she eventually "saw that he intended it for general man, that is to say every man, who is sinful and will be until the last day. Of which man I am a member, as I believe," she confesses, "and there I was taught that I ought to see my own sin and not other men's, unless it may be for the comfort and help of my fellow Christians."[51]

Because of her belief in the presence of God's love in each person, Julian possesses a very optimistic anthropology. Everything she studied and reflected upon during her entire life brought her to her concluding words in *Showings*: "And I saw very certainly in this and in everything that before God made us he loved us, which love was never abated and never will be. And in this love he has done all his works, and in this love he has made all things profitable to us, and in this love our life is everlasting. In our creation we had our beginning, but the love in which he created us was in him from without beginning. In this love we have our beginning, and all this shall we see in God without end."[52] Such unconditional, total love is comforting, to say the least, and sets the stage for much happiness. All a person has to do to receive such happiness is exercise his or her free will, for "any man or woman who voluntarily chooses God in his lifetime for love, he may be sure that he is endlessly loved with an endless love."[53] But Julian even goes further than to claim that Christ's loving presence alleviates the existential pain of the human condition; she exalts the human condition as perfect. "If the blessed Trinity could have created man's soul any better, any fairer, any nobler than it was created, the Trinity would not have been fully pleased with the creation of man's soul. But because it made man's soul as beautiful, as good, as precious a creature as it could make, therefore the blessed Trinity is fully pleased without end in the creation of man's soul," Julian argues. "For as well as the Father could create a creature, and as well as the Son could create a creature, so well did the Holy Spirit want man's spirit to be created, and so it was done. And therefore the blessed Trinity rejoices without end in the creation of man's soul, for it saw without beginning what would delight it without end."[54] She does not deny that sin has dire effects on human lives, saying that sin "has no kind of substance, no share in being, nor can it be recognized except by the pains which it causes."[55] It is purgative pain, unfortunately needed, "for all who will be saved" because "it purges and makes us know ourselves and ask for mercy."[56] She provides an example of such beneficial pain when relating her Seventh Revelation. Here she experienced the extremes of pleasure and pain "now the one and now the other, again and again, I suppose about twenty times." She soon understood why: "This vision was shown to teach me to understand that some souls profit by experiencing this, to be comforted at one time, and at another to fail and to be left to themselves. God wishes us to know that he keeps us safe all the time, in sorrow and in joy; and sometimes a man is left to himself for the profit of his soul."[57] Her conclusion, that "sin is necessary, but all will be well, and all will be well, and every kind of thing will be well,"[58] is well known, thanks to T. S. Eliot's use of it in *Four Quartets,*[59] but it captures her pervasive optimism quite powerfully. Sin occurs, pain follows, but life is still good. The key is to remember that "bliss lasts forevermore, and pain is passing, and will be reduced to nothing for those who will be saved."[60] Moreover, knowledge of this reality should take the sting out of the pain, temporary though it is, "for he wants us to pay true heed to this, that we are as certain in our hope to have the bliss of heaven whilst we are here as we shall be certain of it when we are there."[61] In a passage which strikingly underlines the strength of Julian's teaching methodology, she makes the same point while contemplating a promise she received in her last vision: "And these words: You will not be overcome, were said very insistently and strongly, for certainly and strength against every tribulation which may come. He did not say: You will not be troubled, you will not be belabored, you will not be disquieted; but he said: You will not be overcome. God wants us to pay attention to these words, and always to be strong in faithful trust . . . and all will be well."[62]

Julian also saw communal life as beneficial and therefore encouraged service to others at every opportunity. God "wants to make us partners in his good will and work" and if we are, "he will repay us, and give us eternal reward."[63] Julian also says that God "wants us to be his helpers, giving all our intention to him, learning his laws, observing his teaching, desiring everything to be done which he does."[64] She repeatedly points out that the goal of her writing is service to others. She states that her First Revelation "was given to my understanding to teach,"[65] and the sentiment is either implicitly or explicitly stated in every consequent revelation. In an unusual passage in mystical writing she even acknowledges the urge to make people laugh as good. After seeing God get the better of the devil in a vision she tells us "I laughed greatly, and that made those around me to laugh as well; and their laughter was pleasing to me. I thought that I wished that all my fellow Christians had seen what I saw. Then they would all have laughed with me; but I did not see Christ laughing, but I know well that it was the vision he showed me which made me laugh, for I understood that we may laugh, to comfort ourselves and rejoice in God."[66] In another atypical passage Julian praises the service of youth. Her Sixth Revelation concerns itself with "the honourable thanks with which our Lord God rewards all his blessed servants,"[67] and the labor of youth is the first type acknowledged: "Our Lord said: I thank you for your service and your labour in your youth." Even the gratitude of God for service is placed within a communal setting: "All the blessed in heaven will see the honour of the thanks. God makes the soul's service known to all who are in heaven; and at this time this example was revealed. If a king thank [sic] his subjects, it is a great honour for them; and if he make this known to all the kingdom, then their honour is much increased." Again she singles out the service of youth within her general praise of all human service: "And I saw that this was familiarly and sweetly revealed, that every man's age will be known in heaven, and he will be rewarded for his voluntary service and for the time that he has served, and especially the age of those who voluntarily and freely offer their youth to God is fittingly rewarded and wonderfully thanked."[68]

Community is not the only contemporary issue that Julian weighed in upon. She was also extremely interested in epistemology, and her views on the nature and value of knowledge are consistent with her optimistic anthropology. Her views on knowledge are formulated in some of her most challenging passages and articulated with commanding authority.[69] Not that her contemporaries were not equally critical of their inherited legacy; John Duns Scotus (ca. 1265–1308), William of Ockham (ca. 1285–ca. 1347) and their Oxford colleagues are often introduced in surveys as intellectuals intent upon rethinking the whole body of ancient and medieval philosophical doctrine.[70] Her contemporary intellectuals were also equally interested in epistemology; Ockham's and Scotus' chief focus was on knowledge of knowing. In trying to situate her in the spectrum of philosophical thought current in her day, though, what becomes apparent is not any adherence to a school of thought but her independence of mind. Here she is agreeing with Augustine, Aquinas, Duns Scotus, and Ockham, there she is disagreeing with them. She accepts, for example, Aquinas' analysis of visions as a valid source of knowledge and his methodology for scriptural exegesis, but she rejects his stance that reason is dependent on the senses and that there is a distinction between faith and reason.[71] Ockham claims that all knowledge is intuitive and based on experience; John Duns Scotus claims that knowledge of God is derived solely from revelation and faith. Julian holds a middle position. God is very knowable in three different ways: "by bodily vision, and by words formed in my understanding and by spiritual vision."[72] To wit, experience, reason, and revelation yield knowledge of God.

In one of her most significant departures Julian rejects a long tradition of God as wrathful, punitive, or interested in retribution. Augustine argues that "the authors of Scripture have decided to use the name wrath for God's vengeance, although God's vengeance is exercised with absolutely no such emotion,"[73] and Aquinas maintains that "in attributing anger to God what is signified is not an emotion but a just judgment and the will to punish sin,"[74] but Julian finds both these formulations troublesome. She comprehends the seriousness of her discomfort, for she realizes that in rejecting this tradition of a wrathful God she is indirectly challenging the church's authority and its monopoly over knowledge. Still, she does not back away from the dilemma, and as she persists in trying to resolve it we see her attitudes toward knowledge, reason, and authority protruding into her discussion:

> The first judgment, which is from God's justice, is from his own great endless love, and that is that fair, sweet judgment which was shown in all the fair revelation [the Ninth Revelation] in which I saw him assign to us no kind of blame. And though this was sweet and delectable, I could not be fully comforted only by contemplating it, and that was because of the judgment of Holy Church, which I had understood before, and which was continually in my sight. And therefore it seemed to me that this judgment I must necessarily know myself a sinner. And by the same judgment I understood that sinners sometimes deserve blame and wrath, and I could not see these two in God, and therefore my desire was more that I can or may tell, because of the higher judgment which God revealed at the same time, and therefore I had of necessity to accept it. And the lower judgment had previously been taught me in Holy Church, and therefore I could not in any way ignore the lower judgment.[75]

Julian captures the dilemma of late medieval intellectuals well in the recitation of her personal conflict: Whence comes true knowledge? Without an answer to this question, resolution of conflicts among different sources of knowledge is impossible. Who or what was the ultimate arbitrator when contradictions arose: Julian's personal experience of visions, the use of reason, revelation, or the church? "Between these two oppositions [reason and church authority]," Julian lamented, "my reason was greatly afflicted by my blindness, and I could have no rest for fear that . . . I should be left in ignorance" as to what was the valid source of knowledge. Still, she persisted in her query, because "three circumstances gave me courage to ask this. The first is because it is so humble a thing, for if it were a great one I should be afraid. The second is that it is so general; for if it were special or secret, I should also be afraid. The third is that it is something which I need to know, it seems to me, if I shall live here, so as to tell good from evil, whereby I may through reason and grace separate them more distinctly."[76] The process she underwent while searching for a resolution became part of her answer. First, God "answered very mysteriously, by revealing a wonderful example of a lord who has a servant,"[77] and then, "for twenty years after the time of the revelation except for three months, [Julian] received an inward instruction." She pondered the meaning of the vision by "seeing inwardly with great care all the details which were at the time revealed, so far as my intelligence and understanding will serve."[78] That is to say, she learned through three different media: an experiential vision, the use of reason, and God's direct communication, the last being the best because "God sees one way and man sees another way."[79] By availing herself to these three ways Julian gained "some understanding of our Lord's meaning."[80] One way often reinforced the validity of another. Once while she reflected upon the contents of a vision she had just received, the Lord reappeared and "gave me true knowledge that it was he who had revealed everything to me before. And when I contemplated this with attention, out Lord very humbly revealed words to me, without voice and without opening of lips, just as he had done before, and said very sweetly: Know it well, it was no hallucination which you saw today, but accept and believe it and hold firmly to it." [81]

Strangely, the explanation she offers does not resolve the original issue of whether the church was superior as a source of knowledge.[82] In the Thirteenth Revelation she brings up the same issue in a different context, whether all non-Christians "will be eternally condemned to hell, as Holy Church teaches me to believe." Here Julian comes closer to an answer by accepting the fact that she will not obtain a resolution in this life. When God tells her "Every kind of thing will be well," she argued "that it was impossible that every kind of thing should be well" if the church teaching be correct. "And to this I had no other answer as a revelation from our Lord except this: What is impossible to you is not impossible to me. I shall preserve my word in everything and I shall make everything well."[83] Church authority is justifiable, but its doctrines are not always within the grasp of human comprehension. Julian accepts the validity of church teaching because in the final analysis all knowledge is from God: "God is the foundation of our natural reason; and God is the teaching of Holy Church, and God is the Holy Spirit, and they are all different gifts, and he wants us to have great regard for them, and to accord ourselves to them. For they work continually in us, all together, and those are great things; and of this greatness he wants us to have knowledge here, as it were in an ABC."[84]

Still, when church teaching seems to contradict either her reason or the experiential knowledge received in visions, Julian does not have a problem with deciding against the church. When discussing the problem of sin, we saw her juxtapose God's justice which is "good and lenient" and assigns "to us no kind of blame," with what she calls "the lower judgment" of the church, which does. Her efforts were then directed and "will until the end of my life," to reconcile these two contradictory views, "for all heavenly things and all earthly things which belong to heaven are comprehended in these two judgments."[85] Julian also employs a rhetorical device to register her discomfort with church doctrine of sin and damnation; thirteen times she mentions the church's teaching but then adds that this was "not revealed" to her.[86] The effect is to make the church teaching appear vulnerable and without support from the other sources of knowledge. She uses the same device when discussing other church doctrines that she apparently had trouble with, always careful to outwardly accept the doctrine so as to appear orthodox, while at the same time undermining it by emphasizing the lack of collaboration for its truth in the other sources of knowledge. "I believe and understand the ministration of holy angels, as scholars tell, but it was not revealed to me" is a statement which typifies her approach, and one that she used twenty-four times.[87] It is a fine line she walks, nevertheless, and she is always conscious of the need to appear orthodox no matter what the issue. At the end of the First Revelation Julian makes a blanket pledge of orthodoxy and promises never to cross the line into heresy: "But in everything I believe as Holy Church preaches and teaches. For the faith of Holy Church, which I had before I had understanding, and which, as I hope by the grace of God, I intend to preserve whole and to practise, was always in my sight, and I wished and intended never to accept anything which might be contrary to it."[88] Being orthodox, however, did not mean accepting things blindly. "God showed the very great delight he has in all men and women who accept, firmly and wisely the preaching and teaching of Holy Church, for he is that Holy Church,"[89] but God also "wants us to understand desiring with all our heart and all our strength to have knowledge."[90] Reason is, after all, "the highest gift we have received."[91]

It should be noted that when John Duns Scotus, William of Ockham, or any of their contemporaries explored the source of knowledge, their search started with a specific goal in mind: knowledge of God.[92] Julian is no exception. Julian is very insistent that while knowledge of God is the primary goal, the secondary goal of self-knowledge must be reached before complete knowledge of God can be attained. "And all this notwithstanding, we can never come to the full knowledge of God until we first clearly know our own soul," she declares.[93] This is not an easy task, to say the least. "And so I saw most surely that it is quicker for us and easier to come to the knowledge of God than it is to know our own soul," Julian proclaims.[94] She then reveals the paradox: "For our soul is so deeply grounded in God and so endlessly treasured that we cannot come to knowledge of it until we first have knowledge of God." The paradox is more apparent than real, given the fact that humans are made in the image and "like to him who is contemplated"[95] and "enclosed" in God, "and so by the leading through grace of the Holy Spirit we shall know them both in one; whether we are moved to know God or our soul, either motion is good and true."[96]

In one passage Julian makes a further distinction concerning self-knowledge. The first kind of knowledge is knowledge of God. The second is "that we know ourselves, what we are through him in nature and in grace," and the third "is that we know humbly that our self is opposed to our sin and to our weakness."[97] Sin, after all, "is incomparably worse, more vile and painful than hell. For it is in opposition to our fair nature; for as truly as sin is unclean, so truly is sin unnatural."[98] Knowledge of one's own nature, therefore, helps one recognize sin as different from one's nature. Julian's independence of mind is evident in these discussions of self-knowledge and sin, because in contrast to the majority of spiritual writers of the period Julian does not dissect personal sin or appear in any way preoccupied with it. Her emphasis is always on God's love for the sinner. God "wants us to know that he takes the falling of any creature who will be saved no harder than he took the falling of Adam, who, we know, was endlessly loved and safely protected in the time of all his need, and now is blissfully restored in great and surpassing joys. For our Lord God is so good, so gentle and so courteous that he can never assign final failure to those in whom he will always be blessed and praised."[99] Self-knowledge, then, must include this fundamental belief in the forgiveable nature of human failings, because "in this our good Lord showed not only that we are excused, but also the honourable nobility to which he will bring us, turning all our blame into endless honour."[100] Julian accepts original sin as the cause of human weakness, but it is a very generous portrait she paints of the fallen sinner. "I understood in this way. Man is changeable in this life, and falls into sin through naivete and ignorance. He is weak and foolish in himself, and also his will is overpowered in the time when he is assailed and in sorrow and woe. And the cause is blindness, because he does not see God," Julian patiently writes. "And, therefore often we fail to perceive him, and presently we fall back upon ourselves, and then we find that we feel nothing at all but the opposition that is in ourselves, and that comes from the old root of our first sin, with all that follow from our own persistence."[101] In the end, it is the same; God "regards sin as sorrow and pain for his lovers, to whom for love he assigns no blame."[102]

Self-knowledge brings Julian to knowledge of God, and when discussing the nature of God Julian is her most scholastic and metaphysical self[103] and at the same time most Augustinian. "It is a great understanding to see and know inwardly that God, who is our Creator, dwells in our soul, and it is a far greater understanding to see and know inwardly that our soul, which is created, dwells in God in substance, of which substance, through God, we are what we are,"[104] Julian explains, "substance" being the equivalent to the scholastic "essence."[105] "And I saw no difference between God and our substance, but, as it were, all God; and still my understanding accepted that our substance is in God, that is to say that God is God, and our substance is a creature in God."[106] Creator and creature and knowledge of both are so intertwined because "the blessed Trinity made mankind in their image and their likeness."[107] Specifically, "God is endless supreme truth, endless supreme wisdom, endless supreme love uncreated; and a man's soul is a creature in God which has the same properties created."[108] In her *imago Dei* anthropology Julian is adhering to a tradition dating from the very origins of Christianity[109] and perhaps most effectively argued by Augustine. Julian accepts Augustine's emphasis on the trinitarian image found in the memory, reason, and will but discusses them as might, wisdom, and love[110] and in terms of being, increasing, and fulfillment: "For all our life consists of three: In the first we have our being, and in the second we have our increasing, and in the third we have our fulfillment. The first is nature, the second is mercy, the third is grace. As to the first, I saw and understood that the high might of the Trinity is our Father, and the deep wisdom of the Trinity is our Mother, and the great love of the Trinity is our Lord; and all these we have in nature and in our substantial creation. And furthermore I saw that the second person, who is our Mother, substantially the same beloved person, has now become our mother sensually, because we are double by God's creating, that is to say, substantial and sensual."[111] Julian scholar Denise Baker argues that Julian contributes new elements to the *imago Dei* tradition "by extending the traditional familial analogies for the Trinity as Father and Son to include Jesus as Mother as well as Brother, [and thus] modifies the ontology and anthropology implied by this Augustinian commonplace into an original theory of an androgynous God who creates the soul in an asexual image."[112]

In the dominant position Julian gives to the *imago Dei* tradition, she has much in common with another group of intellectuals, the humanists. In his groundbreaking magisterial work *In Our Image and Likeness* Charles Trinkhaus demonstrated how central the *imago Dei* doctrine was to the thought of Renaissance humanists.[113] More than any other single work Trinkhaus' study established the extent to which Italian humanists were immersed in and contributed to theology, a thesis which, according to John O'Malley, would have been summarily dismissed as absurd[114] by centuries of scholars who preceded him and deemed the Renaissance pagan and anti-theological. Trinkhaus also showed how steeped in Augustinian and Platonic thought the humanists were, "not only in the realm of religion and moral philosophy, but also on the political level."[115] Chief among the humanists' theological interests was the *imago Dei* tradition in which they saw the key of all human creativity, an emphasis which differed somewhat from medieval writers' preoccupation with mainly human intellectual creativity; humans are creative because they are the image of the creator.[116] The creation of humans in God's image "is also the cause and the condition of the dignity of the human being,"[117] a key concern among humanists.[118]

Julian has more in common with her humanist counterparts than previous generations of historians ever imagined. As Trinkhaus' students continue his research,[119] it becomes more and more apparent how correct Trinkhaus was in his initial evaluation of the Christian and theological content in Renaissance thought. It is now up to the students of late medieval theology to examine their subjects and identify the humanist elements present in mystical thought. Julian is thoroughly engaged in the *imago Dei* tradition, she is heavily influenced by Augustine in religious, moral, philosophical, and political matters, she continually stresses community and human participation in creation, and she bestows utmost dignity to humanity. Her arguments are constructed on different evidence than ones that humanists employ, and her presuppositions often differ from humanists' assumptions, but their goals, motives, and conclusions are often similar. We have noted that Italian humanists interpreted the traditional *imago Dei* doctrine in a new way from their medieval predecessors, emphasizing creativity. Julian too rejected the dominant Augustinian interpretation of *imago Dei* doctrine pertaining chiefly to male reason and instead proposed through her God-as-mother theology that the *imago Dei* applies to all male and female persons.[120] Lorenzo Valla asserts that God is knowable through revelation and through "things created by Him."[121] We have seen example after example of Julian proclaiming likewise. Leonardo Bruni emphasized the civic responsibilities one has to community; so too did Julian.[122] Petrarch based his awe of the human mind and his understanding of nature on the knowledge he received in a quasi-mystical experience on a mountain while reading Augustine's *Confessions* after which he concluded that "nothing is admirable besides the mind; compared to its greatness nothing is great;"[123] Julian wrote of the same judgments. There is no need at this time to assess the relative value of the mystics' intellectual contributions next to the humanists'; it is enough for now to recognize through this limited comparison similarity to humanism, a characteristic too frequently ignored.

Catherine of Siena

One should keep this point in mind as we begin discussing the work of the first officially acknowledged woman doctor of the church, Catherine of Siena.[124] Born in fourteenth-century Siena (1347–1380) and a frequent traveler to the major Renaissance cities of Florence, Pisa, and Rome, Catherine lived and functioned in the heartland of early Renaissance humanism. Catherine's Italy was the Italy of Petrarch (1304–1374) and Boccaccio (1313–1375)—Dante (1265–1321) had died a generation before Catherine's birth—and her church was the Roman church of Avignon and the Great Schism. She lived through the Hundred Years' War and the Black Death and corresponded with secular leaders throughout Europe and Italy and with ecclesiastical leaders including popes. In an age so filled with activity and significant movements Catherine enjoyed an unsullied reputation for wisdom as well as holiness. Her immediate influence was acknowledged by her supporters and opponents alike, and her long-term influence is perhaps best captured by the fact that *Dialogue,* her masterpiece, has been in continuous circulation since she first wrote.[125] Throughout the centuries scholars have stressed different aspects of Catherine's life, some focusing on her political and ecclesiastical activities, some on her mystical experiences, and still others on her preaching and teaching.[126] Here we will look at these activities only insofar as they were motivated by her thought, emphasizing not her political involvement, but the political philosophy that informed her behavior, not her social work but the anthropology that motivated her work.[127]

As typical of so many mystics and humanists of her day, all Catherine's beliefs are grounded in Genesis 1:26: "O supreme goodness that for love alone made us in our image and likeness! For when you created humankind you did not say (as when you created the other creatures); 'Let it be made.' No, you said—O unutterable love!—'Let us make humankind in our image and likeness.' "[128] To Catherine, this is amazing: " 'Think of it! I gifted you with my image and likeness,' God exclaimed."[129] This image and likeness gives humans their beauty, but more importantly it gives them their dignity. Catherine first established this in her prologue to *Dialogue,* and it is a constant theme throughout. It is a fact all thinking people must discover: "Open your mind's eye and look within me, and you will see the dignity and beauty of my reasoning creature."[130] In her spiritual direction she guides her directees to reflect upon the magnitude of this gift. "What heart will be so hard and stubborn," Catherine writes Bartolomeo Smeducci of Sanseverino, "as not to be moved at the sight of such infinite love and the great dignity we have been given."[131] When Catherine asks, "Why did you so dignify us?" her answer is simple: "It was love that made you create us and give us being."[132]

This dignity is at the core of all humanity. It is a dignity "greater than that of the angels," and "this greatness is given to every person."[133] Catherine learned of this dignity by "coming to know herself and God," for the two are inseparable. "As the soul comes to know herself she also knows God better," Catherine explains. "In the gentle Mirror of God she sees her own dignity: that through no merit of hers but by his creation she is the image of God."[134] Once given to humans, dignity is theirs to increase or decrease, and sin, of course, eliminates it. "By our sin we lost the dignity you had given us," Catherine admits, whereas God tells her that it is the contrast between humanity's natural dignity and sin that brings to light the extensive harm sin does to humanity. "I wanted you to experience this mercy as well as your own dignity as I showed you before, so that you would better understand this cruelty and baseness of the wicked," God explains.[135] To those who do sin God decries the loss not of love or virtue but of dignity: "O brutish souls! What have you done with your dignity?"[136] This loss of dignity is not selective but inclusive, and Catherine does not hesitate to remind even the most powerful rulers of the day that they too must guard their dignity closely, as we see her do in a letter to Bernabò, Visconti of Milan: "In that event we become servants and slaves of sin; we become nothings, bereft of any dignity we had."[137] Fortunately, through the Incarnation, by which God "ha[s] become our image," he provided "a way to reconciliation" and to the restoration of human dignity.[138]

Catherine describes humanity's likeness to God in the Augustinian model of the three powers of the soul: memory, understanding, and will.[139] "The understanding is the most noble aspect of the soul" which "is moved by affection ... is love's hand, and this hand fills the memory with thoughts of [God]" and "moves the understanding, saying, as it were. 'I want to love, because the food I feed on is love.' " Understanding, consequently, "is aroused by the consideration of the soul's dignity and the indignity into which she has fallen through her own fault. In the dignity of her existence she tastes the immeasurable goodness and uncreated love with which I created her."[140] Catherine is quick to stress time and again that any indignity a human experiences is because of choices freely made by the will, to which memory and understanding are bound. "The soul is free, liberated from sin in my Son's blood, and she cannot be dominated unless she consents to it with her will, which is bound up with free choice. Free choice is one with the will, and agrees with it. It is set between sensuality and reason and can turn to whichever one it will."[141] According to Catherine, it is hard to place too much importance on the will. It alone decides our fate. "No one can force us to commit the slightest sin, because God has put *yes* and *no* into the strongest thing there is, into our will," Catherine counsels Bernabò in her letter to him.[142] In *Dialogue* she states it thus: "In her freedom she can choose good and evil as it pleases her. But such is the freedom of your humanity, and so strong have you been made by the power of this glorious blood, that neither the devil nor any other creature can force you to the least sin unless you want it. You were freed from slavery so that you might be in control of your own powers and reach the end you were created for."[143]

Catherine's conclusions are simple yet profound. Because all humans are *imago Dei* they have an inherent natural dignity manifest in memory, understanding, and will. Key to understanding Catherine's thought is the idea that each and every individual has this dignity. This fundamental equality of all humans is the foundation upon which all of Catherine's other social theories rest. The world and all creatures in it are made "and put in order to serve the needs of humankind,"[144] not one special class or privileged group. Yet, as we all know, not all people are equally endowed. Vast discrepancies can and do exist among families, friends, and communities. "Why have I established such differences? Why do I give this person one virtue and that person another, rather than giving them all to one person?" God rhetorically asks Catherine. "I give them in different ways so that one virtue might be, as it were, the source of all the others."[145] To one God primarily gives charity, to another justice, and to yet another patience, and so on. Catherine's explanation for this unequal distribution is intriguing. "The same is true of many of my gifts and graces, virtue and other spiritual gifts, and those things necessary for the body and human life. I have distributed them in such a way that no one has all of them. Thus have I given you reason—necessary in fact—to practice mutual charity. For I could well have supplied each of you with all your needs, both spiritual and material. But I wanted to make you dependent on one another so that each of you would be my minister, dispensing the graces and gifts you have received from me." Catherine finds in the equal distribution of traits to humans a justification for class structure. A class society insures social adhesion by making every person's unique contribution indispensable to the whole. Society cannot afford to neglect anyone, because each person's contribution is needed for the good of the whole. "So you see, I have made you my ministers, setting you in different positions and in different ranks to exercise the virtue of charity. For there are many rooms in my house."[146]

Clearly, Catherine thought long and hard about the social conditions of her world. She traveled freely among the poor, the rich, the powerful, and the powerless and assiduously contemplated the inequalities she saw in society. Her need to reconcile these real inequalities with the theoretical equality of all people was inescapable to her personally, and she pursued a solution relentlessly throughout all her writings. She maintains that God "provided for everything in soul and body, for the imperfect and the perfect, for the good and the bad, spiritually and temporally, in heaven and on earth, in this mortal life and in the immortal," but he provides according to a basic need of humanity, the need for community. Catherine held that the solitary life was contrary to human nature. Humans are happiest in community and the inequalities that exist among people is present in order to foster communal life and inhibit isolation. "Whether you want it or not, you are so bound" to each other "by force." In *Dialogue* God expounds upon this at length. "I in my providence did not give to any one person or to each individually the knowledge for doing everything necessary for human life. No, I gave something to one, something else to another, so that each one's need would be a reason to have recourse to the other," He begins. Even if sin perverts a person's will to be kind to others and cooperate with them in community, "you will at least be forced by your own need to practice it in action. Thus you see the artisan turn to the worker and the worker to the artisan: Each has need of the other because neither knows how do to what the other does." Catherine very carefully includes the division of roles within the church in her schema: "So also the cleric and religious have need of the layperson, and the layperson of the religious; neither can get along without the other. And so it is with everything else."[147]

The paradox is deep. The community is composed of people with unequal gifts, talents, and virtues, yet once in community, community makes all people equal. Catherine uses an analogy from the body to clarify: "Your bodily members put you to shame, because they all together practice charity, while you do not. Thus, when the head is aching, the hand helps it. And if the finger, that tiniest of members, hurts, the head does not snub it because it is greater and more noble than all other parts of the body. No, it comes to its aid with hearing and sight and speech and everything it has."[148] For those who still see the unequal distribution of traits as unjust, Catherine resorts to plain talk and asks the question of God directly. His answer is equally direct: "Could I not have given everyone everything? Of course. But in my providence I wanted to make each of you dependent on the others, so that you would be forced to exercise charity in action and will at once." This force is necessary, a fact that coincided with Catherine's personal experience. Some "see a poor person, one of their members, sick and in need, and do not help. They refuse to give not only of their possessions but even a single word. Indeed, they reproachfully and scornfully turn away. They have plenty of wealth, but they leave the poor to starve." Yet, community is so essential to the human condition that it extends even into the next world. "I have so ordered their charity that no one simply enjoys his or her reward in this blessed life that is my gift without its being shared by the others," God proclaims. "The great find joy in the reward of the small, and the small find joy in the reward of the great."[149]

Catherine believed that community is also the birthplace of all personal virtue and vice. "Your neighbors are the channel through which all your virtues are tested and come to birth, just as the evil give birth to all their vices through their neighbors," Catherine declares, so "attend well." All actions good and bad are so because of the impact they have on the community. "All I want is love," God instructs Catherine, but "in loving me you will realize love for your neighbors, and if you love your neighbor you have kept the law."[150] It is impossible therefore to love in isolation. To truly love one must "give their neighbors what is due them: first of all, loving charity and constant humble prayer—your mutual debt—and the debt of teaching, and the example of a holy and honorable life, and the counsel and help they need for their salvation."[151] It is also impossible to exercise the will properly in isolation, for "the principle of holy will means that each of you must work for the salvation of souls according to your own situation."[152] To reinforce the fact that love and proper exercise of the will and service to the community is a responsibility shared by every individual equally, Catherine specifically adds before ending that this applies to each person "whatever your state in life may be—whether noble or superior or subject."[153] In a letter to Joanna, Queen of Naples, Catherine daringly reminds her of this principle, that "neither power nor wealth nor nobility can exempt anyone from service." If Joanna still thought herself an exception, Catherine eliminated that possibility by explicitly commanding Joanna's obedience to this dictate: "I beg you, venerable mother in Christ Jesus," Catherine writes, "behave like a servant too."[154]

It is likewise true that bad actions are judged so because of their relationship to the community. "There is no sin that does not touch others," whether it be done "secretly" or "openly." Even sins against God are "done by means of your neighbors."[155] Catherine expounds further: "Every sin is done by means of your neighbors, because it deprives your neighbors of your charity, and it is charity that gives life to all virtue. So that selfish love which deprives them of your loving charity, and it is charity that gives life to all virtue. So that selfish love which deprives your neighbors of your charity and affection is the principle and foundation of all evil." This is the root cause of "everything unbecoming" and "it has poisoned the whole world and sickened the mystic body of holy church and the universal body of Christianity."[156] Just as "the soul in love with my truth never ceases doing service for all the world, universally and in particular,"[157] so too the reverse is true: Love of the untrue "deprives your neighbors of your charity."[158] Service to the community, then, is not an option, "so whether you will it or not, you cannot escape the exercise of charity!"[159]

Given the high priority Catherine gives to community and to individual involvement in civic affairs it comes as no surprise to see her continually involved in the politics of her own community. Medieval theorists and politicians alike considered society's institutions as the product of one single unified community with two complementary types of rulers, secular nobility and ecclesiastical leaders. There was no distinct line separating the two. All authority came from God, and *regnum* and *sacerdotium* were simply two avenues through which God's authority was made manifest.[160] Each fulfilled indispensable functions for the good of the whole society, and each needed the other. The nature of the relationship between the two was not clearly defined, though, and throughout the centuries this had been a near-constant source of friction. Reasons for continued friction between *regnum* and *sacerdotium* were plentiful in Catherine's day. The increased strength of monarchies and the nascent centralization, constitutionalism, and growth of nation states placed *regnum* in position to upset the balance between itself and, thanks to problems within the papacy, a weakened *sacerdotium*. Secular powers were growing independent and demanding more. They found support in the theories of Dante, Marsilio of Padua, and William of Ockham, all of which challenged not only the authority of *sacerdotium* but even the validity of the concept of Western Christendom.[161] Meanwhile, sacerdotal authority was being attacked within by theorists who promoted conciliarism over traditional papalism. The friction between *regnum* and *sacerdotium* caused by these new theories never really weakened the central Augustinian presuppositions of the age, though; all authority, secular and ecclesiastical, was still believed to come from God. As Catherine says to the signori of Florence, "Human power would be of little use without divine power."[162]

Catherine was intent upon keeping the traditional tenuous balance between *regnum* and *sacerdotium*. She fully acknowledged the rightful power of secular systems of government and argued for total compliance with it no matter what the circumstances. Secular laws must be obeyed, and proper avenues of administration of those laws must be respected. "How unbecoming it would be for a servant to decide to seize power from the judge's hands in order to punish a criminal!" Catherine decried. "We might say, 'The judge isn't doing it, so isn't it good for me to do it?' No, you will be held accountable every time."[163] Even just economic laws must be observed; Catherine urged Pietro del Monte Santa Maria, a Sienese senator, to submit "to the right of justice" and "be conscientious about settling with Messer Matteo and to do so without delay."[164] More important to Catherine, though, is the fact that secular law is valid only if it includes God. In making her case against Florence's formation of an anti-papal league in 1376, Catherine argues that all secular efforts to secure people's happiness are doomed if the *regnum* does not acknowledge their dependency on God. Addressing Nicolò Soderini, one of the city's ruling *priori,* she admits that "since you have been placed in leadership and appointed to the *Signoria,* you could be the means of helping bind all of your townspeople, so that they might not be in such physical and spiritual danger." Nicolò must remember, however, that his secular power will be effective only if he realizes his place in the mystic body, because "a member cut off from its head cannot live, for it is not joined with the source of its life."[165] Any action from those in the secular world which harms or harasses the ecclesiastical world, such as the league would, is wrong. True, "once the league is sealed," Florence would "be in league with many persons and cities. But if God's bonding and help are not there, they would be useless to us. You know that those who guard the city are wearing themselves out for nothing if God is not keeping guard."[166] What Nicolò should do instead is abandon the idea of the league and "try as hard as you can (for God has put you in your position not without great mystery) to bring about peace and unity between yourselves and holy church"—that is, between *regnum* and *sacerdotium*—"so that you and all of Tuscany may not be endangered. It doesn't seem to me that war is so lovely a thing that we should go running after it when we can prevent it."[167] In Catherine's mind, then, conflicts are avoided if the proper balance between *regnum* and *sacerdotium* are maintained, and both must remember that mutual dependency. "The Church is in need, and so are you," Catherine writes to Elizabeth, queen mother of Hungary. "The Church needs your human aid; you need her divine help."[168]

In Catherine's letter to Charles V of France[169] she identifies "three specific things" she believes Charles should do as *regnum* ruler. Her first request is that he acknowledge the nature of his power and his position: "Hold your kingdom as something lent to you, not as if it were your own. For you know well that life, health, wealth, honor, status, dominion—none of those belongs to you." Part of the frustration of the human condition is a result of this knowledge. Charles' power is temporary and his role is that of steward, not owner. If one does not owe something then ultimately he or she does not control it. "The foolish pleasures of the world pass and come to naught," because they do not rightfully belong to humans. They are on loan. Humans "cannot hold on to them, cannot keep life or health or any created thing from passing away like the wind,"[170] because only the owner can control his possessions. Humans are not owners of anything, but only the steward, of those things which God so deigns. No matter what things we enjoy in this world "we can keep them only as much and as long as it pleases the One who has lent them to us."[171] This theme of stewardship is central to Catherine's political thought,[172] for just as stewards have responsibilities, so too do secular leaders.[173] "Every grace you have is from [God] and for his sake," Catherine lectures Queen Joanna of Naples; she does dryly add that Joanna can take ownership for what she rightfully does possess: "Give yourself credit for what is yours—that is, poverty and sin."[174] The upper class "are not so much possessors of [earthly goods] as distributors for the poor."[175] The king of France is "a father to the poor as a dispenser of what God has given you."[176] Catherine's advocacy of stewardship led her to follow the principle to its logical conclusion. In one of her more radical letters Catherine challenges Bernabò to rethink his very identity. "No lordship that we possess in this world allows us to consider ourselves lords. I don't know what sort of lordship that would be, that could be taken away from me and would not be within my control! It seems to me that no man ought to consider or call himself lord, but rather administrator. And this administration is not for always, but only for a time—as it pleases our gentle Lord. And if you should ask me, 'Then don't we have any lordship at all on this earth?' I would answer, yes, we have the most satisfying, most gratifying, most mighty lordship there is—lordship over the city of our own soul."[177]

Catherine combines her understanding of these two elements, stewardship and lordship, to construct an original political concept, the city on loan. She starts her presentation with the proposition that a person "can hardly have lordship over what is being lent to him unless he has started by ruling himself." Only a person who can properly do that is capable of exercising lordship over other things "as something given on loan, not as if it were his own property." She defines the situation thus: "Lordship on loan are cities and other temporary dominions which are lent to us and to others all over the world for a given lapse of time, according to the pleasure of divine bounty, and after local ways and customs so that, either by death or even during our lifetime, they come to an end. They prove, at any rate, that they are on loan." As such, "when we are asked to return the loan, we should do so." A good secular ruler realizes his temporary status but will live up to the responsibilities of governing "with fear of and respect for the entruster."[178]

Catherine's second request of Charles V is "that you uphold true holy justice."[179] Justice and the lack thereof in the world is one of Catherine's favorite themes. "I want you, therefore, to know that nothing causes as much darkness and division in the world among both laypeople and religious, clergy and shepherds of holy Church, as does the lack of the light of justice and the invasion of the darkness of injustice," Catherine wrote in *Dialogue*. Justice is a trait necessary to the functioning of both *regnum* and *sacerdotium*. "No rank whether of civil or divine law can be held in grace within holy justice."[180] With leadership comes power, and the power can easily distort justice, be it secular or ecclesiastical. "There are others who are so bloated with the power in their hands that the standard they carry is injustice" instead of justice, Catherine writes in *Dialogue,* and consequently "they inflict their injustice on God and their neighbors and even on themselves."[181] To Pietro del Monte Santa Maria, a senator of Siena, Catherine expounds that the first rule for administrating justice. "A true minister of real justice" attends to his or her own self first, because "you cannot dispense justice to others in good faith unless you are just with yourself, for what you do is only as just as your will is just and pure." She tells Pietro to "take your place on the judgment seat" of his reason, will, and understanding. Reason should identify the sins, will should be remorseful "and ask for sentencing," and understanding should determine and administer the penalty. "The just Judge will then be appeased. Not only will he pardon your offense, but he will make you who have judged yourself justly become a just judge of others. This is how we become true ministers of justice, by ourselves submitting to the rule of justice."[182] Inversely, Catherine reminds Queen Joanna that false ministers of justice "look only to their own glory, [and] never accomplish anything good. If they are in authority they never reward or punish fairly."[183] The good ruler must do both with justice. "You must, because of your position, see that this is upheld in your kingdom. So I beg you in Christ Jesus not to close your eyes to injustice. See to it that everyone is given his or her just due—the lowly as well as the great, the great as well as the lowly. Take care no human respect diverts you from this."[184] Catherine warns Pope Gregory XI that "those who are in authority, I say, do evil when holy justice dies in them because of their selfish self-centeredness and their fear of incurring the displeasures of others."[185]

Catherine is well aware that even if one follows these rules, human administration of justice is difficult at best and faulty at worst. A leader must firmly believe in justice, in the penalties justice often demands—"justice wants vengeance for the wrong done to God"[186]—and, most importantly, be willing to impose those penalties despite personal discomfort. "This is why the body's [that is, the church's] limbs are rotting—for lack of correction!" Catherine observes. "A firm justice is needed to correct" those clergy "who care for nothing but pleasure, positions of power, and wealth … for while correction should be given with justice and mercy, excessive leniency is the greatest of cruelties."[187] Catherine outright accuses Pope Gregory XI and his clergy of such leniency, and even attributes that leniency to personal failings. These ecclesiastical leaders "see those under them sinning but it seems they pretend not to see and do not correct them. And if they do correct, they do it so feebly and halfheartedly that it is worthless, only a plaster over the vice." Catherine admits the difficulty involved in discerning when and how to administer justice, but again, no justice is the greatest injustice. "Sometimes it's just that they would like to keep peace, and this, I tell you, is the worst cruelty one can inflict. If a sore is not cauterized or excised when necessary, but only ointment is applied, not only will it not heal, but it will infect the whole [body] often fatally." This being so, Catherine asks Gregory in frustration why he and his fellow "shepherds keep using so much ointment?" The obligation to administer justice is so grave a responsibility that those who fail to do so "end up in hell!" because "not only does [the shepherd] fail to rescue his little sheep from the clutches of the wolf; he devours them himself!"[188] Leaders' failure to insure justice may even provoke those to engage in more injustice, because "injustice cannot harmonize with justice."[189] This is Catherine's explanation for the anti-papal league fomenting against Gregory XI: "Even though there is no excuse for wrongdoing, still, because of all the suffering and injustice and unfairness they [members of the league] were enduring from bad pastors and administrators, it didn't seem to them they had any alternative."[190] Not one to mince words, Catherine places responsibility for justice squarely on those in power. "If I were in your place I would be afraid of incurring divine judgment," she rails against Gregory. "See to it, as you value your life, that you are not guilty of irresponsibility. Don't make light of the works of the Holy Spirit that are being asked of you. You can do them if you *want* to. You *can* see that justice is done."[191]

The third request of Charles V is that the "friendship and love between you and your neighbor with whom you have been so long at war" is realized. As Colish points out, all the major issues in medieval political theory were "responses to actual events"[192] and in this Catherine's political thought is no exception. Catherine is reacting here to France's involvement in what posterity has called the Hundred Years' War. Her ideals of human community, dignity, equality, and service come into play here as she pragmatically applies them to the war. Charles' first priority should be his community. "Don't be concerned about losing your earthly possessions, for the loss will be gain to you if only you can make peace with your brothers and sisters," Catherine warns him. The welfare of the community is of utmost importance, and as its secular ruler he is responsible for it. "I am surprised you aren't willing to sacrifice even your life if you could—to say nothing of material things—at the sight of all the physical and spiritual destruction there has been, and all the religious and women and children who have been abused and driven away by this war. No more, for love of Christ crucified! Don't you realize that you are the cause of this evil if you don't do what you can?" Part of Catherine's solution to war within the Christian community is unpalatable to modern critics, but it rests firmly on her conception of community. One must do everything possible to promote love within the community, but one must also defend the community against outsiders who do not share this love. "What a scandal, humanly speaking, and what an abomination before God, that you should be making war against your brothers and leaving your enemies alone, and that you should be seizing what belongs to another and not get back what is yours!" To wit, the evil Catherine perceives is the harm war does to her own community, not war in and of itself. "You and the other Christian lords ought to be ashamed of such a thing," the "thing" being the damage inflicted on the community, so "Make peace! Make peace, and turn the whole war against the unbelievers!" Before ending her letter she issues one last warning: "God will hold you and the others responsible for this at the moment of your death."[193]

Echoes of this plea are found in Catherine's letter to Elizabeth, queen mother of Hungary, begging her to "ask your dear son to offer himself with love to serve holy church ... to make this sweet holy crusade against the wicked unbelieving dogs who have possession of what is ours." After all, "we ought to be lovers of this holy Church, members bound together in this bride, a mystic body."[194] Writing to mercenary John Hawkwood, currently involved in the Italian cities' internecine fighting, Catherine reiterates these themes yet again: "You find so much satisfaction in fighting and waging war, so now I am begging you tenderly in Christ Jesus not to wage war any longer against Christians (for that offends God), but to go instead to fight the unbelievers, as God and our holy father have decreed. How cruel it is that we who are Christians, members bound together in the body of holy Church, should be persecuting one another!"[195] Catherine also brings in her conception of civic service to bear on the matter. "I see in myself no service I can give except tears and sighs and constant prayer. But you, mother and my lord the king, your son—*you* are in a position to help her in prayer," Catherine writes, carefully making the following distinction, "and you can also help in your love with voluntary human aid. Do not refuse this task."[196]

Catherine theoretically opposes the anti-papal league, because the league disrupts the community as Catherine defines it, the mystic body. Members of the league, however, define community as co-existent with their political entity, the city-state. Hints of this fundamental difference can be detected in Catherine's letter to the ruling elders of Lucca. Upholding her understanding of community as church, she answers the elders thus: "And if you tell me, 'It seems that she [the church] is getting weak and can't help herself, let alone her children,' I tell you it is not so. It may well seem that way from appearances, but look within and you will find there that strength of which her enemy [the league] has none. ... And if you should say, 'I don't know about that; I see these members thriving and getting ahead'—wait a while, for it should not and cannot go on like this. For the Spirit says in Holy Scripture, 'In vain and futilely does the guard work to keep the city from harm if God is not guarding it.' " Catherine considers the city-state that sees itself as an independent entity to be like a gangrenous limb severed from the body. At the time that Catherine writes, the Luccan elders had not formally joined the league, and she was trying to dissuade them of making that final step. She reminds them that as of yet "have not been cut off from your head, from the one who is strong. Nor are you bound to the weak and gangrenous limb that has been cut off from his strength. Be careful, be careful, that you do not make such a bonding!"[197]

Birgitta of Sweden

Many of these ideas and principles form the backbone of the writings of a third great woman intellect of the period, Birgitta of Sweden. Birgitta (1303–1373) came from a wealthy, powerful family in Sweden. Married early to Ulf and mother of eight children (the fourth of which was Catherine; saint and probably author of a work, *The Consolation of the Soul*[198]), Birgitta was called to court ca. 1336 to be a *magistra* in the royal household of the newly married King Magnus and Blanche de Namur. The year 1344 was a turning point in her life; she was widowed, and soon after she began receiving "revelations, not while she slept, but while she was awake."[199] Her political life in the European arena began in earnest five years later when she moved to Rome where her visions told her to remain until instructed otherwise. This resulted in a lengthy residence lasting over two decades.[200] During her stay she engaged in many diplomatic efforts to establish peace between the empire and the papacy, to free the papacy from French control, and to rally the West to another crusade. She stayed involved in Swedish politics, though, and as such she was often a thorn in the side of King Magnus; in the book of *Revelations* Birgitta chastises the king for becoming an instrument of the devil when he disobeyed her previous instructions concerning her Russian crusade. Her "insurrection" revelation which calls for the king to step aside and give the rein of power to his son contributed greatly to his overthrow in 1364.[201]

Her reputation was such that in a mere five years after her death she was already being artistically represented in churches in Rome and Naples. Her daughter Catherine claimed that Pope Gregory XI had such a representation in his chamber.[202] Birgitta was canonized only eighteen years after her death. Her formal canonization was not the final word on her doctrine, though. Her thought remained controversial well into the next century, so much so that she was an object of discussion at both the Council of Constance (1414–1418) and the Council of Basel (1431–1439) and in the work of church doctors Pierre d'Ailly and Jean Gerson.[203] Her body of work prevailed, and she remained highly influential until her homeland became Lutheran in the sixteenth century and officially abolished her cult. She enjoyed much attention among English mystics where testimony to her influence abounds. Margery Kempe (ca. 1373–1439) was much taken with her, and even made a pilgrimage to her Roman home where she interviewed Birgitta's previous servants and neighbors for insight into Birgitta's life. When Margery visited the chamber where Birgitta died, "she heard a German priest preach of her there, and of her revelations, and of her manner of life," thereby indicating that within years of her death a cult grew up around her which drew admirers throughout Europe.[204] In a vision the Lord told Margery "that every word that is written in Bridget's book is true."[205] Birgitta's writings are quoted in defense of Richard Rolle's mystical writings. Birgitta's *Revelations* are found as gifts bequeathed among nobility such as the Yorkists and royalty such as Emperor

Wenceslaus IV. Her prophecies were gathered together in various pamphlets and treatises throughout the fifteenth century and often quoted in support of religious and political issues.[206] Her influence is particularly strong even to this day in the art world, both through the adaptation of her imagery of the nativity, crucifixion, and the Pietà, as discussed in Chapter 5, and through the presence of statues, sculpture, frescoes, and altarpieces of Birgitta herself found throughout Scandinavia and northern Europe.[207] As Joseph Cardinal Ratzinger summarizes, "her *Revelations* have for centuries shaped in a very decisive manner, the portrayal of the life and of the human sufferings of Jesus, in one word the image of Christ in the Church."[208]

As in Catherine of Siena's work the theme of justice pervades Birgitta's work. In *Revelations,* the fifth and key book called *Book of Questions,* Birgitta presents her thought through a dialogue between "a certain religious, known to her and at the time still alive in the body—a man of great erudition in the science of theology but full of guile and diabolic malice," and Christ "seated on a wonderful throne like a judge judging."[209] Birgitta's purpose throughout this book is to rationally inquire into the justice of those areas of the human condition which often are obstacles to those who resemble the said religious,[210] as when in the Second Interrogation the religious asks, "Item. Why have you given law and justice if not for doing vengeance?" For Birgitta vengeance and justice are incompatible. Rather, the Judge replies, "Justice and law have been instituted by me that they may be accomplished with supreme charity and compassion and that divine unity and concord may be strengthened among humans."[211] These are the reasons for and the goal of justice: love within the community. Always justice, both divine and human, must be measured with mercy. "We know very well that it is rightful that his sins are punished, but be merciful so that he may be converted and do penance and reverence to God," a voice proclaims to God who answers that mercy is always included in the "fourfold justice of God."[212] Divine justice, which "had no beginning nor end, no more than God himself,"[213] may not always be readily apparent to humans, but that is a result of the limitations of the human condition. "Why are you disturbed because I put up with that man so patiently," God asks Birgitta. "Was it you that bore him, or do you know his interior as I do?" he continues. "I suffer him in order that in him my justice may be manifested to others. And so, wherever dye-plants have been sown, if they are cut before their time, they do not have the strength to color a thing as well as if they were cut in due time. Thus, my words—which are to be manifested with justice and mercy and ought to grow and bear fruit even to the fullness of maturity—then indeed will be more fit for the thing to which they will be applied."[214]

In Birgitta's specific instructions to Peter II, King of Cyprus and John, prince of Antioch, she repeatedly advises them to rule with justice and mercy. Human justice and mercy must imitate divine justice and mercy in both *regnum* and *sacerdotium.* In her Fifth Counsel, for example, she urges them to "will to love the souls of your subjects, advising your military people that all who have in any way offended God should quickly and humbly correct themselves" and "that they should reconcile themselves to those neighbors they have offended and establish a concord with them." Her counsel deals with the secular rulers' obligation to insure the establishment of justice throughout the church: "The sixth counsel is that you should tell all prelates that they must effectively and frequently admonish all their clerics, namely, the rectors of churches, that each of them is to inquire diligently in his parish as to whether there be any of his parishioners who persist in living wickedly in public sins." If they persist in their sin then their "prelates may juridically correct the forwardness of such obstinate persons by means of an ecclesiastical censure." If this still does not help, "then you, my lords, are advised to be, with your powerful hands, co-workers with the lord prelates so that by help the said sinners may be brought to correct themselves and that having amended their lives they may attain God's mercy." It is Peter II and John's duty as secular rulers to promote justice and mercy in all human matters, no matter what the realm. "Since divine providence has appointed you the governors of the kingdom, you should use all possible diligence in speaking to all the prelates" and advise them "that they and their subjects should all correct themselves in all those matters in which they have in any way deviated spiritually or temporally."[215]

In an edited medieval version of *Revelations* Birgitta's advice to a secular king is recorded. Here we see an even stronger connection made between justice and good government:

> For the king was stirred and counseled to beware of all sins forbidden by holy Church and to have moderate fastings, so that he might hear and answer his subjects' complaints, and be ready to do right to rich and poor who asked it; so that for much abstinence the good of the community of the people of the realm and the governance of the common profit not be lessened, nor that he should not be the more slothful from overmuch excess to give audience to all. Also the king was counseled and stirred how he should serve God and pray, and which days and times he should leave other occupations and purposes for the common profit of his realm. Also the king was counseled which days he should treat all his counsels with men who loved Truth and with the friends of God; and that he should never knowingly pass over truth nor law; and that he should not put any unwanted grievance to the common people of his realm but for the defense of the same, and for war against the pagans. Also the king was counseled to have a number of servants in his household, according to the faculty of livelihood and rents of the exchequer of his realm. And all that was left over, he should share with his knights and friends. Also the king was counseled wisely to admonish them who were insolent and lewd with charitable words, and manfully to correct them; ... and he should judge rightfully both men of the land and strangers.[216]

Birgitta's respect for community is as evident in her counsels to secular rulers as is her demand of justice. She advises Peter II of Cyprus and John of Antioch that they themselves must "be united in true love so that you may be one heart toward God and his honor, ruling the kingdom for the honor of God and the good of your subjects." Community must continue to grow from mutual love, so "both of you are to be united in true charity with your subjects." Any division within the community harms it, so Peter II and John must even "forgive and spare all" who differed from them in their political interests and "by advice, deed, or approbation, cooperated in the death of your father King Peter. Include them in your charity with all your heart in order that God may deign to include you in his mercy."[217] In a revelation concerning

Cyprus the communal relationship of the people Birgitta's Jesus is addressing is underlined by continually referring to "the inhabitants of the kingdom of Cyprus as if about one human being."[218] In the same revelation Birgitta discusses the wider Christian community of the Roman Church and how essential its unity is; those outside that community, specifically, the Greeks, who "will not spiritually subject and humbly subjugate themselves to that same Roman Church," unfortunately in justice "are unworthy to obtain pardon and mercy." For Birgitta lack of unity to the Roman Church community carries grave political consequences and so warns them: "Let the Greeks also know that their empire and kingdoms or domains will never stand secure and tranquil in peace, but that they themselves will always be subject to their enemies from whom they will always sustain the gravest of losses and daily miseries until, with true humility and charity, they devoutly subject themselves to the Church and faith of Rome, totally conforming themselves to the sacred constitutions and rites of that same Church."[219] The unity within the community must extend to matter and form.

Birgitta shares Catherine of Siena's high regard for the intellectual capacity of humanity and sees in its rational powers a source for its dignity. Although the *imago Dei* imagery is not as frequently employed in Birgitta's writings, it is implied throughout. In one of her few explicit statements on the *imago Dei* Birgitta writes thus: "Truly, the soul is more worthy and more noble than the whole world and more stable than all things. It is more worthy because it is spiritual and equal to the angels and created for eternal joy. It is more worthy because it was made, in the image of my Godhead, both immortal and eternal." Birgitta then uses this likeness to establish humanity's dignity through its rational powers: "Therefore, because man is more worthy and more noble than all creatures, man ought to live more nobly than all; for he, in preference to others, has been enriched with reason." The gift of intellect comes with a high price, that of responsibility, for "if man abuses reason and my divine gifts, what wonder is it if, at the time of justice, I punish that which was passed over in the time of mercy?"[220] One must be most careful with this gift of intelligence, for "erudition, without a good life, does not please me; therefore, it is necessary that those who abuse rationality be corrected." Only if "rationality and life are in agreement" is it beneficial to a person; "it is not without cause that in some, rationality is great but useless, as in those who have knowledge but not life." Every person is "given a measure of rationality by means of which he can obtain heaven if he lives piously." However, because "rationality varies in many according to their natural and spiritual dispositions," the responsibility owed to that rationality varies. To those with more, more is expected: "Let everyone who has the grace of intelligence therefore fear that, because of it, he will be judged more heavily if he is negligent. Let him who has no intelligence or talent rejoice and do as much as he can with the little that he has, for he has been freed from many occasions of sin."[221] Reason is what distinguishes humans from animals. Because God created a world in which everything is "for man's use or for his needs and sustenance or for his instruction and reproof or for his consolation and humiliation," he did not give animals reason. If they possessed "intelligence as man does, they would certainly be a trouble to him, causing harm rather than profit."[222] True, humans also have emotions, but emotions only will not bring happiness. "Friend, I gave man [bodily] sense and intelligence that he might consider and imitate the ways of life and flee the ways of death," the Judge in Birgitta's interrogations declares,[223] but it is rationality in whatever proportion one possesses it, that is of utmost importance. Simply put, humans "have reason and understanding. If they use these they shall be saved."[224]

One of the more striking characteristics of Birgitta's writing is her preoccupation with body parts. From the simple instructions Mary gives Birgitta to possess "a mouth clean of all detraction, ears closed to idle talk, modest eyes, hands busy with good works" to Birgitta's more detailed discussions in her *Prayers* of body parts, her concern for body parts permeates her work. As unusual as it may be in our contemporary world, Bynum reminds us that such preoccupation was somewhat typical in Birgitta's world. A glance at the art of the period certainly verifies this fact; even Herrad's *Hortus deliciarum* and Hildegard of Bingen's *Scivias* give witness to the era's propensity for body parts.[225] Birgitta's third prayer[226] composed in honor of Jesus' body and "to offer to all the members of your precious body such thanks as I can,"[227] while her fourth prayer is dedicated to Mary's body "to render here on earth such praise and thanks as I can to all your precious limbs."[228] The detail given to the body in the prayers is quite minute and thorough. "Blessed, therefore, be your eyes, your eyelids, and your glorious eyebrows," "your kindly ears," "your most sweet and blessed nostrils," "your venerable mouth and your lips," and "your most clean teeth" with which "you most moderately chewed physical food" are addressed and described at length. "Blessed be your throat, your stomach, and your viscera," "your holy shoulders and neck," "your most worthy blood," "your magnificent heart," "your precious ribs and your back," "your blessed feet," and "your knees with their hams and your shins" round out Birgitta's praise of Jesus' body parts.[229] Lest one think Birgitta exhausted her knowledge and appreciation of the body, she focuses on specific female anatomical parts in her prayer to Mary. "Praise be your hair with all its strands," "your most honest face," "your most blessed cheeks," "your most sacred breasts giving milk to the Son of God," "your glorious bosom," and "your most blessed womb above all fruitfully sprouting fields" are praised in addition to the limbs and organs singled out in her prayer for Jesus' body.[230]

Revelations is also filled with praise of body parts. The first interrogation of the key *Book of Questions* is a series of five questions on the function of body parts. "First question: 'O Judge, I ask you: You have given me a mouth. May I not say the things that please me?' Second question: 'You have given me eyes. May I not see with them those things that delight me?' "[231] The second interrogation asks, "why have you given me limbs for my body," while the third asks, "why did you give us bodily senses," and so on throughout the interrogations.[232] In all these instances Birgitta's high regard for the body is obvious. In one revelation Birgitta communicates her love of the part through a proclamation of Jesus to Mary on the beauty and value of her mother's body. Mary is told "your head was like gleaming gold, and your hair like the rays of the sun," "your cheeks were of the finest color—namely, white and ruddy," "your mouth was like a lamp—burning within shining without," "your neck is nobly erect and beautifully elevated," "your breast was so full of all the sweetness of the virtues," and "your womb was as perfectly clear as ivory and shone like a place built on exquisite stones."[233] In *Sermo Angelicus*[234] Birgitta makes it clear that Mary's body was as essential to salvation history as her soul. "At her funeral [the apostles] humbly venerated her," Birgitta writes, "exalting with laud and glory her dead body. Doubtless it should be believed that, as the dead body of the most Blessed Virgin was carried by the friends of God to be buried, so by God himself, her most beloved son, her body with her living soul was venerably assumed to perpetual life."[235] Just as Mary's "soul was the origin of all her good deeds, so too her honorable body was a most apt and ready instrument for the carrying out of these deeds," and so too is this true for our bodies. Therefore, Birgitta concludes, "all bodies will arise at the last days and together with their souls receive fitting rewards," joining Mary's body which had already been "assumed with the soul of the most holy Virgin into heaven."[236]

Contrary to stereotypes concerning medieval intellectual disdain for the body, in Bynum's opinion, "it is patently not true (however much passing remarks about Platonic dualism may suggest it) that twelfth-, thirteenth-, and fourteenth-century thinkers who attributed some independent substantial reality to matter and/or body were inclined to see such entities as unreal or (in a simple, categorical sense) evil."[237] Birgitta was no exception. Rather than view the body as evil, she saw it as worthy of praise, and her appreciation of the human body extends to its reproductive organs and activities. As Birgitta explains it, with the first sin came "the arrival of shame for the violation," and then "inordinate impulses soon increased, and most of all in that organ which was set in place for the sake of fruitfulness. But so that this impulse might not be fruitless, by the goodness of God it was converted into something good; and through the institution of a divine command, the work of carnal intercourse was granted as the means by which nature could bear fruit." Her belief that sexual intercourse was basically good had the practical effect of rendering her opinion of marriage as high. She accepted the value of virginity but did not use that to devalue marriage. As she eloquently stated it, "virginity is a most beautiful path to heaven—while marriage, is, as it were, a road."[238] When discussing her position on clerical marriage, her appreciation of marriage seeps through even her argument against clerical marriage. She calls an archbishop who made a statement that "if he were pope, he would give leave for all clerics and priests to contract marriage in the flesh," confused but nevertheless, "still a friend of God" because "through such marriage the greater carnal sins might be avoided."[239] Interestingly, Birgitta's conclusion that "it has been justly ordained that priests who do not live in chastity and continence of the flesh are cursed," she uses a metaphor of body parts to describe that curse: "God will condemn him to a sentence as great, in a spiritual way, as that which the law justly inflicts in a corporeal way on a man who has transgressed so gravely that he must have his eyes gouged out, his tongue and lips, nose and ears cut off, his hands and feet amputated, all his body's blood spilled out to grow completely cold, and finally, his whole bloodless corpse cast out to be devoured by dogs and other wild beasts. Similar things would truly happen in a spiritual way."[240] As Bynum argues, underlying most of the late medieval discussions of body parts are the theses that "material continuity is crucial to identify" personhood and "that the material body we occupy in this life is integral to person."[241] If the body is essential for personhood, then it is also essential for eternal happiness. Bonaventure wrote concerning Mary's assumption that because "the person is not the soul; it is a composite." Mary's body must be in heaven with her soul or "otherwise she would not be there [in heaven] in perfect joy."[242] Birgitta is very much a member of this school of thought. While certainly no pioneer in these positions, Birgitta was, on the other hand, one of its chief promoters, given how pervasive is her theme and the influence of her work. Rather than see Birgitta's constant reference to body parts as a quirk or a distraction, we must see it for the strong intellectual statement that it was. The person is a composite being of soul and body, and thus when considering any aspect of a person, the physical must be taken into consideration.

7

Women Humanists

We have already recounted how influenced Margery Kempe was by the writings of Birgitta of Sweden; in this Margery was one of many. There are indications that Birgitta's work was well-known in England and that her *Revelations* were among the most bequested books in fourteenth- and fifteenth-century English wills.[1] The renowned Birgittine monastery at Syon, the only new female monastery founded in England after 1377 until modern times, did much to make the cult of St. Birgitta visible and her works known. Laity such as Margery Kempe tell us that she made the popular pilgrimage to Syon herself "to obtain her pardon" during Lammastide, just as many people did.[2] Nor can it be said that England was unique in its devotion to Birgitta, for we know of many other instances of her work being reproduced throughout the West for lay consumption. Thomas of Štítné (ca. 1331–1401), for example, translated *Visions of Saint Bridget of Sweden* into Czech specifically for the education of young women, including his daughter Agnes,[3] only years after Birgitta's death. The following century saw *Revelations* translated and printed in various languages, thus making it both famous and influential in a relatively short period.[4] Likewise did Catherine of Siena's fame and influence parallel Birgitta's. Catherine's *vita* was among the most bequested works in late medieval English wills,[5] and her *Dialogue* was translated into English for the Birgittines at Syon. Known as *The Orcherd of Syon* it was printed in 1519.[6] When Sir Richard Sutton, steward of Syon Abbey, directed the printing of *The Orcherd of Syon* he stated that it was for the laity as well as for religious.[7] According to Tommaso Caffarini, Catherine's disciple and the chief promoter of her canonization, Catherine's letters were already circulating less than eighteen years after her death. He tells us that Christofano Gani "gathered together almost all of the virgin's letters that had been scattered here and there, so that he made of them two volumes, which I, when I was in Siena in 1398, brought back with me to Venice."[8] The first printed edition of her letters appeared in 1492, the same year Birgitta's *Revelations* was first printed.[9] Clearly the works of women intellectuals were being read and were being included in the early modern literary canon.

Christine de Pizan

Chief among those women whose works formed that canon was Christine de Pizan. France's first woman of letters and probably the first Western person to support herself and her family solely through writing, Christine de Pizan is a major intellectual force to be reckoned with in any intellectual history. Accolades abound. "An uncommon scholar" whose "works represent some of the richest poetry and prose writings of her era" and "are rich in philosophic argument and thought" is Waithe's description of Christine.[10] Charity Cannon Willard, a scholar whose pioneering research and excellent translations are largely responsible for our current appreciation of and access to Christine, tells us that Christine is "altogether phenomenal" because of the "scope and variety of her works." A participant in the first public literary debate, one on misogyny, "Christine is equally important as a vivid witness of the times in which she lived" as an educator and political commentator.[11] Daniel Poirion declares that Christine "in the true sense of the word, is our first *author,* and that author is a woman."[12] With continued research surely other areas of significance in Christine's work will emerge and reinforce the truth of Martin le France's epitaph uttered in 1442: "Though death may draw the curtain around her body, her name shall still endure."[13]

These were Christine's own sentiments about fame, as recorded in the concluding sections of *The Book of the Body Politic.* So confident was she of her own importance that she based her compensation on that fame. "And I beg in payment from those living and their successors, the very noble kings and other French princes, in remembrance of my sayings in times to come when my soul is out of my body, that they would pray to God for me, requesting indulgence and remission of my sins," Christine writes.[14] Her request is also addressed to people other than nobility, thus indicating how wide Christine believed her audience to be. "And likewise, I ask of French knights, nobles, and generally of all, no matter from where they might be, that if they have any pleasure in the hours they saw or heard read from my little nothings, that they think of me and say an Our Father. And in the same way, I wish the universal people—the three estates and the whole together—that God by His holy mercy desire to maintain and increase them."[15] In *The Book of Three Virtues* (also known as *The Treasury of the City of Ladies*) we see Christine's belief in the superiority of her insights become the motivation in her pursuit of even wider fame and influence. Indeed, her ambition seems to have no limits in time, place, or class:

> As I looked at [the Three Virtues: Reason, Rectitude, and Justice] written down and reviewed them, they seemed to me more and more profitable for the improvement of virtuous habits, increasing ladies' honor, and good for the whole community of women, now living and those in the future, wherever this work may reach an audience. Therefore I, their servant, though not always adequate in serving them well (though I always desire to be so), began thinking that I would make many copies of this work and would distribute it throughout the world, no matter what the cost. It would be presented in many different places to queens, princesses, and noble ladies so that it would be more honored and exalted—for it is most worthy—and through them it could be disseminated to other women. Once this idea is executed and my wish fulfilled—and I have already started on this—the work will circulate and be published in all countries, even though it is written in French. But since this language is more common in the world than any other, this work will not remain unknown and useless but will remain in the

> world without fail in many copies. Many valiant ladies and women of authority will see and hear it in present and in future times, and they will pray to God for their servant Christine, wishing that she should have lived during their lifetime so that they could have known her.[16]

Such explicit, self-conscious reflection on fame is highly significant, because it is a characteristic common to humanists. Burchhardt claimed long ago that "the idea of fame, that is, of distinction won by a man's personal efforts" was a major characteristic of Italian humanism. According to this master historian of the Renaissance, "boundless ambition and thirst after greatness" was a major motivation of the humanists and as such resulted in the birth of "the modern idea of fame."[17] Too often she is readily classified as the first woman writer of the French Middle Ages;[18] too rarely is she considered to be the first woman humanist of the French renaissance. As literary historian Diane Bornstein argues, "if Christine's work is read without preconceptions" the conclusion the reader would in fact reach is that Christine "deserves to be considered one of the first humanists of the French Renaissance," no less the first woman humanist.[19] In two of her books Christine deals specifically with the history and education of women, *The Book of City of Ladies* and *The Book of Three Virtues,* and these preoccupations "place her squarely into the forefront of humanist thinking," according to historian Susan Bell.[20] Her autobiographical writings possess the same degree of self-revelatory, introspective writing as does the writing of her model Petrarch.[21] Concern for the political is another characteristic of Renaissance humanism, and literary scholar Earl Jeffrey Richards claims that "Christine, particularly in her use of national images, marks a significant departure from the medieval universalist tradition" and that she "goes farther than Petrarch" in some political causes.[22] Christine's analysis of the realities of power and the ethics which must regulate public life are as plain and directly written as Machiavelli's later writing; Bell calls Christine "an earlier female Machiavelli,"[23] Christine believes that every noble child should "understand Latin" because "the greater good would ensue and virtue would increase for them and their subjects."[24] Her view of civic life also "differs from the traditional medieval understanding" of social classes based on religious criteria and instead endorses a secular basis.[25] Bornstein concludes that Christine "does not have the international, Catholic focus of the Middle Ages, but the national, secular one of the Renaissance," and that her emphasis on civic virtue and on an active civic life is similar to Italian humanists.[26] These are just some of the features in Christine's work that remind us how incomplete is the scholarly assessment of her thought.

This is not to deny Christine's position in medieval culture; again as Bornstein reminds us, the Renaissance owes much to the Middle Ages and their respective "realms of ideas were not antithetical."[27] Much scholarship during the latter part of the twentieth century has been devoted to softening the contrast between the two periods and emphasizing their continuity.[28] As we shall see, Christine is a prime example of this continuity, much in the same way that Dante's work is the culmination of medieval worldview and the origin of the early modern.

Even Christine's life embodies characteristics typical of both medieval and Renaissance societies; Willard entitles her first chapter in Christine's biography,

"A Child of Two Worlds."[29] Born in 1364 in Venice, Christine's early years were spent there and in Bologna, and although she was too young to be influenced directly by the Renaissance culture flourishing in these cities, her father, Thomas de Pizan, certainly was not. Christine tells us much about herself in *Visions*. Here she explains that her father was at the very center of Venetian intellectual culture, revered for "the importance and authority of his learning." Soon the king of France and the king of Hungary both extended him offers of employment in their courts "for the great fame of his scholarly authority" had spread far and wide. Thomas decided to go to the French court of Charles V "as he wanted to see the colleges of Paris," and in 1369 he moved his family to that city.[30] When Christine became of marriageable age her father "looked to a young scholar and graduate" for a suitable match, "since my father thought that the most worthy man possessed both great learning and good character."[31] It was a happy marriage but short, for ten years later "Death deprived me of him when he was thirty-four years old." Christine's father had died some two years before her husband's death, and she "was justifiably filled with bitterness" as she became the sole support of her own three children and her mother's households.[32] Christine's first hurdle was untangling the massive confusion of her husband's finances, a situation which led her repeatedly to court "because of inherited properties on which old revenues and large arrearages were demanded."[33] It also led to the composition of one of her earliest ballads, an emotional condemnation of French society's unconscionable treatment of widows, and, as she reflected on her past happiness, to the penning of *One Hundred Ballads,* ca. 1394.

As her mourning passed and her days in court ended Christine was able to return "to the life that naturally pleased me the most, that is, the solitary and tranquil life." In her widow's solitude "there came back to me from the earlier days memorized passages of Latin and the languages of the noble sciences—various sententia and polished rhetoric that I had heard in the past when my dear, dead husband and father had been alive." Admitting that she "was naturally inclined to scholarship from birth,"[34] she confesses that once married she ignored the fonts of philosophy and "took not my fill of them." Her frustration only increased as she realized that the loss of her husband and father meant the loss of scholarship. "Alas! when I had masters of knowledge beside me, I neglected learning," Christine lamented, so now her only option was to undertake a course of self-education. "Like the child one first puts to his ABC's, I went to the ancient histories from the beginning of the world," Christine confides, "and thereafter to the deductions of the sciences, according to what I could understand in the time I had studied them. Then I went to the books of poets, and as they continued to increase the good of my understanding, I was content inasmuch as I had found the style natural to me." In due time her studies gave birth to a desire to make her own contributions: "At this point, my mind and feelings were unsatisfied; indeed, Nature wanted new volumes brought forth from me through the engenderment of study and the things [I had] seen. She told me, 'Take the tools and strike the anvil. The material I will give you is so durable that neither iron nor fire nor anything else will be able to destroy it. So forge pleasing things.'"[35]

Write she did. "From the year 1399 when I began until this year of 1405" (the year her autobiographical *Visions* from which these comments are taken), "fifteen principal volumes were compiled, excluding other individual small poems."[36] *Letter of the God of Love, Letter of Othea, Book of Human Integrity, Debate of Two Lovers, Book of Three Judgments, Tale of Poissy, Tale of the Shepherdess, Book of the Long Road of Learning,* and the famous *Letters from the Debate on the Romance of the Rose* were written between 1399 and 1403. The years 1404–1405 were most productive, for during this period she published her longest and most learned poem, *Book of Fortune's Change.* She also published many of her most important prose works: *Book of the Deeds and Good Customs of Wise King Charles V, Book of the City of Ladies, Book of Three Virtues,* and *Visions.* These are by and large historical and instructional works; *Book of the Duke of True Lovers,* a rather rebellious interpretation of courtly love, was probably composed during these years too. In her last writing phase, 1407–1418, Christine wrote nine major works, chiefly political in nature. *Book of the Body Politic, Book of Deeds and Arms and Chivalry, Letter in the Prison of Human Life, Lamentations on the Troubles of France,* and *Book of Peace* all reflect both the civil unrest of the day and Christine's own political theories about that unrest. *The Tale of Joan of Arc* (1429) is the last known work by Christine and the only contemporary narrative about Joan written before her fall from grace. Joan was executed in May 1431, and Christine may or may not have survived her.

Being the first woman intellectual to earn her living as such, the question of Christine's influence is of historical interest. That Christine was held in high esteem by her contemporaries is beyond doubt. Contemporary poet Eustache Deschamps wrote that she was "without equal today in acquired wisdom and all doctrine, science, philosophy, knowledge."[37] Most interest in her work today centers around her feminist apologia, particularly as expressed in her utopian *Book of the City of Ladies* and *Book of the Three Virtues,* and in her literary debate, the famous *querelle de la rose;* it is fair to say her contemporaries shared these interests. Christine's participation in the latter debate not only earned her visibility among the reading public, but it also marks her acceptance within Parisian intellectual circles. The debate was initiated by Jean de Montreuil in 1401 and concerned the very popular thirteenth-century poem, *The Romance of the Rose.* The allegorical poem was a hybrid. The first four thousand verses were written by Guillaume de Lorris ca. 1236, and some forty years later Jean de Meun added another 17,000 lines. According to Christine, Jean de Montreuil expressed his high opinion of the poem, particularly Jean de Meun's section, in a private conversation with her and then in a written treatise. A copy of the treatise was sent to Christine, to Gontier Col, who, like Jean de Montreuil, was a royal secretary, and to Pierre d'Ailly, bishop of Cambria and an intellectual of some stature. Within a few months Christine wrote a response to Jean de Montreuil's critique, and the most famous literary debate of the period had begun. "Moved rather by my contrary opinion of your words," Christine decided to write a formal response because "you have committed a grave error without reason in giving such perfect praise to the foresaid work, which could better be called utter idleness than a useful work, in my judgment."[38] Christine qualifies her criticism of *The Rose* by acknowledging that "there are certainly some good things well stated in it," but then she is quick to point out that the dual nature of the work is "the work's greatest danger: for evil is rendered more believable by putting it together with good to make it more respectable."

She spells out her reasons for reaching this conclusion. The humanist promotion of civic duties, moral philosophy, individualism, respect for history, and love of antiquity, all goods, are embraced as fully as the poem's disrespect for women, an evil. Therefore, *Romance of the Rose* "is not worthy of a judgment being imputed to it," and by so magnifying its worth "you do a great injustice to all valuable books: for a work without usefulness to the common or private good—no matter how delightful or at what labor and cost—is not worthy of praise."[39] She continues:

> And just as in olden times when the triumphant Romans would give neither praise nor honors to anything that was not useful to the public, let us look at their example before attempting to crown this romance. For I find, it seems to me, these forementioned things and others considered, better that it be shrouded in fire than crowned with laurel, even though you call it a "mirror of good living, a model for political self government and for living religiously and wisely;" on the contrary, with all respect, I say that it is an exhortation to vice seeking to comfort a dissolute life, a doctrine full of deception, a path to damnation, public defamation, a cause of suspicion and heresy, shame in several people, and perhaps a source of error.[40]

What Christine finds especially offensive is the misuse of Reason in the allegory, "that the lofty personage of Reason, whom he himself calls the daughter of God, must be the one to enunciate" the false premise that "it is better to deceive than be deceived." Jean de Meun's crude, graphic language is also inexcusable to Christine, because she sees no benefit gained by its employment. "What use or advantage can it be for the listener to hear such vileness?" she asks in an argument revealing her underlying belief in the power of literature to instruct intellectually and to mold morally. "What great benefit can be noted, what need to record the dishonest and ugly words," she persists in her argument. "What good example or initiation can this possibly provide?"[41]

Christine's objections to the romance's portrayal of women and Jean de Montreuil's defense of this portrait are the objections perhaps most remembered by posterity. Her arguments have earned Christine the label of being an early feminist in some scholars' eyes,[42] but it is key to remember that at this stage of the *querelle de la rose* Christine's intent was to expose faulty intellectual reasoning as the cause of licentious and hypocritical behavior[43]: "My motive is nothing more than to uphold pure truth." Since, however, one of the contentious points in the debate involves women, Christine argues, she is well situated to rebut an argument experiential as well as rationally: "In that I am indeed a woman, I can better bear witness on this aspect than he who has no experience of it and who speaks only out of supposition and haphazard guessing."[44] This is the issue that seems to frustrate Christine above all others, that Jean de Meun bases his generalization not on logic but on experience, experience which is so limited as to void their ability to generalize properly. Since Jean de Meun "blamed all women in general, I am forced to believe that he has never made the acquaintance nor known the company of an honorable and virtuous woman." If he had condemned only dishonest women then "his teachings would be good and just. But no! He accuses all women of this without exception. But if the author takes it upon himself so much beyond the limits of reason to accuse them or judge them untruthfully, no blame should be imputed to them, but rather to him who tells a lie so far beyond the boundaries of truth that it is totally unbelievable."[45]

When Christine does rely on experiential knowledge it is usually historical rather than personal. She reminds Jean de Montreuil that Jean de Meun had had many historical examples that contradicted his generalizations available to him if he had truly cared to discover the truth, "for there have already been, there are and will be many of the most valiant women, more honest, better raised and even more learned, whose greatest worth is revered throughout the world where that author has never been—even in worldly affairs." The proof is readily found "in the Bible and in other ancient histories" and "even in our time." Christine reminds Jean de Montreuil that they all have "seen in France many valiant women, great ladies and others of our ladies of France; the holy devoted Queen Joan, Queen Blanche, the Duchess of Orléans, daughter of the King of France, the Duchess of Anjou, who is now named the Queen of Sicily—all of whom had such beauty, chastity, honesty, and wisdom—and still others" hidden more from the public eye. On the other hand, Christine is not averse to using personal experience to bolster logical arguments. She caustically does so when refuting Jean de Meun's stance that all women criminally prey on men. Given male dominance physically and socially "what can these women do if you don't give them a chance to deceive you?" Christine sarcastically asks. If they ask you for money, "don't give it to them if you do not wish to! And if you say that you were besotted at the time, don't let yourself get drunk! What are these women going to do, track you down in your home and take it from you by force?" Christine uses this kind of biting humor to expose the irrational nature of Jean de Meun's claim. Given these realities Christine concludes derisively: "It would be good to know just how women deceive you."[46]

Soon after Christine's written response another high-profile intellectual entered into the debate, Jean Gerson. Gerson was the revered chancellor of the University of Paris, and on August 25 he chastised Jean de Montreuil in a sermon, thus offering public support for Christine's interpretation. On September 13 Gontier Col wrote Christine a threatening, offensive letter demanding that she amend her argument, and two days later he wrote "a second, more insulting letter, criticizing me as a member of the female sex (which you claim to be excessively emotional by nature) and accusing me of folly and presumption in daring to correct and contradict a teacher as renowned, well qualified and learned as you declare the author [Jean de Meun] of the work to be. Therefore you urge me insistently to recant and repent." Christine adroitly negates Gontier Col's presupposition concerning women's emotional excess by directing her argument to intellectual reasoning and resisting the temptation to answer his offensive letter emotionally with anger and outrage. She insinuates that he, in fact, is the emotional one and calmly counsels him to "not deliberately allow your keen mind to be clouded and narrow in its views. Consider the matter clearly and fairly, guided by the methods of the queen of learning—theology." She has no fear that his "belittling [of] my forceful arguments with your anti-feminist attacks" will render her thesis false, for it is Col's arguments that rest on shaky emotional grounds, hers on the solid ground of reason. "So," she concludes, "even if you threaten me with your insults and subtle reasoning, methods that generally create fear in the faint-hearted, do not for one moment think that I am fickle in my opinions or that my mind might easily be changed."[47]

The debate continued for some time, although Christine's reposte apparently silenced Gontier Col. Christine tried to enlist the aid of the French queen, Isabeau of Bavaria, by sending her and William of Tignonville, provost of Paris, copies of the debate to date. Gontier's brother Pierre attempted to prolong the debate with an attack on both Christine's and Jean Gerson's opinions. When Gerson's response effectively rebuked Pierre, the debate died a natural death. Christine's reputation was made, and she remained a professional writer for some years. Those traits that she identified in her parting shot to Gontier, that she is neither fickled nor easily changed in her ideas, remain visible in all her remaining writing. She is always highly opinionated, but her intransigency is rooted in her confidence in reason's ability, or, more precisely, woman's reasoning powers. In her most extensive critique of misogyny, *City of Ladies* Christine allows a personified Reason to answer her question on whether God endowed women "with great intelligence and knowledge." Reason answers in the affirmative, claiming that if girls were sent to school "they would grasp and learn the difficulties of all the arts and sciences just as easily as the boys do." The explanation for why women know less than men is simple: "It's because they are less exposed to a wide variety of experiences since they have to stay at home all day to look after the household. There's nothing like a whole range of different experiences and activities for expanding the mind of any rational creature." In a typical humanistic vein, Christine's Reason concludes that it "all comes down to their lack of education."[48] Women's ignorance then is due the lack of that knowledge, not absence of intelligence, and this gap is easily remedied by education. "God has given every woman a good brain which she could put to good use, if she so chose, in all the domains in which the most learned and renowned men excel;" women merely have to gain "confidence in their own intellectual abilities" and stop "letting themselves be discouraged and saying that they are fit for nothing but fussing over men and bearing and bringing up children."[49] Christine brings this a step further, maintaining that not only could women be as educated as men, but they actually should be "because there is no excuse for plain ignorance."[50] She reminds the reader that this is a constant theme of hers and that she has "made these points elsewhere in [her] writings."[51] As with most of her arguments, she then turns to history to support what she has argued logically: "I'll now go on to prove to you that the female sex is just as clever as the male sex, by giving you some examples of women who had fine minds and were extremely erudite."[52]

Employment of what literary critics call catalogues was popular during the late Middle Ages. Common in ancient literature but rarely present in early or central Middle Ages, catalogues use applicable historical examples of people to illustrate the virtue or vice being discussed.[53] The revival of their presence in literature during this period by such literary giants as Chaucer and Boccaccio is not surprising according to literary historian Glenda McLeod, because the audience these writers addressed "wanted edification, a moral example to imitate, and (in an age when books were expensive items) ample erudition and facts,"[54] all things catalogues do. Christine takes full advantage of the catalogue, using *exempla* of historical women for edification, imitation, and erudition. She borrows so extensively from Boccaccio's best known catalogue, *Concerning Famous Women,* when writing *City of Ladies* that in the past some have claimed that Christine's work is merely a translation, a claim recent critics have put to rest.[55] *Concerning Famous Women* is itself the result of much literary borrowing, for such were the normal practices of the catalogue genre. When Christine's catalogue is compared with Boccaccio's *Concerning Famous Women* and another popular catalogue, Jacobus de Voragine's *Golden Legend*[56] which she also relied on for her *City of Ladies,* we gain a clearer view of how Christine used history with originality and purpose. Boccaccio's catalogue starts with Eve and proceeds chronologically to discuss various women who are known for their virtue or their vice, and he does so to entertain. Christine's catalogue, on the other hand, is selective and didactic. She has a specific purpose in mind, to argue that women are not guilty "of such horrors as so many men seem to say,"[57] "to prevent others from falling into the same error," and "to ensure that, in future, all worthy ladies and valiant women are protected from those who have attacked them." To attain these goals Christine's strategy is to select only *exempla* of "ladies who are of good reputation and worthy of praise" for habitation in her city. "It's no wonder that women have been losers in this war against them since the envious slanderers and vicious traitors who criticize them have been allowed to aim all manner of weapons at their defenceless targets," Christine writes. Judicious utilization of history, however, will give women the necessary defense they need, because "even the most undeserving case will win if there is no one to testify against it."[58] Thus Christine selects and edits traditional *exempla* to shape her argument. She includes *exempla* from hagiographical literature to boost her claims of women's historical worth, for instance, in contradistinction to Boccaccio who claimed that hagiographical material should not be mixed with pagan literature; he, therefore, excluded women saints from his catalogue.[59] When she does present women saints found in *The Golden Legend* the editing is readily apparent. She adds, modifies, and embellishes, so says literary historian Christine Reno, when it suits her didactic "purpose of presenting women in a more favorable light."[60]

Christine is particularly intent upon presenting women as active contributors to intellectual history, earning her perhaps the distinction of being the first women's intellectual historian. She dedicates much of books one and two in *City of Ladies* to proving women's participation in intellectual activity. To begin with, Christine chooses Lady Reason and not one of the more traditional theological or cardinal virtues[61] as her first guide "to help you get rid of those misconceptions which have clouded your mind and made you reject what you know and believe in fact to be the truth just because so many other people have come out with the opposite opinion."[62] It is Lady Reason whose task it is "to help you begin by giving you tough, indestructible cement which you will need to set the mighty foundations" of the City of Ladies.[63] Christine allows Reason to begin her historical tour in the Field of Letters, where Reason tells Christine to "take the spade of your intelligence" and begin digging the foundation, following "the line that I [Reason] have traced."[64] Christine wastes no time but attacks Ovid and Virgil forthwith for their "derogatory remarks about women" in their writings.[65] Here Christine shows her diplomatic skills. Instead of ignoring the authoritative texts of the classical past which contain arguments contrary to her thesis, she has Reason meet the arguments head-on. As editor Rosalind

Brown-Grant observes, Christine knew her voice would not drown out the authoritative voices of the past, so she decided "selective quotation was a game that two could play." Christine proceeded to plunder "the misogynists' favorite scriptural and classical authorities in order to come up with a mass of examples that support her thesis against theirs."[66] Boccaccio's Eve is countered with Christine's Judith, Esther, and Susanna;[67] she uses Medea to her advantage by omitting Medea's dismembering of her brother's body.[68] She refutes classic Greek scientific views of women being physically weaker than men and, therefore, morally diminished by having Reason declare that such was "a false conclusion which is completely untenable" because Nature "very often compensates for [defects] by giving that body some greater quality." She offers Aristotle and Alexander the Great as examples to prove this.[69] Not content to simply disprove the conclusion of the ancients, Christine instead turns it on its head and declares that "women are lucky" to be physically weak "because they are at least spared from committing and being punished for the acts of appalling cruelty, the murders and terrible violent deeds which men who are equipped with the necessary strength have performed in the past and still do today."[70] When Christine asks Reason if "God ever chose to honour any [woman] with great intelligence and knowledge" or "an aptitude for learning," Reason replied: "Although women may have weaker and less agile bodies than men, which prevents them from doing certain tasks, their minds are in fact sharper and more receptive when they do apply themselves."[71]

Christine also argues that not only were women's minds endowed "with the capacity not simply to learn and grasp all kinds of knowledge, but also to invent new ones by themselves, discovering sciences which have done more good and have been more useful to humanity than any others."[72] Christine even has Reason claim after her recitation of women's contributions "that the teachings of Aristotle, which have so greatly enriched human knowledge and are rightly held in such high esteem, put together with all those of every other philosopher who ever lived, are not worth anything like as much to humankind as the deeds performed by these ladies, thanks to their great ingenuity."[73] Christine relies heavily on *exempla* and on authoritative male texts to persuade her readers her argument is correct. Anticipating her critics, Reason declares: "But don't let it be said that I'm telling you these things out of bias: these are the words of Boccaccio himself and thus the truth of them is indisputable."[74] That Christine's adherence to Boccaccio's text is superficial and only when to her advantage is plainly seen in her willingness to attack his conclusions, particularly when she can employ even more authoritative texts in her service. When presenting the *exempla* of Arachne, the inventor of the arts of dyeing wool and weaving tapestries and of fishing and trapping, Reason concludes that "in my view, this woman did no small service to humanity, which has since derived great pleasure and profit from her inventions." Christine argues here for progress and for abandoning false reliance of authoritative texts merely because it was traditionally done. "Certain writers, including Boccaccio, who is our source on these matters, maintain that the world was a better place before human beings learnt more sophisticated ways," but Reason tells Christine differently. "With all due respect to him and to those other authors who claim that the world has been harmed by these inventions,"[75] Christine still continues to advocate progress[76] and reason's role in progress. "If human beings misuse the inventions" that are part of creation "this is not because the things in themselves are not good and invaluable when used correctly and wisely. Rather, it is because those who misuse them are wicked and perverse in the first place." Then Christine plays her trump card: "The life of Jesus Christ himself proves my point,"[77] thereby using a greater authoritative text to undermine a lesser one.[78]

Besides using *exempla* in her pursuit of an intellectual history of women, Christine also employed them in another genre, that of the "mirror for princes." This popular genre was fundamentally a handbook for the upbringing of princes, but it was also a vehicle for theories on education and political life.[79] The genre's form is simple and strictly adhered to. It starts with a disclaimer or humility topos where the author denies any special talent or authority for instructing a superior, that is, a prince. Some basis for writing the handbook is then established (often because it was commissioned), and the author then begins a discussion of how one should mold a prince into an ideal king. Characteristic of the genre is the inclusion of *exempla* illustrating the vices and virtues of bad and good kings. Christine had always shown a keen interest in education and in the relationship between education and civic duties, so it is not surprising to see her use this genre in her later years. In early discussions on the education of youth she often wrote in allegorical poetry; *The Letter of Othea,* her first major work, is an example. Written ca. 1400 this work was one of her most popular.[80] Here Othea, which "in Greek can be taken to mean 'woman's wisdom,'" writes a letter to Hector of Troy (whom Christine's contemporary society revered as the ancestor of the French royal family[81]) "for the edification of the soul residing in this miserable world."[82] The lessons expounded in the letter are similar to those found in Christine's earlier instructions for her son, Jean du Casel, and in *Moral Proverbs* and *Moral Teachings.*[83] "Son, I have no great treasure/To make you rich, but a measure/Of good advice which you may need," Christine modestly begins Jean's instruction,[84] and she maintains this approach in all her pedagogical works. In *The Book of Three Virtues,* an educational handbook for "those whose royal or noble blood" Christine mandates that princes "must be better educated than others." Her "first lesson, therefore, will be directed at them—the queens, princesses, and other great ladies. Then, step by step, we will begin to set forth our doctrine for women of the lower degrees."[85]

Christine's contributions to humanistic pedagogy is actually quite significant in *Three Virtues,* and in many instances she anticipates educational methods made popular by other contemporary and even later humanists. For example, Christine advocates a governess "to direct her charge with a pleasant and courteous manner, giving her mistress inconsequential gifts of the sort which please young people." She should indulge "in games and diversions when she and the young princess are alone," and tell first "fables or stories of the type customarily told to young children" and then relate "histories of ladies and maidens who have governed themselves intelligently, thus having turned out well." A good teacher disguises her educational method; at no time must the governess "appear to be giving examples, only recounting adventures." These adventures should be taken from "stories of the saints, their lives, and their passions" and to guarantee "her tales won't become boring, she will interrupt them to tell some little jokes."[86] In this manner a student will more readily respond to a teacher's direction. Advocation of similar methods are found in humanists Giovanni Dominici's

Rule for the Government of Family Care, Peter Vergerius' *De ingenuis moribus,* and Francesco Barbaro's *De re uxoria.*[87] Willard reminds us, though, that "Christine's ideas about the instruction of children with kindness in order to awaken their curiosity naturally have never been given the attention they deserve."[88]

It is with the *Book of the Body Politic* that Christine produced a *bona fide* mirror for princes which conforms fully to the genre's standards. Written for the dauphin, Louis of Guyenne, sometime before the 1407 assassination of his uncle Louis, Duke of Orleans, the probable commissioner of the work,[89] Christine begins with the traditional humility topos, stating her unworthiness because of her sex. Contrary to the typical topos, though, she swiftly and very adroitly twists this weakness into strength: "If it is possible for vice to give birth to virtue, it pleases me in this part to be as passionate as a woman, since many men assume that the female sex does not know how to silence the abundance of their spirits." Because of the passion she possesses "many inexhaustible springs and fountains of my courage" sustain her in the task before her, "to speak about the way of life for higher ranks." Christine implores the princes "not to take wrongly nor distain such small intelligence as mine," but rather "to remember the teaching of the Philosopher, who said, 'Do not distain the wise words of the insignificant despite your own high position.' " After she addresses the main purpose of her handbook, the dauphin's education, she extends her educational platform "to speak on the manner of life of knights and nobles. And, then, thirdly, on the whole universal people."[90] Her exposé of the dauphin's education takes up thirty-three chapters; those on knights and nobles, twenty-one; and those on the common people, eleven. In all three sections Christine uses popular *exempla* to illustrate her lesson. "Let us look at the Romans again as an example," Christine writes, in Part One, as she offers *exempla* from Valerius[91] "and since we are on the subject of these noble Roman princes, since their noble virtues ought to be an example and a mirror to every good prince and worthy man, let us tell more of them."[92] The concluding chapter repeats the humility topos, begging "the King of France and afterwards the princes" to pardon her "if by ignorance any faults are found."[93]

John of Salisbury's *Policraticus,* the first medieval attempt to reconcile the theory and practice of politics in a Christian society, is often assumed to be the chief source and influence on Christine's *Body Politic.*[94] Both works are handbooks for the education of princes, and both assign much weight to the body politic metaphor as a vehicle for grasping the political realities of their day. In Christine's time it was receiving increased attention from such scholars as Jean Gerson, Egidio Colonna, and Philippe de Mézières, the latter of whom had used it in his own handbook for the education of Charles VI.[95] While Christine does not acknowledge John's *Policraticus* as her source, she does write that "these three estates [royalty, nobility, and the people] ought to be one polity like a living body according to the words of Plutarch,"[96] an attribution which scholars argue Christine received from John.[97] When trying to identify the unique intellectual contributions of Christine, however, it is more expedient to determine what aspects of Christine's work are different from John's. Intellectual historian Kate Forhan argues that when this approach is taken the uniqueness of Christine's political thought is more sharply drawn. Both John and Christine divide their work into three parts, but John writes for princely advisors while Christine addresses the princes themselves. John stresses interdependent responsibilities; Christine emphasizes individual and collective obligations.[98] Perhaps the biggest difference between the two works, and perhaps even between Christine's and all other preceding works, is that Christine's view of society is secular. No longer adhering to a more typical medieval division of society into prayers, fighters, and farmers,[99] Christine envisions a society in which clergy are simply part of the masses and rather low in the social hierarchy. First come the "prince or princes as the head of the body politic," then the "nobles and knights, which are the arms and the hands," and, finally, "the whole of the people in common, described as the belly, legs, and feet, so that the whole be formed and joined in one whole living body, perfect and healthy."[100] Christine does designate the clergy as "high, noble and worthy of honor amongest the others," but only those clerics who are "students, whether at the University of Paris or elsewhere."[101] Equally surprising is the esteem in which Christine holds the emerging middle class, recognizing that "it is a very good and honorable thing when there is a notable bourgeoise in a city. It is a great honor to the country and a great treasure to the prince." Christine emphasizes their many responsibilities rather than their rights. "They are to ensure that everything concerning commerce and the situation of the population is well governed," and that they "take care that the common people are not hurt." If perchance something does aggravate the people, "the merchants ought to assemble and from among them choose the wisest and most discreet in action and in speech, and go before the prince or council."[102] In this emphasis on the responsibility of the upper ranks of citizens to act as intermediaries between the people and the ruler, Forhan argues that Christine is articulating theory that "develops later into a French political theory of representation."[103]

Christine's opinion of the people and their relationship to political authority brings us to another issue of the late Middle Ages, the question of the people's role in government. Here Christine has been labeled "conservative," a label whose connotations in modern politics are often so personalized by the readers' own experience that little clarity is gained by its use.[104] What is clear is that Christine pays attention to the people and their political voice, and this is significant in and of itself. It places her, says historian Enin McLeod, "on new and interesting ground" and earns her recognition for her contributions to social history.[105] The people Christine defines as artisans and agricultural workers "who are like legs and feet." Their power comes from the rest of society's dependence upon them, "for that which hurts them can dangerously knock the whole body down." Their work is "necessary for the human body and it cannot do without them," and a government that excludes them "could not sustain itself." Contrary to the opinion of some intellectuals these people are "good, noble, and necessary." Interestingly and yet consistent with Christine's high opinion of intellectual pursuits, Christine praises the class of artisans, because "this one comes closest to science. Artisans put into practice what science teaches, as Aristotle says in *Metaphysics,* because their work demands the use of certain sciences, such as geometry. Christine singles out masons, carpenters, painters, and sculptors for particular notice and links this class in a special way to art. "When a painter who is a great artist makes the portrait of a man so lifelike, and so well, that everyone recognizes him," the rest of society, including the upper ranks "ought to praise the skillful in art and believe those who have experience in it."[106]

Christine also champions the agricultural workers whom, she knows, "so many people despise and oppress," despite the fact that "they are the most necessary." Christine appeals to reason, noting that "anyone who considers himself a rational creature will hold himself obligated to them." Christine even proclaims it "a sin to be ungrateful for as many services as they give us!" She makes repeated pleas to the upper class to revise any low opinion of laborers that they may harbor. "The estate of the simple laborer or others of low rank should not be denigrated," because they are so essential to the well being of society and because "there is no doubt that the estate of the poor which everyone despises has many good and worthy persons in purity of life."[107] This positive image of the people, however, does not lead Christine to conclude that they should have a direct role in government. Her reason rests more on her expressed loyalty and pride in France's contemporary form of government that does not give the people a political voice than on any fundamental fear of people's power. "Throughout the whole world, lands which are governed by humans are subject to different institutions according to the ancient customs of places," Christine explains. "Some are governed by elected emperors," some are "self-governed and are ruled by princes which they choose among themselves," some, like Venice, are ruled by powerful families, some by aldermen, "and in some places, the common people govern and every year a number of persons are installed from each trade." Christine believes that such government "is not profitable at all for the republic," yet rather than provide a reasoned rebuttal of these various forms of government, she merely offers the example of France as her proof: "I consider the people of France very happy," Christine writes, "and for this reason and the grace of God of all the countries and kingdoms of the world, the people of France has the most natural and the best love and obedience for their prince, which is a singular and very special virtue and praiseworthy of them and they deserve great merit."[108] So convinced is Christine of France's political superiority that she proclaims it to be a "good example in all other regions where good and correct understanding is desired."[109]

Crucial to understanding Christine's opinion in this matter is remembering who her audience was and the time in which her work was written. The work is addressed to members of the royal family at a time of political instability. Surely an author who desired the patronage of this family would realize patronage could be possible only if her work was seen to be supportive of the family's political power. Christine writes such a book. In all probability she sincerely believed it; certainly the efforts she put forth on the side of the dauphin in her *Book of Peace* indicate she was in fact a firm supporter of the royal family and thus a "conservative" political theorist. Her interest and respect for the middle class and even the lower classes and her emphasis on the interdependence of all classes upon each other should give us pause, nevertheless, before we allow a label to limit her historical significance. In her insistence on cooperation among all classes she was relentless, that "everyone should come together as one body of the same polity, to live justly and in peace as they ought." She was equally insistent upon the individual and communal obligation to maintain the body politic. There is even an insistence upon a moral equality among the classes, since "each estate in the polity, and each individual person" must embrace the same standards of behavior, "to be humane, liberal, and merciful, to love the wise and good."[110] In these aspects her position is neither conservative nor revolutionary; it is the position of the future.

France's future was indeed a major concern of Christine's, and, as noted, her later writings quite frequently dwell on this theme. In *Book of Peace* Christine reiterates the principles of unity articulated in her *Body Politic* as she warns the French of the danger of civil war. "No kingdom divided can stand; nor can cities or households divided against their own good endure,"[111] she begins and then resorts to the body politic metaphor to reinforce her point. So, "Let us consider the absolute folly of seeing a man driven so greatly by anger that he wants to destroy himself: his teeth tearing at his own feet, his hands striking great blows at each other, and his feet tripping each other up and kicking out his eyes, so that the whole body seemed to be an insane spasm against itself."[112] When Agincourt decimated the ranks of the French upper class Christine expressed her love of France and her grief at "the great loss of French knighthood and so many noble and worthy royal princes of France" who "in the just defense of battle, obedient unto death in order to sustain justice, along with the rights of the French crown and their sovereign lord"[113] died in this battle. This same loyalty and pride in time of national crisis is expressed in what was probably her last work, *The Poem of Joan of Arc*. "And now let us receive our king!" Christine rejoices, "Let all of us, the great and small, advance" and rejoice in the fact "that this France (of whom they said/That she was overthrown and done)/Be brought from evil days to fair/By means of God's divine command."[114] The images of national identity that Christine uses in such discussions lead literary critic Earl Jeffrey Richards to conclude that Christine plays a significant role in the development of nationalism during the late Middle Ages; she "attempted to invest French cultural identity with a spiritual, transcendent quality, anticipating the very modern claims of a Maurice Barrès on *les traits, éternels de la France*."[115]

Interestingly, while twentieth-century scholars tend to overlook Christine's political and military works such as those just mentioned in favor of her courtly love literature and feminist writings, the reverse was true of fifteenth-century society. In a study of early English translations of Christine's works, Finke reveals that it was precisely the military and political works that were in demand in England; only one minor work (*Letter to Cupid*) outside these genre was translated during the fifteenth century.[116] Despite Christine's stated trepidation of impinging on male literary territory, she proceeded to write *The Book of Deeds of Arms and of Chivalry*, a manual on warfare, "encouraged, in the light of my other writings, to undertake to speak in this book of the most honorable office of arms and chivalry."[117] Her decision was obviously correct, because, Finke argues, not only was Christine's work translated with her authorship intact, but the work also led to her being cited as an authority herself; she was "given prominence equal to that of other great authorities both classical and contemporary."[118] One of famed printer William Caxton's later works was his own translation of Christine's *Fayttes of Armes and of Chyralrye* (1489), and in his epilogue he explains how he was asked to translate it by "the most Christian king and redoubted prince, my natural and sovereign lord King Henry the vii king of England and of France." Henry VII possessed the French version and sent it to Caxton, because "every gentylman born to armes and all manere of werre, captayns, souldyours, vitallers and all other should have knowledge of how they ought to behave in the fayetts of werre and of batagle."[119] Caxton evidently concurred that the book was an essential and "as necessary a boke and as reguysite as ony may be for every estate hye and lowe that entende the faytes of werre."[120] Fortunately, recent military historians are finally beginning to acknowledge Christine's crucial contribution to the discipline. Her *Deeds of Arms and of Chivalry* signaled the resumption of military studies after centuries of silence, and it was an admirable commencement.[121] With the continued critical editions and translations of her political and military works, indeed, of her entire corpus, perhaps we will finally be able to offer a more complete assessment of Christine's position in all these fields of intellectual endeavor.

One thing she was right about, though, was that even if she did not receive the accolades she deserved while living, her effort to keep her name and works alive through the passage of time succeeded. We have heard her confess how actively she pursued fame and how little she left to chance. Other women writers of the fourteenth and fifteenth centuries had designs similar to Christine's, but they were not as successful. They also were neither as prolific nor as visible in their society, which may account for their different fates. On the one hand we have the daughters of James I of Scotland. They were visible in the political circles of their day as first their father and then their brother James II used them in their matrimonial diplomacy. Two of them, Margaret and Eleanor, deserve mention in an intellectual history, but on the basis of contemporary opinion more than on the slim amount of material that has survived. Margaret of Scotland (1424–1445), wife of the dauphin, the future Louis XI, was well known throughout French society as being the center of a small clique of court poets. The poetry of Jeanne de Filleul, her lady-in-waiting, has been preserved, but, unfortunately, none of Margaret's own poetry has survived. Margaret was said to have written some dozen rondeaux and ballades a day.[122] Her sister Eleanor (ca. 1433–1480) was married to Sigmund, archduke of Tyrol. She corresponded in German, Latin, French, and English, and many of her letters have survived. She was a bibliophile, and her contemporaries recognized her as the cultivated, educated student of letters that she was.[123] The most important reason for inclusion of Eleanor in an intellectual history is her translation of *Pontus und Sidonia,* a work considered by some as a "landmark in the history of German prose literature,"[124] and one that is, fortunately, extant. The Paston women, on the other hand, were very prolific but not visible in English society. Their contribution to the famous collection of the Paston family letters preserved from fifteenth to seventeenth centuries is quite significant. An excellent primary source for social history, the degree of education the Paston women enjoyed is evident upon first reading, as is the degree in which they participated in a literate society.[125]

During the early days of Italian humanism women were present in that society as audience, and the importance of that role, Nadia Solamone states, cannot be overestimated. "Women were regarded to a great extent as the reference public for the vernacular literature that was produced," and their presence "affected the literary scene in a radical way;" it "modified that literature, led to the questioning of its forms and impelled it toward the acquisition of new ones."[126] Exactly how much women shared in the increase in literacy or benefited directly from humanistic educational platforms remains to be seen, for the identification and examination of women's writing in Italy has barely just begun.[127] A few decades after Christine de Pizan's death we find two Florentine women enjoying some visibility as poets. Lucrezia Tornabuoni, mother of ruler-poet Lorenzo de Medici, was known as a renowned writer of *Laudi,* religious hymns, and Antonia Pulci was well received as a poet and playwright. Antonia's religious plays were known to have been performed by lay guilds.[128]

Isotta Nogarola

There were a limited number of women who actually joined the ranks of Italian humanists. All of the women were from the upper class, so they enjoyed some degree of visibility, but none of them was particularly prolific. Neither was any of them especially remarkable, but in the opinion of Renaissance scholars Margaret King and Albert Rabil, "the women compare favorably with much that humanism produced."[129] The first generation of women humanists are so designated more on the strength and type of their education than because of any tangible contribution to humanism they made. The letters of Maddalena Scrovegni provide testimony to the fact that women were present in the humanistic movement even at its beginning, as do the orations of Battista da Montefeltro Malatesta and Costanza Varanza.[130] During this period the brightest of these women humanists, Isotta Nogarola (1418–1466), wrote what King judges to be "the most important [work] written by a woman in the early Italian renaissance: the *Of the equal or unequal sin of Adam and Eve*."[131] This dialogue was based on a series of letters exchanged between Isotta and the Venetian humanist Ludovico Foscarini written at mid-century, after Isotta had retired into near-seclusion in 1441. Her retirement only makes her life and work more noteworthy, for they are a testimony to a new option, the possibility of maintaining an intellectual life outside the structure of marriage or a religious order.[132] In a society where individualism, humanism, and the intellectual life were greatly valued, Isotta found a unique way to combine and nourish them, and did so until her death twenty-five years later. This accomplishment was apparently not lost to some of her contemporaries, for a few years after Isotta began her life as an independent lay woman scholar, another woman humanist wrote praising Isotta's contributions. "I congratulate you, for you have advanced to the highest peaks, to the great splendor and glory of your name," Costanza Varano proclaimed, repeating the message of Lactantius Firmianus, "for nothing could be more expedient and fruitful for women than to forget the needs of the body and to reach out strenuously for those goods which fortune cannot destroy." As "those who neglect the goods of the soul will live in shadows and death," so too will Isotta live in fame. "This being so, you must be judged the equal of those most excellent learned women of whom in antiquity there was no small multitude."[133]

The treatise *Of the equal or unequal sin of Adam and Eve* is hard to evaluate. Isotta's thesis is that Eve's sin is less than Adam's, and she defends the thesis by paradoxically arguing that "where there is less intellect and less constancy, there there is less sin; and Eve [lacked sense and constancy] and therefore sinned less."[134] One may rightly question, however, whether this approach was a rhetorical ploy of the type frequently found throughout Western intellectual history, to propose the weakness or limitation of something and then prove the proposal by contrarily using the strength of that something to persuade one's opponent. Peter Damian, for example, argued the limits of philosophy and then supported his premise by employing sophisticated philosophical arguments.[135] Here Isotta uses the full strength of her well-endowed intellect to argue that women are less intelligent than men. If Isotta truly believed her own thesis, she would not have believed it possible to match wits with Ludovico nor countered his arguments with her own. In essence she said to Ludovico that she is going to prove women are less intelligent than men by presenting arguments more intelligent than he was capable of presenting. In Ludovico's closing words he bows to Isotta's superior intelligence, calling her "most learned," "most brilliant," and "always more learned and more ready," yet few reading his conclusion miss the rhetorical nature of his comments and think he truly believed that Isotta was more intelligent than he.[136] Unfortunately, most readers miss the rhetorical nature of Isotta's claims.

Laura Cereta

The second generation of women humanists differed little from the first, except, perhaps, that they were more mediocre. Ippolita Sforza belongs to this group, and she is best remembered for her oration before humanist Pope Pius II, who himself recorded that, "Bianca's daughter Ippolita delivered a speech before the Pope in such elegant Latin that all present were lost in wonder and admiration."[137] Ippolita was best known, though, as a patron of humanists, as was her mother Bianca Visconti, and other members of the ruling families: Isabella d'Estes, Marchioness of Mantua, and Elizabeth Gonzana, Duchess of Urbino.[138] Whereas this second generation exhibited only modest confidence, the same cannot be said of third generation humanist Laura Cereta, who unabashedly confesses, "My heart chafes and swells with a burning desire for fame."[139] She knows that she has the talent and can honestly "boast, I admit, about the intellectual gifts the omnipotent lord has given me." She also acknowledges that "the road to fame is everlasting, runs along the precipices and is difficult and narrow," but that has never stopped her from pursuing it. "I preferred to please the crowd rather than myself," and thus "stimulated by the desire for fame" she embarked upon a course of self-education that would yield her the desired fame.[140] "Though I was untrained and scarcely exposed to literature, through my own intelligence and natural talents I was able to acquire the beginnings of an education," she tells us, emphasizing her self-direction, "and, although I remained ill-equipped for the task despite my passion for learning, I reached a decision that awakened in me a desire for fame and honor, as though my mind were challenging itself to scale new heights."[141] Laura's firm conviction that such fame was hers is based on the confidence that she possessed "small (though I hope adequate) gifts from the secret places of my mind." These intellectual abilities will "cause new amazement to draw many people throughout the world to the greenness of my glory for centuries to come."[142]

Laura's open pursuit of fame and her confidence in obtaining it was rewarded within her own lifetime at least to some degree. Sometimes between 1486 and her death in 1499 she offered a series of public lectures in Brescia over a seven-year period, a clear indication of her acceptance into the humanist academic circle.[143] These lectures were probably those discussions found among her public letters that deal with stock humanist themes: friendship, the coming of the Turks, a defense of Epicurus, a discussion of the solitary life, marriage, and education.[144] She also reports that when she moved to Chiari in 1486 "all the men most zealous about the study of literature at Santa Chiara hurriedly rivaled one another to write me when I first arrived here."[145] She did not win over Cassandra Fedele, a Venetian scholar and probably the most respected women writer in Europe at the time.[146] When Laura's attempt to begin a literary correspondence with Cassandra was met with rebuff, Laura was incensed. "I know you will consider this first gift worthy enough so I won't think that you've rejected me or turned your back on my work," Laura had confidently written, but when her confidence proved to be misplaced Laura accused Cassandra of rejecting her scholarship out of envy: "And so it would appear that she either has contempt for her peers or heaps more abuse on people who are more knowledgeable than she."[147]

Laura also reports that Cassandra "believes that the things I have written are not mine but came from the pen of the father who educated me" and that "she doesn't pursue these baseless thoughts alone." Laura's wound is superficial, though, and the conviction of her scholarly worth rebounds immediately. "There isn't anyone who doesn't know of my literary gifts," she proclaims, so why should it be surprising "if illiterate grammarians, who are contemptuous of the work of so many celebrated minds, disapprove of my pen?"[148]

Posterity has sided more with Cassandra Fedele's evaluation than with Laura's. While Laura's written works certainly earn her a position as a humanist, her contributions to Western intellectual literature were modest. Perhaps more contributions would have been forthcoming if her love of learning had not been tempered when her husband died. We know, for instance, that before his death after only eighteen months of marriage she spent her time consumed with a desire to master astronomy. "I could observe the wandering, falling planets and those bodies which sometimes move in a retrograde position, sometimes a descending course, and at other times with more velocity under the continual revolutions of the rising and sinking stars, since I was trying to find out, using rigorous proofs, whether the stars remained fixed while the heavens were descending or whether they were propelled in a circular orbit away from us, equidistant in a vast orbit." After her husband's death Fortune threw "the serenity of my study into confusion" and "redirected my investigations into the subtleties of heavenly things to grim mourning." Laura did regain most of her "love of active study," as witnessed in her subsequent career as a humanist, but there is no evidence in her extant work that she ever again pursued the "search for the cause of things" that she had abandoned at her husband's death.[149]

She did make significant contributions to the *querelle des femmes,* following closely in the footsteps of Christine de Pizan. In a letter to Bibolo Semproni,[150] Laura presents an extensive formal argument against misogyny, particularly as found in

Boccaccio's *Concerning Famous Women.* Like Christine she challenges Boccaccio's main theme that intellectual women are an exception to the rule and then proceeds to prove the reverse thesis by carefully manipulating Boccaccio's catalogue. Whereas Christine de Pizan places her history of brilliant women within a metaphorical city, Laura places it on a metaphorical family tree. She begins her treatise by admitting that she writes because her intellect and her emotions are disturbed by the falseness of Bibolo's claim that Laura's "extraordinary intellect of the sort one would have thought nature would give to the most learned of men" was rarely if ever seen in any other woman. After calling such remarks "typical of the lowborn, plebian mind," Laura readily acknowledges that "I am angry and my disgust overflows." She is careful to emphasize that not simply are her passions aroused, but that this "red-hot anger lays bare a heart and a mind long muzzled by silence."[151] This deliberate fusion of thinking and feeling is unusual in humanistic writings,[152] but Laura makes it clear that in her the two are one: "Because of this [attack] a mind thirsting for revenge is set afire."[153]

Her defense begins, as did Christine's, with a discussion of women's history, a recitation of "that noble lineage which I carry in my own breast . . . a lineage that knowledge, the bearer of honors, has exalted in every age." Most of her *exempla* are taken from Boccaccio, but her alternations of those *exempla* are even more blatant than Christine's. She presents ancient female prophets as learned women, women like Amalthea, "a woman erudite in the knowledge of the future" who "sold books full of oracles," and Nicostrata who was "very learned in prophecy as well as literature."[154] This effectively places prophecy within the framework of scholarship and gives Laura many more *exempla* to rest her argument on. She continues her review of history up to the present day, ending with mention of her contemporaries Isotta Nogarola and Cassandra Fedele. At this point she adds her most innovative twist to her defense; she proclaims the existence of a universal right to education. Her belief in this right could not be more clearly stated: "Nature imparts one freedom to all human beings equally—to learn."[155] Literary scholar Diana Robin notes that such a stance is "a radical statement for a fifteenth-century humanist," for it takes the commonplace humanist belief that intellectual gifts are not dependent upon social status and extends the premise to women.[156] Once equality of aptitude and opportunity are established, Laura pinpoints that element responsible for knowledge. It is free will: "Choice alone, since it is the arbiter of character, is the distinguishing factor." Women scholars are "endowed by God the grantor with any giftedness or rare talents." Indeed, "nature has granted to all enough of her bounty, she opens to all the gates of choice, and through these gifts, reason sends legates to the will, for it is through reason that these legates can transmit their desires." Laura grants all humans, male and female, control over their lives with this argument. It is up to the individual whether he or she becomes a scholar, "for knowledge is not given as a gift but by study."[157]

Notes

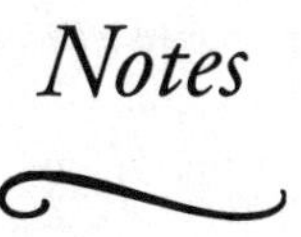

Abbreviations

AASS *Acta Sanctorum.* 70 vols. Paris, 1863–1940.
MGH *Monumenta Germaniae Historica.* Edited by G. H. Pertz *et al.* Hanover, 1826–1913.
PL *Patrologia curcus completus: Series Latina.* Edited by J.-P. Migne. Paris, 1844–1864.

Introduction, pp. ix–xi

1. Laurie A. Finke, *Women's Writing in English: Medieval England* (London: Longman, 1999), 213.
2. *Her Immaculate Hands: Selected Works By and About the Women Humanists of Quattrocento Italy,* eds. Margaret L. King and Albert Rabil (Binghamton, NY: MRTS, 1983), 28–29.
3. This is Carolyn Walker Bynum's summation of the skeptical school of women's history, not her own opinion. Quote in *Hildegard of Bingen: Scivias,* tr. M. Columba Hart and Jane Bishop, pref. Carolyn Walker Bynum, intro. Barbara Newman (New York: Paulist Press, 1990), 4. The work of Brigitte Cazelles, *The Lady as Saint: A Collection of French Hagiographical Romances of the Thirteenth Century* (Philadelphia, PA: University of Pennsylvania Press, 1991), 29, takes the argument a step further and argues that most women's voices are heard only if the women embody female sanctity and, therefore, is "located in Heaven and, consequently, set at a safe distance from earthly reality." A good analysis of the many flaws in Cazalles' thesis is found in Elizabeth D. A. Weber, "The Power of Speech: Models of female martyrdom in medieval and early modern French literature," PhD Diss. University of Wisconsin-Madison, 1994, 4–9.
4. See Andrea Dworkin, *Our Blood: Prophecies and Discourses on Sexual Politics* (New York: Harper & Row, 1976).
5. See Peter Dronke's magisterial work, *Women Writers of the Middle Ages* (Cambridge: Cambridge University Press, 1984); *Medieval Women Writers,* ed. Katharina M. Wilson (Athens, GA: University of Georgia Press, 1984); Weber, "The Power of Speech"; and Carolyn Walker Bynum, *Holy Feast and Holy Fast* (Berkeley, CA: University of California Press, 1989).
6. See Patricia Ranft, "A Key to Counter Reformation Women's Activism: The Confessor-Spiritual Director," *Journal of Feminist Studies in Religion* 10:2 (1994), 7–26.

7. Carolyn Walker Bynum, *Fragmentation and Redemption: Essays on Gender and the Human Body in Medieval Religion* (New York: Zone Books, 1991), 5:156.
8. For those readers who desire a better background in Western intellectual history, Marcia L. Colish, *Medieval Foundations of the Western Intellectual Tradition 400–1400* (New Haven, CT: Yale University Press, 1997) is an excellent reference work; I refer to it continually throughout the study. For a history more strictly of philosophy, see Frederick Copleston's multi-volume classic, *A History of Philosophy,* 7 vols., repr. (Garden City, NY: Image Books, 1963) and *History of Women Philosophers,* 4 vols., ed. Mary Ellen Waithe (Dordrecht: Kluwer Academic Publishers, 1989). Central Michigan University offered some support for this study through its Research Professorship program.

Chapter 1, pp. 1–34
The Early Renaissance

1. M. T. W. Laistner, *Thought and Letters in Western Europe A.D. 500 to 900,* 2nd ed. (Ithaca, NY: Cornell University Press, 1976).
2. David Knowles and D. Obolensky, *The Christian Centuries,* Vol. 2: *The Middle Ages* (New York: Paulist Press, 1983), 129. For years standard textbooks have gone from Augustine to Anselm with little or no apology. See, for example, the international favorite, Julián Marías, *The History of Philosophy* (New York: Dover Publications, 1967), which went through twenty-three editions by 1967 and is still being reprinted: "There is, in the first place, a long gap of four centuries, from the fifth to the ninth, in which there is no philosophy" (p. 25).
3. The term "renaissance" has a long history of use and abuse, starting with Charles Homer Haskins challenge to the academic world with his *The Renaissance of the Twelfth Century* (Cambridge, MA: Harvard University Press, 1927). I use the term here without any hidden agenda and only because, even given its problems, it is common and convenient.
4. Marcia L. Colish, *Medieval Foundations of the Western Intellectual Tradition 400–1400* (New Haven, CT: Yale University Press, 1997), 62.
5. Pierre Riché, *Education and Culture in the Barbarian West from the Sixth through the Eighth Century,* tr. John J. Contreni (Columbia, SC: University of South Carolina Press, 1976), 311.
6. See *AASS,* January 15, 1:1062–1068, for Ida's *vita.*
7. See Riché, *Education,* 312; John Lanigan, *An Ecclesiastical History of Ireland . . . from Irish Annals and Other Authentic Documents, Still existing in Manuscripts,* 2nd ed. (Dublin: J. Cumming, 1829); Roger Reynolds, "*Virgines subintroductae* in Celtic Christianity," *Harvard Theological Review* 61 (1968), 547–566; and John Ryan, *Irish Monasticism: Origins and Development* (repr., Dublin: Irish Academic Press, 1986).
8. Patricia Ranft, *Women and the Religious Life in Premodern Europe* (New York: St. Martin's Press, 1996), 17. Besides instructing boys, Cogitosus writes that Brendan of Clonfert asked Brigid of Kildare for instruction.
9. Laistner, *Thought,* 143–148.
10. Bede, *A History of the English Church and People,* tr. Leo Sherley-Price, repr. (Harmondsworth: Penguin Books, 1986), 3:3 (p. 144).
11. Ibid. (p. 145).

12. Ibid., 3:19 (p. 172).
13. Hilda's *vita* is in ibid., 4:23 (pp. 245–250).
14. Ibid., 4:24 (p. 250). See Laistner's comments, *Thought,* 372–373.
15. Bede, *History,* 4:24 (pp. 250–253).
16. *The Earliest Life of Gregory the Great,* tr. Bertram Colgrave (Lawrence, KS: University of Kansas Press, 1968); and John Godfrey, "The Double Monastery in Early English History," *The Ampleforth Journal* 79 (1974), 19–32.
17. Bede, *History,* 4:23 (p. 249).
18. Riché, *Education,* 377, claims that "the culture of nuns was, in fact, more developed in Wessex than elsewhere—another mark of Irish influence."
19. See Laistner, *Thought,* 152.
20. Riché, *Education,* 379.
21. PL 89, 103–104.
22. Colish, *Foundations,* 64.
23. Aldhelm, *De laudibus virginitate,* 2, in *MGH,* AA, xv, ed. R. E. Ehwald, 228–229.
24. PL 89, 106.
25. See examples of curriculi in male monasteries in Riché, *Education,* 369–399.
26. Aldheim, *De virginitatis,* 60, p. 323.
27. There exists a questionable charter of freedom for the monks at Malmesbury that Aldhelm signed "at the convent of Wimbourne." William of Malmesbury, *De gestis pontificium Anglorum,* ed. N. E. S. Hamilton, *Rolls Series* 52 (1870), 378.
28. Bede, *History,* 3:25 (p. 187).
29. Godfrey, "Double Monastery," 29.
30. So says Rosamond McKitterick, "Women and Literacy in the Early Middle Ages," in idem, *Books, Scribes and Learning in the Frankish Kingdoms, 6th–9th Centuries* (Brookfield, VT: Variorum, 1994), 13:33. McKitterick agrees with P. Sims-Williams, *Religion and Literature in Western England, 600–800* (Cambridge: Cambridge University Press, 1990), 209, that this Eadburg may have been an abbess of Wimbourne and a different Eadburg was Boniface's correspondent.
31. Ep. 12, Pope Gregory II to Boniface, in *The Anglo-Saxon Missionaries in Germany,* tr. C. H. Talbot (London: Sheed & Ward, 1954), 68.
32. Within the extant correspondence there are letters to Bugga and to Abbess Bugga; it is also known that one Bugga became Abbess Eadburg.
33. PL 89, 691–692.
34. PL 89, 731.
35. PL 89, 712.
36. Ep. 30, in Michael Tangl, *Die Briefe des heiligen Bonifatius und Lullus, MGH,* Epistolae Selectae I.
37. Ep. 13, ibid.
38. Ep. 29, in Talbot, *Anglo-Saxon Missionaries,* 87–88; PL 89, 720–721.
39. Rudolf of Fulda, *The Life of St. Leoba,* in Talbot, *Anglo-Saxon Missionaries,* 214.
40. His thirst for knowledge and his reliance on books is evident in many of his letters and not just the ones to women. To Abbot Duddo, for example, he writes: "Extending prayers to God, I continue to be zealous in learning, in the Holy Scriptures and in the Holy Fathers' spiritual writings on how to become an eloquent teacher of holy books, and for

this purpose I, an apprentice in the sacred sciences, need a portion of St. Paul's writings, which I asked you to send to me. I already have two of his epistles, that is, Romans and First Corinthians. Likewise, any books in your monastery's library that I do not have or information that is not in my other books, and would be useful to my work, like a faithful son with an uneducated father, redirect my thoughts to be worthy of your happiness" (PL 89, 740–741).

41. *Life of St. Leoba,* 214.
42. Ibid., 215.
43. Ibid., 214.
44. Wolfhard, *Miraculis S. Waldburgus Monheimensibus,* in MGH, SS, xv, p. 1, 535–555. See the portrait of Walburga summarized in M. Emmanuel, "Saint Walburga Benedictine Abbess and Missionary (710–779)," *Word and Spirit* 11 (1989), 50–59; and *Heilige Walburga, Leben und Wirken* (Eichstatt: Abtei St. Walburga, 1979).
45. Bernhard Bischoff, "Wer ist die Nonne von Heidenheim?" *Studien und Mitterlungen zur Geschichte des Benediktinerordens und seiner Zweige* 49 (1931), 387–397. Text is found in MGH, SS, xv, p. 1, 86–117. It was written in 778.
46. Hugeberc of Heidenheim, *The Hodoeporicon of St. Willibald,* in Talbot, *Anglo-Saxon Missionaries,* 153. Boniface established such an atmosphere of scholarship among his disciples that it would be unlikely that those close to him or his bishops would be illiterate. Even his last wishes expressed concern for his books, as his hagiographer, coincidentally Willibald, tells us. Cf. *Life of St. Boniface,* in Talbot, *Anglo-Saxon Missionaries,* 54.
47. Ibid.
48. *Medieval Women's Visionary Literature,* ed. Elizabeth Alvilda Petroff (New York: Oxford University Press, 1986) 87.
49. Talbot, *Anglo-Saxon Missionaries,* 152.
50. Riché, *Education,* 474.
51. Talbot, *Anglo-Saxon Missionaries,* 152, says the work is "of highest interest" and "of great archaeological value."
52. Lina Eckenstein, *Women under Monasticism* (Cambridge: At the University Press, 1896), 140.
53. *Hodoeporicon,* 153.
54. Ibid., 154.
55. Ibid., 156.
56. Ibid., 161.
57. Ibid., 165–166. Mention of the church of Calvary with three crosses of stone being a replica is not found elsewhere.
58. Ibid., 171–172.
59. Ibid., 164.
60. Ibid., 162.
61. Ibid., 163.
62. Ibid., 170.
63. Ibid., 169.
64. Ibid., 172–173.
65. Ibid., 175.
66. Talbot, *Anglo-Saxon Missionaries,* xii–xiii.

67. See Riché, *Education,* 393–399, for discussion.
68. Talbot, *Anglo-Saxon Missionaries,* xii–xiii.
69. Ibid, xiii.
70. Bernhard Bischoff, "Die Kölner Nonnenhandschriften und das Skriptorium von Chelles," *Mittelalterliche Studien* 1 (1965), 17–35.
71. Rosamond McKitterick, "Nuns' scriptoria in England and Francia in the eighth century," *Francia* 19:1 (1989), 7:33. McKitterick remains careful, however, to always couch her conclusions as conjectures. See her collection of essays on the topic in *Books.* "Nuns' " is included there.
72. PL 89, 726–727.
73. For one of the most compelling discussions of this task, see William Bark, *Origins of the Medieval World* (Stanford, CA: Stanford University Press, 1958).
74. Riché, *Education,* 393.
75. Ibid., 496.
76. Laistner, *Thought,* 141–152.
77. *Life of Boniface,* in Talbot, *Anglo-Saxon Missionaries,* 47.
78. Bede, *History,* 3:8 (pp. 153–55).
79. See above, p. 5.
80. Bede, *Lives of the Abbots of Wearmouth and Jarrow,* 11, in *The Age of Bede,* tr. D. H. Farmer (repr., Harmondsworth: Penguin Books, 1985), 196. Benedict also brought back "no less a stock of sacred pictures . . . which he had built within the main monastery and church." Ibid., 194. When Alcuin is made Abbot of St. Martin's in his retirement he sent his monks back at York where he was schooled to obtain copies of books missing from Frankish libraries.
81. Boniface, Ep. 34, cited in Riché, *Education,* 435.
82. Suzanne Fonay Wemple, *Women in Frankish Society* (Philadelphia, PA: University of Pennsylvania Press, 1981), 179.
83. Bischof, "Die Kölner Nonnenhandschriften."
84. McKitterick, "Nuns' scriptoria," 7:4, 33.
85. While the historical veracity of the work is in question, the fact that a biographer would make such a claim tells us something about society's expectations. See *Vita ss. Herlindis et Regnildae,* 4–5, in AASS, March 22, 3, 384–385. McKitterick, "Women and Literacy," in *Books,* 13:27, argues that a woman from their community is the author.
86. Venantius Fortunatus, *Life of Radegund,* 3, in *Sainted Women of the Dark Ages,* tr. JoAnn McNamera and John E. Halborg with E. Gordon Whately (Durham, NC: Duke University Press, 1992), 72.
87. Baudonivia, *Life of Radegund,* 8, ibid., 91: "She so loved her flock, which, in her deep desire for God, she gathered in the Lord's name, that she no longer remembered that she had a family and a royal husband. . . . So she would often say when she preached to us: 'Daughters, I chose you. You are my light and my life.' " See Wemple, *Women in Frankish Society,* 183–185, for more comparisons.
88. Bischoff, "Die Kölner Nonnenhandschriften."
89. *Alcuini epistolae,* MGH, EPP aevi merov. et karl., II.
90. See examples in Laistner, *Thought,* 203.

91. See MGH, Capit, II, 327; and MGH, Concil, II, 581.
92. MGH, Concil II, 581, tr. in Laistner, *Thought,* 208.
93. *The Handbook of Dhuoda: A Carolingian Woman's Counsel for Her Son,* tr. with intro. Carol Neel (Lincoln, NE: University of Nebraska Press, 1991), incipit (p. 2).
94. M. A. Claussen, "Fathers of Power and Mothers of Authority: Dhuoda and the *Liber Manualis,*" *French Historical Studies* 19:3 (Spring 1996), 788, says almost a third of her references are to the psalter.
95. Peter Dronke, *Women Writers of the Middle Ages* (Cambridge: Cambridge University Press, 1984), 46.
96. See Bernadette Janssens, "L'influence de Prudence sur le *Liber manualis* de Dhuoda," *Studia patristica* 17:3 (1982), 1366–1373.
97. Claussen, "Fathers of Power," 808.
98. *Handbook,* 3:10 (p. 35).
99. Ibid., xvi–xvii.
100. Wemple, *Women in Frankish Society,* 187. Wemple's work was groundbreaking at the time and given the status of research at the time of completion, her conclusions were understandable. It is harder to understand why JoAnn McNamara, *Sisters in Arms* (Cambridge, MA: Harvard University Press, 1996), 169, did not take recent research into account before stating her conclusions.
101. See the vast work of McKitterick, *Books;* Elisabeth van Houts, *Memory and Gender in Medieval Europe* (Toronto: University of Toronto Press, 1999); Janet L. Nelson, "Women and the Word in the Earlier Middle Ages," in *Women in the Church,* eds. W. J. Sheils and Diana Wood (Oxford: Basil Blackwell, 1990), 53–78; M. A. Claussen, "God and Man in Dhuoda's *Liber manualis,*" ibid., 43–52; Rosemond McKitterick, "Women in the Ottonian Church: An Iconographic Perspective," ibid., 79–100; Bernhard Bischoff, *Katalog der festaendischen Handschriften des neuten Jahrhunderts,* Vol. 1: *Aachen-Lambach,* ed. Birgit Ebersperger (Washbaden: Harrasswitz, 1998); and the excellent Steven A. Stofferahn, "Changing views of Carolingian women's literary culture: the evidence from Essen," *Early Medieval Europe* 8:1 (1999), 69–97.
102. Pierre Riché, "Les bibliothèques de trois aristocrates laics carolingiens," *Moyen Ages* 69 (1963), 87–104.
103. Claussen, "God and Man," 43.
104. As James Marchand, "The Frankish Mother: Dhuoda," in *Medieval Women Writers,* ed. Katharina M. Wilson (Athens, GA: University of Georgia Press, 1984), 4, says, "Too often intellectual history turns out to be the history of professional intellectuals; from Dhuoda we learn how a private person viewed the Carolingian world."
105. Neel, *Handbook,* xvii, says this is one of Dhuoda's principal models for her work.
106. Neel, *Handbook,* incipit (p. 1).
107. Until recently only two incomplete texts were available. In the 1950s a complete text was found, and in 1975 Riché's critical edition of the work was published in the *Sources Chretiennes,* No. 225. Since its availability has been widespread only for a relatively short period, lack of due respect for Dhuoda is not surprising. *Dhuoda: Manuel pour mon fils,* intro., texte critique, notes par Pierre Riché, tr. Bernard de Vregille et Claude Mondésert (Paris: Editions du Cerf, 1975).
108. *Webster's New Collegiate Dictionary* (1973), s.v. political.
109. Neel, *Handbook,* incipit, (p. 2).

110. Ibid., pref. (p. 6). Marchand, "Frankish Mother," 1–3, summarizes the political realities of the family well; he calls William a "semi-hostage."
111. Neel, *Handbook,* 1:5 (p. 11).
112. Ibid.
113. Ibid., 10:4 (p. 100).
114. Ibid., 8:14 (pp. 87–88).
115. Ibid., 3:8 (p. 33).
116. This tradition thrived among some Church Fathers and was revived to a degree in the eleventh century. Tertullian is the most noted spokesman for the tradition among the Fathers, while Peter Damian, quite unfairly I believe, is usually named as representative of the eleventh-century revival. See Richard Niebuhr, *Christ and Culture* (New York: Harper Torch Books, 1951), and Patricia Cricco, "Monasticism and Its Role as a Liminal Community in Medieval Society," PhD Diss., West Virginia University, 1981.
117. Neel, *Handbook,* prol. (p. 5).
118. Ibid., 3:10 (p. 34); Riché, *Dhuoda: Manuel,* 3.10.27.
119. Ibid., 1:2 (p. 8).
120. Ibid., 1:6 (p. 12).
121. Ibid., 2:2 (p. 17).
122. Ibid., 4:1 (p. 45).
123. Ibid., 4:1 (p. 43); Riché, *Dhuoda: Manuel,* 4.1.1.
124. Ibid., 4:2 (p. 45).
125. Ibid., 3:4 (p. 25).
126. Ibid., 3:4 (pp. 26–27).
127. Ibid., 3:8 (p. 31).
128. Ibid., 3:8 (p. 32).
129. Ibid., 3:11 (p. 39).
130. Ibid. (p. 42).
131. Ibid., 3:9 (p. 33).
132. Ibid., 3:10 (pp. 34–35).
133. Ibid., 4:8 (pp. 55–56).
134. Ibid., 5:2 (p. 69).
135. Ibid., 7:1 (p. 79).
136. Ibid., 4:4 (p. 49).
137. Ibid. (p. 48). Dronke, *Women Writers,* says not only is it one of the earliest articulations of chivalry but that in this matter Dhuoda "anticipates the radical close of Dante's *Monarchia"* (p. 47 and p. 42, respectively).
138. Claussen, "Fathers of Power," 801–802.
139. Neel, *Handbook,* 3:1 (p. 21).
140. Ibid., 3:2 (p. 23).
141. Ibid., 3:3 (p. 25).
142. Ibid. (p. 24).
143. Ibid., 3:10 (p. 36); Riché, *Dhuoda: Manuel,* 3.10.98 and 101.
144. Ibid. (p. 38).
145. See Cricco, "Monasticism;" and M. D. Chenu, "Monks, Canons and Laymen in Search of the Apostolic Life," in *Nature, Man, and Society in the Twelfth Century,* tr. Jerome Taylor and Lester K. Little (Chicago: University of Chicago Press, 1968), 202–238.

146. Glenn W. Olsen, "One Heart and One Soul (Acts 4:32 and 34) in Dhuoda's 'Manual,'" *Church History* 61:1 (March 1992), 23–33, discusses the novelty of Dhuoda's exegesis at length.
147. *Handbook,* 4:8 (p. 58); see also 4:9 (pp. 62–63); and 4:8 (p. 56).
148. Ibid., 4:8 (pp. 58–59).
149. Claussen, "Fathers of Power," 807.
150. *Handbook,* 3:10 (p. 37). The poet is unknown.
151. Ibid., 4:9 (p. 62).
152. Olsen, "One Heart," 28, and Pierre Toubert, "La théorie du marriage chez les moralistes carolingiens," in *Il matrimonio nella società altomedievale,* 2 vols. (Spoleto: Presso la seda del Centro, 1977), 1:233–282.
153. Neel, *Handbook,* 4:6 (pp. 52–3)
154. Ibid., 10:4 (pp. 99–100); incipit (pp. 1–2); prol. (p. 5); pref. (p. 6).
155. Ibid., 3:5 (pp. 28–29).
156. Ibid., 8:15 (p. 88).
157. Ibid., 7:2 (p. 79).
158. Ibid., 7:3 (p. 80).
159. Ibid., 1:1 (p. 7); 5:1 (p. 67); and 7:1 (p. 79); and Riché, *Dhuoda: Manuel,* 1:1.15–16; 5:1.68; and 7:1.13–14. Her use of the concept of humanity in some key passages has already been noted above. See notes, nos. 118, 123, and 143 above.
160. See Claussen, "God and Man," 44: "Dhuoda's disclaimer has nothing to do with her status as a woman or a lay person, but rather as a human."
161. Dronke, *Women Writers,* 36–37.
162. Neel, *Handbook,* 7:1 (p. 79).
163. Bernard took the youngest child from Dhuoda after birth.
164. Ibid., 1:7 (p. 13). See also ibid., 10:4 (p. 100).
165. That she uses the rhetoric of humility typical of the age is not to deny that Dhuoda appears sincerely aware of the limitations of both her education and her intellectual prowess. This realization, however, never stops her from proceeding with the task at hand.
166. Neel, *Handbook,* 1:2 (p. 8).
167. See Marie Anne Mayeski, *Dhuoda: Ninth Century Mother and Theologian* (Scanton, PA: University of Scanton Press, 1995), 65–92, for full exposition of Dhuoda's exegesis of the story.
168. Neel, *Handbook,* 1:2 (p. 8).
169. Ibid., 1:1 (p. 7).
170. Ibid., 6:1 (p. 75). Claussen, "Fathers of Power," 800, agrees.
171. Ibid., 1:1 (pp. 7–8).
172. Ibid., prol. (p. 5).
173. Ibid., 1:7 (p. 13). See also ibid., 10:1 (p. 95) and 10:4 (p. 100).
174. Ibid., prol. (p. 2).
175. Ibid., 1:7 (p. 13).
176. Ibid., 1:1 (p. 7).
177. Ibid., 2:2 (p. 17).
178. Ibid., 4:5 (p. 50).

179. Ibid., epigraph (p. 4). See also ibid., 1:5 (p. 11): "I think about such things as I have heard read."
180. Ibid., 1:7 (p. 13).
181. Ibid., 4:1 (p. 44).
182. Ibid., 4:1 (p. 44); 7:6 (p. 81); 4:4 (p. 48), and 4:1 (p. 44), respectively.
183. Ibid., 10:2 (p. 97).
184. Ibid., 1:7 (p. 13).
185. Ibid., 4:8 (p. 56).
186. Ibid., 8:1 (p. 83).
187. Ibid., 4:8 (p. 55).
188. Ibid., 10:2 (p. 96).
189. Ibid., 5:9 (p. 73).
190. Ibid., epigraph (p. 4).
191. Ibid., prol. (p. 5).
192. Ibid., 1:2 (p. 8).
193. Ibid., 1:5 (p. 10).
194. Ibid., 9:1 (p. 91).
195. Ibid., 6:1 (p. 75).
196. Ibid., 10:1 (p. 95).
197. Ibid., 4:4 (p. 48).
198. Ibid., 4:1 (p. 45).
199. Ibid., 4:2 (p. 45).
200. Ibid., 6:4 (p. 77). Dhuoda's numerology is, unfortunately, little explored. See *Medieval Numerology,* ed. Robert L. Surles (New York: Garland, 1993); in the Introduction Surles comments that medieval numerology is still under-valued and not properly appreciated, but that it had a profound influence on medieval thought. It certainly had an influence on Dhuoda.
201. E. Ann Matter, "Exegesis and Christian Education: The Carolingian Model," in *Schools of Thought in the Christian Tradition,* ed. Patrick Henry (Philadelphia, PA: Fortress Press, 1984), 91.
202. See, in particular, Books Four and Six.
203. Neel, *Handbook,* 4:8 (p. 59); passage is Ps 10:6.
204. Ibid., passage is 1 Jh 2:17.
205. Ibid., 4:8 (p. 55); passage is Js 1:19.
206. Ibid. (p. 59); and ibid., 1:2 (p. 8); parable is in Mt 14:21–28 and Mk 7:24–30.
207. See ibid., 3:10 (pp. 34–38) and 2:2 (pp. 16–17). References to body and soul are probably the most common in the manual.
208. Mayeski, *Dhuoda,* argues for the term "practical theology" to summarize Dhuoda's thought.
209. Neel, *Handbook,* 11:2 (p. 106).
210. See John Newell, "Education and Classical Culture in the Tenth Century: Age of Iron or Revival of Learning?" in *Hrotsvit of Gandersheim: Rara Avis in Saxonia?,* ed. Katharina M. Wilson (Ann Arbor, MI: Marc, 1987), 127–141.
211. M. A. Meyer, "Women and the Tenth-Century English Monastic Reform," *Revue bénédictine* 87 (1977), 34–35.

212. Constance Bouchard, "Family Structure and Family Consciousness among the Aristocracy in the Ninth and Tenth Century," *Franciá* 14 (1986), 639–658.
213. Suzanne Fonay Wemple, "Monastic Life of Women from the Merovingians to the Ottonians," in Wilson, *Hrotsvit: Rara Avis,* 41. See also Karl Leyser, *Rule and Conflict in an Early Medieval Society* (Bloomington, IN: Indiana University Press, 1979), 63–73.
214. Elisabeth van Houts, "Women and the writing of history in the early Middle Age: the case of Abbess Matilda of Essen and Aethelweard," *Early Medieval Europe* 1:1 (1992), 59.
215. Van Houts, *Memory,* 70–77.
216. Van Houts, "Women and the writing of history," 58.
217. Agius, *Vita et Obitus Hathumodae,* Ch. 9, in MGH, SS, iv, 166–189.
218. Beryl Smalley, *The Study of the Bible in the Middle Ages,* 3rd ed. (Oxford: Basil Blackwell, 1983), xxvii.
219. Katharina M. Wilson, "The Saxon Canoness Hrotsvit of Gandersheim," in *Medieval Women Writers,* 31–32.
220. Newell, "Education," 132.
221. McKitterick, "Women and literacy," in *Books,* 13:15–16.
222. The codex is Düsseldorf, Landes-und Universitäts-bibliothek Sammelhandschrift B.3; it consists of 306 folios. Stofferahn, "Evidence from Essex," Appendix. See also Bernhard Bischoff, "Die liturgische Musik und das Bildungswesen im frühmittelalterlichen Stift Essen," *Annales des Historischen Vereins für den Niederrhein* 157 (1955), 191.
223. Bischoff, "Die liturgische Musik," 192–194.
224. Stofferahn, "Evidencc from Essen," 73.
225. Ibid., 72.
226. Ibid., 88.
227. *Vitae Liutbergae,* c.35, in MGH, SS, iv, 44.
228. *Vitae Mathildis reginae antiquor,* ed. R. Kopke, MGH, SS, x.
229. Pref. to legends, tr. M. Gonsalva Wiegand, "The Non-Dramatic Works of Hrotsvit," in *Hrotswitha of Gandersheim: Her Life, Times, and Works, and a Comprehensive Bibliography,* ed. Anne Lyon Haight (New York: Hroswitha Club, 1965), 14.
230. Dronke, *Women Writers,* 74 n.46. Passage is from *Letter to Learned Patrons,* pref. to plays.
231. See Rosamond McKitterick, *The Carolingians and the Written Word* (Cambridge: Cambridge University Press, 1989), 155–164, 244–250, 252–261.
232. See McKitterick, "Women and Literacy," 13:41, for a list of citations to these charters.
233. Ibid., 13:21.
234. Particularly convincing is her argument concerning an illumination of Jerome and Paula in which, she believes, "the wisdom and learning of women vowed to the religious life is thus stressed." McKitterick, "Women in the Ottonian Church," 93.
235. Rosemary Sprague, "Hrotswith—Tenth-Century Margaret Webster," *Theatre Annual* 13 (1955), 19, comments that Constantine's love of theatre "has gone down in history as without precedent, even for an *aficionado.*"
236. See Haskins, *Renaissance,* 19–21.
237. William Hudson, "Hrotsvitha of Gandersheim," *English Historical Review* 3 (1888), 437.

238. A study of the history of technology reminds us how simple inventions are usually the most significant and influential. See Lynn White, *Medieval Technology and Social Change* (Oxford: Clarendon Press, 1962).
239. See Cornelia C. Coulter, "The 'Terentian' Comedies of a Tenth-Century Nun," *The Classical Journal* 24 (1929), 527.
240. For Hrotsvitha's complete works, see Helen Homeyer, ed., *Hrotsvithae opera* (Munich: Schöningh, 1970); and K. A. Barack, *Die Werke der Hrotsvitha* (Nürnberg: Bauer u. Raspe, 1858). For plays only see *The Plays of Hrotsvit of Gandersheim,* tr. Katharina M. Wilson (New York: Garland, 1989); and *The Plays of Roswitha,* tr. Christopher St. John (pseudonym for Christabel Marshall) (London: Chatto & Windus, 1923). For English translations of the historical works, see Mary B. Bergman, *Hrotsvithae Liber Tertius* (Covington, KY: Sisters of St. Benedict, 1943); and Wiegand, *Non-Dramatic Works.* Hrotsvitha's works are composed of three books. The first contains eight legends, the second has six dramas, and the third has two historical epics. Eight prefaces are found among the works.
241. Pref. to *Gesta Ottonis,* in *Plays of Roswitha* (www.fordham.edu/halsall/basis/roswitha-gerberg.html); Homeyer, *Hrotsvithae opera,* 385–386.
242. Katharina M. Wilson, "The Old Hungarian Translation of Hrotsvit's *Dulcitius:* History and Analysis," *Tulsa Studies in Women's Literature* 1:2 (1982), 177.
243. See Kenneth DeLuca, "Hrotsvit's 'Imitation' of Terence," *Classical Folio* 28 (1974), 89–102.
244. Wilson, *Plays,* 3–4; Homeyer, *Hrotsvithae opera,* 233–234.. Unfortunately, many today still do not see beyond Hrotsvitha's contemporaries and agree with them.
245. Edward H. Zeydel, "Ekkehard's Influence upon Hrotsvitha: A Study in Literary Integrity," *Modern Language Quarterly* 6 (1943), 339.
246. *Letter to learned patrons,* in Wilson, *Plays,* 4–5; Homeyer, *Hrotsvithae opera,* 236.
247. Pref. to legends, in *Plays of Roswitha;* Homeyer, *Hrotsvithae opera,* 38. Dronke, *Women Writers,* 66, comments that "the suggestion that writing in classical metres is especially hard for women, because they are frail, is deliberately preposterous and is said tongue in cheek."
248. Pref. to legends, in *Plays of Roswitha;* Homeyer, *Hrotsvithae opera,* 38.
249. Dennis Kratz, "The Nun's Epic: Hrotswitha on Christian Humanism," in *Wege de Worte,* ed. Donald E. Riechel (Cologne: Böhlau, 1978), 132, says that "Hrotswitha's deliberate departure from tradition raises it above any other Christian epic of the period."
250. Preface to epics, *Plays of Roswitha;* Homeyer, *Hrotsvithae opera,* 385.
251. Dronke, *Women Writers,* 76.
252. *Founding,* 185–226, in Homeyer, *Hrotsvithae opera,* 457–458. See Dronke's analysis, ibid., 80–82.
253. Dronke, *Women Writers,* 82, 71, 66, and 65. References to her weakness and the frailty of women are strewn throughout the prefaces. Hrotsvitha's statement in her preface to the dramas, Wilson, *Plays,* 3, that she is "the strong voice of Gandersheiem" is often taken as her moniker.
254. I agree with the conclusion of Sprague, "Hrotswitha," 30: "A great deal of ink has been spilled in an attempt to determine whether or not Hrotsvitha's plays were performed.

This is rather foolish, for from what is known of Gandersheim and its patrons, the plays must certainly have been performed." See Mary M. Butler, *Hrotsvitha: The Theatricality of Her Plays* (New York: Philosophical Library, 1960) for a detailed argument for their performance.

255. *Dulcitius,* Wilson, *Medieval Women Writers,* 55; Homeyer, *Hrotsvithae opera,* 2.2 (p. 270).
256. Wilson, ibid., 58; Homeyer, ibid., 12.1 (p. 275).
257. Wilson, ibid., 56; Homeyer, ibid., "*in derisium,*" 7:1 (p. 272).
258. Wilson, ibid., 55–56; Homeyer, ibid., 4:2–3 (p. 271).
259. See Barbara K. Gold, "Hrotswitha Writes Herself: *Clamor Validius Gandershemensis,*" in *Sex and Gender in Medieval and Renaissance Texts: The Latin Tradition,* eds. Barbara K. Gold, Paul A. Miller, and Charles Platter (Albany, NY: SUNY Press, 1997), 41–70.
260. I agree with Gold, "Hrotswitha Writes Herself," 52.
261. *Sapientia,* in Wilson, *Plays,* 135; Homeyer, *Hrotsvithae opera,* 5:4 (p. 365).
262. Wilson, ibid., 129; Homeyer, ibid., 3:10 (p. 361).
263. Wilson, ibid., 132; Homeyer, ibid., 3:22 (p. 363).
264. Wilson, ibid., 132–133; Homeyer, ibid., 3:24; 4:1–4 (pp. 363–364).
265. Wilson, ibid., 139; Homeyer, ibid., 5:17 (p. 368).
266. Wilson, ibid., 138; Homeyer, ibid., 5:13 (p. 367).
267. See Patricia Ranft, *Women and Spiritual Equality in Christian Tradition* (New York: St. Martin's Press, 1998), 17–71.
268. Newell, "Education," 134.
269. *Pafnutius* is often considered to be Hrotsvitha's masterpiece. See Sprague, "Hrotsvitha," 28.
270. Katharina M. Wilson, *Hrotsvit of Gandersheim: The Ethics of Authorial Stance* (Leiden: E. J. Brill, 1988), 96. After agreeing with Sandro Sticco, Helena Homeyer, and David Chamberlain that the way Hrotsvitha's combines learning and poetry is to be admired, she adds: "That Hrotsvit's practice of scientific interpolation might be reciprocal—that is, that her incorporation of details of the *artes liberales* as ornaments of her didactic moral poetry might, in turn, be intended to confer a value on the *artes* as well—on the other hand, has not been suggested. Yet Hrotsvit's dual purpose in providing her dramas with scientific interpolations is equally arguable, especially in light of her Boethian reference explaining the practice."
271. *Pafnutius,* in Wilson, *Plays,* 96, 97, 100–101; Homeyer, *Hrotsvithae opera,* 1:5–7 (pp. 329–330); and 1:18–20 (pp. 333–334).
272. Preface to *Gesta,* in St. John; Homeyer, ibid., 386.
273. Preface to legends, in Homeyer, ibid., 38.
274. Preface to legends, in St. John; Homeyer, ibid., 37.
275. See William Provost, "The Boethian Voice in the Dramas of Hrotsvit," in Wilson, *Hrotsvit: Rara avis,* 71–78.
276. Letter to patrons to dramas, in Wilson, *Plays,* 5; Homeyer, *Hrotsvithae opera,* 236.
277. Wilson, ibid., 3; Homeyer, ibid., 235.
278. Hrotsvitha's repeated self-deprecating remarks are occasionally judged out of context, especially in women's studies but are really nothing more than the expected rhetoric of all writers, male and female.
279. Letter, in Wilson, *Plays,* 5.

280. Pref. to dramas, in ibid., 3; Homeyer, *Hrotsvithae opera,* 233. A few sentences later she repeats the sentiment: "My intent" was to "have rendered the praise of the innocent as well as I could."
281. Ibid.
282. See G. R. Coffman, "A New Approach to Medieval Latin Drama," *Modern Philology* 22 (1925), 262–263. This is not the same as claiming Hrotsvitha influenced all future medieval drama, for that is a topic still open to debate and is related to how well known her dramas were prior to Conrad Celtis' rediscovery of her manuscript in 1494.
283. E. Blashfield, *Portraits and Backgrounds* (New York: Charles Scribner's Son, 1917), 23–24; and Bulter, *Hrotsvitha,* 79–80.
284. Hrotsvitha does tell us, though, that Otto II had "ordered it to be presented to your keen gaze." Prol., *Gesta,* in Haight, *Hrotswitha of Gandersheim,* 33; Homeyer, *Hrotsvithae opera,* 388.
285. Haight, ibid., 31; Homeyer, ibid.
286. See "The *Gesta Ottonis* in Its Contexts," in Wilson, *Hrotsvit: Rara avis,* 201–209.
287. Haight, *Hrotswitha of Gandersheim,* 33; Homeyer, *Hrotsvithae opera,* 388.
288. Cf. 2 Kings 24:17 and *Gesta Ottonis,* lines 266–275 and 292–296; Homeyer, ibid., 416–417.
289. Line 139: "ut credas regem David regnare fidelem." Ibid., 411.
290. Haight, *Hrotswitha of Gandersheim,* 31; Homeyer, *Hrotsvithae opera,* 387.
291. Kratz, "*Gesta,*" 204.
292. Homeyer, *Hrotsvithae opera,* 243–244. She repeats this belief in both prefaces to *Gesta Ottonis* and in the text.
293. Kratz, "*Gesta Ottonis,*" 205–206.
294. See Chenu, *Nature, Man,* 162–201, especially 164.
295. Preface to epics, *Plays of Roswitha;* Homeyer, *Hrotsvithae opera,* 385.
296. Note before pref. to dramas, Haight, *Hrotswitha of Gandersheim,* 189; Homeyer, ibid., 227.
297. Haight, ibid., 30; Homeyer, ibid., 385.
298. Prol., *Gesta Ottonis,* 387, in Haight, ibid., 31; Homeyer, ibid. In Hrotsvitha's history of the foundation of her own monastery at Gandersheim, she is similarly careful to establish the validity of her sources. Her opening comment sets the criterion: "As the report of many well-informed people tells." In Dronke, *Women Writers,* 80; *Primordia,* 185, in Homeyer, *Hrotsvithae opera,* 457.
299. Thomas Head, "Hrotsvit's *Primordia* and the Historical Traditions of Monastic Communities," in Wilson, *Hrotsvit: Rara avis,* 143–155.
300. Dronke, *Women Writers,* 81; *Primordia,* 185–226, in Homeyer, *Hrotsvithae opera,* 457–58.
301. Pref. to legends, *Plays of Roswitha;* Homeyer, *Hrotsvithae opera,* 38.
302. Homeyer, *Hrotsvithae opera,* 38; Katharina M. Wilson, "Hrotsvit and the Sounds of Harmony and Discord," *Germanic Notes* 14:4 (1983), 55.
303. Dronke, *Women Writers,* 68; *Primordia,* 10–11, in Homeyer, *Hrotsvithae opera,* 177.
304. Dronke, *Women Writers,* 82.
305. See comments by A. Daniel Frankforter, "Hrotswitha of Gandersheim and the Destiny of Women," *The Historian* 41:2 (February 1979), 314: "Male strength, if misdirected, is not always virtue; female weakness, if properly utilized, is not always vice."

306. Pref. to dramas, Wilson, *Plays,* 3; Homeyer, *Hrotsvithae opera,* 234.
307. Letter, in Wilson, ibid., 5; and pref. to dramas, 1; Homeyer, ibid., 236, 233.

Chapter 2, pp. 35–70
The Creation of a Literate Society

1. The literature for all these changes is vast and readily accessible. Rather than present a bibliography here, I will refer the reader to perhaps the best source currently available for recent research, the journal *Early Medieval Europe,* published by Blackwell.
2. See Jean Leclercq, *Love of Learning and the Desire for God,* tr. Catharine Misrahi, 2nd rev. ed. (New York: Fordham University Press, 1974).
3. The great exception to this generalization is Frederick Copleston. It should be noted, however, that Frederick Copleston wrote his masterpiece, *A History of Philosophy,* 7 vols., repr. (Garden City, NY: Image Books, 1963) specifically for a Catholic audience, which partially accounts for the different approach.
4. C. Stephen Jaeger, *The Envy of Angels* (Philadelphia, PA: University of Pennsylvania Press, 1994), 4.
5. Brian Stock, *Listening for the Text* (Baltimore, MD: Johns Hopkins University Press, 1990), 19, 13.
6. Besides ibid., see Stock's groundbreaking *The Implications of Literacy: Written Language and Models of Interpretation in the Eleventh and Twelfth Centuries* (Princeton, NJ: Princeton University Press, 1983).
7. B. B. Price, *Medieval Thought: An Introduction* (Oxford: Blackwell, 1992), vii.
8. Stock, *Listening,* 124.
9. Ibid., 34.
10. Price, *Medieval Thought,* viii.
11. Stock, *Listening,* 14, adds that it also became a new source of subjection (for example, the codification of laws).
12. She writes: "si que forte fila vel etiam floecos de panniculis, in veste philisophiae abruptis, evellere quivi, praefato opusculo *inserere* [to incorporate, weave] curavi." K. A. Barack, *Die Werke des Hrotsvitha* (Nürnberg: Bauer u. Raspe, 1858), 142. See ibid., 41.
13. Stock, *Listening,* 42.
14. Ibid., 35–37.
15. Ibid., 122.
16. Ibid., 125.
17. McKitterick, "Nuns' scriptoria," 7:3–4.
18. See discussion of this in Patricia Ranft, *Women and the Religious Life in Premodern Europe* (New York: St. Martin's Press, 1996), 9. I have discussed women's participation in book production above in reference to Boniface's missionary needs.
19. See chapter 1, pp. 11–12, and Rosamond McKitterick, "Nuns' scriptoria in England and France in the eighth century," *Francia* 7 (1989), 1–35. Bischoff's article in 1965 began the research in earnest ("Die Kölner Nonnenhandschriften und das Scriptorium von Chelles," *Mittelalterliche Studien* 1 (1965), 17–35), and works such as Alison Beach, "The Female Scribes of Twelfth-Century Bavaria," PhD Diss., Columbia University,

1996, continue it. Beach presents "criteria for identifying female scribes and establish[es] a framework for analysis" and hopes that the "potentially rich material from the tenth and eleventh century" (p. 377) will also be explored.

20. Matilda did so; see next paragraph.
21. I am being restrained here; I have never seen them included.
22. Turgot, "*Life of St. Margaret of Scotland,*" 2, 12, *AASS,* June 10, 2, 328, in *Medieval Saints: A Reader,* tr. William Forbes-Seith, ed. Mary-Ann Stouck (Peterborough, CAN: Broadview Press, 1999), 279.
23. Ibid., 2, 13 (p. 280).
24. Ibid., 3, 33 (p. 290).
25. For Eve's collaboration with Goscelin, see A. Wilmart, "Eve et Goscelin," *Revue bénédictine* 46 (1934), 414–438.
26. William of Malmesbury, cited in *The Writings of Medieval Women: An Anthology,* tr. and ed. Marcelle Thiébaux, 2nd ed. (New York: Garland, 1994), 298.
27. Turgot, *Life,* prol., 1, 1 (p. 274).
28. Ibid., 1, 2 (p. 274).
29. Matilda to Anselm, Letter 1, in Thiébaux, *Writings of Medieval Women,* 301.
30. Dhuoda's manual is replete with unacknowledged citations.
31. Matilda, letter 1, 301–302.
32. Ibid., 302–303.
33. Ibid., 303.
34. Ibid., 308.
35. *Regesta: Regesta Regum Anglo-Normannorum,* 3, Nos. 808, 809, cited in Marjorie Chibnall, *The Empress Matilda* (Oxford: Basil Blackwell, 1991), 10.
36. Ibid., Nos. 565, 567, in ibid.
37. Ibid.
38. For a concise summary of his reign, see C. Warren Hollister, *The Making of England,* 6th ed. (Lexington, MA: D. C. Heath, 1992), 126–138.
39. Matilda, Letter 5, in Thiébaux, *Writings of Medieval Women,* 307. Anselm went into exile in 1097 after a quarrel with William II Rufus, but Henry invited him back once he came to the throne. They too soon quarreled, and Anselm returned to exile in 1103. The quarrel (over lay investiture) was resolved in 1107.
40. "*litterarum pluremum emicuit scientia*" (*Vita Wolfhelmi,* c.25, in MGH, SS, 12, 190).
41. See Albert Groeteken, *Die heilige Adelheid von Vilich und ihre Familie* (Kevelaer: Verlag Butzon und Bercker, 1937).
42. *Mater Spiritualis: The Life of Adelheid of Vilich,* tr. Madelyn Bergen Dick (Toronto: Peregrina Publishing, 1994), prol. (p. 15).
43. Ibid., 1 (p. 16).
44. Ibid., 1 (pp. 16–17).
45. Ibid., 2 (p. 18).
46. Ibid., 1 (p. 17).
47. Ibid., 2 (p. 17).
48. Ibid. (p. 18).
49. The poem is found in a manuscript of verse (British Library, Add. 24199, fol. 77v), probably originating at Bury St. Edmunds. It is edited in André Boutemy, "Recueil poétique du

manuscrit Additional 24199 du British Museum," *Latomus* 2 (1938), xiv, 42–44. An English translation is found in Gerald Bond, *The Loving Subject: Desire, Eloquence, and Power in Romanesque France* (Philadelphia, PA: University of Pennsylvania Press, 1995), 166–169; and in Constant J. Mews, *The Lost Love Letters of Heloise and Abelard: Perceptions of Dialogue in Twelfth-Century France* (New York: St. Martin's Press, 1999), 164–166.

50. Mews, *Lost Love Letters,* 164–165.
51. Ibid., 165.
52. Ibid., 166.
53. Marcia L. Colish, *Medieval Foundations of the Western Intellectual Tradition 400–1400* (New Haven, CT: Yale University Press, 1997), 268.
54. Monica Green and John F. Benton maintain that there was no eleventh-century Trotula but that there was a twelfth-century woman physician called Trota. She wrote a *practica* but not the three treatises usually attributed to Trotula or her. See John F. Benton, "Trotula, Women's Problems, and the Professionalization of Medicine in the Middle Ages," *Bulletin of the History of Medicine* 59 (1985), 30–53.
55. *The Letters of Abelard and Heloise,* tr. Betty Radice (London: Penguin Books, 1974), 66 (Abelard) and 277 (Peter the Venerable).
56. PL 178, 325–336 (Abelard); and *The Chronicle of Guillaume Godel* cited in Mary Ellen Waithe, "Heloise," in *A History of Women Philosophers,* 4 vols., ed. Mary Ellen Waithe (Dordrecht: Kluwer Academic Publishers, 1989), 2:69.
57. *Historia calamitatum,* in Radice, *Letters,* 66–67.
58. M. T. Clancy, *Abelard: A Medieval Life* (Oxford: Basil Blackwell, 1999).
59. Elizabeth Mary McNamer, *The Education of Heloise* (Lewiston, NY: Edwin Mellen Press, 1991), 52–54.
60. Joseph T. Muckle, "The Personal Letters between Abelard and Heloise," *Medieval Studies* 15 (1953), 51.
61. McNamer, *Education,* 57–58.
62. See Ewald Könsgen, *Epistolae duorum amantium: Briefe Abaelardus und Heloises?* (Leiden: E. J. Brill, 1974); and Mews, *Lost Love Letters,* for complete argument.
63. Helen Moody, *The Debate of the Rose* (Berkeley, CA: University of California Press, 1981), 117, cited in McNamer, *Education,* 50–51, for citations from all the above.
64. Mews, *Lost Love Letters,* 41.
65. Bernhard Schmeidler, "Der Briefwechsel zwischen Abälard und Heloise eine Fälschung?" *Archivum für Kulturgeschichte* 11 (1913), 1–30; and Etienne Gilson, *Héloïse et Abélard* (London: Hollis & Carter, 1953).
66. John Benton, "Fraud, Fiction, and Borrowing in the Correspondence of Abelard and Heloise," in *Pierre Abélard-Pierre le Venerable,* eds. René Louis, Jean Jolivet, and Jean Châtillon (Paris: Editions du Centre national de la recherche scientifique, 1975), 469–512; and *idem.,* "A Reconsideration of the Authenticity of the Correspondence of Abelard and Heloise," *Petrus Abaelardus (1079–1142),* eds. Rudolf Thomas *et al.* (Trier: Paulines-Verlag, 1980).
67. Hubert Silvestre, "Die Libesgeschichte zwischen Abaelard und Heloise: de Anteil des Romans," in *Fälschungen im Mittelalter* 5, MGH, Schriften, 33.5, pp. 121–165.
68. See John Marenbon, "Authenticity Revisited," in *Listening to Heloise,* ed. Bonnie Wheeler (New York: St. Martin's Press, 2000), 19–33.

69. Radice, *Letters,* 278.
70. Anyone who has assigned the *Letters* in class can verify how "modern" they still are.
71. Radice, *Letters,* 114.
72. I am referring, of course, to his revelatory *Confessions,* tr. R. S. Pine-Coffin, repr. (Harmondsworth: Penguin Books, 1978).
73. Jaeger, *Envy of Angels,* 3–4.
74. See Carolyn Walker Bynum, *Docere Verbo et Exemplo: An Aspect of Twelfth Century Spirituality* (Missoula, MT: Harvard University Press, 1979).
75. Patricia Ranft, "The Concept of Witness in the Christian Tradition from Its Origin to Its Institutionalization," *Revue bénédictine* 102:1–2 (1992), 9–23.
76. PL 204, 1016.
77. PL 172, 1380.
78. Patricia Cricco, "Monasticism and Its Role as a Liminal Community in Medieval Society," PhD Diss., West Virginia University, 1981, 112–168.
79. PL 172, 1380.
80. See, for example, *Lettres des Premiers Chartreux,* tr. par un Chartreux (Paris: Editions du Cerf, 1962); *Annales Camaldulenses ordinis sancti Benedicti,* eds. J. Mittarelli and A. Costadoni, 2 vols. (Venice, 1756).
81. For summary, see Ranft, *Women and the Religious Life,* 47–49.
82. Radice, *Letters,* 176.
83. Ranft, *Women and the Religious Life,* 49.
84. Jaeger, *Envy of Angels,* 218.
85. M. Tullius Cicero, *De amicitia* (London: W. Heinemann, 1927), 9, 14, 27.
86. Radice, *Letters,* 117.
87. Ibid., 113.
88. Ibid., 66.
89. Ibid., 147.
90. Ibid., 133.
91. Ibid., 147.
92. Ibid., 132.
93. Ibid., 116.
94. Ibid., 135.
95. See Andrea Nye, "A Woman's Thought or a Man's Discipline? The Letters of Abelard and Heloise," *Hypatia* 7:3 (Summer 1992), 25–47. Nye disagrees that Heloise's love was Ciceronian (43 n.10). *Ethics* (or *Know Yourself*) was begun ca. 1138, but not completed. Abelard died in 1142. Ibid., 44 n.15.
96. Radice, *Letters,* 115.
97. Ibid., 131–132.
98. Abelard adds no such qualifier: "The merit or the praiseworthiness of the doer is not in the deed but in the intention." *Peter Abelard's Ethics,* ed. David Luscombe (Oxford: Clarendon Press, 1971), 28.
99. Particularly disappointing is its absence in Wheeler, *Listening to Heloise,* otherwise an excellent source.
100. His treatises on creation and on the study of literature, a book of 133 hymns, numerous liturgical compositions, and a collection of sermons were all written at Heloise's

request. Peter Dronke, *Women Writers of the Middle Ages* (Cambridge: Cambridge University Press, 1984), 134.

101. *Problemata,* tr. in McNamer, *Education,* Appendix, 111–112.
102. Dronke, *Women Writers,* 112.
103. Radice, *Letters,* 133.
104. Ibid., 114.
105. Dronke, *Women Writers,* 138.
106. *Problemata,* 35 (p. 165).
107. Ibid., 8 (p. 127).
108. Ibid., 12 (p. 132).
109. Ibid., 18 (p. 152).
110. Ibid., 22 (p. 154).
111. Ibid., 19 (p. 152).
112. Ibid., 20 (p. 153).
113. Ibid., 13 (p. 133).
114. Ibid., 16 (p. 147).
115. Ibid., 14 (p. 136).
116. Ibid., 34 (p. 165).
117. See Junita Feros Ruys, "*Quae Maternae Immemor Naturae:* The Rhetorical Struggle over the Meaning of Motherhood in the Writings of Heloise and Abelard," in Wheeler, *Listening to Heloise,* 323–339.
118. *Problemata,* 5 (pp. 119–120).
119. Ibid., 40 (p. 172).
120. Ibid., 9 (p. 129).
121. Ibid., 24 (p. 156).
122. Ibid., 26 (p. 159).
123. Ibid., 18 (p. 152).
124. Ibid., 42 (p. 174).
125. Stock, *Listening,* 33.
126. *Problemata,* 39 (p. 170).
127. Ibid., 2 (p. 113).
128. Ibid., 6 (pp. 121–122).
129. Ibid., 7 (p. 124).
130. Ibid., 28 (p. 159).
131. Stock, *Listening,* 40.
132. See *Jutta and Hildegard: The Biographical Sources,* tr. Anna Silvas (University Park, PA: State University of Pennsylvania, 1998). Hildegard was never canonized.
133. *Life of Lady Jutta the Anchoress,* 1, in ibid., 65.
134. Ibid., 1, in ibid., 66.
135. Guibert to Bovo, Letter 38, 8, in ibid., 109.
136. Jaeger, *Envy of Angels,* 7.
137. Letter 38, 6, in *Jutta and Hildegard,* 106.
138. Ibid., 38, 7, in ibid., 107.
139. *Life of Lady Jutta,* 2, in ibid., 67.
140. Ibid., 3, in ibid., 68.

141. Ibid., 5, in ibid., 73.
142. *Life of Hildegard,* 1, in ibid., 139. Godfrey could be using allegorical language here. See Barbara Newman, *Symphonia: A Critical Edition of the "Symphonia armonie celestium revelationium,"* (Ithaca, NY: Cornell University Press, 1988), 22–23.
143. *Life of Jutta,* 4, in *Jutta and Hildegard,* 71. The passage is adopted from the Rule of St. Benedict 6, 8.
144. Letter 38, 8, in ibid., 109.
145. Ibid., 6, in ibid., 72.
146. Ibid., 8, in ibid., 78–79.
147. Letter 38, 7, in ibid., 109–110.
148. *Life of Hildegard,* 5, in ibid., 144.
149. Letter 38, 10, in ibid., 111.
150. Ibid., 3, in ibid., 102.
151. Ibid., 3, in ibid., 101.
152. Declaration, in *Hildegard of Bingen: Scivias,* tr. M. Columba Hart and Jane Bishop, intro. Barbara Newman, pref. Carolyn Walker Bynum (New York: Paulist Press, 1990), 59–60.
153. Ibid., 60; and *Life of Hildegard,* 2, in *Jutta and Hildegard,* 159.
154. No scholar of repute today questions Hildegard's authorship, even though Hildegard did not hand-write her works. Volmar was her secretary for over thirty years, and she was also served by Richardis of Stade and Guibert of Gembloux.
155. Declaration, in *Scivias,* 59–60.
156. Newman, intro., ibid., 23, compares the contents with Hugh of St. Victor's summa, *On the Sacraments of the Christian Faith.*
157. Declaration, ibid., 60–61.
158. Letter 103r, Hildegard to Monk Guibert, in *Letters of Hildegard of Bingen,* tr. Joseph L. Baird and Radd K. Ehrman (New York: Oxford University Press, 1998), 2:24.
159. In its final form Theodoric included lengthy passages of Hildegard's own autobiographical writings.
160. *Life of Hildegard,* 2, in *Jutta and Hildegard,* 160.
161. Augustine, *Confessions,* 4:16 (p. 87).
162. Peter Dronke, "Problemata Hildegardiana," *Mittellateinisches Jahrbuch* 16 (1981), 107.
163. Ibid., 107–108.
164. Michael Camille, *Gothic Art: Glorious Visions* (Upper Saddle River, NJ: Prentice-Hall, 1996), 22.
165. *Scivias,* 3.2.9 (p. 329).
166. Ibid., 1.4.24 (p. 123).
167. Hugh of St. Victor, *Joel,* PL 175, 355.
168. Richard of St. Victor, *In apocalypsim Joannis,* PL 196, 686.
169. See Copleston, *History of Philosophy,* 2:1: 203; and Steve Chase, *Angelic Wisdom* (Notre Dame, IN: University of Notre Dame Press, 1995), 48–51, especially n.4.
170. *Life of Hildegard,* 8, in *Jutta and Hildegard,* 150.
171. *Scivias,* 1.4.24 (p. 123).
172. *Book of Divine Works,* Book 4, 98, in PL 197, 738–1035. It is interesting to note Hildegard's use of eye imagery in her drama *Ordo virtutum.* Here *oculus* means either eye or the bud of a plant ("the eye of a potato"). In the prologue of the play the

Patriarchs and Prophets declare that they are "the fruit of the living bud." In scene two Hope says that she is the "sweet viewer of the living eye," and in the epilogue she declares "that thy eye should never yield, until thou mightest see my body full of buds." See Bruce W. Hozeski, "Hildegard of Bingen's *Ordo Virtutum:* The Earliest Discovered Liturgical Morality Play," *American Benedictine Review* 26:3 (September 1975), 251–259; and idem, "*Ordo Virtutum:* Hildegard of Bingen's Liturgical Morality Play," *Annuale Medievale* 13 (1972), 45–69.

173. Dronke, *Women Writers,* 144.
174. Ibid., 171.
175. Letter 23, *Letters of Hildegard,* 1:76–79.
176. Colish, *Foundations,* 143, notes, however, that Avicenna tended to "Platonize Aristotelianism."
177. It was chronologically possible but highly unlikely that Aristotle's writings were available to her, except, of course, through Boethius, whose *Philosophia* resembles Hildegard's *Sapientia.* See Barbara Newman, *Sister of Wisdom* (Berkeley, CA: University of California Press, 1989), 74.
178. Ibid., 247.
179. Helen J. John, "Hildegard of Bingen: A New Twelfth-Century Woman Philosopher?," in *Hypatia's Daughters,* ed. Linda Lopez McAlister (Bloomington, IN: Indiana University Press, 1996), p. 19.
180. *Scivias,* 3.13.12 (p. 533).
181. Declaration, *Scivias,* 60.
182. PL 197, 979–81; Newman, *Sister,* 52–53.
183. *Scivias,* 3.2.9 (p. 329). Light is one of the root words Hildegard uses to create new names in her imagery language. See M. L. Portmann and A. Odermatt, *Wörterbuch der unbekannten Sprache (Lingua ignota)* (Basel: Basler Hildegard-Gesellschaft, 1986).
184. See R. W. Southern, *The Making of the Middle Ages* (New Haven, CT: Yale University Press, 1978), 234–235.
185. Ibid., 237.
186. Anselm, *Cur Deus Homo,* 1, 7, in *St. Anselm: Basic Writings,* tr. S. N. Deane, 2nd ed., (LaSalle, IL: Open Court, 1968), 187.
187. Ibid., 1, 3 (pp. 182–183).
188. Hildegard does retain, though, the imagery of cosmic war in some letters. See Dronke, *Women Writers,* 184.
189. *Scivias,* 2.6.100–102 (pp. 288–289).
190. Ibid., 3.1 (p. 310).
191. Ibid., 3.4.1 (p. 358).
192. Southern, *Making,* 237–241.
193. *Scivias,* 3.8 (p. 425).
194. Ibid., 3.8.13 (p. 435).
195. Jeffrey Schnapp, "Virgin Words: Hildegard of Bingen's *Lingua Ignota* and the Development of Imaginary Languages Ancient to Modern," *Exemplaria* 3:2 (1991), 278.
196. Ibid., 287.
197. Ibid., 283.
198. Ibid., 284. The language has survived in two manuscripts. In the Wiesbaden manuscript there are six categories, and in the Berlin manuscript there are fifteen.

199. *Causae et curae,* ed. Paul Kaiser (Leipzig: Teubner, 1903), 65, cited in Heinrich Schipperges, *Hildegard of Bingen: Healing and the Nature of the Cosmos,* tr. J. Broadwin (Princeton, NJ: Markus Wiener, 1997), 10.
200. Newman, *Sister,* 19. Newman uses the title found in the earliest manuscript, *De operatione Dei,* translates it as *On the Activity of God. Liber divinorum operum (The Book of Divine Works)* is the title given it in most other manuscripts and in Migne's edition. We will use its more common designation here.
201. *Scivias,* 1.2.27 (p. 86).
202. Preface, *Physica,* PL 197, 1125.
203. Hildegard of Bingen, *Book of the Rewards of Life,* tr. Bruce W. Hozeski (Oxford: Oxford University Press, 1994), 1:118 (p. 62).
204. Ibid., 6:17 (p. 271).
205. Ibid., 1:40 (p. 28).
206. Ibid., 4:59 (pp. 208, 209).
207. Ibid., 1:40 (p. 28).
208. Ibid., 3:28 (p. 139).
209. Ibid., 6:17 (p. 271).
210. Ibid., 4:30 (p. 192).
211. Ibid., 3:23 (p. 137).
212. Letter 192, *Letters of Hildegard,* 2:162.
213. *Book of the Rewards,* 4:59 (p. 208).
214. Ibid., 4:8 (p. 180).
215. Ibid., 5:3 (p. 221).
216. *Scivias,* 3.10.2 (p. 473).
217. *Causae,* 41–45, in Dronke, *Women Writers,* 243.
218. *Scivias,* 1.4.21 (pp. 121–122).
219. *Causae,* 104; Dronke, *Women Writers,* 244, 176.
220. *Causae,* 55–56, in Marcia Chamberlain, "Hildegard of Bingen's *Causes and Cures:* A Radical Feminist Response to the Doctor–Cook Binary" in *Hildegard of Bingen: A Book of Essays,* ed. Maud Burnett McInerney (New York: Garland, 1998), 64–65.
221. Ibid., 18, in ibid., 65.
222. Letter 155r, *Letters of Hildegard,* 2:100.
223. Letter 156r, ibid., 2:103.
224. Hildegard's influence and role as advisor is discussed at length in Patricia Ranft, *A Woman's Way: The Forgotten History of Women's Spiritual Direction* (New York: Palgrave, 2000), 74–79.
225. See Elizabeth Gössmann, "Hildegard of Bingen," in Waithe, *History of Women Philosophers,* 2:53–54; and Newman, *Sister,* 91–94.
226. *Scivias,* 3.1.7 (p. 314).
227. Ibid., 3.1.8 (p. 315).
228. *Book of Divine Works,* 4.103, in PL 197, 888, tr. in Schipperges, *Hildegard,* 38.
229. Ibid., 4.100, in PL 197, 885, tr. in Newman, *Sister,* 96.
230. *Scivias,* 1.2.12 (p. 78).
231. Ibid., 3.2.23 (p. 337).
232. Ibid., 3.2.22 (p. 336).
233. Ibid., 1.2.29 (p. 87).

234. Ibid., 1.2.27 (p. 86).
235. *Book of the Rewards,* 4.20 (pp. 185–186).
236. Laurence Moulinier, "L'abbesse et les poissons: un aspect de la zoologie de Hildegarde de Bingen," in *Exploitation des animaux sauvage à travers le temps* (Juan-les-Pin: APDCA, 1993), 461–472.
237. Kenneth Kitchell and Irven Resnick, "Hildegard as a Medieval 'Zoologist': The Animals of the *Physica,*" in McIerney, *Hildegard,* 48.
238. Albert was born a generation after Hildegard's death and benefited greatly by the influx of Greek texts into the West that was too late for Hildegard. Quote is ibid., 32.
239. Sabina Flanagan, *Hildegard of Bingen, 1098–1179: A Visionary Life* (London: Routledge, 1989), 82.
240. Kitchell and Resnick, "Hildegard," 45.
241. *Scivias,* 1.3.18 (p. 98).
242. Quoted in Flanagan, *Visionary Life,* 95.
243. *O quam mirabilis* (No. 60), tr. in ibid., 111.
244. *Divine Works,* 4.100, 104–105, in PL 197, 885.
245. PL 197, 743–744, tr. in Newman, *Sister,* 69, 70.
246. Ibid.
247. See Otto von Simson, *The Gothic Cathedral* (Princeton, NJ: Princeton University Press, 1956), 21–24.
248. Letter 23, *Letters of Hildegard,* 1:77–79.
249. *Scivias,* 3.13.12 (p. 533).
250. *Life of Hildegard,* 2.1, in *Jutta and Hildegard,* 155.
251. Barbara Jeskalían, "Hildegard of Bingen: Her Times and Music," *Anima* 10:1 (Fall 1983), 8.
252. Peter Dronke, *Poetic Individuality in the Middle Ages* (Oxford: Clarendon Press, 1970), 151.
253. Jeskalían, "Hildegard," 11.
254. Kathryn L. Bumpass, "A Musical Reading of Hildegard's Responsory 'Spiritui Sancto,'" in McInerney, *Hildegard,* 157.
255. See ibid., and Marianne Pfau, "Hildegard von Bingen's *Symphonie armonie celestium revelationum:* Analysis of Musical Process, Modality, and Text–Music Relations," PhD Diss., State University of New York at Stoney Brook, 1990.
256. Simson, *The Gothic Cathedral,* 22.
257. See Pozzi Escot, "Gothic Cathedral and the Hidden Geometry of St. Hildegard," *Sonus* 5:1 (Fall 1984), 14–31; Robert Cogan, "Hildegard's Fractal Antiphon," *Sonus* 11:1 (1990), 1–19; and Jan S. Emerson, "A Poetry of Science: Relating Body and Soul in the *Scivias,*" in McInerney, *Hildegard,* 77–101.
258. In Dronke, *Poetic Individuality,* 161–162.
259. Ibid., 153.
260. Dronke, "Problemata," 100. The text of the play is reproduced in idem, *Poetic Individuality,* 180–192.
261. This is unfortunate, because these works are still used extensively. See Karl Young, *The Drama of the Medieval Church* (Oxford: Oxford University Press, 1933) and O. B. Hardison, Jr., *Christian Rite and Christian Drama in the Middle Ages* (Baltimore, MD: Johns Hopkins University Press, 1965).

262. See Patricia Ranft, *Women and Spiritual Equality in Christian Tradition* (New York: St. Martin's Press, 1998), 171–172 and Fletcher Collins, *The Production of Medieval Church Music-Drama* (Charlottesville, VA: University of Virginia Press, 1972), 57.
263. See Robert A. Potter, "The Idea of a Morality Play," and "Images of the Human Predicament: Some Ancient and Modern Visualizations of the Morality Play," *Research Opportunities in Renaissance Drama* 13–14 (1970–1971), 239–247 and 249–258.
264. Dronke, *Poetic Individuality,* 169, dismisses the idea that Hildegard's play is merely a dramatization of Prudentius' *Psychomachia.*
265. Ibid., 179.
266. Scene 1, line 18, ibid., 172, 181.
267. Scene 1, lines 45–47, ibid., 173, 182.
268. Ulrike Wiethaus, "Cathar Influences in Hildegard of Bingen's Play 'Ordo Virtutum,' " *American Benedictine Review* 38:2 (June 1987), 192–203, suggests that *Ordo Virtutum* was intended as a defense against Cathar heresy. Hildegard's portrayal of the Devil and the human body offers strong support for her thesis.
269. Scene 4, lines 229–231, Dronke, *Poetic Individuality,* 176–177; 190.
270. Dronke, *Women Writers,* 201.
271. Letter 1, *Letters of Hildegard,* 1:28.
272. Letter 35, ibid., 102.
273. Ranft, *A Woman's Way,* 74–79.
274. Letter 40, *Letters of Hildegard,* 1:110.
275. I tend to think Dronke, *Women Writers,* 149, is underestimating the esteem in which Hildegard's reasoning powers were held, for, as he comments, Odo "credited Hildegard with a means of judging different from and superior to normal methods of metaphysical enquiry."
276. Readings, 7, in *Jutta and Hildegard,* 217–218.
277. *Life of Hildegard,* 12, in ibid., 173.
278. There is no evidence that Hildegard's gender caused problems. This is a bit surprising, for this period saw many new groups of laity claiming the right to preach as part of their witness to the *vita apostolica,* and clergy were becoming more and more protective of their preaching rights. See Carolyn Muessig, "Prophecy and Song: Teaching and Preaching by Medieval Women," in *Women Preachers and Prophets through Two Millenia of Christianity,* ed. Beverly M. Kienzle and Pamela J. Walker (Berkeley, CA: University of California Press, 1998), 146–158.
279. *Life of Hildegard,* 17, in *Jutta and Hildegard,* 191.
280. See Kathryn Kerby-Fulton, "Self-Image and the Visionary Role in Two Letters from the Correspondence of Elizabeth of Schönau and Hildegard of Bingen," *Vox Benedictina* 2–3 (1985), 204–223.
281. Anne L. Clark, *Elizabeth of Schönau* (Philadelphia, PA: University of Pennsylvania Press, 1992), 80.
282. *Scivias,* intro., 46.
283. Ibid., 47.
284. Kathryn Kerby-Fulton, "Prophecy and Suspicion: Closet Radicalism, Reformist Politics, and the Vogue for Hildegardiana in Ricardian England," *Speculum* 75:2 (April 2000), 322–323.
285. Ibid., 319, 341.

Chapter 3, pp. 71–90
The Coming of the Vernacular

1. Charles Homer Haskins, *The Renaissance of the Twelfth Century* (Cambridge, MA: Harvard University Press, 1927).
2. Marcia L. Colish, *Medieval Foundations of the Western Intellectual Tradition 400–1400* (New Haven, CT: Yale University Press, 1997), 182, 175.
3. See *The Idea of the Vernacular: An Anthology of Middle English Literary Theory, 1280–1520,* eds. Jocelyn Wogan-Browne and others (University Park, PA: Pennsylvania State University Press, 1999). Alastair J. Minnis, *Medieval Theory of Authorship,* 2nd ed. (Aldershot: Wildwood, 1988); Ernest R. Curtis, *European Literature and the Later Middle Ages,* tr. W. R. Trask (Princeton, NJ: Princeton University Press, repr., 1990); and Marcia L. Colish, *The Mirror of Language: A Study in the Medieval Theory of Knowledge,* rev. ed. (Lincoln, NE: University of Nebraska Press, 1983).
4. See Friedrich Heer, *The Medieval World,* tr. Janet Sondheimer, repr. (New York: New American Library, 1962), 356–376. This is not to say that medieval people were self-consciously aware of this relationship. As H. J. Claytor, *From Script to Print* (Folcroft, PA: Folcroft Library Editions, repr., Norwood Editions, 1977), 22–47, points out, "language had little or no political significance in the middle ages" (p. 22) and medieval people would never have regarded language as a mark of nationality. Eventually, however, it was so regarded and even became "a national possession for which a people will fight and die" (p. 45).
5. G. Turville-Petre, *The Origins of Icelandic Literature* (Oxford: Clarendon Press, 1953), 213.
6. See Terry G. Lacy, *Rings of Seasons: Iceland—Its Culture and History* (Ann Arbor, MI: University of Michigan Press, 1998) and Jesse L. Byock, *Medieval Iceland* (Berkeley, CA: University of California Press, 1988). An example of contemporary awareness of the relationship between the vernacular and national identity is seen in Iceland's policy toward legal birth names; parents must choose from an approved list of names.
7. Heer, *Medieval World,* 360.
8. Gabrielle Spiegel, *Romancing the Past: The Rise of Vernacular Prose Historiography in Thirteenth Century France* (Berkeley, CA: University of California Press, 1993), 3.
9. Katherine Gill, "Women and the Production of Religious Literature in the Vernacular, 1300–1500," in *Creative Women in Medieval and Early Modern Italy,* eds. E. Ann Matter and John Coakley (Philadelphia, PA: University of Pennsylvania Press, 1994), 64–104; and Carlo Delcorno, "Predicazione volgare e volgarizzamenti," *Melanges de l'Ecole Française de Rome, Moyen Age, Temps Modernes* 89 (1977), 679–689.
10. See Herbert Grundmann, "Die Frauen und die Literatur im Mittelalter," *Archiv für Kulturgeschichte* 26:2 (1936), 133.
11. Colish, *Medieval Foundations,* 206, hints ever so slightly at this when she mentions celebration, but I think it deserves more attention.
12. Ibid., 202–204.
13. *The Writings of Medieval Women: An Anthology,* tr. and ed. Marcelle Thiébaux, 2nd ed. (New York: Garland, 1994), 279.
14. Marie de France, *Fables,* tr. and ed. Harriet Spiegel (Toronto: University of Toronto Press, 1987), epilogue, 4,

15. Ibid., lines 9–10 and *The Lais of Marie de France,* tr. and intro. Robert Hanning and Joan Ferrante (New York: E.P. Dutton, 1978), lines 43–48 (p. 29), respectively.
16. See discussion in Emanuel J. Mickel, *Marie de France* (New York: Twayne Publishers, 1974), 19–21.
17. Marie, *Fables,* lines 3–8 (p. 257).
18. "Guigeman," lines 7–17, in Thiébaux, *Writings,* 279.
19. *Saint Patrick's Purgatory,* tr. and intro. Michael J. Curley (Binghamton, NY: MRTS, 1993), lines 2297–2300 (p. 171).
20. See the rebuttal of this criticism in Joan M. Ferrante, *The Glory of Her Sex* (Bloomington, IN: Indiana University Press, 1997), 195.
21. Quoted in Thiébaux, *Writings,* 279.
22. See Verger, *Men of Learning in Europe at the End of the Middle Ages,* tr. Lisa Neal and Steven Randall (Notre Dame, IN: University of Notre Dame Press, 1997), 9–15, especially 10.
23. Robert Sturges, *Medieval Interpretation* (Carbondale, IL: Southern Illinois University Press, 1991), 74.
24. Heer, *Medieval World,* 368.
25. Raymond E. Brown, "Hermeneutics," in *Jerome Biblical Commentary,* eds. Roland Murphy, Raymond E. Brown and Joseph Fitzmeyer (Englewood Cliffs, NJ: Prentice-Hall, 1968), 71:41. See above, p. 4.
26. Ironically, Jerome's *Vulgate* translation of the bible was a translation into the vernacular.
27. Sturges, *Medieval Interpretation,* 74.
28. Mikhail Bakhtin, quoted in Spiegel, *Romancing,* 9.
29. Herbert Grundmann, *Religious Movements in the Middle Ages,* tr. Steven Rowan (Notre Dame, IN: University of Notre Dame Press, 1995), 187.
30. See his comments throughout in Curley, *Purgatory.*
31. Ibid. In addition, see *Das Buch vom Espurgatoire S. Patrice der Marie de France und seine Quelle,* ed. Karl Warnke (Halle: Max Memeyer, 1938); and *Saint Patrick's Purgatory, a Twelfth Century Tale of a Journey to the Other World,* tr. Jean-Michel Picard (Dublin: Four Court Press, 1985).
32. Jacques LeGoff, *The Birth of Purgatory,* tr. Arthur Goldhammer (Chicago: University of Chicago Press, 1984), 108. In my opinion LeGoff's secular analysis fails to appreciate or comprehend the theological origins of the doctrine.
33. Curley, *Purgatory,* lines 2299–2300 (p. 171).
34. Quoted in intro., ibid., 21.
35. Ibid., lines 3–6 (p. 47).
36. Ibid., lines 9–12.
37. Ibid., lines 17–20.
38. Ibid., lines 25–30 (pp. 47–49).
39. Ibid., intro., 24.
40. Ibid., lines 1908–1914, 1925, 1927–1932 (p. 151).
41. Curley, *Purgatory,* 26; Warnke, *Das Buch,* 16; and Picard, *Saint Patrick's Purgatory,* 46.
42. Ibid. It is revealed later in the poem that this person is Gilbert of Louth.
43. Curley, *Purgatory,* line 204 (p. 57).
44. Cited in Curley, *Purgatory,* intro., 30.

45. Curley, *Purgatory,* lines 257–262 (p. 59).
46. Ibid., 30.
47. Warnke, *Das Buch,* 68; Picard, *Saint Patrick's Purgatory,* 58; discussion in Curley, *Purgatory,* 31.
48. Curley, *Purgatory,* lines 1542–1543 (p. 133); ibid., intro., 32–33 for discussion.
49. Ibid., lines 181–184 (pp. 55–57); analysis, pp. 25–26.
50. Ibid., lines 1411–1412, 1415–1418 (p. 127); analysis, p. 23.
51. Spiegel, *Fables,* intro., 3–6; Warnke, *Das Buch,* 279; and Curley, *Purgatory,* 37.
52. Spiegel, *Fables,* intro., 6.
53. Ibid., lines 23–27 (pp. 29–31).
54. Ibid., lines 1–10 (p. 29).
55. See Mickel, *Marie,* 34; and Paula Clifford, *Marie de France: Lais* (London: Grant & Cutler, 1982), 10.
56. Kornei Chukovsky, *The Art of Translation: A High Art,* tr. and ed. Lauren Leighton (Knoxville, TN: University of Tennessee Press, 1984), xxii.
57. See Bonaventure's discussion, cited in Wogan-Browne, *Idea of the Vernacular,* 3: "People compose books in four different ways. One person writes material composed by other people, adding or changing nothing; and this person is said to be merely the scribe. Another one writes material composed by others, joining them together but adding nothing of his own; and this person is said to be the compiler. Another one writes both materials composed by others and his own, but the materials composed by others are the most important materials, while his own are added for the purpose of clarifying them; and this person is said to be the commentator, not the author. Another one writes both his own materials and those composed by others, but his own are the most important materials and the materials of others are included in order to confirm his own; and this person must be called the author."
58. Spiegel, *Fables,* lines 1–2 (p. 257).
59. Ibid., lines 11–19 (pp. 257–259). For prologue, see lines 17–20 (p. 29). Marie is mistaken in her belief in Aesop's identity. The tradition through which Aesop's fables reached medieval society is more complicated than Marie could have known. See Spiegel, *Fables,* intro., 6.
60. Ibid., 7.
61. Ibid.
62. Ibid., 9–10.
63. Fable 29, ibid., lines 12–15, 115–122 (pp. 101 and 107).
64. Fable 46, ibid., lines 2–4, 51–54, 64–74 (pp. 141–145).
65. Fable 47, lines 49–62 (p. 147).
66. Hanning, *Lais,* intro., 1.
67. Ibid., "Equitan," line 9 (p. 60).
68. Ibid., "Chevrefoil," line 5 (p. 190).
69. Ibid., "Le Fresne," line 2 (p. 73).
70. Ibid., lines 39–42, 47–48 (p. 29), respectively.
71. Ibid., lines 28–33 (pp. 28–29).
72. Literature on individualism during the twelfth century is abundant. See Colin Morris, *The Discovery of the Individual* (London: Camelot Press, 1972).

73. Hanning, *Lais,* lines 1–8 (p. 28).
74. See above, p. 126; and Curley, *Purgatory,* lines 2299–2300 (p. 171).
75. Hanning, *Lais,* lines 9–20 (p. 28).
76. Ibid., "Bisclavret," lines 125–126 (p. 95).
77. Ibid., lines 157, 165, 178–180 (pp. 96–97).
78. Colish, *Medieval Foundations,* 279.
79. Peter Lombard, *Book of Sentences,* 2, cited in ibid., 284.
80. See Monica Brzezinski Potkay and Regula Meyer Evitt, *Minding the Body: Women and Literature in the Middle Ages, 800–1500* (London: Twayne Publishers, 1997), 77–87, for discussion of Marie and her audience.
81. Meg Bogin, *The Women Troubadours* (New York: W. W. Norton, 1980), 11–13.
82. Cited in Thiébaux, *Writings,* 247.
83. For background, see Linda M. Paterson, *Troubadours and Eloquence* (Oxford: Clarendon Press, 1975).
84. Bogin, *The Women Troubadours,* 13, says women engage in less play or the exercise of craft, prefer direct conversation, do not idealize relationships, and do not use allegorical figures. When Joan Ferrante, "Notes toward the Study of a Female Rhetoric in the Trobairitz," in *The Voice of the Trobairitz,* ed. William Paden (Philadelphia, PA: University of Pennsylvania Press, 1989), 63–72, compared the poetry of the two groups, she found, albeit tentatively, only minor differences in their rhetoric.
85. Bogin, *The Women Troubadours,* 68, is the exception. She concludes "that the women troubadours were doing something unique in medieval art: they were writing in a true first person singular at a time when almost all artistic endeavor was collective."
86. Alais, Iselda and Carenza, ibid., 144–145.
87. Ibid., 65–69, quote 68.
88. Countess of Dia, ibid., 3 (pp. 88–89).
89. Ibid., 2 (pp. 86–87).
90. Razo for Maria de Ventadour, in ibid., 168.
91. Ibid., 98–99.
92. Bogin, ibid., 11, note, justifies her exclusion of Gormonda's poem from her otherwise complete anthology of trobairitz poetry with the bizarre excuse that because it is a rebuttal of the troubadour William Figuerira's attack on Rome it "is of interest only for Church history."
93. François Zufferey, "Toward a Delimitation of the Trobairitz Corpus," in Paden, *Voice,* 33–34.
94. Dietmar Rieger, "Die französische Dichterin im Mittelalter: Marie de France, die 'trobairitz'—Christine de Pisan," in *Die Französische Autorin vom Mittelalter bis zur Genenwart,* eds. Renate Baaden and Dietar Fricke (Wiesbaden: Akademische Verlagsgesellschaft Athenaion, 1979), 39.
95. Katharina Städtler, "The *Sirventes* by Gormonda de Monpeslier," in Paden, *Voices,* 151.
96. Gormonda, 7, in ibid., 132–133; discussion, 144.
97. Ibid., 13 (p. 135).
98. Ibid., 5 and 6 (p. 132).
99. Ibid., 7 (pp. 132–133).
100. Ibid., 11 (p. 134).
101. Sumption, 215, cited in ibid., 146.

102. Gormonda, ibid., 14 (p. 135).
103. Ibid., 20 (p. 137).
104. Ibid., 19 (p. 137).
105. See Elisabeth van Houts, "Women and the writing of history in the early Middle Ages: the case of Abbess Matilda of Essen and Aethelweard," *Early Medieval Europe* 1:1 (1992), 59; and *Vita Mathildis reginae antiquior,* ed. R Köpke, MGH, SS, 10 (1849), 573–582; *Vita Mathildis reginae posterior,* ed. G. Pertz, MGH, SS, 4 (1841), 282–302; and Janet Nelson, "Perceptions du pouvoir chez les historiennes de Haut Moyen Age," *La Femme au Moyen Age,* ed. M. Rouche (Paris: Diffusion, J. Touzot, 1990), 77–85.
106. See Ferrante, *The Glory of Her Sex* (Bloomington, IN: University of Indiana Press, 1997), 68–106; van Houts, "Women and the writing of history," and Nelson, "Perceptions."
107. Patricia Ranft, "Maintenance and Transformation of Society: Cluniac Eschatology," *Journal of Religious History* 17 (1987), 246–255.
108. See Patrick Corbet, *Les Saints ottoniens* (Sigmaringen: Jan Thorbecke, 1986), 256–268.
109. *The Chronicle of Aethelweard,* ed. Alistair Campbell (London: T. Nelson, 1962), 1.
110. William of Malmesbury, *De gestes regum Anglorum,* ed. William Stubbs (London: Eyre & Spottiswoode, 1887); *Vita S. Margaretae Scotorum Reginae,* in *Symeonis Dunelmensis Opera et Collectanea,* I, ed. Hodgson Hinde (Durham, MD: Andrews, 1868); *Encomium Emmae Reginae,* tr. and ed. Alistair Campbell (London: Royal Historical Society, 1949); and *Lives of Edward the Confessor,* ed. Henry Luard (London: Longman, 1858). Henry I's *vita* by David is not extant.
111. Ferrante, *Glory,* 106,
112. Spiegel, *Romancing,* 216. She adds (215–216): "Aristocratic patronage of contemporary chronicles can be seen as a form of political action, an attempt to control the subject matter of history and the voices of the past as a means of dominating the collective memory of feudal society. To the extent that the patronage of contemporary history in the thirteenth century is prompted by political goals, it signals the beginning of an overt contest over the past that would scarcely have been conceivable in an earlier period when history represented primarily the trace of God's operation in human affairs."
113. The desire for vernacular texts can be seen in the new demand for translations of Latin works into the vernacular. Diana B. Tyson, "Patronage of French Vernacular History Writers in the Twelfth and Thirteenth Centuries," *Romania* 100 (1979), 183.
114. Ö. Södergaard, ed., *La vie seinte Audrée* (Uppsala: no publisher, 1955), lines 4619–4620.
115. Jocelyn Wogan-Browne, "'Clerc u lai, muïne u dame': women and Anglo-Norman hagiography in the twelfth-thirteenth centuries," in *Women and Literature in Britain, 1150–1500,* ed. Carol M. Meale (Cambridge: Cambridge University Press, 1993), 66.
116. Guernes de Pont-Ste.-Maxence, *La vie de saint Thomas Becket,* ed. E. Wallberg (Lund: Glemp, 1922), 8, cited in ibid., 61.
117. See ibid., 62–63; and Elisabeth van Houts, "Latin Poetry and the Anglo-Norman Court 1066–1135: The Carmen de Hastingae Proelio," *Journal of Medieval History* 15 (1989), 39–62.
118. R. Lejeune, "Rôle littéraire d'Aliénor d'Aquitaine et de sa famille," *Cultura Neolatina* 14 (1954), 5–57, holds strongly to the thesis that Eleanor was Wace's patron.
119. Ferrante, *Glory,* 111. It should be remembered that the vernacular of the English court was French after the Norman Conquest.

120. Geffrei Gaimar, *Estoire des Engleis,* ed. A. Bell (Oxford: Blackwell, 1960), lines 6430 ff, cited in ibid., 239 n.72.
121. This lack of clear motive leads one to wonder how many similar texts were written and did not survive.
122. See I. Short, *The Anglo-Norman Pseudo-Turpin Chronicle of William de Briane* (Oxford: ANTS, 1973).
123. Spiegel, *Romancing,* 12.
124. Kimberly Lo Prete, "Adela of Blois: Familial Alliances and Female Lordship," in *Aristocratic Women in Medieval France,* ed. Theodore Evergates (Philadelphia, PA: University of Pennsylvania Press, 1999), 43.
125. Wemple and McNamara argue that women lost all their political power during the Middle Ages, as Duby argues. Lo Prete and Evergates, ibid., 1–5, point out that their theses have unfortunately been widely accepted without evidence and that when noble women's lives during the high Middle Ages are actually studied the fallacy of this stance is revealed. See Wemple and MacNamara, "The Power of Women through the Family," in *Women and Power in the Middle Ages,* eds. Mary Erler and Maryanne Kowaleski (Athens, GA: University of Georgia Press, 1983), 83–101.
126. Lo Prete, ibid.; and Amy Livingstone, "Aristocratic Women in the Chartrain," ibid., 44–73; Theodore Evergates, "Aristocratic Women in the County of Champagne," ibid., 74–110; Karen S. Nicholas, "Countesses as Rulers in Flanders," ibid., 111–137; and Fredric L. Cheyette, "Women, Poets, and Politics in Occitania," ibid., 138–177.
127. Ibid., intro., 5,4.
128. Ferrante, *Glory,* 3.

Chapter 4, pp. 91–117
The Vernacular Mothers

1. Charles Homer Haskins, *The Renaissance of the Twelfth Century* (Cambridge, MA: Harvard University Press, 1927), 275, summarized the coming of vernacular history thus: "By 1200 vernacular history had come to stay, and this fact is one of more than linguistic or literary significance, since it involved ultimately the secularization and popularization of history. So long as history was confined to Latin, it perforce remained primarily an affair of the clergy and reflected their preoccupations and view of the world. When it came to be written for laymen, it must make its appeal to them, first at the courts which gave its writers their support, later in the towns whose chronicles meet us in the later period of the Middle Ages. History for laymen and history for the people necessarily meant history in the language of the lay world, that world of courts and towns which had grown so fast in the course of the twelfth century."
2. Herbert Grundmann, "Die Frauen und die Literatur im Mittelalter," *Archiv für Kulturgeschichte* 26:2 (1936), 133.
3. Herbert Grundmann, *Religious Movements in the Middle Ages,* tr. Steven Rowan (Notre Dame, IN: University of Notre Dame Press, 1995), 193.
4. Interestingly, the only known German vernacular prayerbook from the twelfth century (the earliest) was for a woman and may have even been compiled by another woman. Ibid., 188, and 387 n.3.

5. Countess of Dia, in Meg Bogin, *The Women Troubadours* (New York: W. W. Norton, 1980), 2 (p. 85), and 1 (p. 83).
6. *Poems in Stanzas,* in *Hadewijch: The Complete Works,* tr. M. Columba Hart (New York: Paulist Press, 1980), 24.7.64–70 (p. 195).
7. Ibid., 10.3.19–27 (p. 153).
8. Ibid., 9 (pp. 149–152). Modern editions usually include the subtitles given her poetry by Jozef Van Mielo, *Hadewijch: Strophische Gedichten,* 2 vols. (Antwerp: Standaard, 1942).
9. *Stanzas,* 9.8, 73–75 (p. 151).
10. *Poems in Couplets,* lines 44–46 (p. 312).
11. *Hadewijch,* 19.
12. Theodoor Weevers, ed., *Poetry of the Netherlands in Its European Context, 1170–1930* (London: Athlone Press, 1960), 27.
13. *Stanzas,* 37.11–12, 41–48 (pp. 236–237).
14. Intro., *Meister Eckhart and the Beguine Mystics,* ed. Bernard McGinn (New York: Continuum, 1994), 6–7.
15. Grundmann, *Religious Movements,* 187.
16. Maud, wife of Henry II; Maud, wife of Stephen; Mary, sister of Thomas Becket; and Maud, daughter of Henry II, were among these abbesses.
17. William McBain, "The Literary Apprenticeship of Clemence of Barking," *AUMLA: Journal of the Australasian Universities Language and Literature Association* 9 (November, 1958), 21, compares the two lives and concludes thus: "Might we not, therefore, be justified in supposing that the *Vie d'Edouard le Confesseur* was written by Clemence of Barking, that it was her first major work . . . that the *Vie de sainte Catherine* is a later work . . . [and], furthermore, that there may exist other, possibly intermediate works by Clemcnce of Barking, which have not yet come to light."
18. *La vie d'Edouard le Confesseur,* ed. Östen Södergard (Uppsala: Almquist & Wiksells, 1948), lines 5308–5311, tr. in M. Dominica Legge, *Anglo-Norman Literature and Its Background* (Oxford: Clarendon Press, 1963), 61.
19. *The Life of St. Catherine by Clemence of Barking,* ed. William Macbain (Oxford: Basil Backwell [sic], 1964), lines 2689–2691 (p. 85).
20. Ibid., lines 109–112 (p. 4); 449–456 (p. 15); 1019–1022 (p. 33); 1025–1030 (p. 33); and *Life of Edward,* lines 535–541; 3129–3136; 3139–3144; 3147–3149; and 3153–3156. See Macbain, "Literary Apprenticeship," for these examples and others.
21. *Edward,* lines 6442–6451, in Legge, *Anglo-Norman Literature,* 62.
22. Ibid., lines 1–10, in ibid., 63.
23. Ibid., lines 5312–5323, in ibid., 65–66. Legge comments on the last line thus: "Many a man could and did do worse."
24. Ibid., lines 35–47, in ibid., 68.
25. Ibid., 67.
26. *Catherine,* lines 2173–2176; 2185–2186 (69).
27. Ibid., lines 2315–2316 (p. 73).
28. Ibid., lines 2351–2352 (p. 75).
29. Ibid., lines 1727–1728 (p. 55).
30. Ibid., lines 1266–1272 (p. 41).
31. Ibid., lines 141–143 (p. 5).

32. Ibid., line 647 (p. 21).
33. Ibid., line 1078–1080 (p. 35).
34. *Life of Catherine of Alexandria* Version B, in Brigitte Cazelles, *The Lady as Saint: A Collection of French Hagiographic Romances of the Thirteenth Century* (Philadelphia, PA: University of Pennsylvania Press, 1991), lines 146–156 (p. 115).
35. Clemence, *Life of St. Catherine,* lines 145–147 (p. 5).
36. Cited in Macbain, "Literary Apprenticeship," 11–20. Examples are ibid.: sin: lines 535–540; injustice: lines 3129–3136; love of God: lines 5336–5340; and miracles: lines 6546–6548.
37. For examples see ibid.: righteous: lines 1019–1030; soul: lines 589–596; original sin: lines 67–72; and goodness of God: lines 1178–1238.
38. Clemence, *Life of St. Catherine,* lines 1361–1364.
39. Cornelia Wolfskeel, "Hadewych of Antwerp," in *History of Women Philosophers,* ed. Mary Ellen Waithe, 4 vols. (Dordrecht: Kluwer Acadermic Publishers, 1989), 2:160.
40. Joan Gibson, "Mechthild of Magdeburg," in Waithe, *History of Women Philosophers,* 2:130.
41. *Hadewijch,* letter 17.112–122 (p. 84).
42. Ibid., intro., 5.
43. John Macquarrie, *Principles of Christian Theology,* 2nd ed. (New York: Charles Scribner, 1977), 57–58.
44. We know that Hadewijch and Beatrice knew Latin and were well educated in many Latin forms, such as the *ars dictaminis*; see *Hadewijch,* 5. Mechthild knew some Latin but had no formal training in it; see *Mechthild of Madgeburg: The Flowing Light of the Godhead,* tr. and intro. Frank Tobin, pref. Margot Schmidt (New York: Paulist Press, 1998), 4. Regardless of the women's knowledge of Latin, they still had a choice. They could have dictated to a scribe to be put in Latin before circulation.
45. *The Life of Beatrice of Narazeth 1200–1268,* tr. Roger De Ganck (Kalamazoo, MI: Cistercian Press, 1991), prol. 4 (p. 5).
46. J. Van Mierlo, *Seven Modes* (Louvain, 1926), 76, believes there are eight lost works and two prayers; he bases this belief on evidence in Beatrice's vita. L. Reypens, *Vita Beatricis* (Antwerp, 1964), 58, disagrees. See Wolfskeel, "Beatrice," in *History of Women Philosophers,* 2:114 for discussion.
47. *Seven Manners of Loving,* in *Medieval Netherlands Religious Literature,* tr. and intro. E. Colledge (New York: London House & Maxwell, 1965), 1 (p. 19).
48. Beatrice, *Seven Manners,* 19. See Wolfskeel, "Beatrice," in Waithe, *History of Women Philosophers,* 2:113 n.18, for her interpretation of this neoplatonic presence in Beatrice's work.
49. Ibid., 7 (p. 29).
50. Ibid., 3 (p. 21).
51. Ibid., 5 (p. 24). Reypens, *Vita,* and Wolfskeel, "Beatrice," in Waithe, *History of Women Philosophers* argue that the seventh mode includes a copyist's interpolations in the extant manuscript.
52. Ibid. (p. 23).
53. Ibid., 2 (p. 20).
54. Ibid., 5 (p. 24).
55. Ibid., 6 (pp. 25–26).
56. Macquarrie, *Principles,* 56.

57. The second mode of Beatrice, *Seven Manners,* 2 (p. 20), discusses how "to serve love with love;" Hadewijch devotes an entire poem "Becoming Love with Love," to the theme. See *Hadewijch,* No. 34 (pp. 224–226).
58. Beatrice, *Seven Manners,* 6 (p. 25). Colledge, *Medieval Netherlands,* p. 9, notes that Mechthild of Magdeburg also has a similar passage.
59. *Stanzas,* in *Hadewijch,* 2.1.6; 2.1.4; 6.1.3; 15.1.2; 21.1.2; and 24.1.2–5.
60. Ibid., poems 19 (pp. 176–179); 22 (pp. 186–189); and 31 (pp. 216–218), refer to the seasons in the body; poem 29 (pp. 207–212) does not.
61. Ibid., poem 40 (p. 243).
62. Ibid., poem 6.1 (p. 141).
63. Ibid., poem 42.1 (p. 248); poem 35.1 (p. 227); and poem 43.1 (p. 250).
64. Ibid., 4.2 (p. 137).
65. See Norbert de Paepe, *Hadewijch: Strofische Gedichten* (Ghent: Koninklijke Vlaamse Academie, 1967), 149–151.
66. A lengthy analysis of her direction is found in my *A Woman's Way: The Forgotten History of Women Spiritual Directors* (New York: Palgrave, 2000), 67–74. What follows is mostly a summary of that work.
67. *Vision* 14, in *Hadewijch,* 304.
68. *Couplets,* 10.71–74, in ibid., 337.
69. *Vision* 8, in ibid., 284.
70. *Vision* 1, in ibid., 263.
71. Letter 14, in ibid., 77.
72. *Vision* 14, in ibid., 305.
73. Letter 4, in ibid., 54.
74. Ibid., 53.
75. Letter 2, in ibid., 51.
76. Letter 13, in ibid., 75.
77. *Vision* 9, in ibid., 286.
78. Letter 30, in ibid., 117.
79. Letter 5, in ibid., 55.
80. Letter 18, in ibid., 86.
81. Letter 2, in ibid., 49.
82. Letter 6, in ibid., 58.
83. Letter 2, in ibid., 49.
84. Letter 6, in ibid., 57.
85. Letter 2, in ibid., 50.
86. *Minne*—Love, God, Divine Love, the soul's relationship to God—as it is used by Beatrice and Hadewijch has been interpreted in many, many ways. All of the sources cited here pertaining to these women discuss *minne, passim.*
87. Letter 2, in ibid., 50.
88. Letter 6, in ibid., 57.
89. Letter 6, in ibid., 58.
90. Letter 13, in ibid., 75.
91. *Vision* 1, in ibid., 268.

92. Letter 6, in ibid., 61.
93. Letter 2, in ibid., 51.
94. *Vision* 1, in ibid., 269.
95. Vision 11, in ibid., 291–292.
96. *Vision* 14, in ibid., 302.
97. *New Catholic Encyclopedia,* s.v. "Exemplarism," by C. J. Chereso. Pseudo-Dionysius was the first major philosopher who tried to Christianize exemplarism and emanation in his *Exordium to the Divine Names.*
98. Thomas Aquinas, *Summa theologica* repr. (Westminster, MD: Christian Classics, 1981), 1a:15.2, *respondeo.*
99. Letter 19, in *Hadewijch,* 90.
100. See McGinn, *Meister Eckhart,* for essays on current opinions about Hadewijch's influence on Eckhart, particularly Saskia Murk-Jansen, "Hadewijch and Eckhart," 17–30. Louis Bouyer, *Women Mystics* (San Francisco, CA: Ignatius Press, 1993), 19, is quite convinced "that Ruusbroec was familiar with what was most personal in Hadewijch's teaching" and that "there can no longer be any doubt that we have here, if not Eckhart's sole sources, assuredly the most invaluable testimony about a spirituality developed well before him and on which he was closely dependent." Jean-Baptiste Porion, "Hadewijch, mystique flamande et poétesse, 13e siècle," in *Dictionnaire de spiritualité,* ed. Marcel Viller (Paris: G. Beauchesne et ses fils, 1937), 7:21, claims that "a fundamental part of his literary resources" are from Hadewijch.
101. Letter 20, in *Hadewijch,* 92.
102. Letter 18, in ibid., 86.
103. *Vision* 4, in ibid., 274–275.
104. *Vision* 8, in ibid., 283.
105. *Vision* 3, in ibid., 272.
106. *Vision* 8, in ibid., 284.
107. *Vision* 11, in ibid., 290–291.
108. Letter 6, in ibid., 61.
109. Ibid., 58.
110. *Vision* 1, in ibid., 269.
111. *Vision* 14, in ibid., 302–303.
112. Ibid., 305.
113. Letter 6, in ibid., 62.
114. Ibid., 62–63.
115. Letter 10, in ibid., 66–67.
116. *Vision* 14, in ibid., 305.
117. Letter 6, in ibid., 63.
118. Letter 11, in ibid., 69.
119. *Vision* 12, in ibid., 295.
120. Letter 6, in ibid., 61.
121. See intro., *Flowing Light,* 9.
122. Wolfgang Mohr, "Darbietungsformen der Mystik bei Mechthild von Magdeburg," cited in ibid., 10.

123. *Flowing Light,* 4:2 (pp. 143–144).
124. Elizabeth Alvilda Petroff, in *Medieval Women's Visionary Literature,* ed. Elizabeth Alvidla Petroff (New York: Oxford University Press, 1986), 208, says that Mechthild wrote Books 5 and 6 during the fifteen years following the completion of Books 1–4.
125. Ulrike Wiethaus, *Ecstatic Transformation* (Syracuse, NY: University of Syracuse Press, 1996), 27.
126. *Flowing Light,* 4:13 (p. 156).
127. Joan Gibson, "Mechtild of Magdeburg," in Waithe, *History of Women Philosophers,* 2:130.
128. *Flowing Light,* 6:36 (p. 261).
129. Ibid., 2:19 (p. 83).
130. Ibid., 2:26 (pp. 96–97).
131. Ibid., 7:1 (p. 274).
132. Ibid., 4:14 (p. 157).
133. Ibid., 5:4 (p. 182).
134. Ibid., 2:19 (pp. 83–84).
135. Ibid., 4:14 (pp. 157–158).
136. Wiethaus, *Ecstatic Transformation,* 160. Wiethaus here is reflecting on the work of Ken Wilbur, "Eye to Eye: Science and Transpersonal Psychology," in *Beyond Ego,* eds. Roger N. Walsh and Frances Vaughan (Los Angeles: J. P. Tarcher, 1980), 216–241.
137. *Flowing Light,* 6:26 (p. 252).
138. Ibid., 6:36 (p. 261). See also ibid., 3:1 (p. 102), 6:20 (p. 249), and 5:12 (p. 190).
139. Gibson, "Mechtild," 2:130–131.
140. *Flowing Light,* 6:23 (p. 251).
141. Ibid., 6:19 (p. 247).
142. Wiethaus, *Ecstatic Transformation,* 102, brings Arthur Deikman's work to bear on Mechthild's distinction between types of knowledge.
143. *Flowing Light,* 2:3 (pp. 70–71).
144. Ibid., 3:21 (p. 131).
145. Ibid., 2:25 (p. 95).
146. Ibid., 2:26 (p. 97). She also uses the word to describe aspects of her relationship with God. See, for example, ibid., 2:25 (p. 93) and 5:32 (p. 32).
147. Ibid., 6:31 (p. 257).
148. Ibid., 3:9 (p. 115).
149. Ibid., 6:30 (p. 256).
150. Ibid., 1:44 (p. 61).
151. Ibid., 6:31 (pp. 256–257).
152. Ibid., 7:17 (pp. 288–289).
153. Ibid., 7:32 (p. 301).
154. Ibid., 5:22 (p. 196).
155. Ibid., 6:4 (p. 231).
156. Ibid., 2:8 (p. 77).
157. Ibid., 4:11 (pp. 151–152).
158. Ibid., 3:3 (p. 109).
159. Ibid., 3:9 (p. 117).

160. Ibid., 1:3 (p. 42), 1:19 (p. 48) and 1:44 (p. 59), respectively.
161. Ibid., 2:19 (p. 81) and 2:26 (p. 97).
162. Ibid., 4:5 (p. 149) and 1:2 (pp. 41–42), respectively.
163. Ibid., 4:14 (p. 157).
164. Ibid., 3:10 (p. 119).
165. Ibid., 4:1 (p. 140), 2:25 (p. 93), 2:20 (p. 85), and 1:44 (p. 61).
166. See Amy Hollywood, *The Soul as Virgin Wife* (Notre Dame, IN: University of Notre Dame Press, 1995), 183–93.
167. *Flowing Light,* 6:7 (p. 233).
168. Ibid., 7:6 (p. 280).
169. Ibid., 6:7 (p. 233).
170. Ibid., 6:19 (pp. 247–248).
171. Ibid., 5:16 (p. 192).
172. Ibid., 7:17 (pp. 288–289).
173. See Romana Guarnieri, *Observatore Romano* (June 1946).
174. Romana Guarnieri, ed., "Il movimento del Libero Spirito," *Archivo Italiano per la storia della pietà,* 4 (1965), 351–708; text, 513–635. The English translation used here is *Marguerite Porete: The Mirror of Simple Souls,* tr. and intro. Ellen L. Babinsky (New York: Paulist Press, 1993).
175. See bibliography in *Mirror,* 235–236.
176. Peter Dronke, *Women Writers of the Middle Ages* (Cambridge: Cambridge University Press, 1984), 217.
177. There is still a debate among scholars as to whether her writings were orthodox or heretical. See Robert E. Lerner, *Heresy of the Free Spirit in the Late Middle Ages* (Berkeley, CA: University of California Press, 1972), 208. Gwendolyn Bryant, "The French Heretic Beguine Marguerite Porete," in Wilson, *Medieval Women Writers,* 208, concludes that she was guilty of pantheism but not antinomianism. Since such a judgment is beyond the scope of this work we will treat her writings here as heretical and discuss them accordingly.
178. See *Mirror,* 25–26.
179. Brian Stock, *Listening for the Text* (Baltimore, MD: Johns Hopkins University Press, 1990), 132.
180. See Maria Lichtmann, "Marguerite Porete and Meister Eckhart," in McGinn, *Meister Eckhart,* 67.
181. *Mirror,* 122 (p. 200).
182. Cited in Bryant, "French Heretic," 205. Marguerite's life is summarized on pp. 204–205.
183. *Mirror,* intro., 25.
184. *Mirror,* explicit (p. 79). It is noteworthy that although she demands humility of her readers, she herself bypasses the traditional humility topos of authorship so common among medieval men and women. See Dronke, *Women Writers,* 226; and Robert E. Lerner, intro., *Mirror,* 3.
185. *Mirror,* 121 (p. 197).
186. Ibid., 13 (p. 94).
187. Ibid., 122 (p. 200).
188. Ibid., 19 (p. 101).

189. Ibid., 2 (p. 81).
190. Lichtmann, "Marguerite Porete," 67–68.
191. *Mirror,* 13 (p. 94).
192. Ibid., 117 (pp. 187–188).
193. Ibid., 110 (p. 182).
194. Ibid., intro., p. 31, 36.
195. Ibid., 13 (p. 95).
196. See Lerner, *Heresy of the Free Spirit,* 204–205.
197. *Mirror,* 9 (p. 87).
198. Ibid., 5 (pp. 82–83).
199. Ibid., 49 (p. 127).
200. Ibid., 81 (p. 157), 86 (p. 161) and 89 (p. 165).
201. Ibid., 91 (p. 167).
202. See above, pp. 107–108 and 110.

Chapter 5, pp. 119–144
Scholastics, Mystics, and Secondary Intellectuals

1. Dorothy Koenigsberger, *Renaissance Man and Creative Thinking* (Atlantic Highlands, NJ: Humanities Press, 1979), 271.
2. Ibid., 5.
3. *Philosophy in the Middle Ages,* eds. Arthur Hyman and James J. Walsh (Indianapolis, IN: Hackett Publishing, 2nd ed., 1986), 454–456, discusses the modern scholarly debate on whether Bonaventure is an Augustinian who uses Aristotelian terminology or an Aristotelian in philosophy but not in theology.
4. *Commentaries in Four Books on the Sentences,* quoted in Julian Marías, *The History of Philosophy,* 23rd ed. (New York: Dover Publications, 1967), 161.
5. Etienne Gilson, *History of Christian Philosophy in the Middle Ages* (New York: Random House,1955), 331.
6. Marías, *History of Philosophy,* 162.
7. Bonaventure, *Commentary in Four Books on the Sentences,* conclusion, in *Readings in Medieval History,* Vol. 2: *The Later Middle Ages,* ed. Patrick Geary (Peterborough CAN: Broadview Press, 1998), 163; and *Breviloquium,* 2, 2, in ibid., 167, respectively.
8. Bonaventure, *Retracing the Arts to Theology or Sacred Theology the Mistress among the Sciences,* 12, in Hyman and Walsh, *Philosophy,* 465.
9. Marcia L. Colish, *Medieval Foundations of Western Intellectual Tradition 400–1400* (New Haven, CT: Yale University Press, 1997), 237.
10. Bonaventure, *Collationes,* 6, 2, in Geary, *Readings,* 166.
11. Bonaventure, *Commentary,* 1 Sent. d.1, a.1, q.2, 3–4, in ibid., 160–161.
12. Marías, *History of Philosophy,* 162.
13. Bonaventure, *Retracing,* 26, in Hyman and Walsh, *Philosophy,* 469.
14. Bonaventure, *Retracing,* 1, in Hyman and Walsh, *Philosophy,* 461.
15. Ibid., 10, in ibid., 465.
16. Beatrice of Nazareth, *Seven Manners of Loving,* 1, in *Medieval Netherlands Religious Literature,* tr. and intro. E. Colledge (New York: London House & Maxwell, 1965), 19.

17. *Vision* 12, in *Hadewijch: The Complete Works,* tr. M. Columba Hart (New York: Paulist Press, 1980), 293–295.
18. *Vision* 9, in ibid., 285–286.
19. Letter 28, in ibid., 112, 111.
20. Letter 22, in ibid., 94.
21. Letter 24, in ibid., 103.
22. *Marguerite Porete: The Mirror of Simple Souls,* tr. and intro. Ellen L. Babinsky (New York: Paulist Press, 1998), 13 (p. 94).
23. Mechthild of Magdeburg, *The Flowing Light of the Godhead,* tr. and intro. Frank Tobin, pref. Margot Schmidt (New York: Paulist Press, 1998), 5:4 (p. 182).
24. Beatrice, *Seven Manners,* in Colledge, *Medieval Netherlands,* 4 (p. 22).
25. Ibid., 6 (p. 25). See Mechthild, *Flowing Light,* 1:44 (p. 61) and 7:27 (p. 297) for examples of her usage.
26. *Stanzaic* 3 in *Hadewijch,* 134.
27. *Stanzaic* 6:1, 3 in ibid., 141–142.
28. Bonaventure, *Retracing,* in Hyman and Walsh, *Philosophy,* 461.
29. Marguerite, *Mirror,* 52 (p. 130).
30. Beatrice, *Seven Manners,* 1 (p. 19).
31. Letter 22, in *Hadewijch,* 99.
32. *Vision* 8, in *Hadewijch,* 284.
33. Mechthild, *The Flowing Light,* 4:14 (p. 157).
34. Ibid., 7:32 (p. 301).
35. Ibid., 6:41 (p. 266).
36. Bonaventure, *Retracing,* 1, in Hyman and Walsh, *Philosophy,* 461, names four sources: the external light of mechanical skill, the lower light of sense perception, the inner light of philosophical knowledge, and the higher light of grace and Scripture.
37. Letter 13, in *Hadewijch,* 75.
38. Letter 4, in ibid., 55.
39. Mechthild, *The Flowing Light,* 4:3 (pp. 144–146).
40. Marguerite, *Mirror,* 13 (pp. 94–95).
41. Ibid., explicit (p. 79). Her emphasis on reason being subjected to love is also part of her offensive against the establishment intellectual and ecclesiastical elite. See the rest of the explicit, and above, pp. 114–117.
42. Intro., ibid., 27.
43. See E. Grant, *Foundations of Modern Science in the Middle Ages* (Cambridge: Cambridge University Press, 1996); A. C. Crombie, *Robert Grossteste and the Origins of Experimental Science* (Oxford: Clarendon Press, 1953).
44. Chiara Frugoni, "Female Mystics, Visions, and Iconography," in *Women and Religion in Medieval and Renaissance Italy,* eds. Daniel Bornstein and Roberto Rusconi, tr. Margery J. Schneider (Chicago: University of Chicago Press, 1996), figure 8.
45. *Birgitta of Sweden: Life and Selected Revelations,* ed. Marguerite Harris, tr. A. Kezel (New York: Paulist Press, 1990), 7:2, 1–22.
46. See discussion of it in Craig Harbison, "Visions and meditations in early Flemish painting," *Simiolus* 15 (1985), 94–95. It is interesting to note that some of Birgitta's visions in turn were stimulated by artistic images. See Sixten Ringbom, "Devotional Images and Imaginative Devotions," *Gazette des beaux-arts,* ser. 6:73 (1969), 161.

47. Patricia Ranft, *Women and Spiritual Equality in Christian Tradition* (New York: St. Martin's Press, 1998), 207–208.
48. Craig Harbison, *The Mirror of the Artist: Northern Renaissance Art in Its Historical Context* (New York: Harry N. Abrams, 1995), figure 56 (p. 86), and p. 97; and Anthony Butkovich, *Revelations: Saint Birgitta of Sweden* (Los Angeles: Ecumenical Foundation of America, 1972), 46.
49. *The Book of Blessed Angela of Foligno: The Instructions,* 4, in *Angela of Foligno: Complete Works,* tr. Paul Lachance (New York: Paulist Press, 1993), 245.
50. See Ranft, *Women and Spiritual Equality,* 177.
51. Gertrude the Great, *The Life and Revelations of Saint Gertrude* repr. (Westminster, MD: Newman Press, 1952), 2:4. It is discussed in ibid., 177–178.
52. *Life of Blessed Juliana of Mont-Cornillon (1192–1258),* tr. Barbara Newman (Toronto: Peregrina Publishing, 1989), 6 (pp. 94–95). That it is a non-visionary, male author who is recording Juliana's reaction makes the case even stronger that the whole of society was well aware of the dual roles the visionary and the scholastic played in the intellectual world.
53. Ibid., 10 (p. 105).
54. Miri Rubin, *Corpus Christi* (Cambridge: Cambridge University Press, 1991), 273; and Ranft, *Women and Spiritual Equality,* 176.
55. Rubin, ibid., 347.
56. William F. Lynch, *Images of Faith: An Exploration of the Ironic Imagination* (Notre Dame, IN: University of Notre Dame Press, 1973), 5, reminds us of the corollary, that "faith is a form of imagining and experiencing the world."
57. What I am arguing here is simply that intellectual historians must make sure their treatment and understanding of intellectual activity is compatible with what we now know about brain activity from a medical view point. Advances in our knowledge of how different areas of the brain work have implications in the humanities as well as in the sciences.
58. *Henrici de Gandavo Opera omnia,* ed. R. Macken (Louvain and Leiden,1979), quolibet 1, q.35 (p. 199), cited in Jacques Verger, *Men of Learning in Europe at the End of the Middle Ages,* tr. Lisa Neal and Steven Rendall (Notre Dame, IN: University of Notre Dame Press, 1997), 125.
59. Ibid., 125–137.
60. See Harbison, "Visions and Meditations," 99.This was particularly true among women. Joanna E. Ziegler, "Reality as Imitation: The Role of Religious Imagery among the Beguines of the Low Countries," in *Maps of Flesh and Light,* ed. Ulrike Wiethaus (Syracuse, NY: Syracuse University Press, 1993), 112, says that this period was a turning point in women's spirituality "when mysticism, once practiced only by an elite few religious specialists, became accessible, because of alternate practices, to many women."
61. *Instructions,* epilogue, in *Angela,* 317. See also Mary Meany, "Angela of Foligno: A Eucharistic Model of Lay Sanctity," in *Lay Sanctity, Medieval and Modern,* ed. Ann W. Astell (Notre Dame, IN: University of Notre Dame Press, 2000), 61–75.
62. Ibid., 267.
63. *Memorial,* approbation, in *Angela,* 123. Early manuscripts identify the scribe as "Bro. A" or "Arnaldus."
64. Ibid., epilogue, 218, 217.

65. See L. Leclève, *Sainte Angèle de Foligno* (Paris: Libraire Plon, 1936), 42–44. The exception is Catherine M. Mooney, "The Authorial Role of Brother A. in the Composition of Angela of Foligno's *Revelations*," in *Creative Women in Medieval and Early Modern Italy*, eds. E. Ann Matter and John Coakley (Philadelphia, PA: University of Pennsylvania Press, 1994), 34–63.
66. Quoted in *Angela*, intro., 110. The Franciscans were in the midst of an internal controversy over the interpretation of poverty during Angela's later years, and her doctrine probably had a great influence in the dispute, even beyond her influence over Ubertino. Lachance maintains, though, that "Angela is concerned with maintaining concord and unity among the factions" (*Angela*, intro., 111). Moreover, her text "also played a role in the quarrel" (112).
67. Ibid., 22.
68. In 1465 Marino di Gionata of Agnone wrote a poem describing her as such. Ibid., 113.
69. Milagros Ortega Costa, "Spanish Women in the Reformation," in *Women in Reformation and Counter Reformation*, ed. Sherrin Marshall (Bloomington, IN: Indiana University Press, 1989), 92.
70. Teresa's poem "Aspirations" contains parallel sentiments and literary composition; see Lachance, *Angela*, 357–358, n.218. María argues for the overall importance of women's spiritual writings and specifically names Angela as an example of whom she is referring. See María de San José, *Book of Recreations*, in Electra Arenal and Stacey Schlau, *Untold Sisters: Hispanic Nuns in their Own Works*, tr. Amanda Powell (Albuquerque, NM: University of New Mexico, 1989), 101; and Patricia Ranft, *A Woman's Way: The Forgotten History of Women Spiritual Directors* (New York: Palgrave, 2000), 140.
71. *Instructions*, epilogue, in *Angela*, 318.
72. Colish, *Medieval Foundations*, 238.
73. See appraisal by Romano Guarnieri in *Angela*, pref., 10–11.
74. *Instructions*, in *Angela*, 240–241.
75. Ibid., 290.
76. Ibid., 300–301.
77. Bonaventure, *The Mind's Road to God*, tr. George Boas (Indianapolis, IN: Bobbs-Merrill, 1953), 3.184 (pp. 22–25).
78. Ibid., 3.6 (p. 26).
79. *Instructions*, in *Angela*, 227.
80. See his prologue to *Mind's Road*, (pp. 3–4): "After the death of that blessed man I ascended to Mount Alverna as to a quiet place, with the desire of seeking spiritual peace; and staying there, while I meditated on the ascent of the mind to God, amongst other things there occurred that miracle which happened in the same place to the blessed Francis himself, the vision namely of the winged Seraph in the likeness of the Crucified."
81. *Instructions*, in *Angela*, 223.
82. Ibid., in ibid., 314.
83. *Memorial* 4.d, in ibid., 154.
84. Ibid., 6, in ibid., 178.
85. Vita of Umiltà of Faenza, 6, in *Medieval Saints: A Reader*, ed. Mary-Ann Stouck (Peterborough, CAN: Broadview Press, 1999), 456.
86. Ibid., 30, in ibid., 467.

87. Umiltà of Faenza, *Sermons,* tr. Richard J. Pioli, 2.1, in *Medieval Women's Visionary Literature,* ed. Elizabeth Alvilda Petroff (New York: Oxford University Press, 1986), 247.
88. Vita of Umiltà, 10, in ibid., 458.
89. Ibid., 13, in ibid., 459.
90. See Michael Richter, *Sprache und Gesellschaft im Mittelalter* (Stuttgart: Anton Hiersemann, 1979), 78; and Bella Millett, "Woman in No Man's Land: English recluses and the development of vernacular literature in the twelfth and thirteenth centuries," in *Women and Literature in Britain, 1150–1500,* ed. Carol Meale (Cambridge: Cambridge University Press, 1993), 86–103.
91. Herbert Grundmann, "Litteratus-illiteratus: Der Wandel einer Bildungsnorm vom Altertum zum Mittelalter," *Archiv für Kulturgeschichte* 40 (1958), 1–65.
92. *Ancrene Wisse,* Part 4, in *Anchoritic Spirituality: Ancrene Wisse and Associated Works* tr. Anne Savage and Nicholas Watson (New York: Paulist Press, 1991), 153.
93. Aelred of Rievaulx, "A Rule for Life of a Recluse," in *The Works of Aelred of Rievaulx,* Vol. 1: *Treatise and The Pastoral Prayer* (Spencer, MA: Cistercian Publications, 1971), 1:7. See also Ranft, *Women and Spiritual Equality,* 140–141.
94. *Ancrene Wisse,* intro.
95. Thomas Hales, lines 193–198, cited in Millett, "Women," 97.
96. *Ancrene Wisse,* Part 2 (p. 72).
97. Much of the discussion of women teachers is based on the fine article by Nicole Bériou, "The Right of Women to Give Religious Instruction in the Thirteenth Century," in *Women Preachers and Prophets through Two Millennia of Christianity,* eds. Beverly M. Kienzle and Pamela J. Walker (Berkeley, CA: University of California Press, 1998), 134–145. For Eustache, see ibid., 138–139; for Robert, see ibid., 139.
98. Ibid., 139.
99. *The Autobiography of Guibert, Abbot of Nogent-Sous-Coucy,* tr. C. C. Swinton Bland (New York: E. P. Dutton, n.d.), 4 (p. 17); discussed in ibid., 135–136.
100. Cited in Jean Richard, *Saint Louis* (Cambridge: Cambridge University Press, 1983), 9.
101. Bériou, "Right of Women," 140, ends the article on a negative note, concluding that the thirteenth-century debates eventually "settled women in a subordinate position for a long time."
102. *The Wohunge of ure Lauerd,* ed. W. Meredith Thompson (Oxford: EETS , 1958), xxii.
103. Millet, "Women," 98.
104. Peter Damian was its chief theologian. See my articles on the subject: "The Concept of Witness in the Christian Tradition from Its Origin to Its Institutionalization," *Revue bénédictine* 102:1–2 (1992), 9–23; *idem,* "Hugh Latimer and Witness," *Sixteenth Century Journal* 11 (1979), 21–34; and "Witness and the Eleventh Century Monastic Renewal," *Journal of Religious History* 16:4 (1991), 361–373.
105. See my article, "The Role of the Eremitic Monk in the Development of the Medieval Intellectual Tradition," in *From Cloister to Classroom,* ed. E. Rozanne Elder (Kalamazoo, MI: Cistercian Publications, 1986), 80–95.
106. PL 145, 489–490.
107. Jacques Verger, *Men of Learning in Europe at the End of the Middle Ages,* tr. Lisa Neal and Steven Randall (Notre Dame, IN: University of Notre Dame Press, 1997), 127.
108. *Testament,* 6, in *Francis and Clare: The Complete Works,* tr. Regis J. Armstrong and Ignatius Brady (New York: Paulist Press, 1982), 227–228.

109. Given the status of the primary sources, confusion reigns supreme in the secondary sources. During the sixteenth century the family of Landsberg tried to claim Herrad as their own. Even though this is greatly disputed today, most twentieth-century sources still use the appellation. See Michael Curschmann, "The German Glosses," in *Herrad of Hohenbourg: Hortus deliciarum,* Vol. 1: *Commentary,* ed. Rosalie Green *et al.* (Leiden: E. J. Brill, 1979), 73. There is also a vast discrepancy about her dates. Joann McNamara, *Sisters in Arms* (Cambridge, MA: Harvard University Press, 1996), 293, mistakenly states that Herrad was abbess from 1160–1170, while a few pages later claims Herrad composed *Hortus* in 1173. William Turner, *The Catholic Encyclopedia* (1910), s.v. Herrad of Landsberg, says Herrad became abbess in 1167, as does Gérard Cames, *Allégories et Symboles dans L'Hortus Deliciarum* (Leiden: E. J. Brill, 1971), 1. Even the definitive work on the book, Green, "Miniatures," *Hortus,* 25, confusingly states that Relinda died in 1176 (typographical error?) and Herrad immediately succeeded her.
110. See fols. 322v/323r in Green, *Hortus,* Figures 331, 332, 333, and 334.
111. *Herrad of Landsberg: Hortus Deliciarum,* commentary A. Straub and G. Keller, ed. and tr. Aristide D. Caratzas (New Rochelle, NY: Caratzas Brothers, 1977), 250.
112. Green, *Hortus,* 24–25.
113. Lina Eckenstein, *Women under Monasticism* (Cambridge: At the University Press, 1896), 254.
114. Curschmann, "Glosses," in Green, *Hortus,* 63. The selections on marriage have made some scholars posit that the intended audience also included lay women. Ibid., 73–74.
115. Christine Bischoff, "Le Texte," in Green, *Hortus,* 37–61. Christian M. Engelhardt, *Herrad von Landsperg Abbtissin zu Hohenburg… und ihr Werk: Hortus deliciarum* (Stuttgart: 1818), studied and traced the manuscript before its destruction in 1870. It is his book and the work of Comte Auguste de Bastard that modern scholarship depends upon. Engelhardt identifies twenty sources that Herrad quotes. See also Eckenstein, *Women under Monasticism,* 245.
116. Curschmann, "Glosses," in Green, *Hortus,* 69 and 68.
117. Caratzas, *Herrad,* 12.
118. The transition text linking the description of philosophy with idolatry, which included Herrad's summary of other philosophers' opinions of the nature of God and the text on the order of the Muses linking them to philosophy and poetry have both been lost. See Joan Gibson, "Herrad of Hohenbourg" in *History of Women Philosophers,* 4 vols., ed. Mary Ellen Waithe (Dordrecht: Kluwer Academic Publishers, 1989), 2:91.
119. Caratzas, *Herrad,* 36.
120. Ibid., 37.
121. Eckenstein, *Women under Monasticism,* 239.
122. Turner, s.v. "Herrad."
123. For the story of the survival of the tracings of the originals, see Green, "Miniatures," in Green, *Hortus,* 17–36. For the problems involved in totaling the number of illuminations in the original manuscript, see ibid., 23–24.
124. Green, ibid., 24, says 54 percent are recorded adequately, 12 percent have one figure or more, 8 percent have only minor details, and 26 percent are missing.
125. Green, *Hortus,* Figures 2, 3, and 4.
126. Ibid., Creation is Figures 6–18; Trinity is Figure 5.

127. Green, "Miniatures,"in Green, *Hortus,* 35.
128. Ibid., 36.
129. Gibson, "Herrad", in *Women Philosophers,* 2:89.
130. Ibid., Figure 34; see also Figure 35.
131. Caratzas, *Herrad,* 36.
132. Green, "Catalogue," in Green, *Hortus,* 104–106.
133. Eckenstein, *Women under Monasticism,* 246.
134. Cited in ibid., 253–254.
135. Green, "Miniatures," 17.
136. Straub, a canon at the cathedral of Strasbourg, was chosen to edit what copies and traces were left after the original was destroyed in 1870. He described them from memory as "brillent de l'éclat des couleurs, rehaussées d'or et dessinées d'une main dont la fermeté nous a toujous remplis d'étonnement" (Green, "Miniatures," in Green, *Hortus,* 30).
137. With all due respect to the artistic merit of the illuminations, the inscriptions written right next to each object it is explaining is a didactic method still popular today in children's books. For example, see Richard Scary's illustrated books.
138. Green, "Miniatures," in Green, *Hortus,* 29.
139. Green, "Catalogue," in Green, *Hortus,* 228, Figure 338.
140. Caroline Walker Bynum, *Jesus as Mother* (Berkeley, CA: University of California Press, 1982) epilogue, 264. Bynum, *The Resurrection of the Body in Western Christianity, 200–1336* (New York: Columbia University Press, 1995), 117–121, and 188–197, also argues that Herrad's summa can tell us much about twelfth-century beliefs in resurrection of the body and attitudes toward the body in general. In these areas Herrad is not original: "The choices made by Herrad and her collaborators were those made generally in twelfth-century theology, iconography, spiritual writing, and popular story" (p. 120). This opinion supports the categorization of Herrad as a secondary intellectual, a disseminator of ideas rather than an originator.
141. Green, "Catalogue," 201.
142. Ibid.
143. Engelhardt, *Herrad,* 104, cited in Eckenstein, *Women under Monasticism,* 247.
144. Caratzas, *Herrad,* 196.
145. Herrad, poem, tr. in Eckenstein, *Women under Monasticism,* 254–255.
146. See Petroff, *Visionary Literature,* 277–280.
147. Marguerite d'Oingt, *The Mirror,* 1 and 2, in Petroff, *Medieval Women's Visionary Literature,* 290–291.
148. Ibid., 292.
149. Marguerite, *Page of Meditation,* cited in ibid., 279.
150. *Writings of Margaret of Oingt,* 72, tr. in Elizabeth Alvilda Petroff, *Body and Soul* (New York: Oxford University Press, 1994), 223 n.33.
151. Ibid., 142 in ibid., 224 n.34. Margaret's use of personal pronouns is confusing here.
152. In this instance, Provençal. See Petroff, *Visionary Literature,* 277–278.
153. *Revelations* in *Margaret Ebner: Major Works,* tr. Leonard P. Hindsley, intro. Leonard P. Hindsley and Margot Schmidt (New York: Paulist Press, 1993), 98.
154. Letter 40, 236, 24–237, 3, cited in *Margaret Ebner: Works,* intro., 35.
155. Letter 13, 188, 19f, cited in ibid., 31.

156. Letter 43, 246, 117–247, 141, cited in Margot Schmidt, "An Example of Spiritual Friendship: The Correspondence between Heinrich of Nördlingen and Margaretha Ebner," in Wiethaus, *Maps of Flesh and Light,* 76.
157. Letter 52, 266, 55–58, cited in *Margaret Ebner: Works,* 41.
158. *Revelations,* in ibid., 87.
159. Ibid., intro., 64.
160. Ibid., 65, 68.
161. *Pater Noster,* in ibid., 176, 177–178.
162. Ibid., 175–178.
163. Ibid., 177, 176.
164. Ibid., 177.
165. PL 152, 529. See also *Autobiography of Guibert,* 34–39; and my article, "The Role of the Eremitic Monk," for a thorough discussion of this process.
166. See AASS, Febuary 3 and PL 162, 1079–1082 for Robert; PL 204, 1005–1046, for Stephen of Muret; PL 172, 1363–1446 and AASS April 2, for Bernard; and AASS April 2, for Stephen Harding.
167. PL 153, 631–760. *Autobiography of Guibert,* 36, reports that the Carthusians are accumulating a large library despite their vow of poverty. Adam of Eynsham, *Magna Vita Sancti Hugonis,* 2:13, comments thus: "It was a very saying of [High of Lincoln] that these books were useful to all monks, but especially to those leading an eremitical life, for they provided riches and delights in times of tranquillity, weapons and armor in times of temptation, food for the hungry, and medicine for the sick." Cited in Ranft, "Eremitic Monk," n.46. See also ibid., 88, for Peter the Venerable.
168. PL 153, 384.
169. Guiges de Chastel, *Meditations of Guigo,* tr. John Jolin (Milwaukee, WI: Marquette University Press, 1951), 225.
170. Ranft, "Eremitic Monk," 84–88.
171. PL 145, 833; see also PL 145, 836.
172. PL 145, 834.
173. PL 144, 476.
174. PL 144, 828.
175. PL 145, 604.
176. Cited in H. O. Taylor, *The Medieval Mind,* 4th ed. (New York: Macmillan, 1925), 1:349; and in Ranft, "Eremitic Monk," 89.
177. PL 183, 967.
178. PL 176, 183–185.
179. *Opus majus of Roger Bacon,* 3 vols., ed. John H. Bridges (London: Williams & Norgate, 1900), 3:36.
180. Bonaventure, *Soul's Journey into God,* tr. Evert Cousins (Ramsey, NJ: Paulist Press, 1978), 4.2; idem, *On Retracing the Arts to Theology,* 7; and in *The Works of Bonaventure,* tr. Jose de Vinck (Paterson, NJ: St. Anthony Guild Press, 1966), 20–21.
181. Ranft, "Eremitic Monk," 90.
182. See Joel Kaye, "The Impact of Money on the Development of Fourteenth-Century Scientific Thought," *Journal of Medieval History* 14 (1988), 251–270; and *The Cultural*

Context of Medieval Learning, eds. John Murdoch and Edith Sylla (Dordrecht: Reidel, 1975), for reflections on similar problems in other fields of scholarly inquiry.

183. See above, ch. 4.
184. *Gertrude of Helfta: The Herald of Divine Love,* tr. Margaret Winkworth (New York: Paulist Press, 1993), 32 (p. 204).
185. Ibid., 68 (p. 231).
186. Ibid. (pp. 231–232).
187. Ibid., 30 (p. 199).
188. *Gertrude the Great of Helfta: Spiritual Exercises,* tr. Gertrud Jaron Lewis and Jack Lewis (Kalamazoo, MI: Cistercian Publications, 1989), 64, 63.

Chapter 6, pp. 145–174
The Great Theologians

1. *The Works of M. de Voltaire,* tr. T. Smollett *et al.,* 25 vols. (London: J. Newberry *et al.,* 1761–1774), 1:82; microfilm: Woodbridge: CT Research Publications, 1985, Reel 1338, No. 04; and Marquis de Condorcet, *Sketch for a Historical Picture of Progress of the Human Mind,* ed. Stuart Hampshire, tr. June Barracleugh (New York: Noonday Press, 1955), 72.
2. Jacob Burkhardt, *The Civilization of the Renaissance in Italy,* tr. S. G. C. Middlemore, rev. and ed. Irene Gordon (New York: New American Library, 1960), 121.
3. John Addington Symonds, *Renaissance in Italy,* Part 1: *The Age of the Despots* (New York: Henry Holt, 1888), 13–15. See also Andrew White, *A History of the Warfare of Science with Theology* (London: Macmillan & Co., 1896).
4. Pierre Duhem, *Les origines de la statique,* 2 vols. (Paris: Hermann, 1905–1906), 1:iv.
5. See William J. Bouwsma, "The Renaissance Discovery of Human Creativity" in *Humanity and Divinity in Renaissance and Reformation,* ed. John W. O'Malley, Thomas M. Izbicki, and Gerald Christianson (Leiden: E. J. Brill, 1993), 17–33, for discussion of the defensive nature of current Renaissance literature and for an example of such a defense.
6. David C. Lindberg, *The Beginnings of Western Science* (Chicago: University of Chicago Press, 1992), 355–360.
7. David C. Lindberg, "Medieval Science and its Religious Context," *Osiris* 10 (1995), 61–79; see 78.
8. Roger French and Andrew Cunningham, *Before Science: The Invention of the Friars' Natural Philosophy* (Brookfield, VT: Scolar Press, 1996), 4.
9. Most scholars would still agree with the reviewer in *The Historical Bulletin,* who wrote thus: "There can be no doubt that this is the best text of the history of philosophy now available in English" (cited in Copleston, *History of Philosophy,* Vol. 1: *Greece and Rome,* Part 2, cover).
10. Ibid., Vol. 3, *Late Medieval and Renaissance Philosophy,* Part 1, *Ockham to the Speculative Mystics,* 166.
11. Juliàn Mariàs, *History of Philosophy* (New York: Dover Press, 1967), 160, 190.
12. Gertrude, *Spiritual Exercises,* 5:12, 91–94, 80–83 (73, 76).
13. Ibid., 5:2, 31–34 (p. 74).

14. See above, Chapter 4, p. 99, for Beatrice; Chapter 2, pp. 63–65, for Hildegard of Bingen.
15. *Elizabeth of Schönau: The Complete Works,* tr. Anne L. Clark, pref. Barbara Newman (New York: Paulist Press, 2000), pref., xi.
16. *Book of the Ways of God,* 1 (p. 161).
17. *Francis and Clare: The Complete Works,* tr. Regis J. Armstrong and Ignatius C. Brady (New York: Paulist Press, 1982), 204.
18. Clare of Assisi, *Testament,* 11, and 14 in ibid., (pp. 229–230).
19. *Julian of Norwich: Showings,* tr. Edmund Colledge and James Walsh (New York: Paulist Press, 1978), long text, Ch. 51 (p. 273). All future references to *Showings* are to the long text, unless otherwise noted.
20. Ibid., intro., 20.
21. Joan M. Nuth, *Wisdom's Daughter: The Theology of Julian of Norwich* (New York: Crossroad, 1991), 9; and *Julian of Norwich: A Book of Showings to the Anchoress Julian Norwich,* tr. Edmund Colledge and James Walsh (Toronto: Pontifical Institute of Medieval Studies, 1978), 1:44 and 43–59.
22. *The Book of Margery Kempe,* tr. B. A. Windeatt, repr. (London: Penguin Books, 1994), Ch. 18 (p. 77).
23. *Julian: Showings,* 51 (pp. 277–278).
24. Nuth, *Wisdom's Daughter,* 103.
25. Julian, *Showings,* 43 (p. 255).
26. Ibid., 59 (p. 296).
27. Ibid., 60 (pp. 297–299).
28. Ibid., 18 (pp. 211, 210).
29. Ibid., 11 (pp. 198–199).
30. Ibid., 18 (p. 211), discussed in Nuth, *Wisdom's Daughter,* 100.
31. See Gregory Baum, *Laborem Exercens* (Toronto: University of Toronto, 1983); and J. L. Illanes, *On the Theology of Work,* tr. Michael Adams (Dublin: Four Court Press, 1982).
32. Julian, *Showings,* 8 (p. 190).
33. Ibid., 5 (p. 183).
34. Ibid., 53 (pp. 283–284).
35. Ibid., 54 (p. 285).
36. Ibid., short text, 6 (p. 134).
37. Ibid., short text, 17 (p. 154).
38. Ibid., 65 (p. 309).
39. Ibid., 9 (pp. 191–192).
40. Ibid., 8 (pp. 190–191).
41. Statements such as C. Warren Hollister, *The Making of England* (Toronto: DC Heath, 6th ed., 1992), 285, that "by the end of 1349 the Black Death had run its course" are misleading. It is often overlooked that the plague struck well beyond its worst years of 1348–1351; it reoccurred in 1361–1362, 1369, 1374–1375, 1379, 1390, 1407, 1413, 1434, 1464, 1471, and 1479.
42. Janet Coleman, *Piers Plowman and the Moderni* (Rome: Edizioni de Storia e Litteratura, 1981), 192; and Christopher Dyer, *Standards of Living in the Later Middle Ages* (Cambridge: Cambridge University Press, 1989), 223.

43. Barbara Hanawalt, *The Ties that Bound* (Oxford: Oxford University Press, 1986), 4.
44. Eamon Duffy, *The Stripping of the Altars* (New Haven, CT: Yale University Press, 1992) and Miri Rubin, *Corpus Christi* (Cambridge: Cambridge University Press, 1991).
45. Frederick Bauerschmidt, *Julian of Norwich and the Mystical Body Politic of Christ* (Notre Dame, IN: University of Notre Dame Press, 1999), 1–14. A presupposition of his work is the thesis "that theology is always already political because it is the 'social theory' underlying the distinctive forms of life of concrete, historical communities that make up the church" (p. 10). See John Milbank, *Theology and Social Theory* (Oxford: Basil Blackwell, 1990) for a defense of the axiom that all politics is theological and all theology is political.
46. Julian, *Showings,* 51 (p. 270).
47. Ibid., 71 (pp. 318–319).
48. Ibid., 86 (p. 342).
49. Ibid., 28 (pp. 226–227).
50. Ibid., 68 (p. 313).
51. Ibid., 79 (pp. 333–334).
52. Ibid., 68 (pp. 342–343).
53. Ibid., 65 (p. 308).
54. Ibid., 68 (pp. 314, 313).
55. Ibid., short text 13 (p. 148).
56. Ibid. (p. 149).
57. Ibid., 15 (p. 205).
58. Ibid., 27 (p. 225).
59. Written in 1942. See Susan McCaslin, "Vision and Revision in *Four Quartets:* T. S. Eliot and Julian of Norwich," *Mystics Quarterly* 12 (December 1986), 171–178.
60. *Julian: Showings,* 15 (p. 205).
61. Ibid., 65 (p. 308).
62. Ibid., 68 (p. 315).
63. Ibid., 43 (p. 253).
64. Ibid., 57 (p. 292).
65. Ibid., 6 (p. 184).
66. Ibid., long text 13 (pp. 201–202) and short text 8 (p. 138).
67. Ibid., 1 (p. 176).
68. Ibid., 14 (pp. 203–204).
69. Elizabeth N. Evasdaughter, "Julian of Norwich" in *History of Women Philosophers,* 4 vols., ed. Mary Ellen Waithe (Dordrecht: Kluwer Academic Publishers, 1989), 2:195, writes that "in her treatment of this issue as of others, Julian acted like an Oxford theologian who had the right to examine theological and philosophical tradition and say *sic et non*—to select, affirm, deny, replace." Much of what follows is developed from Evasdaughter's article.
70. David Knowles and D. Obolensky, *The Christian Centuries,* Vol. 2: *The Middle Ages* (New York: Paulist Press, 1983), 444–449.
71. See Thomas Aquinas, *Summa Theologica,* Part 1, q.12, art 13; Part 1, q.1, art 8; for Julian, see *Showings,* long text, 53 (p. 284) and ibid., 55 (p. 286).
72. *Julian: Showings,* long text 9 (p. 192).
73. Augustine, *Eighty-Three Different Questions,* tr. David Mosher (Washington, DC: Catholic University of America Press, 1982), 89.
74. Aquinas, *Summa,* 1a, 2a, 47,1.

75. *Julian: Showings,* 54 (p. 257).
76. Ibid., 50 (p. 266).
77. Ibid., 51 (p. 267).
78. Ibid. (p. 270).
79. Ibid., 52 (p. 281).
80. Ibid., 51 (p. 276).
81. Ibid., 68 (p. 314).
82. For full discussion of how Julian "negotiates both the conformity of the doctrine between her personal mystical experience and . . . traditional patriarchal and theological authority" (p. 3), see Sandra J. McEntire, "The Likeness of God and the Restoration of Humanity in Julian of Norwich's *Showings*" in *Julian of Norwich: A Book of Essays,* ed. Sandra J. McEntire (New York: Garland, 1998), 3–33; Lynn Staley and David Aers, *The Powers of the Holy* (University Park, PA: University of Pennsylvania Press, 1996), 141, call the whole of the long and short text "an extended dialogue between her spiritual understanding and her belief in the teachings of Holy Church."
83. *Julian: Showings,* 32 (p. 233).
84. Ibid., 80 (p. 335).
85. Ibid., 45 (pp. 256–257).
86. Evasdaughter, "Julian," in *History of Women Philosophers,* 2:216.
87. Ibid. Evasdaughter says that some of these "not shown" statements are probably in reply to questions about why a certain topic was not included. Again, though, she still uses it even here to show her orthodoxy and her lack of experiential knowledge of it.
88. *Julian: Showings,* 9 (p. 192). Nuth, *Wisdom's Daughter,* 16–22, discusses the possibility of Julian being concerned with accusations of heresy.
89. Ibid., 34 (pp. 235–236).
90. Ibid., 56 (p. 290).
91. Ibid., 83 (p. 340).
92. See Marcia L. Colish, *Medieval Foundations of the Western Intellectual Tradition 400–1400* (New Haven, CT: Yale University Press, 1997), 304–315.
93. *Julian: Showings,* 56 (p. 289).
94. Ibid., 56 (p. 288).
95. Ibid., 68 (p. 314).
96. Ibid., 56 (pp. 288–289).
97. Ibid., 72 (p. 321).
98. Ibid., 63 (p. 304).
99. Ibid., 53 (p. 282).
100. Ibid., 52 (p. 282).
101. Ibid., 47 (pp. 260–261).
102. Ibid., 39 (p. 245). Denise Baker, *Julian of Norwich's Showings: From Vision to Book* (Princeton, NJ: Princeton University Press, 1994), 111, believes that Julian does resolve the problem of evil with her "concept of the godly will, by astutely integrating the doctrines of predestination and imago Dei." See below, pp. 157–158.
103. Conrad Pepler, *The English Religious Heritage* (London: Blackfriars, 1958), 306, comments that the long text reads as if Julian had been studying Aquinas's *Summa* since she first wrote the short text." Cited in Evasdaughter, "Julian," 2: 195.
104. *Julian: Showings,* 54 (p. 285).

105. Nuth, *Wisdom's Daughter,* 109.
106. *Julian: Showings,* 54 (p. 285).
107. Ibid., 10 (p. 194).
108. Ibid., 53 (p. 256).
109. See discussion of imago Dei in early Christianity in Patricia Ranft, *Women and Spiritual Equality in Christian Tradition* (New York: St. Martin's Press, 1998), 37–41.
110. Nuth, *Wisdom's Daughter,* 105.
111. *Julian: Showings,* 58 (p. 294).
112. Baker, *Julian of Norwich's Showings,* 113.
113. Charles Trinkhaus, *In Our Image and Likeness: Humanity and Divinity in Italian Humanist Thought,* 2 vols. (Chicago: University of Chicago Press, 1970).
114. Intro., O'Malley, *Humanity and Divinity.*
115. Charles Trinkhaus, *Renaissance Transformations of Late Medieval Thought* (Brookfield, VT: Ashgate, 1999), ix.
116. Bouwsma, "Discovery of Human Creativity", in O'Malley, *Humanity and Divinity,* 26.
117. Charles Trinkhaus, "From the Twelfth-Century Renaissance to the Italian: Three Versions of 'The Dignity of Man,' " in Trinkhaus, *Renaissance Transformations,* 4:80.
118. One of the literary masterpieces of the movement is Pico della Mirandola, *Oration on the Dignity of Man,* tr. E. L. Forbes in *The Renaissance Philosophy of Man,* eds. E. Cassirer *et al.* (Chicago: University of Chicago Press, 1948), whose thesis was simply that humans have dignity because they are God's image.
119. O'Malley, *Humanity and Divinity* is a *Festschrift* for Trinkhaus; it is an excellent presentation of the latest research on the topic by the period's most noted scholars.
120. So says Baker, *Julian of Norwich's Showings,* 166. I am not totally convinced that Augustine limited his *imago Dei* to males.
121. Cited in Trinkhaus, *Renaissance Transformations,* 4:73.
122. See *The Humanism of Leonardo Bruni: Selected Texts,* tr. Gordon Griffiths, Jane Hankins, and David Thompson (Binghamton, NY: MRST, 1987). Evasdaughter, "Julian," in *History of Women Philosophers,* 2:217, says Julian promotes education in at least twenty-eight passages.
123. Petrarch, Letter of 1353, in Cassirer, *Renaissance Philosophy,* 44.
124. So declared on October 4, 1970 by Pope Paul VI.
125. It circulated in the vernacular and in Latin in manuscript form during the century following her death in 1472, just years after printing found its way to Italy; Azzoguidi published the first printed edition. See Guiliana Cavallini, *Catherine of Siena* (London: Geoffrey Chapman, 1998), 19.
126. See Karen Scott, "St. Catherine of Siena, 'Apostola,' " *Church History* 61:1 (March 1992), 34–46, discusses the historiographical emphases. Scott emphasizes her apostleship.
127. See Francis Luongo, "The Politics of Marginality: Catherine of Siena in the War of Eight Saints (1374–1378)," PhD Diss., University of Notre Dame, 1997; he believes Catherine's thought is intrinsically intertwined with Tuscan politics.
128. *Prayer of Catherine of Siena,* tr. Suzanna Noffke (New York: Paulist Press, 1983), 1, (p. 16). It should be noted at the beginning of this discussion of Catherine that she explicitly includes women in the *imago Dei* doctrine, a fact the Noffke emphasizes in her translation. To Joanna, Queen of Naples, she writes: "You are called daughter by First

Truth because we were created by God and came forth from him. This is what he said: 'Let us make humankind in our image and likeness.'" Letter t143/G313/DT39 in *Letters of Catherine of Siena,* tr. Suzanna Noffke (Tempe, AZ: Arizona Center for Medieval and Renaissance Studies, 2000), p. 147.

129. *Catherine of Siena: The Dialogue,* tr. and intro. Suzanna Noffke (New York: Paulist Press, 1980), 12 (p. 46).
130. Prologue, p. 26. Noffke notes (p. 26 n.3) that "'la mia creatura che à in sé ragione' is one of Catherine's favorite expressions for the human person."
131. Letter I/DT52, *Letters* (2000), p. 188.
132. *Dialogue,* 13 (p. 49).
133. Ibid., 110 (p. 205).
134. Ibid., 13 (p. 48).
135. Ibid., 31 (p. 72).
136. Ibid., 32 (p. 74).
137. Letter T28/G191/DT17, *Letters* (2000), p. 133.
138. *Dialogue,* 13 (p. 50).
139. Ibid., 54 (p. 108).
140. Ibid., 51 (pp. 103–104).
141. Ibid., (p. 105).
142. Letter T28, *Letters* (2000), p. 133.
143. *Dialogue,* 14 (p. 53).
144. Ibid., 140 (p. 288).
145. Ibid., 7 (p. 37).
146. Ibid., 7 (p. 38).
147. Ibid., 148 (p. 311).
148. Ibid. (p. 312).
149. Ibid. (pp. 311–312).
150. Ibid., 8 (p. 38).
151. Ibid., 9 (p. 41).
152. Ibid., 66 (p. 127).
153. Ibid., 9 (p. 41).
154. Letter T133/G312/DT32, *Letters* (2000), p. 122.
155. *Dialogue* 6 (p. 35).
156. Ibid., 7 (pp. 35–36).
157. Ibid. (p. 37).
158. Ibid. (p. 35).
159. Ibid. (p. 38).
160. See Walter Ullmann's classic work on the subject, *The Growth of Papal Government in the Middle Ages*, 3rd ed. (London: Methuen, 1970); and Brian Tierney, *Religion, Law, and the Growth of Constitutional Thought, 1150–1650* (Cambridge: Cambridge University Press, 1982).
161. Colish, *Medieval Foundations,* 335–40.
162. Letter 68, *Letters of St. Catherine of Siena*, tr. Suzanna Noffke (Binghampton, NY: MRTS, 1988), 215.
163. Letter T28/G191/DT17, *Letters* (2000), 135.

164. Letter T135/G209/DT42, ibid., 163.
165. Letter 60, *Letters* (1988), 187.
166. Ibid. (p. 188).
167. Ibid. (p. 191).
168. Letter 40, ibid. (p. 132).
169. Catherine met Charles V's brother, Louis, Duke of Anjou, while she was in Avignon. Louis asked her to write to Charles, but it is unknown whether the king received or answered her letter. Letter 78, ibid., 237.
170. Letter T28/G191/DT17, *Letters* (2000), 132.
171. Letter 78, *Letters* (1988), 238.
172. Stewardship was also used by scholastics to explain certain aspects of the economy. See Thomas Aquinas' application of stewardship to the question of stealing when in need. *Summa* 2.2, q.66, art.7.
173. Secular leaders' obligation to stewardship is not exclusive; it extends to religious leaders as well. Catherine writes to Fr. Mariano, a priest in Siena: "Be a good provider for the needy poor. And let fear of God always attend your association with the people there. If you are able to defend humbly what belongs to the poor, do so." Letter T261/G49, *Letters* (2000), 58.
174. Letter T133/G312/DT32, ibid., 124.
175. *Dialogue,* 151 (p. 319). In the same section Catherine elaborates on what she calls God's general providence for the poor. This includes God bringing the poor sometimes "to the brink so that they will better see and know that I can and will provide for them," and then inspiring with mercy "the very persons who treat them ill to give them alms and help." Ibid., 314.
176. Letter 78, *Letters* (1988), 238.
177. Letter T28/G191/DT17, *Letters* (2000), 133.
178. Letter 123, tr. in Cavallini, *Catherine,* 120.
179. Letter 78, *Letters* (1988), 238.
180. *Dialogue,* 199 (p. 224).
181. Ibid., 34 (p. 75).
182. Letter T135/G209/DT42, *Letters* (2000), 162–163.
183. Letter T138/G314/DT41, ibid., 100.
184. Letter T133/G312/DT32, ibid., 124
185. Letter 54, *Letters* (1988), 167.
186. Letter 64, ibid., 204.
187. Letter T109/G41/DT51, *Letters* (2000), 268.
188. Letter 54, *Letters* (1988), 167.
189. *Dialogue,* 159 (p. 342).
190. Letter 64, *Letters* (1988), 205.
191. Letter 72, ibid., 223, 222.
192. Colish, *Medieval Foundations,* 335.
193. Letter 78, *Letters* (1988), 239.
194. Letter 40, ibid., 132.
195. Letter 31, ibid., 106.
196. Letter 40, ibid., 132.

197. Letter T168/G206/DT53, *Letters* (2000), 241–243.
198. Although never formally canonized, Catherine is included in the Roman martyrology, and her feast is celebrated on March 24 throughout the Scandinavian world. See *Butler's Lives of the Saints,* 4 vols., eds. Herbert J. Thurston and Donald Attwater, repr. (Westminister, MD: Christian Classics, 1998), 1:671. She had an interesting life in her own right. She was Birgitta's constant companion for the last twenty-five years of her mother's life, which meant that she traveled in the same influential circles as Birgitta did. During the Great Schism Pope Urban VI turned to her and her friend Catherine of Siena for help in gathering support for his papacy. He proposed sending the two as his emissaries to Joanna, Queen of Naples. However, in the *vita* of Catherine of Siena its author, Raymond of Capua, says that he himself dissuaded the pope from doing so, because it was too dangerous. Catherine of Sweden's most important accomplishment was the establishment of a community at Vadstena in Sweden according to her mother's rule and wishes. This was the mother house of the Birgittine Order (Order of the Most Holy Savior). Ibid.
199. Petrus Olai, *Acta et processus canonizaciones beate Birgitta,* ed. Isak Collijn (Uppsala: Almquist & Wiksells, 1924–1931), 570. *The Life of Blessed Birgitta by Prior Peter and Master Peter,* 28, in *Birgitta of Sweden: Life and Selected Revelations,* ed. Marguerite T. Harris, tr. Albert R. Kezel (New York: Paulist Press, 1990), 78, says that "even before her husband's passing, she saw certain things."
200. Her intended destination was Jerusalem, which she finally did travel to in 1372, the year before she died. See Cornelia Wolfskeel, "Birgitta of Sweden," in *History of Women Philosophers,* 2:168.
201. Bridget Morris, *St. Birgitta of Sweden* (Woodbridge, GB: Boydell Press, 1999), 85–86.
202. Ibid., 1.
203. Birgitta's canonization was reaffirmed by Pope John XXII. Gerson reminded the concilarists that a church council can not revoke Birgitta's canonization. See *Oeuvres complètes de Jean Gerson,* intro., text, and notes M. Glorieux (Paris: Desclée & Cie, 1973), art. 5, 9:177.
204. *The Book of Margery Kempe,* tr. S. A. Windeatt, repr. (London: Penguin Books, 1994), Ch. 39 (pp. 131–133), quote (p. 132).
205. Ibid., Ch. 20 (p. 83).
206. Morris, *Birgitta,* 2.
207. Harris, *Birgitta,* pref., 9.
208. Joseph Ratzinger, "The relevance of Saint Bridget of Sweden for our times," *Santa Brigida Profeta dei Tempi Nuovie: Proceedings of the International Study Meeting Rome Oct. 3–7, 1991* (Rome: Casa Generalizea Suore Santa Brigida, 1996), 86.
209. *Revelations,* 5, in Harris, *Birgitta,* prol. (p. 101).
210. Morris, *Birgitta,* 87, states that this book is Birgitta's "most sustained expression of anti-intellectualism." I believe this is much too strong and wrong-ended a conclusion. Granted, Birgitta bows profoundly before faith in this dialogue, but I do not think that that diminishes either her appreciation of rational inquiry or her recognition that it is a part, a good part, of the human condition. Unless the religious asked his probing questions he would not have been able to receive answers. Moreover, the form in which she constructs her book gives witness to her appreciation of scholastic methodology. In much of the religious' attitudes and questions Birgitta is but capturing the prevailing

intellectual stances of the Occamists who dominated her contemporary intellectual world. As such, *Revelations* is an interesting, reasoned response to these contemporaries.

211. *Revelations,* 2nd interrogation, q.4 (pp. 103–104).
212. *Saint Bride and Her Book: Birgitta of Sweden's Revelations,* tr. Julia Bolton Holloway (Cambridge: D.S. Brewer, 2000), Ch. 22 (p. 65).
213. Ibid., Ch. 23 (p. 80).
214. *Revelations,* Bk. 5, 12th rev., in Harris, *Birgitta* (p. 153).
215. *Revelations,* Bk. 7, Ch. 18, in ibid. (pp. 195–196).
216. *Revelations,* Ch. 23, in Holloway, *Bride* (pp. 83–84).
217. *Revelations,* Bk.7, Ch. 18, in Harris, *Birgitta* (pp. 194–195).
218. Ibid., Bk. 7, Ch. 19 (p. 197).
219. Ibid. (p. 199).
220. Bk. 5, 16th interrogation, ibid. (p. 152).
221. Bk. 5, 13th interrogation, response 4 q, ibid. (p. 136).
222. Bk. 5, 9th interrogation, ibid. (p. 117).
223. Bk. 5, 3rd interrogation, ibid. 104.
224. Holloway, *Bride,* Bk. 4:37 (p. 35).
225. See Carolyn Walker Bynum, *Fragmentation and Redemption: Essays on Gender and the Human Body in Medieval Religion* (New York: Zone Books, 1991), Figures 7:2–7.17, for examples of this preoccupation.
226. The four main *orations* were received in Birgitta's visions.
227. *Prayers,* in Morris, *Birgitta,* 3:64 (p. 229).
228. Ibid., 4:85 (p. 232).
229. Ibid., 4 (pp. 229–232).
230. Ibid., 4:85–100 (pp. 232–234).
231. *Revelations,* Bk. 5, 1st interrogation (p. 102).
232. Ibid. (pp. 103–104).
233. Ibid., Bk. 5, Rev. 4 (pp. 119–120).
234. *Sermo Angelicus* is comprised of a series of three long lectures on Mariology broken up into twenty-one parts. Birgitta wrote them in Swedish as readings for the Office, telling us that Christ sent her an angel "who will reveal to you the lections in honor of my Mother, the Virgin, which should be read by the nuns at Matins in your monastery. He will dictate them to you; you will write down exactly what he tells you." After doing so, she gave them to her confessor, who then translated them into Latin. Much discussion has been expended on whether the translation which, with the exception of two fragments, are all we have of the lectures, are therefore true reflections of Birgitta's work. Given that Birgitta approved the Latin translation before it was dispersed and given the above instructions from her vision, I conclude that she believed the translation to be faithful to her original composition. See *Birgitta of Sweden, The Word of the Angel: Sermo Angelicus,* tr. John E. Halborg (Toronto: Peregrina Publishers, 1996).
235. *Sermo,* Sat., Lesson 2, Ch. 20 (p. 66).
236. Ibid., Lesson 3, Ch. 21 (p. 67).
237. Bynum, *Fragmentation,* 256.
238. *Revelations,* Bk. 5, 12th interrogation (p. 129). Her appreciation for carnal pleasures does not, of course, interfere with her admiration for virginity. She continues:

"However, it is more glorious to extend oneself beyond a command by doing whatever additional good one can out of love; and this is virginity." Positing that virginity is "more virtuous and more magnificent" than non-virginity does not negate or even diminish her position that sexual intercourse was "something good." Ibid.

239. Ibid., Bk. 7, Ch. 10 (p. 172).
240. Ibid. (p. 173).
241. Bynum, *Fragmentation* (p. 266).
242. Bonaventure, *De assumptione B. Virginis Mariae,* Sermon 1, Sect. 2, quoted in ibid. (p. 257).

Chapter 7, pp. 175–194
Women Humanists

1. Margaret Deanesly, "Vernacular Books in England in the Fourteenth and Fifteenth Centuries," *Modern Language Review* 15 (1920), 349–358; and Hilary M. Carey, "Devout Literate Laypeople and the Pursuit of the Mixed Life in Later Medieval England," *Journal of Religious History* 14 (1987), 370.
2. *The Book of Margery Kempe,* tr. B. A. Windeatt, repr. (London: Penguin Books, 1994), 2:10 (p. 290). The Pardon of Syon was an indulgence granted to pilgrims to the women's monastery during Lammastide.
3. Alfred Thomas, *Anne's Bohemia: Czech Literature and Society, 1310–1420* (Minneapolis, MN: University of Minnesota Press, 1998), 45.
4. *The Life of Blessed Birgitta: Life and Revelations,* ed. Marguerite T. Harris, tr. Albert R. Ketzel (New York: Paulist Press, 1990), pref. (pp. 3–4).
5. Carey, "Devout Laypeople," 370.
6. Ibid., 376. See *The Orcherd of Syon,* eds. Phyllis Hodgson and Gabriel Liegey (London: Oxford University Press, 1966).
7. *Orcherd,* prol., 1.
8. Cited in *The Letters of St. Catherine of Siena,* tr. Suzanna Noffke (Binghampton, NY: MRTS, 1988), intro., p. 12.
9. Ibid., p. 14, and Harris, *The Life of Blessed Birgitta,* p. 3.
10. *History of Women Philosophers,* 4 vols., ed. Mary Ellen Waithe (Dordrecht: Kluwer Academic Publishers, 1989), 312.
11. *The Writings of Christine de Pizan,* ed. Charity Cannon Willard (New York: Persea Books, 1994), ix.
12. Daniel Poirion, *Littérature Français: Le Moyen Age, 1300–1480* (Paris, 1971), 206, cited in Charity Cannon Willard, *Christine de Pizan: Her Life and Works* (New York: Persea, 1984), 223.
13. Martin le Franc, *Le Champion des Dames,* Brussels, bibl. Roy. ms. 9281, fol. 151, cited in ibid.
14. Christine de Pizan, *The Book of the Body Politic,* ed. and tr. Kate Langdon Forhan (Cambridge: Cambridge University Press, 1994), 3:11 (p. 109).
15. Ibid., 109–110.
16. Christine de Pizan, *The Book of Three Virtues,* 3:14, in *The Selected Writings of Christine de Pizan,* tr. Renate Blumenfeld-Kosinski and Kevin Brownlee, ed. Renate Blumenfeld-Kosinski (New York: W. W. Norton, 1997), 172–173.

17. Jacob Burchhardt, *The Civilization of the Renaissance in Italy,* tr. S. G. C. Middlemore, rev. and ed. Irene Gordon (New York: New American Library, 1960), 133, 128.
18. Jacqueline Cerquiglini, "The Stranger," in *Selected Writings,* 265.
19. Diane Bornstein, "Humanism in Christine de Pisan's *Livre du corps de policie,*" *Bonnes feuilles* 3 (Fall 1974), 113. She believes this unfair treatment is evident when Christine's *Corps de policie* is compared to Erasmus' *Institution of a Christian Prince*: "Both belong to a long line of mirrors for the prince, ... Yet the *Institution of a Christian Prince* is usually classified as an important humanist document, whereas the *Corps de policie* is dismissed as a conservative piece of chivalric." Ibid.
20. Susan Bell, "Christine De Pizan (1364–1430): Humanism and the Problem of a Studious Woman," *Feminist Studies* 3:3–4 (1976), 177.
21. Willard, *Christine de Pizan,* 15.
22. Earl Jeffrey Richards, "French Cultural Nationalism and Christian Universalism in the Works of Christine de Pizan," in *Politics, Gender, and Genre: The Political Thought of Christine of Christine de Pizan,* ed. Margaret Brabant (Boulder, CO: Westview Press, 1992), 90.
23. Bell, "Christine de Pizan," 179.
24. *Body Politic,* 1:13 (p. 7).
25. Laurie A. Finke, *Writing in English: Medieval Engalnd* (London: Longman, 1999), 209.
26. Bornstein, "Humanism," 104.
27. Ibid., 101.
28. Willard, *Christine de Pizan,* 31. Willard infers here that Christine's literary inspiration came from "the two worlds that formed her," the humanist culture of Renaissance Bologna and Venice and the medieval culture of the French court.
29. Ibid., 15–31. Willard emphasizes how much Venice was involved in early humanism, thanks in large part to the fact that during this time Petrarch was residing in Venice for much of the year and drew visitors such as Boccaccio to his home.
30. Christine de Pizan, *Christine's Vision,* tr. Glenda K. McLeod (New York: Garland, 1993), 3:3 (p. 108).
31. Ibid., 3:4 (p. 110).
32. Ibid., 3:6 (p. 111).
33. *Christine's Vision,* 3:6 (p. 112).
34. Ibid., 3:8 (p. 117).
35. Ibid., 3:10 (p. 119).
36. Ibid., 3:10 (pp. 119–120).
37. *Oeuvres Complètes de Eustache Deschamps,* SATF 9, vol. 6, ed. le Marquis de Queux de Saint-Hilaire (Paris: Firmin Didot, 1889), balade 1242, cited in Joan Ferrante, *The Glory of her Sex* (Bloomington, IN: University of Indiana, 1997), 176.
38. "Christine's response to the Treatise on the Romance of the Rose by John of Montrevil, June–July 1401," tr. Nadia Margolis, in *Medieval Women's Visionary Literature,* ed. Elizabeth Alvilda Petroff (New York: Oxford University Press, 1986), 341.
39. Ibid., 345.
40. Ibid., 345–346.
41. Ibid., 342.

42. See discussion in Enid McLeod, *The Order of the Rose: The Life and Ideas of Christine de Pizan* (London: Chatto & Windus, 1976), 73.
43. Willard, *Christine de Pizan,* 80–81.
44. "Response," 345.
45. Ibid., 344.
46. Ibid.
47. *Christine's Letter to Gontier Col (1401),* 25/19, in *Woman Defamed and Woman Defended: An Anthology of Medieval Texts,* eds. Alcuin Blamires with Karen Pratt and C. W. Marx (Oxford: Clarendon Press, 1992), 287–288. Jean Gerson's treatise is found in his *Oeuvres complètes* 7.1.301–316; and in *Jean Gerson: Early Works,* tr. Brian P. McGuire (New York: Paulist Press, 1998), 378–398.
48. Christine de Pizan, *The Book of the City of Ladies,* tr. Rosalind Brown-Grant (London: Penguin Books, 1999), 1:27 (pp. 57–58).
49. Ibid., 1:28 (pp. 58–59).
50. Ibid., 1:8 (p. 17).
51. Ibid., 1:8 (p. 18).
52. Ibid., 1:27 (p. 58).
53. See Glenda McLeod, *Virtue and Venom* (Ann Arbor, MI: University of Michigan Press, 1991), 1–9, 141, for discussion of catalogues; and Patricia Ranft, *Women and Spiritual Equality in Christian Tradition* (New York: St. Martin's Press, 1998), 204–207, for discussion of woman's image in these catalogues.
54. McLeod, *Virtue,* 3. Chaucer's *Canterbury Tales* and Boccaccio's *Concerning Famous Women* are the prime examples of the catalogue's effectiveness.
55. A. Jeanroy, "Boccace et Christine de Pizan: le 'De Claris Mulieribus' Principale Source du 'Livre de la Cité des Dames,'" *Romania* 48 (1922), 92–105 and Willard, *Christine de Pizan,* 135–136.
56. Christine also liberally used Jean de Vignay's French translation of Vincent of Beauvais' *Speculum historiale* as a source, particularly for Part 3 of *City of Ladies.* The framework of the entire book was inspired by Augustine's *City of God;* Boccaccio's *Decameron* was likewise a source. See *City of Ladies,* xviii.
57. *City of Ladies,* 1:1 (p. 7).
58. Ibid., 1:3 (p. 11).
59. Blumenfeld-Kosinsky, *Selected Writings of Christine,* 118.
60. In Part 3, ten of the nineteenth chapters are based on the *Golden Legend.* Christine M. Reno, "Christine de Pisan's Use of the *Golden Legend* in the *Cité des dames,*" *Bonnes feuilles* 3 (Fall 1974), 97, 90, 93. Christine's presentation of St. Natalie is an example of her adaptation of *Golden Legend* material to suit her own purposes.
61. Faith, hope, and charity are the theological virtues; prudence, temperance, fortitude, and justice are the cardinal virtues.
62. *City of Ladies,* 1:2 (p. 8).
63. Ibid., 1:4 (pp. 12–13).
64. Ibid., 1:8 (p. 16).
65. Ibid., 1:9 (p. 20).
66. Ibid., xxx–xxxi.

67. Ibid., 2:31 (Judith; pp. 131–132); 2:32 (Esther; pp. 133–134); and 2:37 (Susanna; pp. 141–142). See Catherine Brown Tkacz, "Susanna as a Type of Christ," *Studies in Iconography* 20 (1999), 101–153, for an excellent study of the tradition Christine drew from.
68. Ibid., 1:32 (p. 63); and 2:56 (pp. 174–175).
69. Ibid., 1:14 (p. 33).
70. Ibid., 1:14 (p. 34).
71. Ibid., 1:27 (p. 57).
72. Ibid., 1:37 (p. 70).
73. Ibid., 1:38 (p. 73).
74. Ibid., 1:37 (p. 70).
75. Ibid., 1:39 (p. 74).
76. This is not to imply that in the high Middle Ages reverence for tradition inhibited or obstructed progress, only that promotion of progress was more explicit in the late Middle Ages. See M. D. Chenu's classic article, "Tradition and Progress," in *Nature, Man, and Society in the Twelfth Century,* tr. and eds. Jerome Taylor and Lester K. Little (Chicago: University of Chicago Press, 1968), 310–330.
77. *City of Ladies,* 1:39 (p. 74).
78. *Body Politic,* xix.
79. For a thorough discussion of the basis of Christine's authority, see Patricia A. Phillippy, "Establishing Authority: Boccaccio's *De Claris Mulieribus* and Christine de Pizan's *Le livre de la cité des dames*" in Blumenfeld-Kosinski, *Selected Writings,* 329–361.
80. Ibid., xii–xiii, 29–41; and Willard, *Writings,* 90, 96–103.
81. Willard, *Writings,* 90.
82. Ibid., 97.
83. Ibid., 90.
84. *Teachings for Jean du Castel,* in ibid., 59.
85. *Treasury of the City,* 1:1, in ibid., 214.
86. *Book of Three Virtues,* 1:24, in ibid., 217–218.
87. Willard, *Christine de Pizan,* 175.
88. Willard, *Writings,* 254. See also C. C. Willard, "Christine de Pizan as Teacher," *Romance Language Annual* 3 (1991), 132–136.
89. Willard, *Christine de Pizan,* 177.
90. *Body Politic,* 1:1 (pp. 3–4).
91. Ibid., 1:12 (p. 21). Valerius Maximus' *Facta et dicta memorabilia* is her main source for exempla. See McLeod, *Order of the Rose,* 123.
92. *Body Politic,* 1:12 (p. 22).
93. Ibid., 3:11 (p. 109).
94. Kate Langdon Forhan, "Polycracy, Obligation, and Revolt: The Body Politic in John of Salisbury and Christine de Pizan," in *Politics, Gender,* 33–34.
95. Willard, *Christine de Pizan,* 177.
96. *Body Politic,* 1:1 (p. 4).
97. For discussion of this issue, see Forhan, "Polycracy," n.2.
98. Ibid., 33–34.
99. See George Duby, *The Three Orders* (Chicago: University of Chicago Press, 1980).

100. *Body Politic,* 3:1 (p. 90).
101. Ibid., 3:4 (p. 95).
102. Ibid., 3:6 (p. 99).
103. Forhan, "Polycracy," 44.
104. Willard in her 1984 biography calls Christine "consistently conservative" (*Christine de Pizan,* 182) in her discussion of *Body Politic.* In her 1994 *Writings* the label is omitted in her discussion of the same.
105. McLeod, *Order of the Rose,* 124–125.
106. *Body Politic,* 3:9 (pp. 105–106).
107. Ibid., 3:10 (pp. 107–109).
108. Ibid., 3:2 (pp. 92–93). In *Book of Peace,* 3:12, Christine repeats this sentiment: "Therefore, for the reasons I laid out in the previous chapter, common people should not hold public office. And if some want to say that the opposite is true because in some cities in Italy and elsewhere, such as Bologna and others, are governed by the common people, I respond that they are, but that I have heard nothing to indicate that they are well governed or that they are at peace for very long." Blumenfeld-Kosinski, *Selected Writings of Christine,* 242.
109. *Body Politic,* 3:2 (p. 92).
110. Ibid., 2:1 (p. 59). In her *Prayers to Our Lady* Willard notes that Christine interestingly "included prayers for all levels of French society": royal family, knights, clergy, bourgeoise, agricultural workers, wives, and maidens. Willard, *Writings,* 319; *Prayers* 6, 8, 17 (pp. 323–324).
111. *Book of Peace,* 1:3, in Willard, *Writings,* 310.
112. Ibid., 3:14, in ibid., 314.
113. *Letter concerning the Prison of Human Life,* in ibid., 339.
114. *Poem of Joan of Arc,* 6, lines 41, 44–45, and 10, lines 77–80, in ibid., 353–354.
115. Richards, "French Cultural Nationalism," 76.
116. Finke, *Writing in English,* 201.
117. Christine de Pizan, *The Book of Deeds of Arms and of Chivalry,* tr. Sumner Willard, ed. C. C. Willard (University Park, PA: State University of Pennsylvania, 1999), 1:1 (p. 12). The work freely borrows from Vegetius' *De re militari* and Honoré Bouvet's *Arbre des batailles.*
118. Finke, *Writing English,* 202.
119. Oxford Bodleian ms. Douce 180, H ii[v], cited in ibid., 210; and in McLeod, *Order of the Rose,* Appendix, 165. Finke also hints that Christine's encouragement of French nationalism might have seemed to be applicable to English nationalism.
120. Cited in McLeod, *Order of the Rose,* Appendix, 165.
121. R. E. Dupuy and N. H. Dupuy, *Encyclopedia of Military History from 1500* BC *to the Present* (New York: Harper & Row, 1986), 400.
122. Priscilla Bawcutt and Bridget Henisch, "Scots Abroad in the Fifteenth Century: The Princesses Margaret, Isabella and Eleanor" in *Women in Scotland, c. 1100–1750,* eds. Elizabeth Ewan and Maureen M. Meikle (East Linton, GB: Tuckwell Press, 1999), 46.
123. As, for example, seen in Heinrich Steinhöwel's dedication of his translation of Boccaccio's *Concerning Famous Women* to Eleanor. Ibid., 52.

124. Ibid. Bawcutt and Henisch also mention another fifteenth-century woman translator of French *chansons de geste,* Elizabeth von Nassau-Saarbrucken, and a noted patron of letters, Isabella of Scotland. They cite (n.43) Reinhard Hahn, " 'Von frantzosischen zungen in teütsch': das literarische Leben am Innsbrucker Hof des späteren 15. Jahrhunderts und der Prosaroman 'Pontus und Sidonia (A),' " (Frankfurt, 1990). Unseen.
125. *The Paston Letters,* ed. James Gairdner, intro. Roger Virgoc, repr. (Gloucester, GB: Alan Sutton, 1986).
126. Nadia Salamone, "Women and the making of the Italian literary canon," in *Women in the Italian Renaissance Culture and Society,* ed. Letizia Panizza (Oxford: Legenda, 2000), 500.
127. Kate Lowe, "History writing from within the convent in Cinquecento Italy: the nuns' version," in ibid., 105: "Studies of women's writing in early modern Italy are in their infancy, but even within this category of writing there are some discrepancies of interest. As far as female secular writing is concerned, there has been a concentration of work on poetry. . . . Religious writing by women . . . is normally treated separately," and "nearly everything remains to be done in relation to the study of women writing histories." Unfortunately, not much progress has been made, for Paul O. Kristeller made the same observation decades ago in "Learned Women of Early Modern Italy: Humanists and University Scholars" in *Beyond their Sex,* ed. Patricia Labalme (New York: New York University Press, 1980), 91.
128. Bibliographical references to the works of these two women are found in Kristeller, ibid., nn. 7, 8.
129. *Her Immaculate Hand: Selected Works By and About the Women Humanists of Quattrocento Italy,* eds. Margaret L. King and Albert Rabil (Binghampton, NY: MRTS, 1983), 28.
130. A text from the pen of each woman is included in ibid., 1:1–1:3 (pp. 33–41).
131. Margaret L. King, "Book-lined Cells: Women and Humanism in the Early Italian Renaissance," in Labalme, ed., *Beyond Sex,* 71. See *idem,* "The Religious Retreat of Isotta Nogarola," *Signs* 3:4 (1978), 807–822, for discussion of this work. I should note here that while I agree with much of what King writes, I am in basic disagreement with her thesis, that women scholars opted not to participate in intellectual matters but instead withdrew "to self-constructed prisons, lined with books—to book-lined cells, my symbol for the condition of the learned women of this age" ("Book-lined Cells," 74). Such interpretation poses a false either/or situation and rests on a faulty understanding of public and private domains. King is implying here that only intellectual developments that take place in the public, i.e., male, arena are significant. This actually reinforces any supposed patriarchal attempt to minimize or negate women's contributions by not acknowledging that intellectual activity can occur in domains traditionally labeled private. An excellent re-evaluation of the whole public versus private domain issue is found in Raymond Geuss, *Public Goods, Private Goods* (Princeton, NJ: Princeton University Press, 2001), especially 106: "There is no such thing as the public/private distinction, or, at any rate, it is a deep mistake to think that there is a single substantive distinction here that can be made to do any real philosophical work."
132. King, "Religious Retreat of Isotta," interprets this in negative terms chiefly on the basis that when Isotta retired she turned to religious intellectual endeavors and away from secular humanism. Research since King's 1978 argument has revealed how much religion was part of so-called secular humanism, and consequently Isotta's change in focus

should not be seen as that dramatic. Isotta's treatise on Eve proves this point. The topic there is superficially religious, yet it contains numerous characteristics consistent with secular humanism. Furthermore, King's thesis assumes that membership in a male humanist community is superior to any other kind of intellectual life, a vulnerable position at best. Finally, it also implies that the intellectual life was monolithic and that anyone not adhering to the "party line" did not merit to be called an intellectual.

133. *Letter of Costanza Varano to Isotta Nogarola,* in King and Rabil, *Her Immaculate Hands,* 56.
134. *Of Equal or Unequal Sin of Adam and Eve,* ibid., 59.
135. Peter Damian claimed to "spurn Plato" and "renounce the much-thumbed books" of the ancients in a letter in which he applied the full strength of his rhetorical abilities and philosophical knowledge. See Letter 28, *Peter Damian Letters,* tr. Owen Blum (Washington, DC: Catholic University of America Press, 1989), 255–89 (known as "Dominus vobiscum,") and Patricia Ranft, "The Role of the Eremitic Monk in the Development of the Medieval Intellectual Tradition," in *From Cloister to Classroom,* ed. E. Rozanne Elder (Kalamazoo, MI: Cistercian Publications, 1986). This "catch 22" is quite common in Western history.
136. *Of Equal or Unequal Sin,* 69.
137. *Memoirs of a Renaissance Pope: The Commentaries of Pius II,* tr. F. A. Gragg (New York, 1962), cited in *Her Immaculate Hands,* 47.
138. Elizabeth Gonzaga was immortalized in Castioglione's *The Courtier.*
139. Letter to Bernardino di Leno (Febuary 26, 1486), in Laura Cereta, *Collected Letters of a Renaissance Feminist,* tr. and ed. Diana Robin (Chicago: University of Chicago Press, 1997), 51.
140. Letter to Cardinal Ascanio Maria Sforza (March 1488), ibid., 39–40. She received more of a formal education that these statements here lead one to believe. She came from an educated family and was "entrusted to a woman highly esteemed" and educated in a convent for two years. Apparently she resented the fact that her family's educational level was not higher, because she also calls her childhood household "drier and less cultivated" than humanist Cassandra Fedele's. See letters in ibid., to Nazaria Olympica (November 5, 1486), 25–26; and to Bonifacio Bembo (August 22, 1487) 146.
141. Letter to Sforza, in Cereta, *Collected Letters,* 37–38.
142. Ibid., 45. This *viriditas,* greenness, is also used by Hildegard of Bingen. See above,
143. So Laura reports in Letter 18. Ottavio Rossi confirmed this in his 1620 history. See Albert Rabil, *Laura Cereta* (Binghamton, NY: MRTS, 1981), 29.
144. Cereta, *Collected Letters,* 151–152.
145. Letter to Clemenzo Longolio (Oct. 1, 1487), in Cereta, *Collected Letters,* 178.
146. Even though some may argue that Cassandra's career peaked in the Quattrocento, she lived well into the sixteenth century (1558) and thus is not included in this work.
147. Letter to Bembo, *Collected Letters,* 145.
148. Ibid., 146.
149. Letter to Agostino Emilio, *Collected Letters,* 100–101.
150. In all probability the addressee is fictional, a common ploy used by Laura.
151. Letter to Semproni, *Collected Letters,* 75.
152. Ibid., 73.
153. Ibid., 75.

154. Ibid., 76.
155. Ibid., 78.
156. Diana Robin, "Humanism and feminism in Laura Cereta's public letters," in *Women in Italian Renaissance Culture,* 379.
157. Letter to Bibolo, *Collected Letters,* 79.

Bibliography

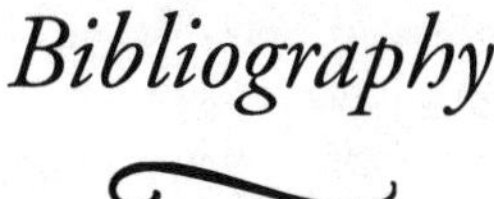

Abbreviations

AASS *Acta Sanctorum.* 70 vols. Paris, 1863–1940.
MGH *Monumenta Germaniae Historica.* Edited by G. H. Pertz *et al.* Hanover, 1826–1913.
PL *Patrologia curcus completus: Series Latina.* Edited by J.-P. Migne. Paris, 1844–1864.

Primary Sources

Aelred of Rievaulx. "A Rule for Life of a Recluse." In *The Works of Aelred of Rievaulx.* Vol. I: *Treatise and the Pastoral Prayer.* Spencer, MA: Cistercian Publications, 1971.

Anchoritic Spirituality: Ancrene Wisse and Associated Works. Translated by Anne Savage and Nicholas Watson. New York: Paulist Press, 1991.

Angela of Foligno. Complete Works. Translated by Paul Lachance. New York: Paulist Press, 1993.

Anglo-Norman Pseudo-Turpin Chronicle of William de Briane. Oxford: ANTS, 1973.

The Anglo-Saxon Missionaries in Germany. Translated by C. H. Talbot. London: Sheed & Ward, 1954.

Annales Camaldulenses ordinis sancti Benedicti. Edited by J. Mittarelli and A. Costadoni. 2 vols. Venice, 1756.

Aquinas, Thomas. *Summa Theologica.* Translated by Fathers of English Dominican Province. Reprint. Westminster, MD: Christian Classics, 1981.

Augustine. *Confessions.* Translated by R. S. Pine-Coffin. Reprint. Harmondsworth: Penguin Books, 1978.

——. *Eighty-Three Different Questions.* Translated by David Mosher. Washington, DC: Catholic University of America Press, 1982.

The Autobiography of Guibert, Abbot of Nogent-Sous-Coucy. Translated by C. C. Swinton Bland. New York: E. P. Dutton, n.d.

Barack, K.A. *Die Werke der Hrotsvitha.* Nürnberg: Bauer u. Raspe, 1858.

Bede. *A History of the English Church and People.* Translated by Leo Sherley-Price. Reprint, Harmondsworth: Penguin Books, 1986.

——. *Lives of the Abbots of Wearmouth and Jarrow.* In *The Age of Bede.* Translated by D. H. Farmer. Reprint. Harmondsworth: Penguin Books, 1985.

Bergman, Mary B. *Hrotsvithae Liber Tertius.* Covington, KY: Sisters of St. Benedict, 1943.

Birgitta of Sweden: Life and Selected Revelations. Edited by Marquerite T. Harris. Translated by Albert R. Kezel. New York: Paulist Press, 1990.

Birgitta of Sweden. *The Word of the Angel: Sermo Angelicus*. Translated by John E. Halborg. Toronto: Peregrina Publishing, 1996.

Bogin, Meg. *The Women Troubadours*. New York: W. W. Norton, 1980.

Bonaventure. *The Mind's Road to God*. Translated by George Boas. Indianapolis, IN: Bobbs-Merrill, 1953.

——. *Soul's Journey into God*. Translated by Evert Cousins. Ramsey, NJ: Paulist Press, 1978.

The Book of Margery Kempe. Translated by B. A. Windeatt. Reprint. London: Penguin Books, 1994.

Das Buch vom Espurgatoire S. Patrice der Marie de France und seine Quelle. Edited by Karl Warnke. Halle: Max Memeyer, 1938.

Catherine of Siena: The Dialogue. Translated by Suzanna Noffke. New York: Paulist Press, 1980.

Cazelles, Brigitte. *The Lady as Saint: A Collection of French Hagiographical Romances of the Thirteenth Century*. Philadelphia, PA: University of Pennsylvania Press, 1991.

Cereta, Laura. *Collected Letters of a Renaissance Feminist*. Translated and edited by Diana Robin. Chicago: University of Chicago Press, 1997.

Christine de Pizan. *The Book of the Body Politic*. Edited and translated by Kate Langdon Forhan. Cambridge: Cambridge University Press, 1994.

——. *The Book of the City of Ladies*. Translated by Rosalind Brown-Grant. London: Penguin Books, 1999.

——. *The Book of Deeds of Arms and of Chivalry*. Translated by Sumner Willard. Edited by C. C. Willard. University Park, PA: State University of Pennsylvania Press, 1999.

——. *Christine's Vision*. Translated by Glenda K. McLeod. New York: Garland, 1993.

Chronicle of Aetheweard. Edited by Alistair Campbell. London: T. Nelson, 1962.

Cicero, M. Tullius. *De amicitia*. London: W. Heinemann, 1927.

Condorcet, Marquis de. *Sketch for a Historical Picture of Progress of the Human Mind*. Edited by Stuart Hampshire. Translated by June Barracleugh. New York: Noonday Press, 1955.

Dhuoda: Manuel pour mon fils. Introduction, text critique, notes by Pierre Riché. Translated by Bernard de Vregille and Claude Mondésert. Paris: Editions du Cerf, 1975.

The Earliest Life of Gregory the Great. Translated by Bertram Colgrave. Lawrence, KS: University of Kansas Press, 1968.

Elizabeth of Schönau: The Complete Works. Translated by Anne L. Clark. Preface by Barbara Newman. New York: Paulist Press, 2000.

Encomium Emmae Reginae. Translated and edited by Alistair Campbell. London: Royal Historical Society, 1949.

Englelhardt, Christian M. *Herrad von Landsperg Abbtissin zu Hohenburg… und ihr Werk: Hortus deliciarum*. Stuttgart, 1818.

Francis and Clare. The Complete Works. Translated by Regis J. Armstrong and Ignatius C. Brady. New York: Paulist Press, 1982.

Geffrei Gaimar. *Estoire des Engleis*. Edited by A. Bell. Oxford: Blackwell, 1960.

Gertrude the Great. *The Life and Revelations of Saint Gertrude*. Reprint. Westminster, MD: Newman Press, 1952.

Gertrud the Great of Helfta: Spiritual Exercises. Translated by Gertrud Jaron Lewis and Jack Lewis. Kalamazoo, MI: Cistercian Publications, 1989.

Gertrude of Helfta: The Herald of Divine Love. Translated by Margaret Wakworth. New York: Paulist Press, 1993.

Guiges de Chastel. *Meditations of Guigo.* Translated by John Jolin. Milwaukee, WI: Marquette University Press, 1951.

Hadewijch: The Complete Works. Translated by M. Columba Hart. New York: Paulist Press, 1980.

The Handbook of Dhuoda: A Carolingian Woman's Counsel for Her Son. Translated with introduction by Carol Neel. Lincoln, NE: University of Nebraska Press, 1991.

Her Immaculate Hands: Selected Works By and About the Women Humanists of Quattrocento Italy. Edited by Margaret L. King and Albert Rabil. Binghamton, NY: MRTS, 1983.

Herrad of Landsberg: Hortus Deliciarum. Commentary by A. Straub and G. Keller. Edited and translated by Aristide D. Caratzas. New Rochelle, NY: Caratzas Brothers, 1977.

Herrad of Hohenbourg: Hortus deliciarum. Vol. 1: *Commentary.* Edited by Rosalie Green, Michael Evans, Christine Bischoff, and Michael Curschmann. Leiden: E. J. Brill, 1979.

Hildegard of Bingen. *Book of the Rewards of Life.* Translated by Bruce W. Hozeski. Oxford: Oxford University Press, 1994.

Hildegard of Bingen: Scivias. Translated by M. Columba Hart and Jane Bishop. Preface by Carolyn Walker Bynum. Introduction by Barbara Newman. New York: Paulist Press, 1990.

Hrotsvithae opera. Edited by Helen Homeyer. Munich: Schöningh, 1970.

The Humanism of Leonardo Bruni: Selected Texts. Translated by Gordon Griffiths, Jane Hankins, and David Thompson. Binghamton, NY: MRST, 1987.

Jean Gerson: Early Works. Translated by Brian P. McGuire. New York: Paulist Press, 1998.

Julian of Norwich: Showings. Translated by Edmund Colledge and James Walsh. New York: Paulist Press, 1978.

Julian of Norwich: A Book of Showings to the Anchoress Julian Norwich. Translated by Edmund Colledge and James Walsh. Toronto: Pontifical Institute of Medieval Studies, 1978.

Jutta and Hildegard: The Biographical Sources. Translated by Anna Silvas. University Park, PA: State University of Pennsylvania Press, 1998.

Könsgen, Ewald. *Epistolae duorum amantium: Briefe Abaelardus und Heloises?* Leiden: E. J. Brill, 1974.

Lanigan, John. *An Ecclesiastical History of Ireland . . . from Irish Annals and Other Authentic Document Still Existing in Manuscripts.* 2nd ed. Dublin: J. Cumming, 1829.

The Letters of Abeland and Heloise. Translated by Betty Radice. London: Penguin Books, 1974.

Letters of Catherine of Siena. Translated by Suzanna Noffke. Tempe, AZ: Arizona Center for Medieval and Renaissance Studios, 2000.

The Letters of St. Catherine of Siena. Translated by Suzanna Noffke. Binghamton, NY: Medieval and Renaissance Texts and Studios, 1988.

Letters of Hildegard of Bingen. Translated by Joseph L. Baird and Radd K. Ehrman. New York: Oxford University Press, 1998.

Lettres des Premiers Chartreux. Translated by a Carthusian. Paris: 1962.

The Life of Beatrice of Nazareth, 1200–1268. Translated by Roger De Ganck. Kalamazoo, MI: Cistercian Press, 1991.

Life of Blessed Juliana of Mont-Cornillon (1192–1258). Translated by Barbara Newman. Toronto: Peregrina Publishing, 1989.

The Life of St. Catherine by Clemence of Barking. Edited by William Macbain. Oxford: Basil Backwell [sic], 1964.

Lives of Edward the Confessor. Edited by Henry Luard. London: Longman, 1858.

Margaret Ebner: Major Works. Translated by Leonard P. Hindsley. Introduction by Leonard P. Hindsley and Margot Schmidt. New York: Paulist Press, 1993.

Marguerite Porete: The Mirror of Simple Souls. Translated and introduction by Ellen L. Babinsky. New York: Paulist Press, 1993.

Marie de France. *Fables.* Translated and edited by Harriet Spiegel. Toronto: University of Toronto Press, 1987.

——. *Saint Patrick's Purgatory.* Translated and introduction by Michael J. Curly. Binghamton, NY: MRTS, 1993.

——. *The Lais of Marie de France.* Translated by Robert Hanning and Joan Ferrante. New York: E.P. Dutton, 1978.

Mater Spiritualis: The Life of Adelheid of Vilich. Translated by Madelyn Bergen Dick. Toronto: Peregrina Publishing, 1994.

Mechthild of Madgeburg: The Flowing Light of the Godhead. Translated and introduction by Frank Tobin. Preface by Margot Schmidt. New York: Paulist Press, 1998.

Medieval Numerology. Edited by Robert L. Surles. New York: Garland, 1993.

Medieval Saints: A Reader. Translated William Forbes-Seith. Edited by Mary-Ann Stouck. Peterborough, CAN: Broadview Press, 1999.

Medieval Women Writers. Edited by Katherine M. Nelson. Athens, GA: University of Georgia Press, 1984.

Medieval Women's Visionary Literature. Edited by Elizabeth Alvilda Petroff. New York: Oxford University Press, 1986.

Mirandola, Pico della. *Oration on the Dignity of Man.* Translated by E. L. Forbes. In *The Renaissance Philosophy of Man.* Edited by E. Cassirer *et al.* Chicago: University of Chicago Press, 1948.

Newman, Barbara. *Symphonia: A Critical Edition of the "Symphonia armonie celestium revelationium."* Ithaca, NY: Cornell University Press, 1988.

Oeuvres complètes de Jean Gerson. 10 vols. Introduction, text and notes by M. Glorieux. Paris: Descleé & Cie, 1973.

Olai, Petrus. *Acta et processus canonizaciones beate Birgitta.* Edited by Isak Collijn. Uppsala: Almquist & Wiksells, 1924–1931.

Opus majus of Roger Bacon. 3 vols. Edited by John H. Bridges. London: Williams & Norgate, 1900.

The Orchard of Syon. Edited by Pyllis Hodgson and Gabriel Liegey. London: Oxford University Press, 1966.

The Paston Letters. Edited by James Gairdner. Introduction by Roger Virgoc. Reprint. Gloucester: Alan Sutton, 1986.

Peter Abelard's Ethics. Edited by David Luscombe. Oxford: Clarendon Press, 1971.

Peter Damian Letters. 4 vols. Translated by Owen J. Blum. Washington, DC: Catholic University of America Press, 1989–1998.

Petrarch, Letters of 1353. In *The Renaissance of Man.* Eds. E. Cassirer *et al.* Chicago: University of Chicago Press, 1948.

Philosophy in the Middle Ages. Edited by Arthur Hyman and James J. Walsh. 2nd ed. Indianapolis, IN: Hackett Publishing, 1986.

The Plays of Hrotsvit of Gandersheim. Translated by Katharina M. Wilson. New York: Garland, 1989.

The Plays of Roswitha. Translated by Christopher St. John (Christabel Marshall). London: Chatto & Windus, 1923.

Poetry of the Netherlands in Its European Context, 1170–1930. Edited by Theadoor Weevers. London: Athlone Press, 1960.

Prayer of Catherine of Siena. Translated by Suzanna Noffke. New York: Paulist Press, 1983.

Readings in Medieval History. Vol. 2: *The Later Middle Ages.* Edited by Patrick J. Geary. 2nd ed. Petersborough, CAN: Broadview Press, 1998.

Richard, Jean. *Saint Louis.* Cambridge: University of Cambridge Press, 1983.

Saint Bride and Her Book: Birgitta of Sweden's "Revelations". Translated by Julia Bolton Holloway. Cambridge: D. S. Brewer, 2000.

Saint Patrick's Purgatory, a Twelfth Century Tale of a Journey to the Other World. Translated by Jean-Michel Picard. Dublin: Four Court Press. 1985.

St. Anselm: Basic Writings. Translated by S. N. Deanne. 2nd ed. La Salle, IL: Open Court, 1968.

Sainted Women of the Dark Ages. Translated by JoAnn McNamara and John E. Halborg with E. Gorden Whately. Durham, NC: Duke University Press, 1992.

The Selected Writings of Christine de Pizan. Translated by Renate Blumenfeld-Kosinski and Kevin Brownlee. Edited by Renate Blumenfeld-Kosinski. New York: W.W. Norton, 1997.

Untold Sisters: Hispanic Nuns in their Own Works. Edited by Electra Arenal and Stacey Schlau. Translated by Amanda Powell. Albuquerque, NM: University of New Mexico, 1989.

Van Mielo, Jozef. *Hadewijch: Strophische Gedichten.* 2 vols. Antwerp: Standaard, 1942.

La vie seinte Audree. Edited by Ö. Södergaard. Uppsala: no publisher, 1955.

Vita S. Margaretae Scotorum Reginae. In *Symemis Dunelmensis Opera et Collectanea.* Edited by Hodgson Hinde. Durham: Andrews, 1868.

Wiegand, M. Gonsalva. "The Non-Dramatic Works of Hrotsvit." 14–16. In *Hrotswitha of Gandersheim: Her Life, Times, and Works, and a Comprehensive Bibliography.* Edited by Anne Lyon Haight. New York: Hroswitha Club, 1965.

William of Malmesbury. *De gestes pontificium Anglorum.* Edited by N. E. S. Hamilton. *Rolls Series.* 52 (1870).

——. *De gestes regum Anglorum.* Edited by William Stubbs. London: Eyre & Spottiswoode, 1887.

The Writings of Medieval Women: An Anthology. Translated and edited by Marcelle Thiebaux. 2nd ed. New York: Garland, 1994.

The Wohunge of ure Lauerd. Edited by W. Meredith Thompson. Oxford: EETS, 1958.

Woman Defamed and Woman Defended: An Anthology of Medieval Texts. Edited by Alcuin Blamires with Karen Pratt and C. H. Marx. Oxford: Clarendon Press, 1992.

The Works of Bonaventure. Translated by Jose de Vinck. Paterson, NJ: St. Anthony Guild Press, 1960.

Works of M. de Voltaire. 25 vols. Translated by T. Smollett *et al.* London: W. Johnson *et al.,* 1770. Microfilm: Woodbridge: CT Research Publications, 1985, Reel 1338 No. 04.

The Writings of Christine de Pizan. Edited by Charity Cannon Willard. New York: Persea Books, 1994.

Secondary Sources

Baker, Denise. *Julian of Norwich "Showings."* Princeton, NJ: Princeton University Press, 1994.

Bark, William. *Origins of the Medieval World.* Stanford, CA: Stanford University Press, 1958.

Baum, Gregory. *Laborem Exercens.* Toronto: University of Toronto Press, 1983.

Bauerschmidt, Frederick. *Julian of Norwich and the Mystical Body Politic of Christ.* Notre Dame, IN: University of Notre Dame Press, 1999.

Bawcutt, Priscilla and Bridget Henisch. "Scots Abroad in the Fifteenth Century: The Princesses Margaret, Isabella and Eleanor." In *Women in Scotland, c. 1100–1750.* Edited by Elizabeth Ewar and Maureen M. Meikle, 45–55. East Linton: Tuckwell, Press, 1999.

Beach, Alison. "The Female Scribes of Twelfth-Century Bavaria." PhD Diss. Columbia University, 1996.

Bell, Susan. "Christine le Pizan (1364–1430): Humanism and the Problem of a Studious Woman." *Feminist Studies* 3:3–4 (1976), 173–184.

Benton, John. "Fraud, Fiction, and Borrowing in the Correspondence of Abelard and Heloise." In *Pierre Abéland-Pierre le Venerable.* Edited by Réne Louis, Jean Jolinek, and Jean Châtillon, 469–512. Paris: Editions du Centre national de la recherche scientifique, 1975.

——. "A Reconsideration of the Authenticity of the Correspondence of Abelard and Heloise." In *Petrus Abaelardus (1079–1142).* Edited by Rudolph Thomas, Jean Jolivet, David Luscombe, and Lambertus M. de Rÿk. Trier: Paulines-Verlag, 1980.

——. "Trotula, Women's Problems, and the Professionalization of Medicine in the Middle Ages." *Bulletin of the History of Medicine* 59 (1985), 30–53.

Bériou, Nicole. "The Right of Women to Give Religious Instructions in the Thirteenth Century." In *Women Preachers and Prophets through Two Millennia of Christianity.* Edited by Beverly M. Kienzle and Pamela J. Walker, 134–145. Berkeley, CA: University of California Press, 1998.

Bischoff, Bernard. "Die Kölner Nonnenhandschriften und das Skriptorium von Chelles." *Mittelalterliche Studien* (1965), 17–35.

——. "Die liturgische Musik und das Bildungswesen im frühmittelalterlichen Stift Essen." *Annales des Historischen Vereins für den Niedershein* 157 (1955), 191–194.

——. *Katalog der festaendischen Handscriften des neuten Jahrunderts.* Vol. 1: *Aachen-Lambach.* Edited by Birgit Ebersperger. Washbaden: Harasswitz, 1998.

——. "Wer ist die Nonne von Heidenheim?" *Studien und Mitterlungen zur Geschichte des Benedicktinerordens und seiner Zweige* 49 (1931), 387–397.

Blashfield, E. *Portraits and Backgrounds.* New York: Charles Scriber's Son, 1917.

Bond, Gerald. *The Loving Subject: Desire, Eloquence and Power in Romanesque France.* Philadelphia, PA: University of Pennsylvania Press, 1995.

Bornstein, Diane. "Humanism in Christine de Pisan's *Livre du corps de policie.*" *Bonnes feuilles* 3 (Fall 1974), 100–115.

Bouchard, Constance. "Family Structure and Family Consciousness among the Aristocracy in the Ninth and Tenth Century." *Franciá* 14 (1986), 639–658.

Boutemy, André. "Recueil poétique du manuscript Aditional 24199 du British Museum." *Latomus* 2 (1938), 30–52.

Bouwsma, William J. "The Renaissance Discovery of Human Creativity." In *Humanity and Divinity in Renaissance and Reformation.* Edited by John W. O'Malley, Thomas M. Izbicki, and Gerald Christianson, 17–33. Leiden: E.J. Brill, 1993.

Bouyer, Louis. *Women Mystics.* San Francisco, CA: Ignatius Press, 1993.

Brown, Raymond E. "Hermeneutics." 71. In *Jerome Biblical Commentary.* Edited by Roland Murphy, Raymond E. Brown and Joseph Fitzmeyer. Englewood Cliffs, NJ: Prentice-Hall, 1968.

Bryant, Gwendolyn. "The French Heretic Beguine Marguerite Porete." In *Medieval Women Writers.* Edited by Katharina M. Wilson, 204–226. Athens, GA: University of Georgia Press, 1984.

Bumpass, Kathryn L. "A Musical Reading of Hildegard Responsory 'Spiritui Sancto.'" 155–73. In *Hildegard of Bingen: A Book of Essays.* Edited by Maud Burnett Mc Inerney. New York: St. Martin's Press, 2000.

Burkhardt, Jacob. *The Civilization of the Renaissance in Italy.* Translated by S. G. C. Middlemore. Revised and edited by Irene Gordon. New York: New American Library, 1960.

Butkovich, Anthony. *Revelations: Saint Birgitta of Sweden.* Los Angeles: Ecumenical Foundation of America, 1972.

Butler's Lives of the Saints. 4 vols. Edited by Herbert J. Thurston and Donald Attwater. Reprint. Wesminister, MD: Christian Classics, 1998.

Butler, Mary M. *Hrotsvitha: The Theatricality of Her Plays.* New York: Philosophical Library, 1960.

Bynum, Carolyn Walker. *Docere Verbo et Exemplo: An Aspect Twelfth Century Spirituality.* Missoula, MT: Harvard University Press, 1979.

——. *Fragmentation and Redemption: Essays on Gender and the Human Body in Medieval Religion.* New York: Zone Books, 1991.

——. *Holy Feast and Holy Fast.* Berkeley, CA: University of California Press, 1989.

——. *Jesus as Mother.* Berkeley, CA: University of California Press, 1982.

——. *The Resurrection of the Body in Western Christianity, 200–1336.* New York: Columbia University Press, 1995.

Cames, Gerárd. *Allégories et Symboles dans L'Hortus Deliciarum.* Leiden: E. J. Brill, 1971.

Camille, Michael. *Gothic Art: Glorious Visions.* Upper Saddle River, NJ: Prentice-Hall, 1996.

Carey, Hilary M. "Devout Literate Laypeople and the Pursuit of the Mixed Life in Later Medieval England." *Journal of Religious History* 14 (1987), 361–811.

Cavallini, Giuliana. *Catherine of Siena.* London: Geoffrey Chapman, 1998.

Chamberlain, Marcia. "Hildegard of Bingen's *Causes and Cures:* A Radical Feminist Response to the Doctor–Cook Binary." In *Hildegard of Bingen: A Book of Essays.* Edited by Maud Burnett McInerney, 53–73. New York: Garland, 1998.

Chenu, M.D. *Nature, Man, and Society in the Twelfth Century.* Translated by Jerome Taylor and Lester K. Little. Chicago: University of Chicago Press, 1968.

Chereso, C.J. "Exemplarism." *New Catholic Encyclopedia.* Washington, D.C. 1967.

Cheyette, Fredric L. "Women, Poets and Politics in Occitania." In *Aristocratic Women in Medieval France.* Edited by Theodore Evergates, 138–177. Philadelphia, PA: University of Pennsylvania Press, 1999.

Chibnall, Marjorie. *The Empress Matilda.* Oxford: Basil Blackwell, 1991.

Chukovsky, Kornei. *The Art of Translation: A High Art.* Translated and edited by Lauren Leighton. Knoxville, TN: University of Tennessee Press, 1984.

Clancy, M. T. *Abelard: A Medieval Life.* Oxford: Basil Blackwell, 1999.

Claytor, H. J. *From Script to Print.* Reprint. Folcraft, PA: Norwood Editions, 1977.

Claussen, M. A. "Fathers of Power and Mothers of Authority. Dhuoda and the *Libes Manualis.*" *French Historical Studies* 19:3 (Spring 1966), 785–809.

——. "God and Man in Dhuoda's *Liber Manualis.*" In *Women in the Church.* Edited by W. J. Shiels and Diana Wood, 43–52. Oxford: Basil Blackwell, 1990.

Clifford, Paula. *Marie de France: Lais.* London: Grant & Cutler, 1982.

Coffman, G. R. "A New Approach to Medieval Latin Drama." *Modern Philology* 22 (1925), 23.

Cogan, Robert, "Hildegard's Fractal Antiphon." *Sonus* 11:1 (1990), 1–19.

Coleman, Janet. *Piers Plowman and the Moderni.* Rome: Edizioni de Storia e Letteratura, 1981.

Colish, Marcia L. *Medieval Foundations of the Western Intellectual Tradition 400–1400.* New Haven, CT: Yale University Press 1997.

——. *The Mirror of Language: A Study in the Medieval Theory of Knowledge.* Revised ed. Lincoln, NE: University of Nebraska Press, 1983.

Collins, Fletcher. *The Production of Medieval Church Music-Drama.* Charlottesville, VA: University of Virginia Press, 1972.

Copleston, Frederick. *A History of Philosophy.* 7 vols. Reprint. Garden City, NY: Image Books, 1963.

Corbet, Patrick. *Les Saints Ottoniens.* Sigmaringen; Jan Thorbecke, 1986.

Costa, Milagros Ortega. "Spanish Women in the Reformation." In *Women in Reformation and Counter Reformation.* Edited by Sherrin Marshall, 89–119. Bloomington, IN: Indiana University Press, 1989.

Coulter, Cornelia C. "The 'Terentian' Comedies of a Tenth-Century Nun." *The Classical Journal* 24 (1929), 515–529.

Cricco, Patricia. "Monasticism and Its Role as a Liminal Community in Medieval Society." PhD Diss. West Virginia University, 1981.

Crombie, A. C. *Robert Grosseteste and the Origins of Experimental Science.* Oxford: Clarendon Press, 1953.

The Cultural Context of Medieval Learning. Edited by John Murdock and Edith Sylla. Dordrecht: Reidel, 1975.

Curtis, Ernest R. *European Literature and the Later Middle Ages.* Translated by W. R. Trask. Reprint. Princeton, NJ: Princeton University Press, 1990.

Deanesly, Margaret. "Vernacular Books in England in the Fourteenth and Fifteenth Centuries." *Modern Language Review* 15 (1920), 349–358.

Delorno, Carlo. "Predicazine volgare e volgarizzamente." *Melanges de l'Ecole Françoise de Rome, Moyen Âge, Temps Modernes* 89 (1977), 679–689.

De Luca, Kenneth. "Hrotsvit's 'Imitation' of Terence." *Classical Folio* 28 (1974), 89–102.

Dronke, Peter. *Poetic Individuality in the Middle Ages.* Oxford: Clarendon Press, 1970.

——. "Problemata Hildegardiana." *Mittellateinisches Jahrbuch* 16 (1981), 97–131.

——. *Women Writers of the Middle Ages.* Cambridge: Cambridge University Press, 1984.

Duby, George. *The Three Orders.* Chicago: University of Chicago Press, 1980.

Duffy, Eamon. *The Stripping of the Altars.* New Haven, CT: Yale University Press, 1992.

Duhem, Pierre. *Les origins de la statique.* 2 vols. Paris: Hermann, 1905–1906.

Duprey, R. E. and N. H. Duprey. *Encyclopedia of Military History from 1500* BC *to the Present.* New York: Harper & Row, 1986.

Dworkin, Andrea. *Our Blood: Prophecies and Discourses on Sexual Politics.* New York: Harper & Row, 1976.

Dyer, Christopher. *Standards of Living in the Later Middle Ages.* Cambridge: Cambridge University Press, 1989.

Eckenstein, Lina. *Women under Monasticism.* Cambridge: At the University Press, 1896.

Emerson, Jan S. "A Poetry of Science: Relating Body and Soul in the *Scivias.*" In *Hildegard of Bingen: A Book of Essays.* Edited by Maud Burnett McInverney, 77–101. New York: Garland, 1998.

Emmanuel, M. "Saint Walburga Benedictine Abbess and Missionary (710–779)." *Word and Spirit* 11 (1989), 50–59.

Escot, Pozzi. "Gothic Cathedral and the Hidden Geometry of St. Hildegard." *Sonus* 5:1 (Fall 1984), 14–31.

Evasdaughter, Elizabeth N. "Julian of Norwich." In *History of Women Philosophers.* 4 vols. Edited by Mary Ellen Waithe, 2:191–222. Dordrecht: Kluwer Academic Publishers, 1989.

Evergates, Theodore. "Aristocratic Women in the County of Champagne." In *Aristocratic Women in Medieval France.* Edited by Theodore Evergates, 74–110. Philadelphia, PA: University of Pennsylvania Press, 1999.

Ferrante, Joan. "Notes toward the Study of a Female Rhetoric in the Trobairitz." In *The Voice of the Trobairitz.* Edited by William Paden, 63–72. Philadelphia, PA: University of Pennsylvania Press, 1989.

——. *The Glory of Her Sex.* Bloomington, IN: Indiana University Park, 1997.

Finke, Laurie A. *Women's Writing in English: Medieval England.* London: Longman, 1999.

Flanagan, Sabrina. *Hildegard of Bingen, 1098–1179: A Visionary Life.* London: Routledge, 1989.

Forham, Kate Langdon. "Polycracy, Obligation, and Revolt: The Body Politic in John of Salisbury and Christine de Pizan." In *Politics, Gender and Genre: The Political Thought of Christine de Pizan.* Edited by Margaret Brabant, 33–52. Boulder, CO: Westview Press, 1992.

Frankforter, A. Daniel. "Hrotswitha of Gandersheim and the Destiny of Women." *The Historian* 41:2 (February 1979), 295–314.

French, Roger and Andrew Cunnigham. *Before Science: The Invention of the Friars' Natural Philosophy.* Brookfield, VT: Scolar Press, 1996.

Frugoni, Chiara. "Female Mystics, Visions, and Iconography." In *Women and Religion in Medieval and Renaissance Italy.* Edited by Daniel Bornstein and Roberto Rusconi. Translated by Margery J. Schneider, 130–164. Chicago: University of Chicago Press, 1996.

Geuss, Raymond. *Public Goods, Private Goods.* Princeton, NJ: Princeton University Press, 2001.

Gibson, Joan. "Mechthild of Magdeburg." In *History of Women Philosophers.* 4 vols. Edited by Mary Ellen Waithe, 2:115–140. Dordrecht: Kluwer Academic Publishers, 1989.

Gill, Katherine. "Women and the Production of Religious Literature in the Vernacular, 1300–1500." In *Creative Women in Medieval and Early Modern Italy.* Edited by E. Ann Matter and John Coakley, 64–104. Philadelphia, PA: University of Pennsylvania Press, 1994.

Gilson, Etienne. *Héloise et Abélard.* London: Hollis & Carter, 1953.

——. *History of Christian Philosophy in the Middle Ages.* New York: Random House, 1955.

Godfrey, John. "The Double Monastery in Early English History." *The Ampleforth Journal* 79 (1974), 19–32.

Gold, Barbara K. "Hrotswitha Writes Herself: *Clamor Validius Gandershemensi.*" In *Sex and Gender in Medieval and Renaissance Texts: The Latin Tradition.* Edited by Barbara K. Gold, Paul A. Miller and Charles Platter, 41–70. Albany: SUNY Press, 1997.

Gössmann, Elizabeth. "Hildegard of Bingen." In *History of Women Philosophers.* 4 vols. Edited by Mary Ellen Waithe, 2:27–65. Dordrecht: Kluwer Academic Publishers, 1989.

Grant, E. *Foundations of Modern Science in the Middle Ages.* Cambridge: Cambridge University Press, 1996.

Groeteken, Albert. *Die heige Adelheid von Vilich und ihre Familie.* Kevelaer: Verlag Butzon und Bercker, 1937.

Grundmann, Herbert. "Die Frauen und die Literatur im Mittelalten." *Archiv für Kulturgeschichte* 26:2 (1936), 129–161.

——. "Litteratus-illiteratus: Der Wandel einer Bildungsnorm vom Altertum zum Mittelalter." *Archiv für Kulturgeschichte* 40 (1958), 1–65.

Guarnieri, Romana, editor. "Il movemento del Libero Spirito." *Archivo Italiano per la storia della pretà* 4 (1965), 351–708.

Hanawalt, Barbara. *The Ties that Bound.* Oxford: Oxford University Press, 1986.

Harbison, Craig. *The Mirror of the Artist: Northern Renaissance Art in Its Historical Context.* New York: Harry N. Abrams, 1995.

——. "Visions and meditations in early Flemish painting." *Simiolus* 15 (1985), 87–118.

Hardison, O.B., Jr. *Christian Rite and Christian Drama in the Middle Ages.* Baltimore, MD: Johns Hopkins University Press, 1965.

Haskins, Charles Homer. *The Renaissance of the Twelfth Century.* Cambridge, MA: Harvard University Press, 1927.

Head, Thomas. "Hrotsvit's *Primordia* and the Historical Traditions of Monastic Communities." In *Hrotsvit of Gandersheim: Rara Avis in Saxony?* Edited by Katharina M. Wilson, 143–155. Ann Arbor, MI: Marc, 1987.

Heer, Friedrich. *The Medieval World.* Translated by Janet Sondheimer. Reprint. New York: New American Library, 1962.

Hollister, C. Warren. *The Making of England.* 6th ed. Lexington, MA: D. C. Heath, 1992.

Hollywood, Amy. *The Soul as Virgin Wife.* Notre Dame, IN: University of Notre Dame Press, 1995.

Hozeski, Bruce W. "Hildegard of Bingen's *Ordo Virtutum:* The Earliest Discovered Liturgical Morality Play." *American Benedictine Review* 26:3 (September 1975), 251–259.

——. "Ordo Virtutum: Hildegard of Bingen's Liturgical Morality Play." *Annuale Medievale* 13 (1972), 45–69.

Hudson, William. "Hrostsvitha of Gandersheim." *English Historical Review* 3 (1888), 431–457.

The Idea of the Vernacular: An Anthology of Middle English Literary Theory, 1280–1520. Edited by Jocelyn Wogan-Browne, Nicholas Watson, Andrew Taylor and Ruth Evans. University Park, PA: Pennsylvania State University Press, 1999.

Illanes, J. L. *On the Theology of Work.* Translated by Michael Adams. Dublin: Four Court Press, 1982.

Jaeger, C. Stephen. *The Envy of Angels.* Philadelphia, PA: University of Pennsylvania Press, 1994.

Janssens, Bernadette. "L'influence de Prudence sur le *Liber Manualis* de Dhuoda." *Studia patristica* 17:3 (1982), 1366–1373.

Jeanroy, A. "Boccace et Christine de Pizan: le 'De Claris Mulieribus' Principale Source du 'Livre de la cité des Dames.' " *Romania* 48 (1922), 92–105.

Jeskalían, Barbara. "Hildegard of Bingen: Her Times and Music." *Anima* 10:1 (Fall 1983), 7–13.

John, Helen J. "Hildegard of Bingen: A New Twelfth-Century Woman Philosopher?" In *Hypatia's Daughters.* Edited by Linda L. McAlister, 16–24. Bloomington, IN: Indiana University Press, 1996.

Kaye, Joel. "The Impact of Money on the Development of Fourteenth-Century Scientific Thought." *Journal of Medieval History* 14 (1988), 251–270.

Kerby-Fulton, Kathryn. "Prophecy and Suspicion: Closet Radicalism, Reformist Politics, and the Vogue for Hildegardiana in Ricardian England." *Speculum* 75:2 (April 2000), 318–341.

——. "Self-Image and the Visionary Role in Two Letters from the Correspondence of Elizabeth of Schönau and Hildegard of Bingen." *Vox Benedictina* 2–3 (1985), 204–223.

Kitchell, Kenneth and Irven Resnick. "Hildegard as a Medieval 'Zoologist': The Animals of the *Physica.*" In *Hildegard of Bingen: A Book of Essays.* Edited by Maud Burnett McInerney, 25–52. New York: Garland, 1998.

King, Margaret L. "Book-lined Cells: Women and Humanism in the Early Italian Renaissance." In *Beyond their Sex.* Edited by Patricia Labalme, 66–90. New York: New York University Press, 1980.

——. "The Religious Retreat of Isotta Nogarola." *Signs* 3:4 (1978), 807–822.

Knowles, David and D. Obolensky. *The Christian Centuries,* vol. 2: *The Middle Ages.* New York: Paulist Press, 1983.

Koenigsberger, Dorothy. *Renaissance Man and Creative Thinking.* Atlantic Highlands, NJ: Humanities Press, 1979.

Kratz, Dennis. "The Nun's Epic: Hrotswitha on Christian Humanism." In *Wege de Worte.* Edited by Donald E. Riechel, 132–142. Cologne: Böhlau, 1978.

Kristeller, Paul O. "Learned Women of Early Modern Italy: Humanists and University Scholars." In *Beyond their Sex.* Edited by Patricia Labalme, 91–116. New York: New York University Press, 1980.

Lacy, Terry G. *Rings of Seasons: Iceland—Its Culture and History.* Ann Arbor, MI: University of Michigan Press, 1998.

Laistner, M. T. W. *Thought and Letters in Western Europe A.D. 500 to 900.* 2nd ed. Ithaca, NY: Cornell University Press, 1976.

La Prete, Kimberly. "Adela of Blois: Familial Alliances and Female Lordship." In *Aristocratic Women in Medieval France.* Edited by Theodore Evergates, 7–43. Philadelphia, PA: University of Pennsylvania Press, 1999.

Leclercq, Jean. *Love of Learning and the Desire for God.* Translated by Catharine Misrahi. 2nd rev. ed. New York: Fordham University Press, 1974.

Leclève, L. *Sainte Angéle de Foligno.* Paris: Libraire Plon, 1936.

Legge, M. Dominica. *Anglo-Norman Literature and Its Background.* Oxford: Clarenden Press, 1963.

Le Goff, Jacques. *The Birth of Purgatory*. Translated by Arthur Goldhammer. Chicago: University of Chicago Press, 1984.

Lejeune, R. "Rôle lettéraire d' Aliénor d' Aquitaine et de sa famille." *Cultura Neolatina* 14 (1954), 5–57.

Lerner, Robert E. *Heresy of the Free Spirit in the Late Middle Ages.* Berkeley, CA: University of California Press, 1972.

Leyser, Karl. *Rule and Conflict in an Early Medieval Society.* Bloomington, IN: Indiana University Press, 1979.

Lichtmann, Maria. "Marguerite Porete and Meister Eckhart." In *Meister Eckhart and the Beguine Mystics.* Edited by Bernard McGinn, 65–86. New York: Continuum, 1994.

Lindberg, David C. *The Beginnings of Western Science.* Chicago: University of Chicago Press, 1992.

——. "Medieval Science and its Religious Context." *Osiris* 10 (1995), 61–79.

Livingstone, Amy. "Aristocratic Women in the Chartrain." In *Aristocratic Women in Medieval France.* Edited by Theodore Evergates, 44–73. Philadelphia, PA: University of Pennsylvania Press, 1999.

Lowe, Kate. "History writing from within the convent in Cinquecento Italy: the nuns' version." In *Women in the Italian Renaissance Culture and Society.* Edited by Letizia Panizza, 105–121. Oxford: Legenda, 2000.

Luongo, Francis. "The Politics of Marginality: Catherine of Siena in the War of Eight Saints (1374–1378)." PhD Diss., University of Notre Dame, 1997.

Lynch, William F. *Images of Faith: An Exploration of the Ironic Imagination.* Notre Dame, IN: University of Notre Dame Press, 1973.

Macquarrie, John. *Principles of Christian Theology.* 2nd ed. New York: Charles Scribner, 1977.

McBain, William. "The Literacy Apprenticeship of Clemence of Barking." *AUMLA: Journal of the Australasian Universities Language and Literature Association* 9 (November 1958), 3–22.

McCaslin, Susan. "Vision and Revision in *Four Quartets:* T.S. Eliot and Julian of Norwich." *Mystics Quarterly* 12 (December 1986), 171–178.

McEntire, Sandra J. "The Likeness of God and the Restoration of Humanity in Julian of Norwich's *Showings.*" In *Julian of Norwich: A Book of Essays.* Edited by Sandra J. McEntire, 3–33. New York: Garland, 1998.

McKitterick, Rosamond. *Books, Scribes and Learning in the Frankish Kingdoms, 6th–9th Centuries.* Brookfield, VT: Variorum, 1994.

——. *The Carolingians and the Written Word.* Cambridge: Cambridge University Press, 1989.

——. "Women in the Ottonian Church: An Iconographic Perspective." In *Women in the Church.* Edited by W. J. Shiels and Diana Wood, 79–100. Oxford: Basil Blackwell, 1990.

McLeod, Enid. *The Order of the Rose: The Life and Ideas of Christine de Pizan.* London: Chatto & Windus, 1976.

McLeod, Glenda. *Virtue and Venom.* Ann Arbor, MI: University of Michigan Press, 1991.

McNamara, Jo Ann. *Sisters in Arms.* Cambridge, MA: Harvard University Press, 1996.

McNamer, Elizabeth Mary. *The Education of Heloise.* Lewiston, NY: Edwin Mellen Press, 1991.

Marchand, James. "The Frankish Mother: Dhuoda." In *Medieval Women Writers.* Edited by Katharina M. Wilson, 1–29. Athens, GA: University of Georgia Press, 1984.

Marenbon, John. "Authenticity Revisited." In *Listening to Heloise.* Edited by Bonnie Wheeler, 19–33. New York: St. Martin's Press, 2000.

Marías, Julián. *The History of Philosophy.* 23rd ed. New York: Dover Publications, 1967.

Matter, E. Ann. "Exegesis and Christian Education: The Carolingian Model." In *Schools of Thought in the Christian Tradition.* Edited by Patrick Henry, 90–155. Philadelphia, PA: Fortress Press, 1984.

Mayeski, Marie Anne. *Dhuoda: Ninth Century Mother and Theologian.* Scranton, PA: University of Scranton Press, 1995.

Meany, Mary. "Angela of Foligno: A Eucharistic Model of Lay Sanctity." In *Lay Sanctity, Medieval and Modern.* Edited by Ann W. Astell, 61–75. Notre Dame, IN: University of Notre Dame Press, 2000.

Medieval Netherlands Religious Literature. Translated and introduction by E. Colledge. New York: London House & Maxwell, 1965.

Meister Eckhart and the Beguine Mystics. Edited by Bernard McGinn. New York: Continuum, 1994.

Mews, Constant J. *The Lost Love Letters of Heloise and Abeland: Perceptions of Dialogue in Twelfth Century France.* New York: St. Martin's Press, 1999.

Meyer, M. A. "Women and the Twelfth-Century English Monastic Reform." *Revue bénédictine* 87 (1977), 34–61.

Mickel, Emanuel J. *Marie de France.* New York: Twayne Publishers, 1974.

Milbank, John. *Theology and Social Theory.* Oxford: Basil Blackwell, 1990.

Millett, Bella. "Women in No Man's Land: English recluses and the development of vernacular literature in the twelfth and thirteenth centuries." In *Women and Literature in Britain, 1150–1500.* Edited by Carol Meale, 86–103. Cambridge: Cambridge University Press, 1993.

Minnis, Alastair J. *Medieval Theory of Authorship.* 2nd ed. Aldershot: Wildwood, 1988.

Moody, Helen. *The Debate of the Rose.* Berkeley, CA: University of California Press, 1981.

Mooney, Catherine M. "The Authorial Role of Brother A. in the Composition of Angela Foligno's *Revelations.*" In *Creative Women in Medieval and Early Modern Italy.* Edited by E. Ann Matter and John Coakley, 34–63. Philadelphia, PA: University of Pennsylvania Press, 1994.

Morris, Bridget. *St. Birgitta of Sweden.* Woodbridge: Boydell Press, 1999.

Morris, Colin. *The Discovery of the Individual.* London: Camelot Press, 1972.

Moulinier, Lawrence. "L'abbesse et les poissons: un aspect de la zoologie de Hildegarde de Bingen." 461–472. In *Exploitation des animaux sauvage à travers de temps.* Juan-les-Pin: APDCA, 1993.

Muckle, Joseph T, "The Personal Letters between Abeland and Heloise." *Medieval Studies* 15 (1953), 47–94.

Muessig, Carolyn. "Prophecy and Song: Teaching and Preaching by Medieval Women." In *Women Preachers and Prophets through Two Millennia of Christianity.* Edited by Beverly M. Kienzle and Pamela J. Walker, 146–158. Berkeley, CA: University of California Press, 1998.

Nelson, Janet. "Perceptions du pouvoir chez les historiennes de Haut Moyen Age." In *La Femme au Moyen Age*. Edited M. Rouche and Jean Heuclin, 77–85. Paris: Diffusion, J. Touzot, 1990.

——. "Women and the Word in the Earlier Middle Ages." In *Women in the Church*. Edited by W. J. Shiels and Diana Wood, 53–78. Oxford: Basil Blackwell, 1990.

Newell, John. "Education and Classical Culture in the Tenth Century: Age of Iron of Revival of Learning?" In *Hrotsvit of Gandersheim: Rara Avis in Saxonia?* Edited by Katharina M. Wilson, 127–141. Ann Arbor, MI: Marc, 1987.

Newman, Barbara. *Sister of Wisdom*. Berkeley, CA: University of California Press, 1989.

Nye, Andrea. "A Woman's Thought or a Man's Discipline? The Letters of Abelard and Heloise." *Hypatia* 7:3 (Summer 1992), 25–47.

Nicholas, Karen S. "Countesses as Rulers in Flanders." In *Aristocratic Women in Medieval France*. Edited by Theodore Evergates, 111–137. Philadelphia, PA: University of Pennsylvania Press, 1999.

Niebuhr, Richard. *Christ and Culture*. New York: Harper Torch Books, 1951.

Nuth, Joan M. *Wisdom's Daughter: The Theology of Julian of Norwich*. New York: Crossroad, 1991.

Olsen, Glenn W. "One Heart and One Soul (Acts 4:32 and 34) in Dhuoda's 'Manual.'" *Church History* 61:1 (March 1992), 23–33.

Paepe, Norbert de. *Hadewijch: Strofische Gedichten*. Ghent: Konenklijke Vlaamse Academie, 1967.

Paterson, Linda M. *Troubadours and Eloquence*. Oxford: Clarendon Press, 1975.

Pepler, Conrad. *The English Religious Heritage*. London: Blackfriars, 1958.

Petroff, Elizabeth Alvilda. *Body and Soul*. New York: Oxford University Press, 1994.

Pfau, Marianne. "Hildegard von Bingen's *Symphonie armonie celestium revelationum:* Analysis of Musical Process, Modality, and Text–Music Relations." PhD Diss., State University of New York at Stoney Brook, 1990.

Phillippy, Patricia A. "Establishing Authority: Boccaccio's *De Claris Mulieribus* and Christine de Pizan's *Le livre de la cité des dames*." In *The Selected Writings of Christine de Pizan*. Translated by Renate Blumenfeld-Kosinski and Kevin Brownlee. Edited by Renate Blumenfeld-Kosinski, 329–361. New York: W. W. Norton, 1997.

Poirion, Daniel. *Littérature François*. Paris: Arthaud, 1971.

Porion, Jean-Baptiste. "Hadewijch, mystique flamande et poetesse, 13e siècle." In *Dictionnaire de spiritualité*. Edited by Marcel Viller, 13–23. Paris: G. Beauchesne et ses fils, 1937.

Portmann, M. L. and A. Odermatt. *Wörterbuch dcer unbekannten Sprache (Lingus ignota)*. Basel: Basler Hildegard-Gesellschaft, 1986.

Potkay, Monica Brzezinski and Regula Meyer Evitt. *Minding the Body: Women and Literature in the Middle Ages, 800–1500*. London: Twayne Publishers, 1997.

Potter, Robert A. "The Idea of a Morality Play," *Research Opportunities in Renaissance Drama* 13 (1970), 239–247.

——. "Image of the Human Predicament: Some Ancient and Modern Visualizations of the Morality Play." *Research Opportunities in Renaissance Drama* 14 (1971), 249–258.

Rabil, Albert. *Laura Cereta*. Binghamton, NY: MRTS, 1981.

Ranft, Patricia. "The Concept of Witness in the Christian Tradition from Its Origin to Its Institutionalization." *Revue bénédictine* 102:1–2 (1992), 9–23.

——. "Hugh Latimer and Witness." *Sixteenth Century Journal* 11 (1979), 21–34.

——. "A Key to Counter Reformation Activism: The Confessor-Spiritual Director." *Journal of Feminist Studies in Religion* 10:2 (1994), 7–26.

——. "Maintenance and Transformation of Society: Cluniac Eschatology." *Journal of Religious History* 17 (1987), 246–255.

——. "The Role of the Eremitic Monk in the Development of the Medieval Intellectual Tradition." In *From Cloister to Classroom.* Edited by E. Rozanne Elder, 80–95. Kalamazoo, MI: Cistercian Publications, 1986.

——. "Witness and the Eleventh Century Monastic Renewal." *Journal of Religious History* 16:4 (1991), 361–373.

——. *A Woman's Way: The Forgotten History of Women's Spiritual Direction.* New York: Palgrave, 2000.

——. *Women and the Religious Life in Premodern Europe.* New York: St. Martin's Press, 1996.

——. *Women and Spiritual Equality in Christian Tradition.* New York: St. Martin's Press, 1998.

Ratzinger, Joseph. "The relevance of Saint Bridget of Sweden for our times." In *Santa Brigida Profeta dei Tempi Nuovie: Proceedings of the International Study Meeting Rome Oct. 3–7, 1991.* 82–120. Rome: Casa Generalizea Suore Santa Brigida, 1996.

Reno, Christian M. "Christine de Pisan's Use of the *Golden Legend* in the *Cité des dames.*" *Bonnes feuilles* 3 (Fall 1974), 89–99.

Reynolds, Roger. "*Virgins subintroductae* in Celtic Christianity." *Harvard Theological Review* 61 (1968), 547–566.

Riché, Pierre. "Les bibliothèques de trois aristocrates laics carolingiens." *Moyen Ages* 69 (1963), 87–104.

——. *Education and Culture in the Barbarian West from the Sixth through the Eighth Century.* Translated by John J. Contreni. Columbia, SC: University of South Carolina Press, 1976.

Richards, Earl Jeffrey. "French Cultural Nationalism and Christian Universalism in the Works of Christine de Pizan." In *Politics, Gender, and Genre: The Political Thought of Christine de Pizan.* Edited by Margaret Brabant, 75–94. Boulder, CO: Westview Press, 1992.

Richter, Michael. *Sprache und Gesellschaft in Mittelalter.* Stuttgart: Anton Hiersemann, 1979.

Rieger, Dietmar. "Die französische Dichterin im Mittelalter: Marie de France, die 'trobairitz' Christine de Pisan." In *Die Französische Autorin vom Mittelalter bis zun Gegenwart.* Edited by Renate Braden and Dietar Fricke, 29–48. Wiesbaden: Akademische Verlagsgesellschaft Athenaion, 1979.

Ringbom, Sixten. "Devotional Images and Imaginative Devotions." *Gazette de beaux-arts,* ser., 6:73 (1969), 159–170.

Robin, Diana. "Humanism and feminism in Laura Cereta's public letters." In *Women in Italian Renaissance Culture and Society.* Edited by Letizia Panizza, 368–384. Oxford: Legenda, 2000.

Rubin, Miri. *Corpus Christi.* Cambridge: Cambridge University Press, 1991.

Ruys, Junita Feros. "*Quae Maternae Immemor Naturae:* The Rhetorical Struggle over the Meaning of Motherhood in the Writings of Heloise and Abelard." In *Listening to Heloise.* Edited by Bonnie Wheeler, 323–339. New York: St. Martin's Press, 2000.

Ryan, John. *Irish Monasticism: Origins and Development.* Reprint, Dublin: Irish Academic Press, 1986.

Salamone, Nadia. "Women and the making of the Italian literacy canon." In *Women in the Italian Renaissance Culture and Society.* Edited by Letizia Panizza, 498–512. Oxford: Legenda, 2000.

Schipperges, Heinrich. *Hildegard of Bingen: Healing and the Nature of the Cosmos.* Translated by J. Broadwin. Princeton, NJ: Markus Weiner, 1997.

Schmeidler, Bernard. "Der Brifwechsel zwischen Abälard und Heloise eine Fälschung?" *Archivum für Kulturgeschichte* 11 (1913), 1–30.

Schmidt, Margot. "An Example of Spiritual Friendship: The Correspondence between Heinrich of Nördlingen and Margaretha Ebner." In *Maps of Flesh and Light.* Edited by Ulrike Wiethaus, 74–92. Syracuse, NY: Syracuse University Press, 1993.

Schnapp, Jeffrey. "Virgin Words: Hildegard of Bingen's *Lingus Ignota* and the Development of Imaginary Language Ancient to Modern." *Exemplaria* 3:2 (1991), 267–298.

Scott, Karen. "St. Catherine of Siena, 'Apostola.'" *Church History* 61:1 (March 1992), 34–46.

Simson, Otto von. *The Gothic Cathedral.* Princeton, NJ: Princeton University Press, 1956.

Sims-Williams, P. *Religion and Literature in Western England, 600–800.* Cambridge: Cambridge University Press, 1990.

Smalley, Beryl. *The Study of the Bible in the Middle Ages.* 3rd ed. Oxford: Basil Blackwell, 1983.

Southern, R. W. *The Making of the Middle Ages.* New Haven, CT: Yale University Press, 1978.

Spiegel, Gabrielle. *Romancing the Past: The Rise of Vernacular Prose Historiography in Thirteenth Century France.* Berkeley, CA: University of California Press, 1993.

Sprague, Rosemary. "Hrotswitha—Tenth Century Margaret Webster." *Theatre Annual* 13 (1955), 16–30.

Städtler, Katharina. "The *Sirventes* by Gormonda de Monpeslier." In *The Voice of the Trobairitz.* Edited by William Paden, 129–155, Philadelphia, PA: University of Pennsylvania Press, 1989.

Staley, Lynn and David Aers. *The Powers of the Holy.* University Park, PA: University of Pennsylvania Press, 1996.

Stock, Brian. *The Implications of Literacy: Written Language and Models of Interpretation in the Eleventh and Twelfth Centuries.* Princeton, NJ: Princeton University Press, 1983.

——. *Listening for the Text.* Baltimore, MD: Johns Hopkins University Press, 1990.

Stofferahn, Steven A. "Changing views of Carolingian women's literacy culture: the evidence from Essen." *Early Medieval Europe* 8:1 (1999), 69–97.

Sturges, Robert. *Medieval Interpretation.* Carbondale, IL: Southern Illinois University Press, 1991.

Symonds, John Addington. *Renaissance in Italy.* Part 1: *The Age of the Despots.* New York: Henry Holt, 1888.

Taylor, H. O. *The Medieval Minds.* 4th ed. New York: Macmillan, 1925.

Thomas, Alfred. *Anne's Bohemia: Czech Literature and Society, 1310–1420.* Minneapolis, MN: University of Minnesota Press, 1998.

Tierney, Brian. *Religion, Law, and the Growth of Constitutional Thought, 1150–1650.* Cambridge: Cambridge University Press, 1982.

Tkacz, Catherine Brown. "Susanna as a Type of Christ." *Studies in Iconography* 20 (1999), 101–153.

Toubert, Pierre. "La théorie du marriage chez les moralists carolingiens." In *Il matrimonio nella società altomedievale.* 2 vols. Spoleto: Presso la sede del Centro, 1977.

Trinkhaus, Charles. *In Our Image and Likeness: Humanity and Divinity in Italian Humanist Thought.* 2 vols. Chicago: University of Chicago Press, 1970.

——. *Renaissance Transformation of Late Medieval Thought.* Brookfield, VT: Ashgate 1999.

Turner, William S. V. "Herrad of Landsberg". *The Catholic Encyclopedia,* 1910.

Turville-Petre, G. *The Origins of Icelandic Literature.* Oxford: Clarendon Press, 1953.

Tyson, Diana B. "Patronage of French Vernacular History Writers in the Twelfth and Thirteenth Centuries." *Romania* 100 (1979), 180–222.

Ullmann, Walter. *The Growth of Papal Government in the Middle Ages.* 3rd ed. London: Methuen, 1970.

Van Houts, Elisabeth. "Latin Poetry and the Anglo-Norman Court 1066–1135: The Carmen de Hastingae Proelio." *Journal of Medieval History* 15 (1989), 39–62.

——. *Memory and Gender in Medieval Europe.* Toronto: University of Toronto Press, 1999.

——. "Women and the writing of history in the early Middle Ages: the case of Abbess Matilda of Essen and Aethelweard." *Early Medieval Europe* 1:1 (1992), 53–68.

Verger, Jacques. *Men of Learning in Europe at the End of the Middle Ages.* Translated by Lisa Neal and Steven Randall. Notre Dame, IN: University of Notre Dame Press, 1997.

Waithe, Mary Ellen. "Heloise." In *A History of Women Philosophers.* 4 vols. Edited by Mary Ellen Waithe, 2: 67–83. Dordrecht: Kluwer Academic Publishers, 1989.

Weber, Elizabeth D. A. "The Power of Speech: Models of female martyrdom in medieval and early modern French literature." PhD Diss., University of Wisconsin-Madison, 1994.

Wemple, Suzanne Fonay. "Monastic Life of Women from the Merovingians to the Ottonians." In *Hrotsvit of Gandersheim: Rara Avis in Saxonia?* Edited by Katharina M. Wilson, 35–54. Ann Arbor, MI: Marc, 1987.

——. *Women in Frankish Society.* Philadelphia, PA: University of Pennsylvania Press, 1981.

Wheeler, Bonnie. *Listening to Heloise.* New York: St. Martin's Press, 2000.

White, Andrew. *A History of the Warfare of Science with Theology.* London: Macmillan & Co., 1896.

White, Lynn. *Medieval Technology and Social Change.* Oxford: Clarendon Press, 1962.

Wiethaus, Ulrike. "Cathar Influences in Hildegard of Bingen's Play 'Ordo Virtitum.'" *American Benedictine Review* 38:2 (June 1987), 192–203.

—— *Ecstatic Transformation.* Syracuse, NY: University of Syracuse Press, 1996.

Wilber, Ken. "Eye to Eye: Science and Transpersonal Psychology." In *Beyond Ego.* Edited by Roger N. Walsh and Frances Vaughan, 216–241. Los Angeles: J. P. Tarcher, 1980.

Willard, Charity Cannon. "Christine de Pizan as Teacher." *Romance Language Annual* 3 (1991), 132–136.

——. *Christine de Pizan: Her Life and Works.* New York: Persea Books, 1984.

Wilmart, A. "Eve et Goscelin." *Revue bénédictine* 46 (1934), 414–438.

Wilson, Katherina M. *Hrotsvit of Gandersheim: The Ethics of Authorial Stance.* Leiden: E. J. Brill, 1988.

——. "The Old Hungarian Translation of Hrotsvit's *Dulcitius:* History and Analysis." *Tulsa Studies in Women's Literature* 1:2 (1982), 177–187.

Wogan-Browne, Jocelyn. "'Clerc u lai, muïne u dame': women and Anglo-Norman hagiography in the twelfth-thirteenth centuries." In *Women and Literature in Britain,*

1150–1500. Edited by Carol M. Meale, 61–85. Cambridge: Cambridge University Press, 1993.

Wolfskeel, Cornelia. "Beatrice." In *History of Women Philosophers.* 4 vols. Edited by Mary Ellen Waithe, 2: 99–114. Dordrecht: Kluwer Academic Publishers, 1989.

——. "Birgitta of Sweden." In *History of Women Philosophers.* 4 vols. Edited by Mary Ellen Waithe, 2:167–90. Dordrecht: Kluwer Academic Publishers, 1989.

——. "Hadewych of Antwerp." In *History of Women Philosophers.* 4 vols. Edited by Mary Ellen Waithe, 2:141–165. Dordrecht: Kluwer Academic Publishers, 1989.

Women and Power in the Middle Ages. Edited by Mary Erler and Maryanne Kowalski. Athens, GA: University of Georgia Press, 1988.

Young, Karl. *The Drama of the Medieval Church.* Oxford: Oxford University Press, 1933.

Zeydel, Edward H. "Ekkehard's Influence upon Hrotsvitha: A Study in Literary Integrity." *Modern Language Quarterly* 6 (1943), 333–339.

Ziegler, Joanna E. "Reality as Imitation: The Role of Religious Imagery among the Beguines of the Low Countries." In *Maps of Flesh and Light.* Edited by Ulrike Wiethaus, 112–126. Syracuse, NY: Syracuse University Press, 1993.

Zufferey, François. "Toward a Delimitation of the Trobairitz Corpus." In *The Voice of the Trobairitz.* Edited by William Paden, 31–43. Philadelphia, PA: University of Pennsylvania Press, 1989.

Index